Books by Lewis Mumford

THE STORY OF UTOPIAS   1922

STICKS AND STONES   1924

THE GOLDEN DAY   1926

HERMAN MELVILLE   1929

THE BROWN DECADES   1931

TECHNICS AND CIVILIZATION   1934

THE CULTURE OF CITIES   1938

MEN MUST ACT   1939

FAITH FOR LIVING   1940

THE SOUTH IN ARCHITECTURE   1941

THE CONDITION OF MAN   1944

CITY DEVELOPMENT   1945

VALUES FOR SURVIVAL   1946

GREEN MEMORIES   1947

THE CONDUCT OF LIFE   1951

ART AND TECHNICS   1952

IN THE NAME OF SANITY   1954

FROM THE GROUND UP   1956

THE TRANSFORMATIONS OF MAN   1956

THE CITY IN HISTORY   1961

THE HIGHWAY AND THE CITY   1963

THE URBAN PROSPECT   1968

THE MYTH OF THE MACHINE:

I. TECHNICS AND HUMAN DEVELOPMENT   1967

II. THE PENTAGON OF POWER   1970

INTERPRETATIONS AND FORECASTS: 1922–1972   1972

FINDINGS AND KEEPINGS   1975

MY WORKS AND DAYS   1979

Sketches from Life

Sketches from Life

THE AUTOBIOGRAPHY OF

LEWIS MUMFORD

The Early Years

Beacon Press   Boston

Grateful acknowledgment is made for permission to reprint lines from
"Nineteen Hundred and Nineteen" from *Collected Poems* of William Butler Yeats
(Copyright 1928 by Macmillan Publishing Co., Inc., renewed 1956 by
Georgie Yeats).

First published as a Beacon paperback in 1983 by arrangement with
The Dial Press

Beacon Press books are published under the auspices
of the Unitarian Universalist Association of Congregations
in North America, 25 Beacon Street, Boston, Massachusetts 02108

Published simultaneously in Canada by
Fitzhenry & Whiteside Limited, Toronto

Printed in the United States of America

(paperback) 9 8 7 6 5 4 3 2 1

Library of Congress Cataloging in Publication Data

Mumford, Lewis, 1895–
  Sketches from life.

  Originally published: New York: Dial Press,
c1982.
  Includes index.
  1. Mumford, Lewis, 1895–   . 2. Social
reformers—United States—Biography. 3. City
planners—United States—Biography. 4. Architects
—United States—Biography. I. Title.
CT275.M734A37 1983   973.9'092'4 [B]   82–73958
ISBN 0–8070–5413–5 (pbk.)

To Elizabeth Mumford Morss
and
James Geddes Morss

Contents

Photographs follow pages 54 and 278

Sketches from Life

CHAPTER ONE

East Side, West Side

I

I was a child of the city, and for the first thirty years of my life I knew the country only as a visitor, though the occasional summers I spent on a Vermont farm before 1910 had first and last an influence on me that offset my long incarceration in what Melville called "the Babylonish brick-kiln" of New York. Not merely was I a city boy but a New Yorker, indeed a son of Manhattan, who looked upon specimens from all other cities as provincial—especially Brooklynites. Deep down, I suppose, some of that original sense of metropolitan superiority, which has nothing to do with me personally, still lurks.

My first dream-swift memory brings forth a sunlit room, with the neighbors' children gaping at goldfish swimming about in a bowl. This dates back, my mother once told me, to our fleeting refuge in a flat on Amsterdam Avenue at the corner of Ninety-seventh Street when I was two. But my earliest clear picture is at three—that of the backyard behind a four-story brownstone front on West Sixty-fifth Street, where my mother, in spring, would thrust a few pansy plants into the ground, not because she wanted a garden, but because she loved pansies. That was before the High School of Commerce was built across the way and long before the Lincoln Arcade—which still later became a refuge for penurious artists—was razed to make way for Lincoln Center. Until the new subway tore up Boss Tweed's tree-lined Boulevard ('Bullavard' is what my young ears heard), as Broadway above Fifty-ninth Street was called, this was a quite respectable street and gave no hint of becoming the sordid red-light area it later turned into.

It was in this typical New York brownstone that my conscious life begins. I clearly recall our front parlor, dominated by a fashionable rubber plant, as well as the back parlor, with its heavy walnut furniture, where my grandmother, Anna Maria Graessel, and her husband were lodged. Even better, I can still feel myself lying in bed alongside my mother in what was originally the 'music room,' between back and front parlors. I would wake regularly at six-thirty or so— I've always been an early riser—chanting in monotonous singsong: "I want my toast and coffee." The last two syllables were drawn out in proportion to my impatience, and the coffee was, of course, slightly tanned milk.

At this point my grandmother steps momentarily into the picture: I see her adjusting her bonnet, with a grimace, in front of the pier mirror of the great walnut wardrobe. A few months later she died of Bright's disease.

The backyard, where I played, was safe from all intruders but cats, by reason of one of the high wooden fences with which New Yorkers always enclosed those dreary areas, though its paved path was too uneven to encourage even tricycle riding. From Sixty-fifth Street up, Broadway was still full of vacant lots, with visible chickens and market gardens, genuine beer gardens like Unter den Linden, and even more rural areas. Since for the first quarter of a century of my life I lived between Central Park and Riverside Drive, wide lawns and tree-lined promenades are inseparable in my mind from the design of every great city; for what London, Paris, and Rome boasted, New York then possessed.

My daily walks with my grandfather in Central Park or along Riverside Drive left an ineffaceable impression of noble leisure, though I did not become actively conscious of beauty till I was thirteen and one morning in Central Park saw a mist-veiled landscape transformed, in Turner's magical fashion, by the sun.

Since I have spent no small part of my life wandering about cities, studying cities, working in cities, stirred by all their activities, this original envelopment by the city constitutes an important clue to my life. Certainly Manhattan provided a far from ideal environment during the years I was growing up in it; but it still had many rewarding features, natural and man-made, that have since dropped away or been wiped out. This has come about partly through the profitable congestion of tenements and skyscrapers, partly through the more ominous spread of violence and lawlessness, which, in the city of my youth, used to be confined, like a carbuncle, to certain self-enclosed areas, like the Bowery and Hell's Kitchen. Such quarters had not yet poured their infection into the whole bloodstream of the city.

For one thing, it was possible then for men, women, or children, even when alone, to walk over a great part of the city, and certainly to walk through Central Park or along Riverside Drive at any time of the day or evening without fear of being molested or assaulted. This is no longer true, even though the poverty and misery that festered in large areas of New York at the beginning of this century have now been mitigated by social legislation, labor union organization, and indeed by the general rise in the material standard of life even in the lowest income groups.

There was a kind of moral stability and security in the city of my youth that has now vanished even in such urban models of law and order as London, where for long the police performed their duties without even the threat of a nightstick. So deep was this sense of security in a period that had not yet multiplied all the current forms of insurance against the mischances of life that the word 'security' did not have a place in our vocabulary. More than once lately in New York I have felt as Petrarch reports himself feeling in the Fourteenth Century, when he compared the desolate, wolfish, robber-infested Provence of his maturity, in the wake of the Black Plague, with the safe, prosperous region of his youth.

That breakdown of law and order at the very peak of metropolitan power and prosperity is, as Barbara Tuchman has discovered, one of the chronic puzzles of history.

I have dealt at length with these negative factors in 'The City in History,' for I believe they give fresh insight into the huge cultural transformation now necessary if we are to undo the radical errors that civilized man originally made during the transition from the early life-nurturing neolithic culture to the 'higher' civilization that ensued: a civilization whose enormous gains in controlling the physical environment and raising the ceiling of human achievement in the arts and sciences were offset by an obsession with power as an end in itself.

This discovery has nonetheless not robbed me of my love of cities or made me forget my quiver of anticipation when I stepped off the train in a strange city and, while waiting perhaps for a taxi, caught my first glimpse of its skyline or my first jumbled earful of sounds from its characteristic activities—the high-pitched whistle of the Chicago traffic policemen, at least of old, or the frantic toots of the taxis in Paris, before those sounds were officially suppressed. The overhead whoosh or sonic boom of a plane today unfortunately wakens no such happy expectations.

I was an Upper West Side boy. The area where I grew up then stretched roughly from Fifty-ninth Street to 110th Street: beyond that, though overeager speculators or homemakers had here and there set down scattered rows of defiantly urban houses, was a sort of no-man's-land, already spoiled for agriculture, neither country or city, still less suburbia. Even in built-up areas there were still many vacant lots, sometimes vacant blocks, until well past 1900. On some of these there were not merely squatters' shacks but thrifty market gardens; indeed, I remember that there was still such a leftover in the lower Nineties as late as 1912, on the Astor estate. And above 125th Street there lingered many tracts that could still be called farms, interspersed as they were with roadhouses and beer gardens where the thirsty cyclists who then filled the highways on Sundays could rest in the shade and down a schooner of beer for five cents.

The two main outdoor excursions of my elders—going to the racetrack and going to the cemetery—were always welcome diversions in my youth, on account of the journey itself if not its somber destination. As to the latter, for long this was at least a monthly visitation, often made in the company of uncles and aunts, for my maternal grandmother had died when I was three, and the regular visit to her grave combined piety with pleasure—and was also favored as good for the health. Above MacComb's Dam Bridge, along Jerome Avenue, was then almost open country, but the monument makers' yards thickened as one got closer to Woodlawn Cemetery. My elders would comment on how well or ill the hired florist was keeping the grave bed in order, on what sort of inscription was to be put on the tombstone when my grandfather died, or on how—dear me!—the cemetery was filling up so fast. After that there would be beer and sandwiches, with glasses of sarsaparilla for the children, before starting home.

But the trip to the horse races at Belmont Park or Sheepshead Bay or Brighton was, of course, far more exciting. East of Prospect Park the houses gave way to wide meadows and farms, and the open Brooklyn trolley cars, with their formidably high steps, used to whizz through this placid countryside, with the south wind bringing the delectable odors of new-mown grass and far-off salt spray.

My area of the city was relatively compact. The rows of Brownstone Fronts that had been so popular in the third quarter of the Nineteenth Century—an ugly chocolate-colored sandstone from the quarries around Hartford had displaced the warm reddish-brown sandstone from Belleville, New Jersey, which one may still find on Brooklyn Heights—were giving way to a more variegated type of domestic architecture, first influenced by Richardson, then by McKim, Mead, and White, with fine ocher Roman bricks and classic details; and then, on West End Avenue, this was followed by gabled houses in the Dutch style, as a new shelf of civic history books brought back into the consciousness of New Yorkers their own Dutch heritage.

On Riverside Drive itself the houses, often spreading mansions, were done in rustic stone and had enough shrubbery around them to give them a suburban air, though in the early part of the present century Bishop Potter's new residence, near the Soldiers' and Sailors' Monument, and a few other palatial houses introduced a more urbane Italian note. Never have rich people in New York had more garden space than they did for a decade or so at this time: the steel magnate Schwab—familiar to my grandfather as Charlie Schwab—even built a Renaissance 'castle' set in the middle of a whole block. But these early settlers had not reckoned with the fact that their

7

handsome Riverside Drive quarters were not sealed against atmospheric pollution. They were soon to find that the fresh west winds that blew across the Hudson also blew the fumes and smoke from noisome factories on the Jersey shore, to say nothing of the odors from the long trains of cattle cars that used to pass down to the slaughterhouses in the West Thirties, along the open tracks between Riverside Park and the Hudson.

Those trains, and those cattle cars particularly, were my delight as a child, and not least because, despite their ugly smell, the plaintive lowing of the cattle, and the grunting of the pigs, they brought a touch of wildness into the tame city. But I can understand the dejection that grew to desperation when a prosperous family, after investing heavily on Riverside Drive, belatedly discovered that the grand sweep of the river did not offset the putrid odors and harsh west winds.

Within twenty years this domestic loss was written off by the building of a great palisade of apartment houses for a less choosy economic group; and within another thirty years scarcely a vestige of these suburban palaces remained on Riverside Drive: one of a hundred examples that bear witness to the swift tempo of construction and destruction that has characterized my native city. If someone were to ask me now for directions in the neighborhoods where I lived the first twenty-five years of my life, I could only say, with a helpless smile: "I'm a stranger here myself." New Yorkers over fifty are all Rip van Winkles.

My memories embrace a series of neighborhoods, from Sixty-fifth Street to 105th Street; but unlike Greenwich Village, Yorkville, or Manhattanville, none of them had ever been a village, and so they were only faintly identifiable in either their physical or social structure. My part of the West Side had taken shape in the late eighties and nineties; and its class structure had a diagrammatic neatness. The poorer classes lived on Amsterdam and Columbus Avenues, in the 'old law' tenement houses—crowded structures with the majority of their rooms on airless airshafts and lightless light wells. Here lived the cabmen and clerks, the mechanics and the minor city employees, the widows who rented their extra rooms and went out sewing or washing or cleaning by the day. Only the rich lived off Central Park or on Riverside Drive; while between them on the cross streets, in their row houses, sometimes uniform for a whole block, sometimes with playful architectural variations—inset balconies, oriels, bay windows—lived the well-to-do and the more ambitious middle classes.

Like most New Yorkers in those days we seemed to be always moving; and it was not till I was twelve years old that we finally settled down in the apartment house on Ninety-fourth Street at the southwest corner of Columbus Avenue, where I was to live for the next dozen or so years. This shifting of residences was typical of the old city, at least among those who did not own their houses; it was due to the fact that, far from there being a housing shortage in middle-class quarters, there was actually a constant vacancy of around 4 percent—if I remember correctly the figure I once stumbled on.

People were tempted to move not merely for the sake of 'modern conveniences,' like electricity and 'open plumbing,' or to lower their expenses by getting the standard concession of a free month's rent; sometimes they even moved, it would seem, as the simplest way of getting through a spring cleaning. At all events, they moved; and Moving Day, the first of May or the first of October, saw vans loading and unloading on every block. This whole scheme of moving, this game of musical chairs in domestic real estate, was based on the scandalously low wages that everyone who assisted in the game received: plasterers, painters, wallpaper hangers, moving men.

As a result of our many moves I came to know from within the quality of the space in an old brownstone, and in a smaller, shallower kind of brown brick house we lived in for a few years on West Ninety-third Street, between Columbus Avenue and Central Park West; I have lived in an old 'railroad flat,' and in a better kind of flat with a central passage, bedrooms on one side, living rooms on the other; I have lived on the top floor of a walk-up and on the second floor of an elevator apartment, to say nothing of a more ancient and dingy flat house on West Fourth Street, where my wife and I started our married life.

In only one of my childhood homes did we have a view over any kind of open space other than the backyards: we were lucky if an ailanthus tree or two raised its head in the distance. Visually my domestic memories are mostly bleak and stuffy; and I hate to think how depressing the total effect would have been had not Central Park and Riverside Park always been there to gladden my eyes and to beckon my legs to a ramble.

2

My picture of the city, which I awakened to gradually and now can only patch together disjointedly, would be incomplete if it did not include the interior of our home: this remained, despite all external changes, pretty much the same throughout my youth, until my mother finally settled in a little wooden house on Cumberland Street in Brooklyn in 1923 and took over the Siebrechts' furnishings when Aunt Dora and Uncle Louis Siebrecht moved to a home for the aged.

The clutter of interior decoration in middle-class homes at this period is almost indescribable. The most contemptuous word that could be applied to an interior in those days was 'bare,'—'as bare as a barn.' I still remember that, in one of Conan Doyle's early novels, 'The Firm of Girdlestone,' the young heroine was almost driven to insanity when her cruel, calculating guardian confined her to a bare, whitewashed room. The bareness did it!

To overcome the least hint of bareness, the walls of comfortable early twentieth-century homes were covered with framed lithographs and engravings, 'Moonlight in Venice,' 'The Stolen Kiss,' and of course Sir Luke Fildes's painting of the portly, bewhiskered doctor at the pallet of the dying slum child; and as an additional mark of respectability, there would be oil paintings, too, *hand painted* in fact, which was often all that could be said for them.

The same scheme of decoration was applied to every room except the kitchen and the bathroom. It was a point of honor for the housewife to cover every square foot available, turning the richly figured wallpaper—then always red or dark green in the dining room—into a barely visible frame. There would even be pictures on the walls of the dark hall: a medley, indeed a distracting chaos, that only imitated at many removes the display of paintings in any great gallery of the period, the last dregs of Renaissance palace decoration. Alfred Stieglitz's photograph of his parents' parlor at Lake George tells the same story. The print my uncle Charley left of our Sixty-fifth Street parlor shows how standard all the components had become.

This visual clutter included the windows: they must not be bare either, and to ensure against this possibility in the old houses and better apartments, there were wooden shutters that folded back into the walls, there were roller shades, too, and there were lace curtains that reached to the floor, usually with heavy drapes covering them. In the winter all these curtainings played a part, no doubt, in keeping in such hot air as might rise to the second floor from the distant furnace; but they also screened out the light, and the smell of the dust in them is one of my very definite childhood memories, to be put alongside the smell of ammonia and wet newspaper wads for laying the dust in sweeping, or the acrid smell of the yellow soap that my mother, like the good housekeeper she was, still made out of the winter's accumulation of fat as late as 1905. "To be on tenterhooks" is an old expression that still summons up a sharp image for me, for curtains had to be tightly stretched at every washing, on the tenterhooks of a curtain frame erected out in the yard.

So much for the wall decorations. But all other kinds of bareness were to be avoided, too. True, we were past the period when the legs of pianos were covered in a sort of frilly trouser, on the prudish Victorian supposition that bare legs of any kind were libidinous; but no table was presentable unless its heavy tapestry table cover was in turn covered by a piece of embroidery or crewelwork or at least hemstitched linen; and that in turn was entitled to a crocheted doily before it was ready to receive a Welsbach reading lamp and an ashtray. (In pre-1900 dwellings electricity came in slowly: till 1922 in my mother's flat gas was the only illuminant.)

But other arts were brought into play to avoid bareness, in particular, all manner of bric-a-brac—vases of china and glass, of cloisonné, or of bronze, statues big and little that ranged from crocodiles to nymphs, along with lamps and lampshades as frilly and pink-bosomy as Lillian Russell or Anna Held, those paragons of feminine beauty in my youth. All through my boyhood my mother added to this dense ornamentation by purchases at the Japanese auction houses on our vacations in Atlantic City: the bidding for 'bargains' gave an extra charm to the purchase itself. And since the tables and mantel shelves were never roomy enough to hold all these esthetic encumbrances or to guard the more costly treasures from a careless gesture or the maid's saucy duster, the china closet and the curio cabinet were introduced, the first into the dining room, the second into the parlor, to hold these dubious objects of art. Without these cabinets a middle-class house could hardly be called furnished.

Don't think I have drawn on these memories for some mocking private satisfaction alone. One cannot properly understand the austere architecture of the period from 1930 to 1945 unless one remembers that the leaders in the modern movement and the critics like myself who abetted them were brought up in these chambers of esthetic horror and had no other thought, when at last they stood on their own legs, than to clear out the rubbish. The revolt against *our* bareness and austerity began around 1950, and in the popular decorating and building magazines one could detect spine-chilling signs that an even baser Victorian cycle was beginning all over again. Indeed, even before that, in my own children's delight in the surviving knickknacks of my mother's home, I discovered the germs of that rebellion decades earlier. But even the most licentious imagination could not then have anticipated the bloated imbecilities of Pop Art decoration.

Some of this effort to restore the human touch, to temper the high-handed rigidities that identified the disciples of Le Corbusier and Mies van der Rohe, had a certain justification. But in my time bareness had the dramatic value of silence descending after a howling storm and disclosing the cluttered and grimy landscape that one had turned one's back on now beatified under a benign mantle of snow. In our first joy at beholding that cold nakedness we did not realize that people might not want to live forever in a Snow Queen's palace.

CHAPTER TWO

All Around
the Town

I

My grandfather, Charles Graessel, introduced me to the city. He was really my mother's stepfather, but our relations were as solid as blood could have made them; and as the reader will presently discover, I had no other visible grandfather. The fact that this genial soul had leisure time to be my daily companion for almost half a dozen years, from 1899 on, tells something about the social background of that period. At sixty he became a 'gentleman of leisure,' for he voluntarily retired from the post he had held for, I suppose, some dozen or more years, as head waiter at Delmonico's, a restaurant that then boasted perhaps the finest cuisine in the city. (The great Delmonico cookbook that its onetime chef and epicure, Ranhofer, produced in the nineties is still in my possession. It is a book full of fabulously rich and time-consuming recipes that pampered the appetites and taxed the stomachs and livers of the restaurant's patrons.) By that time my grandfather had saved what seemed to him then a sufficient sum of money to ensure a decent old age. In all, I don't think that this amounted to as much as twenty thousand dollars; but in purchasing power, of course, it was the equivalent of many times that sum today—and that is more than I could show in savings at the same age.

My grandfather's ideals belonged to an early part of the Nineteenth Century, when even successful merchants often prided themselves, not on their ability to continue amassing an ever larger fortune, but on their being fortunate enough to retire in middle life on a 'competency,' as they called it—enough to enable them to enjoy their leisure and their good health before their bodies became enfeebled. "Enough is plenty" was a saying I can remember from my youth, before this became a heresy against the American way of life. Certainly my grandfather gave no appearance of feeling frustrated or depressed by his retirement. Quite the contrary; he had worked hard enough to earn this final respite, a welcome relief after keeping up a brave front under trying conditions—sometimes on board the yachts of the rich, where there were no lavatory accommodations for extra servants, or in strange houses in Newport or Narragansett.

My grandfather was a man of middle height, portly but solid, with a big head, a high forehead, and sideburns which he kept darkened by daily dabs of a vile-smelling liquid: but no mustache covered his broad upper lip. His heavy eyebrows, brushed upward, gave him a roguish look even in old age, though it is more evident in an earlier photograph. For me he was the dear *Doppelgänger* of my favorite childhood comic-strip character, Foxy Grandpa, who was always up to counter-mischief against his own mischievous imps.

Despite his obvious dignity in the Prince Albert coat he regularly wore on our afternoon sorties, he was always up to sly jokes and teases, like suddenly vanishing behind a tree when one's back was turned, or at home, planting a huge sprig of parsley the day after I had planted parsley seed in the backyard garden and pretending that the plant had shot up while I was at school. When I was little, some of his tricks used to frighten me. The false faces and masks he brought home from Delmonico's—those were still the days of masked balls—always filled me with unmitigated terror at the sudden disappearance of the person I loved; even the Santa Claus mask upset me, though I delighted to make my own face disappear in the same terrifying way. But I still remember the taste of boned turkey with truffles or lobster à la Newburg which he sometimes brought home in generous samples.

My grandfather was undeviatingly kind and good-humored; and his willingness, on our afternoon walks, to look at his watch repeatedly, so that I might guess the time—he usually rewarded me with a penny or a candy when I guessed right—is probably responsible for what might otherwise seem my uncanny sense of time, which still operates.

2

My grandfather was born in the Black Forest in Germany, the son of a miller. He came over to this country in the sixties, after a tour of Europe as apprentice waiter, mainly in order to escape military service, though a certain contempt for German discipline and a comic distaste for German arrogance—typical of many Republican forty-eighters—underlay this departure. But he did not hesitate to return to his native country in the eighties to visit his family and especially his nephew, Franz Graessel, who had achieved some local fame in Munich as a painter of farmyard fowl.

Franz was always proudly referred to in the family as *der Enten-maler*—the duck painter—the name his fellow townsmen had bestowed on him, for the Kaiser had once acquired one of his pictures, and they were reproduced in color on postcards, too. The admirable pencil drawing Franz did of my grandfather, in its hand-carved oak-leaved walnut frame, was to my bitter regret lost or left behind in my mother's move to Brooklyn. But I still have two small portraits in oil of peasants, done when Franz was sixteen, earthy faces that show the imprint of a sound esthetic tradition, faces that might once have served for 'The Disciples at Emmaus.'

My grandfather was a servant of the rich, at a time when to be rich, like being white in the deep South, was itself a respectable occupation; and to be one of the Four Hundred in New York was to be securely fixed in the ranks of metropolitan plutocracy, fortified against the moral contempt of Boston or the icy snobbism of London. Just because he was a servant, my grandfather had many more of the traits of the leisured people whom he cajoled and set at ease than their more active, hardfisted business rivals from the hinterland could have boasted. Both in dress and in deportment he was a gentleman of the old school. At ten-forty-five every morning he inaugurated the day with a Manhattan cocktail, decanting the whiskey from a half-gallon demijohn enclosed in wicker, a type of container one can now find, if at all, mainly in antique shops. After that, except on festive occasions, he drank nothing but beer. In all such matters he was on the moderate side. Having partaken all his life of luscious foods, he had had his fill of them; and there was no dish he relished more than the plain 'plate' of fatty boiled beef with mustard, a taste he shared with many French gastronomes—and one that I share, too. The old-fashioned boots my grandfather wore were made to order; so too, were his suits. Every item of the clothing he owned was "the best that money could buy"—and they wore accordingly. Without any conscious imitation, I find, looking back, that even in the days of pinching poverty I followed my grandfather's example, preferring suits of British woolens purchased at long intervals to a new suit of sleazier fabric once or twice a year. Fortunately for the exponents of an expanding economy, not too many people like us are left in the world.

Until I was eight or nine I spent almost every afternoon in the company of my grandfather, in saunters around Central Park or along Riverside Drive. These walks furnished the esthetic background of my childhood. Along Fifth Avenue or Riverside Drive my grandfather could tell me who lived in nearly every great mansion. Often we would sit down on a bench before the west carriage drive in Central Park to watch the regular afternoon procession of broughams, victorias, and hansom cabs in a sort of parkwide carrousel, which mingled self-display with 'taking the air.' (The air was as yet unpoisoned.) My grandfather could identify by name, sometimes with a little personal history, almost everyone of consequence who passed by: the Astors, the Vanderbilts, the Goelets, and the rest of the Four Hundred, as well as rich outsiders, like Russell Sage, who usually drove in an unfashionable surrey with a fringed top. ("A miser," my grandfather once said of Sage. "He watches every penny; but the Old Lady is very nice.")

Oddly enough I still recall the getup of an Astor—or was it a Vanderbilt?—who often drove through the park in a four-in-hand tallyho, with a coachman on the box behind, blowing a horn: a fresh-looking man, with red cheeks and a black, pointed beard above a

16

white stock. Chauncey Depew remains in memory, too: he whose white sideburns contrasted with my grandfather's gray. Depew was so feeble, back in 1904, that he had to be accompanied by an attendant; and my grandfather, looking down at him from the parapet on Riverside Drive, said: "Poor devil, he hasn't long to live." Two years later my grandfather was dead; while Depew continued to fence with death for not a few more years.

On Saturdays or Sundays my grandfather would take me on much farther excursions to visit friends or old cronies like the Bastians. Old Bastian, a kindly white-bearded bookbinder, with a head a little like General Grant's, was one of those gentle, idealistic Germans who came to the New World lured less by the promise of a better income than by the desire for freedom, a desire nourished mainly by Cooper's 'Leatherstocking Tales'; and it was Bastian indeed who, when I was only eight, urged me to read James Fenimore Cooper. I have him to thank for my early initiation into 'The Spy,' 'The Pilot,' and my favorite Leatherstocking novel, 'The Pioneers.' Frank Weitenkampf, the onetime head of the Print Department of the New York Public Library, writing me only a little while before his own death, told me that he had known Bastian well, a painstaking craftsman who used to bind the Astor Library's books.

Before Bastian retired to the lower Bronx, he had a flat above his shop in University Place. Mrs. Bastian, the most hospitable of souls, with a wrinkled moon face and an embarrassed mouth she was always hiding with her hand, would regale us there with coffee and cake; but as her *Pfeffernüsse* were as hard as hickory nuts, my grandfather used cannily to bring a box of more edible cakes from our local bakery, to preserve his teeth and her feelings.

Such visits took us to every part of the city; for we might go down to Canal Street, where my grandfather's boots were made, or over to the East Fifties to pick up the box of moderately expensive handmade cigars he always bought direct from the manufacturer, Keyser and Klug. Sometimes we would go to Brooklyn, on a Saturday afternoon, to listen to a band concert in Prospect Park with my granduncle Louis Siebrecht and his orphaned grandchild, Hewel, a somewhat sissy lad almost my own age. Sometimes my grandfather would encounter one or another of his old Delmonico cronies strolling in Central Park; and they would be as rigorously dressed and as finely polished in manner as he: particularly the debonair Phillipini, then chef at Delmonico's, in a gray Prince Albert and a gray high-crowned hat to match (a perfect Ascot costume!), setting off his gray Napoleonic imperial. I remember the torrential flow of his French!

Grandfather was a fine, upstanding man: there was not a wrinkle of servility in him; nor was he nearly so attached to German ways as Uncle Louis or Aunt Dora, who both came from Hannover, where my mother's family, the Hewels, had originated. Though he often spoke German with my mother at home, my grandfather never attempted to inflict the language upon me, as Uncle Louis had done with Hewel. The only language he gave me a faint smattering of was dinner-table French, chiefly because I was curious about it. Indeed his German was full of French words left over from the Napoleonic occupation: he spoke of *ein Billett,* not *eine Fahrkarte,* and said *adieu* (pronounced 'acheu'), not *auf Wiedersehen,* as people did, I found, in Munich as late as 1932.

These excursions gave me my first impression of the city that lay beyond my neighborhood; and if my grandfather introduced me to a whole variety of strange streets and occupations, he also made me at home in the Metropolitan Museum of Art and the American Museum of Natural History. It was with him that I explored these fascinating institutions long before organized excursions became a regular part of school routine. When, from 1915 on, I began to walk systematically over every neighborhood of my city and its surrounding regions, beholding its life with my own eyes, reading the buildings as if they were so many pages of a book, I was but continuing in solitude these early rambles.

All in all there was a reassuring solidity and poise about my grandfather, the poise of a "man of the world"; and the saddest thing about his long final illness was the shriveling up of his body as he lost the use of his legs and wasted away into a gray shadow. But a flickering sense of humor remained to the end. When I said good-bye to him one morning in late July 1906—he died in September—he knew it was our final parting, and he said: "Remember, Lewlie, all the things your mother used to blame me for, she'll blame on you when I am gone. . . . Be good to her and take care of her."

Much as I loved my grandfather, I had a child's self-protective callousness about his death. When the telegram announcing it came to Mrs. Josephine French's farm in Vermont, where I was again spending the summer, I took it coolly and talked matter-of-factly about what would happen to my mother and our household. Never a tear. He had been out of my active life for well over a year, and it was only in maturity that I at last, contemplating my childhood, realized all he had meant to it, and not least to my studies of the city.

3

Though my grandfather's presence is central to these youthful memories, other parts of the city revealed themselves to me under other auspices, and these more fragmentary impressions long sustained me, too. My Irish nurse, Nellie Ahearn—for a decade she was our cook and maid of all work—introduced me to the Middle West Side, the grimy tenements in the Forties, and those along nearer Amsterdam and Columbus Avenues, where her relatives and friends lived. My nose still wrinkles in disgust at the unsavory smell in the hallways of those tenements, compounded of overcooked cabbage and furniture polish, mingled with the most ugly smells of all, those of the bedbug poisons and the disinfectants that were supposed, in proportion to the offensiveness of the odor, to fortify the sanitary work of soap in cleaning.

But though the nose is the key to so many childish memories, I remember wistfully the unstinting hospitality that even the poorest of Nana's Irish friends would always show; and alongside the taste of Proust's *madeleine* I would place the taste of the Sultana Crackers and the extra-strong Irish tea which Mary Grogan, with her pinched white face, battered black teeth, and kind heart, used to offer me in the cellar flat on West Seventy-third Street, where she and her man were janitors. For me those thin, white, raisin-filled crackers evoke a whole period.

In time I was to know even poorer quarters from the inside,

for, as a lad of nineteen, I would visit my friend Irwin Granich, later Michael Gold, the author of 'Jews Without Money,' who lived far down on the East Side on Chrystie Street. There only one room received outside light and, the tenement being older, whole colonies of cockroaches and bedbugs had had time to entrench themselves in the woodwork. But even in the most elegant parts of the West Side, I must add, just as in Carlyle's Chelsea, these insect companions of man were then far from scarce. The difference between the better apartments and the inferior kind was due partly to the fact that the former were regularly visited by exterminators. (In those halcyon days no one thought of exterminating anything but rodents and insects: human beings were still supposed to be immune.)

Thanks to these contacts, I grew up in the real world, aware of its many social stratifications and faults; not least aware of its poverty, its sordor, and the unflinching efforts of so many of the poor to maintain their respectability and decency in the face of odds one might have thought overwhelming. Later, in the mid-thirties, this underlying experience of the human diversity of New Yorkers made it easy for me, once the ice was broken, to get closer to my Tammany colleagues on the Board of Higher Education. They might call me Professor at first, but they would soon recognize that I was one of them in my understanding and boyhood love of the city. Like them I had gone through the public schools and was at home everywhere.

4

Looking back now, I can see how deeply my walks with my grandfather influenced my later life; not least, how important they were in counteracting the narrow, secondhand learning and the bureaucratic routines of the elementary schools I attended. Being a passive, timid child, weakened before seven by a prolonged case of measles followed by mastoiditis and a long, violent bout of whooping cough, I might have found my life completely desiccated by the current academic drilling, but for the peephole glimpses into other lives and other ways that these walks under the tutelage of my grandfather had given me.

During the period when I was growing up, a series of gigantic shifts and upheavals took place in the urban scene around me; and many of these were, astonishingly, changes for the better. It was then that the first new patch of open play space was carved out of one of the worst slum areas on the East Side, to become Jacob Riis Park; it was then that the first freestanding skyscraper, the Flatiron Building, was built by Daniel H. Burnham, the successor of Burnham and Root, the Root who had built that other freestanding office building, the Monadnock Block, in Chicago. It was then that the series of bridges north of the Brooklyn Bridge was built, culminating in the most handsome one after the Brooklyn Bridge, the Hellgate Railroad Bridge. In the first decades of the Twentieth Century, Park Avenue likewise achieved a moment of exemplary urbanity and good form, with a broad green strip down the middle that made a pleasant pedestrian walk; and it was then that a great tidal movement of population took place, into the Bronx for the lower-income groups and out into the suburbs for the well-to-do.

I was there as a boy; I saw it all. The city grew along with the visible proofs of my own growth. The disappearance of 'Little Coney Island,' an amusement park at 110th Street and Broadway; the rise of Columbia University on the site of the old Bloomingdale Insane Asylum; the slow, tortuous building of St. John's Cathedral, never again to be such a satisfactory monument as in the brute stone of its original Romanesque form; the main building of the New York Public Library on the site of the old reservoir at Forty-second Street, which I used to follow as a high-school student on occasional walks home in the afternoon. All this went on before my eyes, like the later covering over of the gaping railroad yards between Vanderbilt and Lexington Avenues. Not least, the new green double-decker motor buses, careening along Riverside Drive, gave one a fresh sense of the city in movement.

The city I once knew so intimately has been wrecked; most of what remains will soon vanish; and therewith scattered fragments of my own life will disappear in the rubble that is carted away. I have not Frank Lloyd Wright's consolation, when he designed that overmassive pillbox, the Guggenheim Museum, that the building made in his image would survive a nuclear bombing, so that even though the rest of the city was destroyed, his spirit would still be present to survey the ruins. In that sense I share the fate of my generation. Whether hilarious or sad, we are all displaced persons.

5

In centering this account of my childhood in New York mainly on my grandfather—my mother and my nurse will follow—and in showing mainly what I saw through his eyes or in his company, I have hardly done justice to the impressions left by other parts of the city that I constantly touched, or to all those celebrations and seasonal events that colored my childhood and made it in so many ways utterly different from that of a child growing up in the homogenized, high-rise environment of the present day.

No picture of growing up in that New York would be true to its special quality if one left out the parades and public celebrations. On those occasions even today the whole city becomes a theater and all its residents actors as well as spectators: for such assemblages, mere numbers justify themselves. But I would cap those early memories by a single episode, perhaps the most exciting of all: the day after Justice Charles Evans Hughes's supposed presidential victory over Woodrow Wilson in 1916. At noon, in the Main Reading Room of the Public Library, I heard the strange, unexpected blare of a brass band, and rushing out onto Fifth Avenue, I beheld a jubilant impromptu procession, led by a pickup band, celebrating Woodrow Wilson's triumph. Everyone was sure then Wilson would *"Keep Us Out of War."*

Even the intimate daily events of the city had a special domestic color: this somehow was most in evidence on a late spring or summer evening, along the streets where private, middle-class row houses prevailed. Each family, or the occupants of each boarding house, would swarm on the high stoops, usually sitting on straw mats, often on hot nights burning incense or acrid Chinese punk to keep off the mosquitoes, waving palm-leaf fans, chatting among themselves, occasionally exchanging greetings with neighbors, whilst keeping an eye on the children having a last game of tag or running a buck-board wagon lighted by a candle in a cigar box, with a little boy as human motor to push it from the rear, up and down the block.

That picture, as I bring it back, has a kind of bucolic innocence and neighborliness which recalls that vanished age. Through flutter-ing lace curtains a lonely piano might be pleading the cause of love, but except for that and the rumble of the elevated or the clop-clop of a cab horse on the cobblestones, the human voice struck the dom-inant note: chuckling, laughing, just idly talking, sometimes whistling and even singing. But if some dire event or some criminal outrage had occurred later in the evening, the raucous shout of a newsboy crying "Uxtry! Uxtry! All about the great explosion!" might chill the spine for a moment.

This life, without motion pictures, without telephones, without radios, without television sets, without motorcars, without the vast volumes of standardized goods that must nowadays be bought promptly and consumed rapidly was not destitute of amusement and color: but it found its variety in little changes, little differences. The neighborhood grocery store may fittingly symbolize this. Every gro-cer's boasted a row of black lacquered bins holding tea and coffee in bulk, which were identified by their place of origin. One bought cof-fees—Santos, Rio, Maracaibo, Java, Mocha—knowing their special flavors and gauging the quality against a wide range of prices.

That colorful, still selective middle-class world began to disappear in New York after the First World War; and since the fifties has been disappearing in Europe, where it clung tenaciously until after the Second World War. (The Monoprix chain in Paris—and Le Drug Store—sounded the new ominous note.) Nothing so well indicates to me the difference between my own generation and the present one as the fact that I do not, without a certain inner resistance and re-sentment, accept a system of marketing in which all the decisions have been taken out of the hands of both the shopkeeper and the customer and put under the remote control of the market researcher and the packaging expert, the advertising agency and the wholesale distributor. Those who have grown up in this packaged world accept such external controls and compulsions as normal: their loss of choice, their loss of taste, they do not even notice, for they have never known anything different. We have now exchanged autonomy for automation.

6

But one thing is missing from this nostalgic picture. What I cannot quite recapture is the little boy who first took this in: or rather, I cannot get inside him, for he, too, flits across my 'finder' as merely part of the scene: much more scenery than person. For the rest, I behold that child as an outsider might, now squatting on the floor, making drawings of battleships or horses, now calling out "Good night! What time is it?" repeatedly, after going to bed, to make sure of the presence of his mother or grandfather in the next room. Often enough the whole family is playing pinochle, and his wakeful inquiries are trying their patience. Or again, he is playing red rover or buttons with the little gang on the block, like any other West Side boy.

Oh! but where is that bright lad himself, growing year by year in his own consciousness of himself? Somehow he eludes me, and I now begin to guess the reason: He is indissolubly part of the self I have become and therefore cannot be viewed from a vantage point outside. When I look too intently at him, I have the horrifying sense one sometimes has if one looks too long at one's image in the mirror. If one keeps on staring, nothing will remain except a mocking mask, detached from any living reality.

CHAPTER THREE

Inscription for
a Headstone

I

Not without premeditation did I begin this account of my life by describing its setting in the great city, for New York exerted a greater and more constant influence on me than did my family. In fact, it will take all my skill to present a family portrait that will, without outraging credibility, tie up with the kind of self that actually emerged. Yet I can see, when I examine matters closely, that I drew some sustenance even from quite distant relatives, not merely from my grandfather, my mother, and my Irish nurse.

In the world I awakened to, my mother, born Elvina Conradina Baron, was, at thirty, already a widow: actually, though I never definitely learned this till I was in my forties, she was twice widowed, and I was orphaned, as it were, even before my birth. More than a decade before I was born, my mother, as a girl of eighteen or so, had married an Englishman fully twice her age, possibly older, not so much because she loved him as because she was desperate to escape the harsh, unloving atmosphere of her own home, where he had lodged and boarded. After little more than six months together in a Harlem flat, they had parted, he to escape some financial embarrassment in New York by seeking his fortunes in Canada while she, despite his tender, earnest, finally heartbreaking letters begging her to join him, remained behind.

Following a period of perturbed indecision, she bowed to the advice of her family, and the marriage was legally annulled—possibly because it had never in fact been consummated. His last letter to her, which she kept through all the years, had the bitterness of a man utterly betrayed; so I suspect that he had found in this good-looking, loving, docile girl the life companion he had been seeking. My mother never saw him again, and yet, even after the annulment, she retained her married name, something that in those days gave a woman status and a certain measure of freedom. His name was John Mumford; and his is the family name that I bear, without a single drop of his blood running in my veins.

Yet John Mumford passed on to me something that my biological father, who but for a single photograph is a complete blank, did not. As "Jack" he had a place in my mother's autograph album during my boyhood, though, foolishly thinking to 'protect' me, she later removed most of those references. But far more than that, Mumford brought to his marriage and to my mother's bookless background a gift I was one day to make my own: a six-volume set of the complete work of Dickens, in a very cheap, double-columned, badly printed Collier edition, inscribed "From Jack to Elvie." Those books are still in my possession; and once I had passed beyond Alger and Henty, Dickens's novels, sketches, and American Notes, with their pathos and sentiment, played a part in shaping my adolescent literary taste. If I have a turn for comic exaggeration and overemphasis which has to be curbed, it is not only my American background but my Dickensian one that is partly responsible for it.

That John Mumford was not in any way related to me was a thought that may have stirred as the dimmest of suspicions in my childhood, although I never put it in words to myself, and certainly never voiced it. But I did not in fact know this to be true until I learned it directly from my mother in 1942, when I was forty-seven years old.

2

My mother was a good-looking woman after the fashion of the day, which emphasized rather than concealed the rondures men have admired since Paleolithic times; and she had a number of suitors during the years that followed, including the rather dashing but oh!-so-Teutonic George Ebeling from Philadelphia, who would later become my uncle. But she hesitated to marry again after her first disappointing experience.

Early in her twenties she accepted a post as housekeeper in the home of an older well-to-do bachelor who lived in the West Seventies. This job had come to her through my uncle Louis Siebrecht's connections with members of the Harmonie Club, where he was Steward. In fact, she first joined the household as helper to Aunt Dora, his wife, who then presided over it as housekeeper. But even earlier, while visiting Aunt Dora, my mother had met this older man and had fallen in love with him. She was so desperately, so hopefully, yes, so madly in love that she had even written him a letter asking him—the little goose!—for his advice on whether or not to seek marriage; and his reply was one of the handful of letters my mother turned over to me before she died. She had sent the letter anonymously, with heaven knows what provisions for getting an answer; but, as if to leave no doubt of the sender, she had written it in her own unmistakable hand.

J.W., as he was referred to in our family, probably did not need even this evidence to detect who the writer was; and he played his own part with a straight face, writing her a gravely bantering letter carefully weighing in the abstract the advantages and disadvantages of the married state, and voting, at the end, for marriage. His letter seems to have marked a spiritual milestone; for at a later period in her life she even copied it out, without making any identification, in her autograph album.

That was the beginning of a new and very teasing period in young Elvina's life; for a little while later she replaced Aunt Dora as housekeeper in his establishment, after a misunderstanding had caused Aunt Dora to resign in a fit of pique.

Overnight part of my mother's wild dream had come true. She had the seeming good fortune to be living without family supervision in the same house as the man she adored, committed by her very position to be of constant service to him—in fact, to care for him in every sense of the word. Instead of having to take the leavings from the table of her mother—an imperious, selfish, egoistic woman—my mother now had the bounty of a generous household; and better than that, the daily companionship of a handsome, cultivated, witty man, a lawyer by profession, astute in finance but at home in the world of literature and art: a quite typical citizen from Goethe's birthplace, Frankfurt-am-Main.

J.W.'s friends and relatives doubtless drew their own scandalous conclusions about this new housekeeper; but as it happened, they were wrong about facts, if not about appearances. What made her post so teasing to my mother was that J.W., far from keeping her at a distance as a housekeeper, treated her as a friend, indeed courted her as if his intentions were serious, whether honorable or otherwise. He filled her autograph album with classic quotations from Goethe, Heine, and many others, in five languages, including Greek. And what was she to make of the little verse in French that he wrote, probably his own composition, which I memorized in my childhood and can still repeat without looking at the album:

> *Je vous aime de tout mon coeur,*
> *Tous les jours, vingt-quatre heures.*
> *S'il vous fâche que je vous aime;*
> *Vengez-vous, et faites le même.*

My mother did not need any admonition to take that command seriously. In February 1891 she wrote in her autograph album: "I have found him at last. My dream is fulfilled." Fifty years later some of the most glowing memories of her life, before her mind failed her, were those of sleigh rides with J.W. through Central Park or spring dinners tête-à-tête at the old Claremont Inn on Riverside Drive. From his yearly trips to Europe he would always bring her back handsome gifts, such as a huge ostrich-feather fan; and my wife still cherishes the richly enameled Russian bracelet he picked out for my mother at the World's Columbian Exposition of 1893. To quicken more heady hopes J.W. once took her on a vacation in the Poconos, where they occupied adjoining rooms—yet nothing happened between them; neither stepped over the imaginary line that kept them apart. My mother was so enamored of him, she confessed at the end of her life, that, failing marriage, she would gladly have been seduced by him then.

The years passed, and still nothing further happened. With two servants under her my mother busied herself with her housekeeping tasks. Trained exactingly by Aunt Elvina, she had become a superb cook, and she prepared a succession of formal bachelor dinner parties, with mounted *printed menus* worthy of Delmonico's itself. Through all this, the presents at parting and the gifts on returning, with many little favors in between, kept coming. But though, as she

Elvina Mumford

neared thirty, my mother's desires and hopes must have challenged her chaste reserves, she did nothing overtly to break down J.W.'s inhibitions—inhibitions or disabilities that caused him to die a bachelor.

As it happened, it was one of J.W.'s favorite nephews, Lewis, who lived in a New Jersey suburb with his family and sometimes stayed overnight in New York, who finally took the initiative his uncle had not exercised. Toward the end of 1894 Lewis, for a few hectic, excited, anxious weeks, became my mother's lover; and in the middle of January 1895 I was conceived. My mother always referred to January as her unlucky month; and she was convinced that she could identify the very night that settled her fate and mine by the sudden tremor and glow of that union. But in old age she innocently confided to my wife, Sophia: "They tell me now it was what they call an orgasm." If that was the beginning of my own life, it also spelled the end of my mother's dearest hope: to be married to J.W. Yet even a decade later she had not in her heart abandoned that dream.

There was panic in her bosom and furor in the household when it became clear that my mother was pregnant. So far as I know, no one suggested the now common solution of abortion; but the question was, should her young lover marry her, or should she face the world alone? Against the open opposition of his family Lewis declared his readiness to marry her; and though that offer must have been a comfort, it did not sufficiently ease her difficult situation; rather, it put the final burden of decision upon her. Elvina recognized that his family's aversion to her marrying their son was based not merely on differences in economic status and education between the two families, one mainly of clerks, bookkeepers, stewards, and waiters, and the other of merchants, manufacturers, and lawyers: but perhaps even more they had the traditional Jewish aversion to mingling their blood with that of Gentiles, a feeling that remained even in those who, like so many liberal German Jews, had drifted away from formal Judaic orthodoxy.

What finally weighed in my mother's decision, she said, was her sense of the difference in their ages—almost half a dozen years—along with a feeling of guilt over the fact that she, the older one, had yielded to her impetuous wooer. She knew what a yearning, worshipful love was, for she was romantically in love—though not with my father. Yet the decision was not an easy one to make. Her diaries over this period no longer recorded her visits to the theater or the number of kittens her favorite cat had littered: they recorded her conflicts, her confusions, her sense of utter desolation, mingled with genuine affection for young Lewis. After her death I discovered that she had carried around in her purse the tiny obituary notice of his death, while he was in his early thirties. On it she had penciled the words, "Yes, dear."

In the end she decided that a marriage under the conditions that presented themselves would be too heavy a handicap for her lover. But when she left J.W.'s household that spring, she left open hopefully the question as to whether, once the baby was born, she might return to her old duties as J.W.'s housekeeper. The Graessels, her mother and stepfather, rose to the occasion by taking a cottage in Flushing, which was then an almost rural suburb; and it was in a house at 10 Amity Street that I was born, at seven in the morning of the nineteenth of October, 1895. Dr. Rau came all the way from Manhattan to attend her. Eight years later this same physician, in the pleasant, informal fashion of those days, held me reassuringly on his lap in the office of the throat specialist who removed my adenoids and clipped my uvula.

3

This culminating disappointment in love hung over my mother's whole life and possibly accounts, in great measure, for her thirty years of exacerbating invalidism. But her unhappiness and her bitterness sank so deep that a silence, more audible than words, covered every aspect of it: a silence so sustained, so respected by all her family, so barricaded against any outside inquiry, that as late as 1942 she believed she would go to her grave without breaking it to me. I myself never once during my own childhood had asked my mother about my father. That makes me seem, I am aware, a singularly incurious and self-contained child; but until adolescence never had I entertained any private speculations on my paternal origins. That part of life was a blank.

Perhaps I was only, all too obediently, responding to my mother's mute command: children have a way of sensing forbidden subjects and may sometimes respect unspoken taboos. As for my mother's family, they never by even a sly allusion touched on my ancestry; and for people who loved gossip and who must have felt me something of an outsider, this abstention showed the most delicate reserve. In my presence, at least, the topic of my parentage was completely out of bounds.

If ever a psychoanalytic biographer should concern himself with my history, he would probably devote no little time to uncovering all the devious ways in which my life was affected by my obstinate collusion in keeping my mother's secret. Almost inevitably, I predict, he would reject what I am now going to say; but that is no reason for my not saying it: namely that my shadowy awareness of my dubious parentage never consciously beclouded my life or raised any vexing personal difficulties, until I myself married and became a father.

Curiously, this insulating void in my own life did not raise the besetting problem of a later generation, the problem of 'identity'—at least in its biological form. This contrasts with my wife's early doubts about her parentage. As a little girl, with her deep yearning for personal freedom, she was convinced that she must be a gypsy's child, whom her mother had introduced into her own sedately conventional nest. Sophia's sense of being misplaced, of being denied her true identity, had no audible echoes in my own life, though, as concerns my innate character and intellectual interests, I could not have found myself in a more foreign human environment.

As the years passed, the barrier between my mother and me on this subject became more formidable: the lock that might have opened easily in my earlier years became rusted. What is more, by burning letters and excising pages in her autograph album and diaries she felt she had safely disposed of the key. All along she feared, as I was sadly to discover when at last I asked for an explanation, that I would be horrified at learning the truth and would reproach her—or that, after I married, Sophia and I might cast her off!

If I had only not vied with my mother in reticence, I might, to her own great solace, have lifted the burden of secret guilt she carried in her bosom, for it had left within a mark no less searing than Hester Prynne's 'A.' Hers had been a heroic decision: particularly heroic in those days, since, unlike the heroine of Grant Allen's contemporary novel, 'The Woman Who Did,' she had no virtuous sense of rising above the petty demands of society in accepting motherhood alone. Had she read that novel at the time it was published, it might well have accounted for her reluctance to tell me about my father, for the illegitimate daughter in that story heaped bitter reproaches on her mother and disowned her when her mother's scorn of formal marriage was unbared.

Many times since I have regretted that I waited so long to violate my mother's taboo; her ultimate confession riled up pools of anguish she had long left unvisited. My mother's sob of relief when my wife and I assured her as to our feelings came from the depths of love: the same depths that had caused her sudden panic when she realized that, for all her precautions, her 'secret' was finally out. She smiled incredulously when I sought to give her comfort by assuring her that I was in good company, witness Leonardo da Vinci and Erasmus! And in the end it was well for all of us to face the whole truth, without reserve and without shame.

The story my mother told me supplanted the far more plausible one that I had over the years put together and confided to a few of my friends. In that story I assigned to J.W. the role that his nephew actually played. The copious references in the autograph album, the fact that he was one of my two legal guardians, the knowledge that for long my mother used to send him proudly, for inspection, my perfect report cards from elementary school—all these bits of circumstantial evidence once seemed overwhelming. While there was no picture of my actual father around, the photograph of J.W., along with a dim oil painting that he had done, a sort of inky Daubigny, always hung over my mother's desk. And though she eventually destroyed both photograph and painting in a general holocaust that marked her abandonment of her Brooklyn menage in 1943, I still remember his features and feel that this particular family strain came out in me.

More dimly, I can remember the man himself. During the first years of my childhood, up to the time I was four or five, he still used to pay Sunday morning visits from time to time: a soft-spoken, kindly, if somewhat austere man. What was better, till I was six, he used to send me enchanting Christmas toys: once a great fortress with a real dungeon, unfortunately studded with nails, another time a big cannon that fired corks with a vicious pop that would slay a whole battalion of lead soldiers.

As for my biological father, he had visited my mother regularly in the early part of her pregnancy. In those 'slow' premotorized days, before there was any subway, he seems to have managed the trip all the way to Flushing—probably via the East Thirty-fourth Street Ferry and a Long Island train—during his lunch period. But his family insisted on his ceasing these visits when my mother's confinement came near: they were afraid that if he saw his child, he might defy them by marrying its mother after all. She lived the last days of her pregnancy, her diary reveals, in foreboding remorse and tears, and my father never laid eyes on me.

When my mother finally identified his single photograph, forty-seven years later, I looked upon the face of a stranger to whom I bear not the slightest resemblance in any feature, though I could recognize some of his characteristics, particularly his small nose, broad at the nostrils, in the face of my own son. I never consciously missed him, and I still find it as hard to acknowledge him as my biological progenitor as if I had been the product of an artificial insemination from an anonymous donor.

4

During the half-year after my birth my mother's fate and mine hung in suspense; for, rather callously, J.W. offered to take my mother back into his household on the same old terms, provided she would abandon me to an orphanage. But much as she loved him, she loved me more; and so a settlement was finally arranged by Lewis's New Jersey family in trust for both of us: a rather niggardly settlement it turned out to be, considering that J.W. himself, with an income, my mother knew, of forty thousand dollars a year—a huge sum in those days before the income tax and inflation—might have doubled the amount out of his own current returns without feeling even a passing pinch. And as the years wore on, as memories staled, as hopes died, as expenses went up, the meagerness of this annuity, some six hundred dollars a year, became a source of increasing bitterness to my mother.

When I was ready for college, without consulting me she even wrote to J.W., trying to enlist his financial aid, and was incensed by his coldly negative reply; all the more because she felt I was the kind of person in whom, apart from family relations, he might well have taken an impersonal interest. But unmoved, he pointed out that the city of New York offered an excellent free college education to all its citizens who qualified, and I followed this advice without any sense of deprivation.

That was the positive benefit I derived from my well-preserved immunity to my mother's secret. Since my father's family did not 'exist' for me, their wealth aroused no hopes and their indifference promoted no resentments. I made my own way without patronage or favor, indeed without any external advantages except those which my native city offered me. That was a far more munificent gift than any family could bestow: New York with its libraries, its museums, its parks; its nearby landscapes, the Palisades and the Westchester hills; not least its multitudinous human richness, with all its choices of lovers and friends. Walt Whitman's Mannahatta was my Mannahatta, too: "City of orgies, walks, and joys." That is why my city, not my family, properly set the stage for this narrative.

And yet, for all his forbidding coldness, at the end J.W. served in a way as a surrogate father. Is my saying this a subtle and belated revenge? Possibly, but I doubt it. A child gets from his parents, almost by a process of osmosis, many feelings and ideas that the parents may not be fully conscious of, or may even want to hide from their child. But in effect J.W. was my father just because, in my mother's unconscious, he remained throughout her life her husband—the husband who met all her ideals and needs except one, since they had never been joined in the flesh; and in that sense I was his son and spiritual heir. The epigrams and snatches of verse J.W. wrote in my mother's autograph album—a source of rainy-day amusement when I was ten or twelve—opened up wider horizons for me: they hinted at a different life from the increasingly sordid and poverty-cramped one that actually began to envelop me. Possibly that album partly accounts for the fact that my earliest vest-pocket notebook, at fifteen, was devoted to what then seemed to me exquisitely pithy comments on life, such as "Girls are like Mr. Toots' description of Burgess and Company, 'Fash'nable, but very dear.' "

At the time that I drew forth my mother's secret, I believed that it really was a secret: known, of course, to her own family and to the intimates of my father's family, and probably also to Nana, my old nurse, but otherwise completely buried. I did not guess then, for she said nothing to indicate it, that she herself had told my wife's mother, Elizabeth Wittenberg, about my parentage. This was altogether to her credit. When she learned that Sophia and I were to be married, she felt it was only honorable to disclose the fact that I had been born out of wedlock, in case this should seem an obstacle to the union, though she doubtless hoped that the fact that my father was a Jew might turn the scales in my favor. I honor my mother for the impulse that prompted her to this act, and I cannot blame her, once the floodgates were opened, for having told the whole story in great detail. I had already told what I knew or guessed to Sophia; but just as my mother had kept the story from me, Sophia's mother honorably kept the story from her—only to let it out, for such is the way of secrets, to her eldest daughter, from whom in time our own troubled daughter learned it, too—without my knowledge until years later.

Had my mother only told her secret to me at the time she told Mrs. Wittenberg, if not five years earlier, when at twenty I received my portion of our meager trust fund, she would have saved everyone, including herself, much tribulation. But from the original error of withholding the knowledge from the one person who was most deeply concerned in it came a whole series of errors and fruitless falsifications, including her tearing from her autograph album the inscriptions I had, as a boy, read many times, and by the time I was fourteen or fifteen had pieced together into a plausible counterfeit of the real story.

If, when I at last extracted her confession from her, she had only told me that she had already confided in Sophia's mother, she would have saved me from my own error—that of repeating hers, by withholding from my daughter the information she repeatedly demanded, unsatisfied as she naturally was by my vague and airy responses.

As I review it, this story sounds like one of Tolstoy's moral tales, which I remember reading the summer I was graduated from high school, in a French translation: 'Le Faux Coupon.' If my memory holds, Tolstoy showed how one small original crime, that of passing a counterfeit bill, set in motion a succession of other errors committed by distant people who passed the counterfeit along. I hardly dare verify my memory, lest it turn out that the moral was a different one! But in my case it would serve well. Had the wall of silence between my mother and me been broken down—my second cousin Adolph Ebeling would have been my proper informant if my mother shrank from the ordeal, for he was one of the two executors of our petty trust fund—I don't think anything about my life would have changed seriously except my unreadiness to share my suspicions and later my knowledge with my children.

My mother should have known me well enough, the foolish woman, to realize that her son at twenty—full of all sorts of fashionable Shavian and Wellsian attitudes about love and marriage, feeling then that sexual relations were entirely private and personal, and that legal marriage was little better than a concession to outmoded, vulgar prejudices—would not have been embarrassed over his illegitimacy. Sophia, as an equally emancipated member of her own generation, who even, as a Lucy Stoner, insisted on keeping her maiden name until our first baby was born, of course shared these 'advanced' views.

Neither of us, indeed, had any backwardness about discussing my speculations about my paternity with our friends in those early days. But I must record that when I referred to my hypothetical parentage in a letter to my friend Thomas Beer, to counteract a bit of gossip he had heard somewhere—that I was really of Italian descent and that my proper name was Monteverde!—he was so shocked—or should I say so discreet?—that he wrote he had burned my letter. That must have been as late as 1929.

As for the fact that my father was a Jew, nothing would have changed there either. I was brought up as a Christian, not as a Jew, and at no point did I ever feel any desire to identify myself with my father's family: nor in that relatively non–anti-Semitic era in New

York did I feel morally obliged, as many people of mixed descent honorably did later, when the Jews came under Nazi-Fascist persecution, to identify myself with those of Jewish blood and faith. But the suppression of this side of my inheritance had little effect on me: on the contrary, I married into a Jewish family; I wrote frequently in the twenties for the 'Menorah Journal'; and my friends were indiscriminately chosen, not because they were or were not Jews, but because they were people whose interests and ideas I shared. Since I never missed my father, I could not picture how different my life might have been had he played an active part in it; and not till I myself became a father did I have the faintest sense of what I had actually missed. The truth is that I took my unmentioned and unmentionable male parent in my stride till I wrote the story of my son's life in 'Green Memories' and discovered that, though I could speak easily about my wife's parents, I must leave out my own, because there was too much to be explained.

A little while ago, in an attempt to give a full picture of my mother's life, I wrote a sixty-page memoir to supplement the family tombstones in Woodlawn Cemetery. On her headstone, by her expressed desire and strict instructions, only these words were to be carved:

Elvina
1865–1950
Mother of Lewis Mumford

It will not be easy now to pick from those well-combed memories the relevant passages that bear upon my own life; all the more difficult because the tale of her early days mingles with the picture of the city that she knew between 1870 and 1900—before the time when I myself became conscious of it.

CHAPTER FOUR

My Complementary Mothers

I

My mother, Elvina Conradina Baron, was thirty when I was born. She was the oldest child in a family of four, three girls and one boy, all born in Manhattan. Her memories of the whole period of her youth, the seventies and early eighties, were all bleak: they go back mostly to a four-story, pre-Civil War brick house at 108 East Tenth Street, which may still be standing, opposite St. Marks in the Bouwerie. Such houses then rented for some twenty-four hundred dollars a year, unfurnished, unheated: no small sum even in that post-Civil War period of inflation. To make a living by keeping lodgers, as my widowed grandmother did after 1870, required scrimping and scrounging, with a cheap 'greenhorn' servant, and her even cheaper three daughters, to whom she never troubled to teach the arts of housekeeping, and for whom she never seems to have shown any tender maternal solicitude. Quite naturally each of the Baron girls in turn sought to escape this domestic prison by finding work in a shop at the earliest possible moment, or by getting married, as my aunt Theresa did at sixteen, my mother at eighteen.

When Elvina was sixteen she had the traumatic experience of having all her upper teeth extracted, to save the money that their proper treatment and filling would have demanded: this coincided with her first hemorrhage from stomach ulcers, the beginning of her chronic invalidism from that emotionally vulnerable organ. Though Elvina never forgave her mother for this callous parsimony, the

39

memory of it did not prompt her to see that better early care was taken of my own teeth: a strange lapse that I cannot account for any more than I can account for weak-eyed Herman Melville's not taking pains to provide his son Stanwix with the eyeglasses he badly needed.

Despite her dark memories of maternal neglect, all the more galling because my grandmother, Anna Maria, did not hesitate to buy new dresses for herself and go to fancy balls, yet I find in my mother's diary, shortly after my grandmother's death, this item: "To know a dear one is left behind in the cold never to see again on earth is terrible. . . . How I miss Mamma. Even if she was cross and scolding, she still was Mother and was there."

2

My mother was a baffling combination of firmness and softness, of traditional pieties and current fashions, of fearsome prudence and unthinking recklessness; but perhaps her dominant trait was her docility, her submissiveness to those around her. Too easily she took on the color of her environment; and if in her happy situation with J.W. this was an admirable trait, under less favorable circumstances it was a handicap. Though there was a core of personality that remained untouched by other people—much as she loved and respected me, she would never regard me as an authority on any subject about which she had definite opinions of her own!—there were large areas of life through which she drifted with those around her, never rejecting or challenging their ways, still less cutting her own path.

In the circle of her immediate family, my mother sank to their level: so hers was a world of racetracks and card tables and stockbrokers' offices; a world inhabited by busily frivolous people who spent repeated vacations at hotels in Saratoga Springs and Atlantic City, playing endless games of poker, euchre, five hundred, and auction bridge; a world where the scandal and gossip of that part of low society that used to be called 'High Society' spiced and in some degree offset its own code of bourgeois respectability. The flavor of that world was caught with great subtlety and amazing penetration in what has long seemed to me one of Henry James's most acute psychological novels, 'What Maisie Knew,' and what Maisie knew was at least a part of what I knew, too; though it took many years before I fully realized how much I knew.

Had my mother married either of the men she loved, she would probably have been capable of giving them a full measure of happiness and of being deeply fulfilled herself, with a family of many children instead of a single one. Failing here, she covered her disappointment by seeking excitement in cards and horse racing. But her luck in gambling was no better than her luck in love: so this outlet confirmed rather than alleviated her debilitating bodily disorders. Without either the education or the natural ability to make a career for herself except in the household arts, my mother's life was not so much 'dissipated' as empty. When my wife, Sophia, asked her once in her old age what she most regretted about her life, she answered: "I never danced enough; I would have liked to have danced more." Yet would not many another woman, even if sated with a string of lovers, say the same thing?

As I recall her at thirty-five, however, she was still a cheerful, bosomy woman, about five foot four or five in height, who went about her work singing songs from the comic opera 'Floradora': "Oh, tell me, pretty maiden, are there any more at home like you?" Often she would vary this with a tuneful whistle, for she had a surprisingly robust whistle for a woman, even in a day when whistling was far more common in all circles, from children up, than it is today. (Only professional whistlers seem to whistle now.) With her long lashes, her well-marked eyebrows, and her firm features, she was a comely, almost a beautiful woman in the bosomy fashion of the period that was passing, but she had a notable, firm nose with a slight bulge at the tip, as had all my great aunts—a Hewel trait. She boasted a mass of chestnut hair that reached down below her waist till she was past seventy and remained brown even longer.

In a period when all these features, not least a prominent nose, were regarded as desirable, she might still have made a good marriage after I was born but for the fact that the man who most deeply loved her through all these years, my great-uncle James Schleicher, was not free to declare his love until after his wife died—and that was some twenty years too late. During the years when choice was open, her loyalty to me conflicted with her desire to marry; and certainly my grandfather didn't improve her prospects by telling me once, on the eve of our going to Atlantic City, that I had better keep my eye on my mother, or someone would run off with her. That was a regrettable trick for him to play on my mother, and not quite so innocently funny as he may have imagined. But she, at the same time, had a certain apprehension, possibly not unjustified, that the suitors she met on her vacations took for granted, from her airy manners, that she had a far bigger income than she actually possessed, and were not exclusively interested in her person.

My mother's four or five years in J.W.'s household had encouraged expensive tastes and upset her sense of the dire realities of the life possible on her scant income, even at the beginning of this century. For until she was past middle age, it was natural for her to live beyond her means: indeed it seemed impossible for her to live otherwise. Once, her unpaid butcher's bills mounted so high that, to my private adolescent humiliation, the friendly butcher she had long patronized actually dunned her through a collection agency: an act she regarded as an unforgivable insult on his part. This indifference to the arithmetic of happiness as expounded by Mr. Micawber, with its infallible formula for avoiding financial misery, prompted my mother to hope that she might pyramid small amounts of money by placing them on a hundred-to-one shot in the races, and so have sufficient capital to support us both in the style she felt life owed us.

These desperate gambles kept her from guarding the small funds that came her way; for in a few years she had frittered away the inheritance she came by from my grandfather in 1906, when I was eleven: some three thousand dollars whose more prudent disposal might have somewhat lightened my bleak adolescence. But in any miserly sense, she was quite indifferent to money: generous to a fault, as the saying is. At no point in her life, even when our poverty was most acute, did she urge me, despite the indignant promptings of her sisters, to get a 'paying job'; rather, during the lean years after our first child was born in 1925, she voluntarily reduced the regular monthly stipend we were giving her. If I have often disregarded financial rewards and been impervious to financial pressures, I have my mother partly to thank, as well as my wife.

3

Running a boardinghouse was the destiny of impecunious windows in the Nineteenth Century; and it was natural that my mother should have sought this means of self-support; but her only fitness for this task was her talent for the household arts. The art of cooking, indeed, ran in the family, but my mother was the best cook of the lot. I, myself, from being called upon even as a child to judge the final seasoning of a stuffing or a croquette, or to drop the egg yolks one by one in the mixing of a sponge cake, served an informal apprenticeship in the kitchen and acquired standards that plagued my wife for many years, till she in self-defense became my superior. My mother's romantic yearnings made her treat her boarders as 'paying guests,' and that term gives the show away. This self-deluding gentility was doubtless what kept her from facing the economic constraints of her life, and charging for her lavish cuisine at full market rates.

The strange contradictions that ran all through my mother's character came out again in her role as a parent. She was, up to a point, devoted to me, in a sense had consecrated her life to me, as the sole reward and justification of her early misstep; and yet, from first to last, though she delighted in the scholastic proofs of my intelligence, she enjoyed far less of me than she might have done. Before I was ten, she often made me part of *her* life, dragging me along on shopping expeditions, or taking me to brokers' offices where one of my aunts would be watching the ticker from ten till three.

Even worse were those frequent family visits on Sundays that began with a poker game in the afternoon, duly resumed after supper, growing more tense and quarrelsome in the evening hours, sometimes keeping me out till one o'clock in the morning. Talk of the deadly solemnity, the somber pall, of a Puritan Sabbath! For me this anti-Puritan ritual was quite as deadly and even more appalling. John Ruskin, with no more lively Sunday amusement than tracing

43

the pattern on the parlor carpet, knew no worse boredom than I did.

I can still recall, with a residue of childish indignation, being put to sleep among the overcoats on my aunt's brass bed in the evening, and being wakened sufficiently to have my coat put on, then being taken out, cross and miserable, but too sleepy to give vent to my misery, into the biting air of a winter's night. Yet one of my most haunting memories of my mother on such an evening is that of her sitting alone, before supper, at the piano in the music room of my aunt Theresa's apartment, playing the piano softly, picking out a melody she had learned in her youth, wistful, as if recalling a vanished promise. At the very moment this happened, I knew I would remember it all my life.

All these routine visits, lightened only by opportunities to play with my older cousins, were somewhat offset by many more exciting jaunts to the horse races. In the last few years of grammar school my mother would even, once in a while, call for me at eleven in the morning and somehow get our staid old Principal, 'Pop' Moore, to excuse me from classes—I can't guess on what pretext or by what charm!—so that she might take me for an outing to the Sheepshead Bay or Brighton track, where in season we would have softshell crabs for lunch.

But she rarely tried to take a more intimate part in *my* affairs. It was my grandfather and Nana who took me on my own terms; and it was with Nana that I used to 'discuss life,' with infant gravity, or read aloud, while she prepared dinner, from 'The Story of the Bible' or 'Two Little Savages': the two books that equally captivated us till I was nine. So my mother missed many passages in my growth that my wife and I have enjoyed with our own children. But perhaps the loss was more hers than mine.

Again, when a medical examination at City College revealed a tubercular lesion, I kept that knowledge to myself, thinking that my mother would be unduly wrought up over it, until the time came when Dr. Storey demanded her presence for a consultation, before I was asked to withdraw. I was surprised, perhaps even a bit hurt, to find that she took my personal crisis with a cool matter-of-factness; and during the whole period of my wavering invalidism she

44

never expressed any undue concern. On the whole that aloofness was fortunate for me. We were close enough together as it was; and had she been more attentive, more overtly solicitous, I might never have been able to sunder the bond between us.

On the other hand, my mother had many admirable traits as a parent, for she never gave unnecessary commands, and when she gave an order, she meant to be obeyed. If once she made a promise or uttered a threat, she never went back on it, even if a few minutes later more tender feelings intervened or her conscience pricked her and she inwardly relented. Such firmness, so deeply embedded in her seemingly too pliable character, served her on other occasions. Even when she spanked me, she did so in a workmanlike manner, with her bare hand on my bare bottom; but she stopped as soon as I showed sufficient signs of early repentance by crying; and my last spanking took place when I was seven.

That resoluteness was confirmed by her handwriting: a beautiful, well-molded hand, full of character, too, especially in capital letters like 'B,' which she fashioned with a certain Bigness and Bounce. Until she was eighty, her bold penmanship held forth a promise that the banal contents of the letters rarely revealed. Yet I like to think that her handwriting perhaps did justice to a potential self that her life had never favored.

Within the range of her understanding, my mother had special moral excellences, too: not least her sense that private letters, though they might lie open on one's desk, were inviolable. Close though the bond between us was, she always respected my privacy, even during my first serious love affair at fifteen; and I never discussed with her my emotional state or my marital hopes and disappointments; nor yet did she even in a roundabout way try to get me to speak of my personal problems in marriage.

4

Since my mother felt that her own life had been warped by the interferences of her family, she leaned over backward in order not to impose her own will upon me. The only subject on which she presumed to interfere was that of smoking, and it may be in openly doing so she was unconsciously treating the cigarette as a substitute symbol for sex; for she begged me to hold off from this habit until I could no longer resist it. (In the light of present medical evidence this has turned out to be not quite so absurd a request as it once would have seemed.)

My breaking of this taboo, secretly, came at sixteen: but since I made my first essay with a noxious 'little cigar,' it nearly ruined my taste for tobacco permanently, as other men have had their taste for sex spoiled by their first encounter with a repulsive prostitute. But— and this would deepen the parallel with sex—though my mother had asked me to tell her when I did begin, I never informed her about these fitful bouts of smoking till I came back from England in 1920 flaunting my bamboo cigarette holder and my Gold Flakes. If she was a little shocked then, she perhaps was not unprepared for my marriage a year later.

My mother's detachment was perhaps encouraged by the style of the period, at least the style of her youth, which put an over-whelming emphasis on adult concerns: so her preoccupation with the rituals of her contemporaries, the unremitting round of card games, social visits, afternoon family kaffeeklatsches, or dinner par-ties, along with horse races and matinees, all sandwiched in between household chores, was possibly the saving element in a relationship that might otherwise have retarded my erotic maturation, as so often happens in the Irish short stories of Frank O'Connor or Sean O'Faolain.

Yet, there were two or three brief episodes in our life together that both my mother and I always looked back to with particular pleasure: not surprisingly, perhaps, they were times when we were alone, and she had broken loose from the family orbit. One occurred during the year of imprudent economic abandon that followed my grandfather's death, when, to efface the memory of his slow, painful wasting away, she decided to put her furniture in storage and spend part of the winter at the boardinghouse of an old friend on West Seventy-third Street. She even took me out of school for this period, and in February decided to rent a whole house in Atlantic City, an even wilder financial move than boarding. Characteristically, before

46

making this change she prepared for my taking dancing lessons by buying me my first tuxedo suit at Altman's in order that I might go to a proper dancing school. (But I never did go; indeed I never learned to dance till I sought to woo Sophia; and I never acquired another dinner jacket till I was over thirty.)

For a couple of months then, when I was eleven years old, we kept house alone in the narrow three-story cottage she found not far from the old Absecon Light, even then blocks away from the sea. We would walk together on the boardwalk; we would haunt the Japanese auction rooms, as of old; and on cool spring nights, before I was ready for bed, we would lie under a top blanket, reading Scott or Dumas together—with my mother occasionally skipping passages in Dumas she thought were not quite proper for my tender years. In the morning I'd trot our French poodle, Zip, down to the railroad station to pick up the 'Morning Telegraph,' whose racing pages my mother faithfully studied; and after she telegraphed her bets, the day was ours: for baking or cooking or idling by the sea. That period she always put alongside the single week she spent in Cambridge in 1918, when I was studying at the U.S. Naval Radio School, whiling away her mornings in the Harvard Yard—there were benches there then!—and seeing me constantly, since after three in the afternoon the day was entirely my own. This proved to be the last period of close intimacy in our lives, before my work and my attachments to other people weakened the close tie between us.

Even more effective, however, in loosening an otherwise too tightly tied knot, was my mother's self-absorbed invalidism, particularly during my adolescence. As her hopes for a better life faded, as her own natural impulses toward marriage became exacerbated by denial and her romantic expectations shriveled, the mental state that might have developed into a neurosis vented itself in chronic ulcers. These intense physiological preoccupations of hers obviously diverted her libido from me; and though there were later moments when we were perilously near the same kind of familiarity that Melville's hero, Pierre, exhibited toward Mrs. Glendinning, it was not my mother but my violent facial eruptions of acne which most embarrassed my relations with girls from the onset of adolescence right

47

up to the time I married—when they vanished almost overnight. The typical afflictions of an excess of maternal affection—homosexuality, or inability to have intercourse with any woman except a professional prostitute—never troubled me.

Sophia would probably have a different account to give of this filial tie: she would see my breaking away as sadly incomplete, and my attachment to my mother in the early years as a handicap if not a serious threat to our marriage. And doubtless she would be right. In her old age my mother often indignantly reproached herself for her submissiveness to events and personal pressures. But this was accompanied by a certain negative boldness that approached the heroic. Even when she was old and lonely, she proudly insisted upon maintaining her own household, for she didn't believe that mother and wife could get along happily under the same roof.

Probably it was the wealth of unexpressed and unreciprocated love in my mother's life that increasingly curdled it. Nothing shows better her latent capacity for love than the series of beautiful afghans she crocheted for us in the late thirties, when she was over seventy. Her own taste in colors was entirely different from ours; and such afghans as she made for herself and Uncle Charley were rather drab and ill chosen in color, revealing like a Rorschach blot her emotional disappointment. Yet without any guidance from us she chose a range of colors, in a series of five afghans, in perfect harmony with our tastes. Love guided her unerringly here, as it did in the far more variegated afghan she made for our young son. This was the same kind of insight that had prompted her, when I was barely seven, to purchase the expensive ten-volume 'Century Dictionary and Encyclopedia,' duly inscribed on each cover with my name in gold letters; as if she had some intuitive anticipation of my future career.

But the death of my mother's old friends and, in 1935, of her brother Charley, left her with fewer secondary objects of love; and our own lives, increasingly preoccupied with the political and moral crises of our times, could not sufficiently meet her need for affectionate intercourse. The stark emptiness of her final years darkened my own life in a period that brought still other reasons for desolation. Yet, had she died soon after coming back from a long visit with her niece Taza Grollman in California in 1938, while Sophia, our son,

Geddes, our daughter, Alison, and I went on to Honolulu, she would have died a happier woman, I think, than she had ever been before.

5

In 1942, after my mother's 'secret' was bared, and while she was still living alone, I suggested to her that she fill her empty days by writing her life story at length. She later confessed that the few pages she had been able to write were inadequate, and in truth they proved all too vague and allusive, too self-consciously 'literary,' in the jargon of a much earlier day, to be of interest to anyone. But in an old account book begun in 1899, I find a passage almost too painful to transcribe. It is dated 1924, but the handwriting indicates that this possibly is an accidental transposition of 1942: it was her final heart's cry—her last judgment.

> A life wasted but for one redeeming feature. To wake up one day and realize life has passed you by without the dreams, hopes, and longings fulfilled, is a thing words cannot tell the meaning of, living always in the thought that a change would come and the ambitions of a lifetime come to pass, to live and feel the bitterness of what might have been, never to have taken the bull by the horns, and in spite of obstacles to have gone ahead, instead of waiting for others to show the way, never knowing it was too late.

In a very real sense, those were my mother's last words. As to her final breakdown, I can add nothing to a fragment from one of Sophocles' lost dramas:

> *There is no burden like a life prolonged.*
> *To extreme old age all ills are natural,*
> *Mind gone, work useless, vain imaginings.*

6

This account of my close family background would be sadly incomplete if I did not bring in Nellie Ahearn, for she became attached to us before I was two years old, coming to my mother after having done a tour of duty with a more comfortably middle-class family, the Deckers, owners of one of New York's leading dairies. For all of us, Nana was always just Nana, not *my* nana; and I never learned till I had grown up that 'nanny' was the generic term for a child's nurse in England. In a very real sense she was a second mother.

Nana came to us before my mother had taken on the burden of a boardinghouse; and instead of remaining just a nana, she became a general houseworker and turned into a capable cook, too, though this imposed much more work at no advance in pay. I feel sure that she knew my mother's secret, though she never by so much as a breath disclosed it to me. I reciprocated her fondness for me; for more than once in the early years when Nana threw up her job, my mother noted in her diary: "Lewis misses her very much. . . . He told her to come home and cried after her."

Nana had been born in the small Irish seaport of Youghal; and she was so deeply dyed with its life that when a heavy storm came up at night she would always cross herself and say, "God pity the poor sailors on a night like this!" Her hard-pressed, but perhaps also hardhearted, widowed mother had—much against the frightened girl's will—sent her to America as a servant when she was sixteen, to improve the family fortunes by mailing back as much as she could spare from the sixteen or twenty dollars a month she earned. Though she sent the money, she never forgave her mother or fully recovered from this cold push into the cold world; so despite later family cajoling she never went back to the Old Country for a visit.

Nana made up for the family love denied her by devoting herself to me with a jealous passion, long after she had ceased in any other sense to be my nurse. And it might be her voice, no less than my mother's, that repeated a German nursery song to lull me to sleep: *"Patsche, patsche Kuchen, Bäcker hat gerufen."* Or she would amuse me by singing:

> *Are thee my darling? Are thee my dear?*
> *Come with me to Grogan's and I'll buy you some beer.*
> *While I have money, I'll spend it quite free,*
> *For I live in Baxter Street, four forty-three.*

Or perhaps she soothed me to the tune of "Casey would waltz with a strawberry blonde/ While the band played on." In Dublin recently I happened to mention at a dinner for me at the Shelburne this Irish

50

fragment of my New York background and found that the words were still familiar even to the younger people around the table, who thought it dated from the First World War and were surprised to find it had been current at least seventy-five years back.

Nana was one of those dark, Spanish-looking Irish types, a descendant perhaps of the original Mediterranean breed who colonized southern England and Ireland, or possibly of some Spanish sailor washed ashore in the wreck of the Great Armada. With her black hair and black eyes and her Roman nose and her sallow complexion, she certainly looked Spanish. In my youth a faint odor compounded of yellow soap, onions, sachet powder, and snuff hung about her. Her schooling had been even more brief than my mother's; she hardly knew any other environment than that of our family or, later, that of The Dakota, where she was private maid to the owner, before she entered the Catholic Home for the Aged—now vanished—which used to be on West Fifteenth Street west of Seventh Avenue.

Though she was actually in our service less than ten years, the relation she established lasted through a whole lifetime. She had her crotchets and her foibles, had Nana; for the real wrongs life had done her made her acutely sensitive to little wrongs or oversights, sometimes only fancied ones. But all this did not lessen her fierce sense of family devotion. During the period when my mother was too weak to do the housework herself and too poor to afford a weekly cleaning woman, Nana would consummate a hard week's work at The Dakota by cleaning our apartment from one end to the other, with her only reward a glass of whiskey from the wine closet. (For all our poverty, my mother still kept the ghost of a wine closet, just as she still went on brief vacations to Atlantic City and still bought dry goods, when she could buy anything, at Altman's.)

One could hardly imagine an existence more limited in scope than Nana's; for when she rejected an early offer by a printer who wished to marry her, despite the more than comfortable thirty-five dollars a week he was earning, she closed the door that might have led her to a more normal and independent family life. Naturally I became her surrogate child, and she devoted her life to my welfare.

Somehow, perhaps out of her peasant and seafaring background, she had acquired a kind of wisdom, and even a turn of speech, that are among the best gifts of a traditional mode of life. When she wanted to say she'd be there soon, she would say: "I'll be there in two shakes of a lamb's tail." And when she expressed surprise, she would say: "I'll take my supper!" Once, in the Home, when she complained about the nuns on her floor, she said: "They're always digging and dogging at you"—a phrase I had the wits to use later in 'The Golden Day.' Even more moving rhythms would sometimes come from her depths, mysteriously, like one whose occasion now mystifies me, though I noted the words on the spot: "And the hunger and

Nellie Ahearn (Nana)

the torture and the blood that was flowing." But one of her best Irishisms—"Never be backward in putting yourself forward"—was, I fear, largely lost on me.

7

The tie between Nana and my mother was naturally an ambivalent one; and their common love for me was not without tension and jealousy, however they might disguise it, or however deep, tenacious, and compassionate Nana's loyalty to my mother might be. At least thrice in the early days she walked out on my mother, only to be drawn back, when tempers had cooled or grievances were rectified, by her fondness for me. The fact that Nana was an utterly simple woman did not of course make her a less desirable companion for a little boy. Holding fast to the Christian faith and all its dispensations, she knew the difference between right and wrong, and in addition believed in good manners; so that, though I can't remember her punishing me, I am sure she corrected me and guided me no less than my mother did. Her admonitions about swearing were exemplary. "There's nothing wrong in just the word," she explained: "Damn, damn, damn—you might say it a thousand times. But it is a sin to swear *at* anyone. Besides, gentlemen never do it!" I can't think of a nicer demonstration in morals, manners—and semantics.

At the time of my christening in an Episcopal church my mother was 'indisposed'—in its vague connotations that is perhaps the correct word. So Nana took her place. But the first church I have any memory of is the solemn Paulist Fathers' church on Columbus Avenue and Fifty-ninth Street, where Nana would often take me to sprinkle me with holy water and light a candle for my health and salvation. If there were to be company for a Sunday dinner, she would go to the earliest possible Mass. Without these rites and the gleams of another life that they promised, I doubt she could have faced the hardships and deprivations of her own existence. She never won me to Catholicism, and except in her prayers she never sought to: at most she would sometimes remind me that I was by christening an authentic Episcopalian and should at least attend an Episcopalian Sunday school, which I finally did at the age of ten or eleven.

Ours was not in any sense a religious family. Even my elderly and sedate Philadelphia and Brooklyn relatives had in my youth drifted away from any formal religion and ceased to be active members of their Lutheran congregations. So until I went to Sunday school, it was through Nana mainly that I became acquainted with the outward forms and observances of Christianity.

As often happens with simple people, Nana somehow had gotten close to the heart of religion, and was not unduly hypnotized by the superficial rituals and claims of the Church. When I was eighteen, I had come on Henley's poem 'Invictus' and used to recite it frequently, as a bandage to my own bloody but unbowed head. One night, listening to me, she said: "That man is a heathen." When I asked her how she had found this out, she answered—and again I pick out the words I had actually set down promptly in my little 'Golden Treasury'—"God is the true Captain of our souls, and a Christian can't hold anything else." Plainly, she had listened not without understanding to her favorite priest, Father Taylor, and her religion, for all its superstitious accompaniments, gave her existence a meaningful destination that enabled her to face death with serenity and dignity.

Nana's life had presented a grim landscape of poverty, misery, loneliness, hard work, and illness, brightened only by fitful patches of sunlight, such as her yearly vacations in Dutchess County, during which, for once, she could take her ease and be waited upon by others. But as her relatives rose in the economic scale, they ceased to welcome her as a companion on these vacations, for she was still the dowdy greenhorn: and at the end her only visitor besides my mother and myself was a colorless orphaned niece, who unfortunately, Nana said, "had no nature."

8

Though Nana did not make a Roman Catholic of me—she always punctiliously insisted on the Roman part of that qualification—she made me feel so much at home in that church that I took easily to the ceremonial of High Church Episcopalianism, in a way that I never have to the barer ceremonies and the more didactic emphases of other Protestant churches, in which all too often the egotism of the preacher invades even the prayers, whose unctuous rhetoric addresses the audience rather than God. Never did I feel more keenly all that two thousand years of tradition can do to cover with seemly ceremony the bare grim act of disposing of the remains of the dead than at the Mass that preceded Nana's funeral.

The church where it was held, on West Forty-second Street, was a sad relic of Victorian red brick Gothic, and its brownish interior

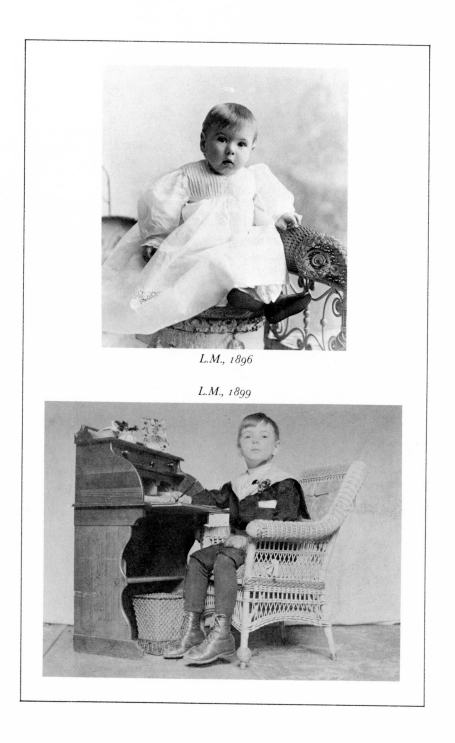

L.M., 1896

L.M., 1899

Grandfather Charles Graessel and L.M., 1902

Aunt Elvina and Uncle James Schleicher   Uncle Louis Siebrecht

Parlor of 105 W. 65th Street, with typical Victorian decoration

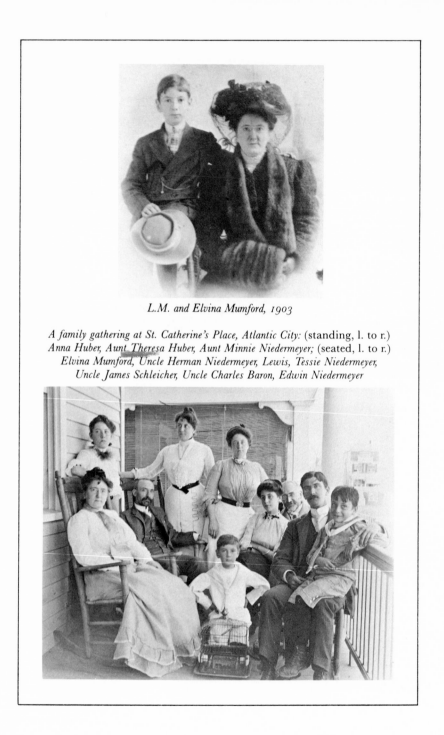

L.M. and Elvina Mumford, 1903

*A family gathering at St. Catherine's Place, Atlantic City: (standing, l. to r.)
Anna Huber, Aunt Theresa Huber, Aunt Minnie Niedermeyer; (seated, l. to r.)
Elvina Mumford, Uncle Herman Niedermeyer, Lewis, Tessie Niedermeyer,
Uncle James Schleicher, Uncle Charles Baron, Edwin Niedermeyer*

Beryl Morse

L.M., 1916

Patrick Geddes, 1930

Sophia at 18

Clarence Britten

L.M., 1922

L.M., sketch by Gladys Mayer, 1922

lacked every esthetic grace. But the fact that this Mass for the Dead was being celebrated had drawn, not only my mother and myself, and Nana's niece Anna, but a fair sprinkling of other communicants, pausing for a moment to face, as the Church constantly made them face, the precarious brevity of their own lives; so that the interior of the building, instead of being unbearably desolate, provided the human companionship such an hour demands, as did the Mass itself, intoned in Latin. What was this mysterious ritual, which may have had its origins in the paleolithic caves, but the most adequate symbol possible for the greater mysteries it pointed to? Even if one did not share the Church's ultimate assurances of heavenly salvation and resurrection, it bestowed a cosmic dignity on these last moments that no secular rite has yet rivaled. I am not sure that translating the Mass into an intelligible national language, still less with jazz music to accompany it, has made it more efficacious.

As life worked out, neither Nana nor my mother would have been an adequate parent alone; but between the two of them I had a sense of being constantly surrounded by love, and needed no extra reassurances. That perhaps explains why I carry so few scars, at least so few that are now visible to me, from what was on the surface a constricted childhood and a bleached, pinched, harried adolescence. Before I could finally draw on my inheritance, there were periods when only a peremptory gift of money from Nana assured me a badly needed overcoat or suit. To the end, she and I had our little jokes and teases, going back to the days when I used to sit in the kitchen and read to her while she peeled the potatoes and chopped the onions. When our Geddes and Alison were born, she gave to them, vicariously, the same fierce devotion she gave to me; talking aloud to their photographs, since visits could only be rare, following anxiously their illnesses; and out of the savings she had put by from her monthly pension from the Clark estate, she left each of them three hundred dollars at her death, after making me solemnly promise not to give this money to her niece.

This, then, was the immediate family ambience of my childhood; and these mixed advantages helped to counterbalance the disorders that came to a head in my adolescence: the thin but overactive body drained of vitality by insufficient food, the defective and too long neglected teeth, the attack of malaria that laid me low in the midst of my final examinations at High School, and the tuberculous lesion that our family friend, Dr. Carlin Phillips, discovered in treating my malaria.

Nana was right: if I had been master of my fate, I should, at the outset, have changed my surroundings and forfended some of these maladies and misfortunes. But for all its deficiencies, this curious family milieu nevertheless provided me with two advantages now often unavailable to the young: long periods of solitude, and the opportunity to explore the world around me and to find myself, before settling down to the task of earning a living. That much of Emerson's self-reliant world was still left in my boyhood; and in effect the Port of New York became my Walden Pond.

In many ways, some of them far from superficial, the family cards may seem to have been stacked against me; and the fact that I survived the limitations of my domestic background and even, in the long run, held a winning hand—a full house if not a royal flush!—seems to call for an explanation. Possibly the best clue to my survival is one that Dr. Sigmund Freud offered about himself, when he said, according to Ernest Jones, that "a man who has been the indisputable favorite of his mother keeps for life the feeling of a conqueror, that confidence of success that often induces real success."

This deep inner confidence, sometimes tactfully covered over as modesty, has never been absent, even during the most disheartening moments of my life. Was it not perhaps due to the fact that I had, in effect, two mothers who accepted my nature and encouraged my gifts, and gave me a sense of inner security? If my own sentimental juvenile attachments did not become an obstacle to further normal growth, it is perhaps because the other women I have loved and who gave me their love—above all the girl I married—called forth in me the passion and strength needed to grapple with life's obstinate realities.

CHAPTER FIVE

Faded Family Album

I

'*Dissipation.*' How full of meaning that word becomes when I reflect on the kind of life that was lived in my mother's family circle. I am not speaking here of sexual looseness, for apart from my Aunt Theresa, who probably had more than one lover, they adhered to current standards of respectability. But it was life itself that oozed away from them, sinking into the quicksand of an endless round of trivial activities.

In all their existence my New York relatives were never touched by an idea or a purpose, however narrow, that might have lifted them above their aimless round. They even turned their recreations into a form of work, as compulsive, as peripheral, yet as inexorable as the routine of office, shop, or factory. On a petty scale they had the superficial vices of the idle rich, of the Four Hundred, as the earlier coven of 'Beautiful People' was called.

Though my mother had qualities that made her appeal to two quite different men whose personalities were visibly elevated by their education, she fell too easily into the family routine, perhaps because her only center of loyalty was the family itself. How I came to detest that treadmill existence filled with empty amusements, empty excitements, empty quarrels—anything for distraction! Yes: a dissipated life. My mother's diaries from the 1890s give an endless record of these inanities: "Lost fifteen cents at pinochle. . . . Went to Proctor's matinee, not so good" and so forth. Her meager notes on my development were equally shallow, though she had sacrificed more attractive prospects in order to keep me by her.

Books played little part in her life, except fitfully, though books might have saved her or at least opened her eyes: it was 'The New York Herald'—particularly the personal and obituary columns—along with 'The Smart Set' and 'Town Topics' that claimed her. Until the radio came, such effortful time killing—what a confession these very words make!—occupied a large part of my mother's life. She was under no obligation to submit to this regime, any more than I was, just because she had been brought up to it; yet her participation was as absolute as my abstention; and in turn my revolt was as complete as her acceptance. "Ten men love what I hate," Robert Browning said, and at least nine were in my own family.

The five first-cousins who always lived within a mile or so of our home partly made up for my lack of brothers and sisters; one, Edwin, was near enough in age to be an occasional playmate. And there was much family visiting, particularly on Sundays, when it began around eleven in the morning with the appearance of one or the other of my uncles by marriage dropping in here or there for a half-hour's chat, whilst their wives were preparing the one o'clock Sunday dinner.

I do not know if this was a general New York custom then; but I suspect that, like the older New Year's Day round, this habit was a common way for those who did not go to church to lighten the tedium of Sunday, especially before the telephone had established a more lazy, disembodied form of communication, and before the Sunday newspaper had become a massive pseudo–encyclopedia-and-shopping-catalog capable of absorbing the whole day. Sometimes old family friends, like Mr. Harry Vogt, as debonair as a clothes dummy, would drop in, and there would be learned discussions of the latest sensation, the Nan Patterson murder trial—was she the murdered or the murderess? I now wonder—or the Pope's death or the Russo-Japanese War; conversations at which I would eavesdrop or occasionally even interject my opinion, as when, against my grandfather's faith in the might of Czarist Russia, I took the side of the Japanese, and Mr. Vogt, gravely nodding his blond head, said mysteriously: "From the mouths of little children!"

Regularly my uncle Herman Niedermeyer would stop by, already stoop-shouldered at forty from his clerical occupation, with haggard white cheeks, a pointed graying beard, and not too rarely, a twinkle of humor in his eyes. He would make ominous prophecies about the Market—it was turning bearish but might rally, as he had heard straight from Morgan's office, indeed almost from J. P. himself. As a bookkeeper in the banking house of Lazard Frères, he looked up to the Great Men of Wall Street like George Blumenthal in the way an ambitious young soldier might have looked up to Napoleon or Lee.

Yet with Uncle Herman this fierce concern for money was only a respectable disguise: the passion for figures, the delight in abstractions, served as his supreme incentive. On its own level this corresponded to the pleasure of a gifted mathematician playing with elegant equations. To my surprise my uncle recognized this esthetic trait in himself, and to that extent he understood and sympathized with my own commitment to literature and philosophy. Almost the last time we talked together, he said to me, in explaining his own life course, "After all, Lewis, you and I are artists." And he was.

My uncle Ernest Huber was of quite a different cut. Whereas the Niedermeyers had come from South Germany, Uncle Ernest had come from Hungary, via Vienna; and he had all the wiliness and *Schlamperei* of a sophisticated Central European: one who would rather get his way by devious tricks and subtly planned moves than by more forthright methods, just for the pleasure of exercising his wits. In the arts of tipping and bribing with just the right amounts to accomplish his purpose, he was a master.

Uncle Ernest had come to this country as an artist, a profession for which he had an insignificant conventional talent, as I judge from the few pictures I can remember. He painted sunsets; and what artist since Turner would paint sunsets? At first he tried to gain a living by keeping an artists' supply store and art gallery; but like all the immediate members of my family, he had no talent for running a business of his own; so he spent the greater part of his life as a china-and-glass salesman at Higgins and Seiter's, at which job his dramatic manner of exploiting the human weaknesses and vanities of his customers made him marvelously successful.

Bald-headed, with a scrubby vandyke beard and mobile, sensuous lips, himself attractive to women, he spent a large part of his life in cagey exercises to pin down his wife Theresa's infidelities; and he so well created an atmosphere of tormenting suspicion that he even conjured up nonexistent lapses. I smile wryly—but how guilt-ily!—at one illustration even now. One evening his wife, after a quarrel, had come to our house and innocently spent the night there. Next day, a Sunday, Uncle Ernest came, full of accusations; and when his wife denied any wrongdoing, he took me aside and asked, con-fidentially and cunningly: Had my aunt Theresa slept there last night? At seven I had not lived in vain in this suspicious atmosphere, so I answered, with equal canniness, "I don't know." Uncle Ernest felt triumphantly vindicated; and since I had committed myself to my 'cleverly' noncommittal answer, even my mother's urgent pleas for me to tell the truth could not budge me from it. Everybody but me got what they deserved.

But apart from his rumpled marriage bed, my uncle Ernest, outside his business hours, led an abortive, secondhand kind of life that matched at every point the empty existence of the women of the family. In summer he followed the baseball games zealously in the evening newspapers, knowing all the teams, keeping in mind the batting averages and games won: yet he boasted that he had never actually witnessed a ball game being played. His world, too, was a chaos of dissociated events, vicarious excitements, numerical abstrac-tions. But since it was his friendship with Mrs. Josephine French, the owner of a farm in middle Vermont, near Bethel, that ultimately led to my spending some enchanting summers there, he has a special niche in my gallery. Not least he, too, set me an example in cooking: his Hungarian goulashes and his sauerkraut with tomatoes and raisins were memorable.

Both Uncle Herman and Uncle Ernest remained lesser people than they might have been; some deficiency of the right elements in their environments, some blockage of their youthful gifts, some fail-ure in judgment or lack of inner pride had made them fall short of their own potentialities. Though economic pressures had doubtless narrowed their choices, the lack of any central personal aim or any broad civic interest limited them more severely.

Strangely enough, the only well-spent life in the New York family circle was that of my maternal uncle, Charles Baron, who was some five years younger than my mother. After growing up as the petted young male of the family, he was apprenticed at an early age to Tiffany's, when its factory was still on Prince Street, and in time he became a silver chaser and later a goldsmith. Uncle Charley was a neat, compact, jaunty little man, not unlike Stubb in 'Moby Dick': a careful workman, thrifty in his habits; and though not averse to the company of young women, he was too prudent to accept the responsibilities of marriage on the twenty dollars a week he earned as a young man, so that technically he remained a bachelor all his life.

Thanks to his being established in a craft and showing an aptitude for goldsmithing when the fashion for chased silver went out, he had a stable and satisfying occupation and the companionship of other competent craftsmen, executing the often admirable designs of Louis Tiffany and his assistants in the great Art Nouveau period of modern jewelry. Though his wages were low, his psychic income, as the economists used to call it, was high; for he took no little satisfaction and pride in meeting the challenges of his daily work. Of all my mother's close family, he was the only one whose potentialities were in any genuine fashion fulfilled. His success even extended to the fact that he died in a few unconscious minutes from a heart attack in the middle of the night, at the age of sixty-five, without any preliminary warnings, and thus escaped, as my mother did not, the humiliations of senile decrepitude.

On his meager pay, even before drawing an inheritance from his stepfather, Uncle Charley had managed in 1904 to visit Europe on a leisurely tour of a few months, and had gone on many later vacation trips—to Arizona and California, to Mexico, Venezuela, to Cuba, and Bermuda—often writing back letters to my mother full of wry humor, sharp observation, and positive enjoyment.

Until I finally had a room of my own, I used to be fascinated by Uncle Charley's den, as such inviolably male chambers used to be called. The den boasted rows of pipes hanging on the wall; a single-shot rifle that my uncle passed on to me at fourteen; a secondhand Civil War sword from Bannerman's, the famous dealers in surplus Civil War stocks; as well as an assortment of deep-sea and freshwater fishing rods, which he used to fashion himself of bethabara wood, and wind with colored silks, before varnishing. The den also flaunted, in the best masculine tradition, a small oil of a nude lady (rear view) surprised in the midst of a tub bath; and I perhaps betray more about myself than about my uncle when I say that this painting, which I felt it was becoming to look at only in passing, as if with complete indifference, made a deeper impression than the accouterments of fishing and hunting.

Since he was a young man when I was born, Uncle Charley did not fall into the role of surrogate father; and my aptitudes and interests were so different from his that we never got as close as we might have through living for a quarter of a century in the same household. Fishing might have brought us together once I was old enough for distant excursions, for Uncle Charley was a notable fisherman, who would return from a day's outing with enough bluefish, weakfish, or flounder for nearby neighbors as well as the family to share. But on our first expedition to his favorite bluefish haunt off Gifford's on Staten Island—I was then fourteen—I became miserably seasick on a perfect day when a long ground swell upset me, so I never went out in a boat with him again. But our son, Geddes, got on famously with my uncle, and, when he was eight or ten, would visit him alone at his summer cabin at Peach Lake near Brewster. My uncle gave him not only fishing tackle but a box of semiprecious stones; and Geddes appreciated, too, more than I could, the big jade ring my uncle had carved, when I passed it on to him.

Except perhaps for my aunt Theresa, an arrogant, selfish woman who yet played a voluptuous substitute role in my infantile fantasies, the immediate members of my family were essentially kindly people: it was the dreary routine of their lives, their painfully limited use of the more significant world around them, that drained away their genuine human qualities and gave more than a flicker of the sordid, the venal, the scheming to all their activities.

I have touched on this background only in order to convey some sense of the nest I flew down from, and to stress why even as a very little boy I never felt at ease in it. On the contrary, the sense of being apart was there from the beginning; and if I were tempted to underestimate this, there remains as verification a photograph of me at the age of four, sitting before the little desk my mother had given me as a birthday present, with an amused, supercilious, quizzical look on my face—a look that, I fear, has not in all these years quite disappeared. I didn't try to be different: I took it for granted that I was different, just as I took it for granted, till I dismally lapsed in high school courses, that I would always be first in my class. Though the latter involved effort, the possibility of my neglecting my homework then for some more interesting task, still less for boyish play, never seriously tempted me. But unlike Goethe, I did not awaken the jealousy or hostility of my peers.

Here we face one of the great teasers of education: What conditions are favorable to human nurture and growth? Can one be sure that what are called the best possible conditions—those free from gross obstacles and pitfalls, from injuries or setbacks, but packed instead with encouragements and rewards—are as life-promoting as we would like to believe? Quite likely I should have profited in my early years by much richer resources than those which I enjoyed; and my wife and I spent much effort in seeking to provide such resources for our children. Yet the things that we did not provide—or sought to avoid—may have counted even more heavily; and what we relied on most confidently as being of benefit, we must ruefully admit, more than once turned into just the opposite, because the personality we were dealing with had other and quite different needs.

3

Fortunately, among the real blessings of my family background were my Philadelphia and my California relatives—yes, and my Brooklyn relatives too—my aunt Dora and her husband Louis Siebrecht. These were people of a quite different caliber from the New York lot; and though I encountered them only occasionally, they reinforced and deepened my native bent. Though my great-grandmother's brother,

Adolph Hewel, had emigrated from Hannover in 1848 to become a forty-niner in California; he ended his life as a judge in Modesto. His widowed sister with her four daughters, Elvina, Dora, Anna Maria—my grandmother—and Theresa, followed him, at least as far as New York. The other three daughters were all better women than my grandmother; or perhaps they had better luck in marriage. When Aunt Dora and Uncle Louis met in America, they were enchanted to discover that they had spent their early lives in Hannover within a block of each other without knowing it.

Like my grandfather, Uncle Louis began life as a waiter and had followed the usual apprenticeship of nineteenth-century waiters in the days before passports and immigration barriers, when the task of serving food was taken seriously and met rigorous standards of deportment. So he had gone the rounds, a typical journeyman's pilgrimage, from small restaurants to big ones, and from provincial capitals like Hannover and Copenhagen to world capitals like Paris, which he saw during the days of Napoleon III's brief glory. It must have been then that he acquired his imperial, the fashion Napoleon had set. He had seen Hans Christian Andersen in the flesh in Copenhagen and had some good stories about his stinginess. One was about an old suit Andersen had given his valet. When the latter had the cloth turned, it looked so sound that the wily master reclaimed the gift! And when Dickens made his last visit to America, my uncle beheld him too at the dinner given at Delmonico's. To Uncle Louis he was always Charley Dickens.

Again like my grandfather, Uncle Louis spoke French as well as German and English, and he admired the novels of George Sand, which he had read in Paris. In 'A New York Childhood,' which I wrote a generation ago for 'The New Yorker,' I fused my grandfather and my granduncle into one figure: but in this portrait it was Uncle Louis who was the model of the stickler for form. He dressed with a strict eye for the occasion, never sitting down to a meal on even the hottest day of summer without wearing a jacket—and not letting any other male do so in his presence! In keeping with his courtly code Uncle Louis addressed even the butcher's boy and the iceman by their last names, prefixed with a 'Mister.' Unlike Shaw's phonetical hero, Henry Higgins, he would not merely have addressed flower girls like duchesses, he would have expected them to treat him with becoming courtesy, too.

Even when he was a young man, Uncle Louis's pale blond hair was almost white and his movements slow; but for all his poky and penurious ways, which my grandfather used to mock—he even sifted the ashes of his furnace to reclaim a few errant coals that had fallen through—he had a deep serenity that may have derived in part from his infallible sense of punctilio. His gravely dramatic conduct of ceremonies made our family Christmas parties at his house notable events, with the candlelighted tree, the magic-lantern show after the presents were distributed, the animal cookies, and the plenteous candy. Even ordinary dinners at this house I remember with respectful pleasure.

True, I was never at ease with their orphaned grandchild, Hewel, almost my age, for he had a tendency to be deviously mischievous, in fact, sneaky. It was Hewel who, at eleven or twelve, smirkily revealed to me the sexual games played by a group of boys and girls he had met on a country vacation: he even spelled out in a mysterious acrostic—Father's Uncle's Cousin Kate—the word that Mellors introduced into Lady Chatterley's vocabulary. Those revelations horrified yet naturally titillated me, somewhat in the way the Witches' Sabbath did Hawthorne's Young Goodman Brown.

Except at Christmas parties there was always an air of studious frugality at the Siebrechts'. This was both natural to their temperaments and necessary in a period when those who retired from work at sixty had no public form of security to fall back on. But despite the narrow margin, everything in the household was the best of its kind. I still have the chessboard and the coffeepot which Uncle Louis had made to order in the seventies, along with the blue-clad papier-mâché Santa Claus who always stood under the tree. The latter became for our children and grandchildren a precious symbol of family continuity.

Sophia and I equally cherish the silver-plated service he passed on to us, via my mother, for it was in the same chastely undecorated form that was once slyly introduced by Philip Johnson, I think, at the first exhibition of Industrial Art at the Modern Museum, as a 'modern' design for a teaspoon, since any genuine equivalent was currently lacking! Their good Limoges ware, of white porcelain with a gold rim, might have been added to that exhibition as an example of similar restraint; and the rich orange-brown plush that covered the furniture was of such good quality that we still have a pillow covered from the remains of it, after some ninety years of continual use.

The whole order of this household was based, not on ephemeral fashions and sensations, on goods deliberately misdesigned or weakened to impose early replacement, but on a lifetime economy. Quality, durability, functional fitness, refined choice—these were the desirable components of the materials and utensils that accompanied that life.

Have we not almost forgotten what such an economy, conceived in terms of generations and centuries, did for the human soul? Good, bad, or mediocre, serene or harried, ailing or healthy, none of my older relatives ever needed to seek the services of a psychiatrist. Though my aunt Dora set a more austere table than my mother originally did, the food was cooked to perfection, for she as well as her sisters had been apprenticed to a hotel in their native town as a young girl, so that they might learn from the bottom how to run a big household competently. That apprenticeship was not enforced by need but rather embarked on in the hope that they would marry well and be prepared to accept heavy domestic responsibilities.

On our almost monthly visits I would adopt Uncle Louis's standards of table behavior with a docility that used to surprise my mother. He and Aunt Dora expected children never to speak at table unless spoken to, and above all to eat whatever their elders put on their plates: strangely, the vegetables I would fuss over or refuse at home I used to tuck away without a murmur under Aunt Dora's eye, since that was the law of the household. In almost everything the strict German note was preserved here no less than in the home of my Philadelphia relatives. The old people prided themselves, for example, on their precise Hannoverian pronunciation—the classic language of the theater, they would always smugly remind us—never turning an 's' into the more usual German 'sch'; and in all other matters their conduct was equally exacting.

Despite this strictness and formalism—or perhaps, with the experience of my later years, it would now be more correct to say *because* of it—I enjoyed their company, and when in my teens I was old enough to pay calls on them by myself, I did so. With a full share of the old German respect for academic advancement, Uncle Louis approved my plan at nineteen to become a Ph.D. in philosophy, and he showed grave disappointment when later I abandoned that ambition.

From both my grandfather and my uncle Louis, who survived him by two decades, I got occasional glimpses of a more sophisticated world, as seen by two upstanding men whose business was to serve it. None knew better than they the demoralization that attends an excess of wealth and power: the imperious vanities and class egoisms, the unscrupulous trickery, the often callous indifference to the many subordinates the rich commanded and controlled. My uncle Louis had higher standards of conduct than most such people. Once, at the Harmonie Club, where he was Steward, the house committee informed my uncle (probably during the great depression of 1893) that it would be necessary to reduce the pay of all the club's employees; but knowing they had a steward of rare probity and ability, they added, "We shall, of course, make an exception in your case." "I regret, gentlemen," Uncle Louis replied, "that I cannot accept your proposal. If it is necessary to reduce salaries"—and he knew quite well that most of these gentlemen were only momentarily, if at all, embarrassed in their finances—"you will please reduce my salary first, in the same proportion as you apply to the men under me."

That anecdote lingers in my mind as one of a dozen little events of the same order of rectitude, and it at least displays a happier aspect of my family heritage, a tradition of personal self-respect and independence, indeed of complete unbribableness, which is still dear to me.

4

Just as rigorous but quite different was the more affluent household of the Schleichers in Philadelphia. They lived in a red brick, white marble-stepped house with a side alley, on North Nineteenth Street, between Arch Street and what was then Logan Square. When I knew the house, it had crept back into the original garden, and some of the floors were half a flight above the others, so that the place was full of dark, twisting passages and unexpected rooms. My mother's memories of this somber house went far back to her girlhood in the seventies, when she began visiting her aunt Elvina while her aunt was married to her first husband, George Ebeling, soon to die.

When my mother was sixteen, she fell in love with James Schleicher, who was then only a boarder in the household of my newly widowed aunt. There is no doubt that James reciprocated her love, for long after, when Aunt Elvina was dead, he declared that the image of my mother had haunted him all through his married life. Suddenly awakened by James, startled, indeed panicked by his attentions, my mother naïvely confessed to her aunt Elvina that this handsome, blue-eyed boarder had kissed her; and Aunt Elvina, frozen with an indignation that turned out to be far from impersonal, sent her packing back to New York—and promptly married James herself. In taking these decisive measures, it turned out that Aunt Elvina wrecked three lives; for she bore Uncle James no child of his own, and if my mother and Uncle James both paid for the separation, so did she.

Aunt Elvina was one of those small, compact women who seem by sheer force of character to tower physically. Once safely married to James, she resumed kindly relations with my mother; for apart from this one ruthless act, she was far from being a selfish monster: rather she was a sensitive, sympathetic, highly intelligent woman, whose worst faults were a passion for cleanliness that no ordinary servant could ever satisfy, and a tendency to be overcensorious and exacting about the moral standards of those around her—a classic psychal compensation for her own lapse.

As for her influence on me, we began badly but ended well. When I was four, she sent me out of the dining room in my own Sixty-fifth Street home—my own home, mind you!—because I had failed to say "Good morning" when I found her there at breakfast; and I still remember my shocked resentment over her having demanded conduct that only my mother, I thought, had a right to require—and rarely did. But in time Aunt Elvina and I became warm friends; and when I was six, at our summer cottage in Atlantic City, she taught me how to make a bed with hospital precision, permitting no slovenliness, her thin lips curling with disdain at those who did these household chores in a more slipshod fashion. She cooked with the same exquisite skill, and it was from her that my mother got her chief instruction in the culinary arts. But no effort on my aunt's part was sufficient to overcome the pall of soot on the curtains and polished furniture that the Pennsylvania Railroad used to dump on the city; and when we visited her Philadelphia home, we would often find her in tears either because another maid had just left her or because the lace curtains she had put up clean a few days before were already blackened—sometimes both.

From Aunt Elvina and from Uncle James I got a glimpse of the aristocratic principle: a life of the mind, with high standards of achievement in every department, exacting much of others but even more of themselves, with a sense of social responsibility on every occasion, and with an utter contempt for any merely fashionable criteria of either conduct or taste. Some of that was part of their family heritage, for Uncle James came from the Belgian branch of the Schleichers, domiciled in Antwerp for at least three centuries but still inveterately German. He could recollect the sixteenth-century mural painting on the walls of their ancient dining room. In his Philadelphia library, moreover, there was a book, or rather a tome, that traced their wide-spreading ancestral line through many generations of generals, African explorers, and public servants. But the essence of the aristocratic principle was in the man himself.

In his white-bearded old age, James [Jakob] Schleicher was a handsome man, short, compact, but delicate, with the hands of an artist and the soul of a poet, for all his devotion to engineering and finance. His pure blue eyes had a sparkling innocence that never left them. Trained as an engineer, he had come to America as representative of the new Otto Gas Engine Company; and in the nineties he had retired from its vice-presidency with what was, in those pre-income-tax days, a comfortable fortune of some half a million dollars.

Being a capitalist by conviction as well as by acquisition, Uncle

James felt morally obliged to invest his fortune, not in safe *rentier's* securities, but in enterprises involving risks. He paid a heavy penalty for this quixotic venturesomeness. But possibly the very riskiness of the stock market played the same role in Schleicher's frustrated sexual life as betting on the horse races did in my mother's—though he always reminded her self-righteously that, even if a confirmed 'bear,' he was a conservative investor, not a gambler like those who bet on horses.

Aunt Elvina had plenty of understanding of the kind of little boy I was, as Uncle James did later of the young man I became, and my only regret is that I did not have more frequent meetings and talks with both of them, or with Aunt Elvina's son, my cousin Adolph Ebeling. For it was Aunt Elvina who first gave me Shakespeare to read, and before that had given me the 'Story of the Bible,' which sufficed until I was ten. It was she who insisted upon meticulous clarity in pronunciation—like all my grandaunts she spoke without a trace of a German accent, though they sometimes kept the intonation. And it was she who, both by example and overt instruction, taught me considerate behavior to other people, high or low, old or young, poor or rich. Aunt Elvina never turned away a beggar who came to her door. Though she was chary of money handouts, she would prepare sandwiches for poor hungry men with the same care that she would for members of her family, only cutting the bread a little thicker; and in winter would sometimes come back from the door with tears of pity in her eyes. One morning in Atlantic City, when a young man at the beach had voluntarily performed some little service for her, perhaps adjusted a backrest, she pointed out to me that men did such things more readily for young, attractive women, and that it was a special grace to do it for an old woman like herself.

As for my uncle James, he had been trained in the classics and had a true taste for literature: it was he who gave me Viktor von Scheffel's 'Ekkehard' to counterbalance the picture of the Middle Ages I had found in Walter Scott; and the more my mind developed, the closer we found ourselves when we met. On my becoming an associate editor of the fortnightly 'Dial' in 1919, he immediately subscribed and, undisturbed by the magazine's political radicalism, he appreciated its excellent literary criticism. When 'The Dial' became a purely literary monthly, he liked it even better and read it with discriminating pleasure, at home with its many European references and not put off by the esthetic experiments it favored.

In that period Uncle James's renewed love for my mother, now openly declared, led him to write verses, some of which he submitted to the monthly 'Dial'; and he once showed them a charming account of his boyhood in Antwerp, which I regret I did not take pains to get a copy of, since it was never published. The sole vestige of that boyhood now is the word 'Antwerp' carved over the doorway of his old dwelling when he turned it into an apartment house. When I taught at the University of Pennsylvania, at intervals during the fifties, I would sometimes go out of my way just to pass that house: a grimy relic, but with the legend over the door still visible.

Perhaps during my adolescence I might have come closer to Uncle James, for we occasionally visited him after Aunt Elvina's death, in his modest suburban home in Merchantville, and were repelled, remembering her standards, by the rancid Maracaibo coffee his housekeeper served us. But the First World War came on, and like so many Germans in America, he was more imperial than the Kaiser, and viewed all of England's traditions with cold contempt, down to the fact that these barbarians degraded the sacred classics by calling Titus Livius 'Livy' and Marcus Tullius Cicero 'Tully.' Before the United States entered the war, he used to bombard my mother and myself with pamphlets arguing the German cause, unaware of the fact that these self-righteous pamphlets so often gave the German cause away. Though I then took a somewhat toplofty view of all these issues, my heart was on the side of the Allies, and my unsympathetic attitude toward the German cause made Uncle James's tirades an obstacle to more intimate intercourse.

Still, Uncle James had a kind of gritty integrity that enabled him to face without quailing the severest shocks of life. When finally his candy business went bankrupt and the factory itself was mortgaged to the hilt, he spent his declining years as night watchman in the plant he had once owned. His stoic sense of duty supported him through all the ordeals and disappointments of his life, even the final one, bitterest of all, that the woman he had always loved, my mother, could not bring herself to marry him and sustain him toward the end.

Fortunately Uncle James had resources within himself that he never permitted to languish. To the end, every week, he would send long letters and tender poems to my mother; he would work in his garden in season, minding his beloved roses; and he would read the fables of La Fontaine and the other classics of his youth. If the political scandals and the economic follies of the twenties aroused his ire and reinforced his contempt for the 'mob,' they also justified the feeling he always cherished, as part of his Germanic heritage, that the government of the best people is the best kind of government. Unfortunately Uncle James's sense of human values was sullied and betrayed by his sentimental attachment to moribund German institutions; and even more perhaps by a failure to appreciate the excellences represented by the democratic traditions of Jefferson and Emerson, a realm he never seriously explored.

My other close Philadelphia relative, Adolph Ebeling, was, until I was twenty, one of my legal guardians. A handsome, genial man with a vandyke beard, looking like the archetypal physician of the 1890s, he was very humane, but perhaps too easygoing and too trusting to be an effective factory manager. On our occasional meetings, up to the time I was eighteen, he had a way of tactfully slipping me a greenback, an English schoolboy's traditional 'tip,' when we said good-bye. We saw each other too little ever to get to the point of exchanging confidences about my origins. Yet of all my relatives he—along with my California cousin, Taza—is the one I most regret not having known more closely as a neighbor and friend.

At a moment in my youth when I was on principle most critical of the capitalist system, it amazed me to find, when I went through the candy factory with Cousin Adolph, on what familiar human terms he was with his workers, calling them by their first names, asking about a sick child or a coming wedding. It was a nonunion shop, and he paid low wages, chiefly to girls and women adding a bit to an insufficient family income; for Camden, Walt Whitman's home, was a low-grade industrial town. But the relation between employer and employed still did not quite correspond to my black-and-white diagram of the exploiter and exploited; and I knew all too well that despite my sympathy with the underdog, I could not then have met any of them halfway, on a human level, as he did. The candy business became bankrupt even before the Great Depression, but he never quite lost his inner buoyancy or his slightly caustic good humor. Though life had treated him harshly—for his wife died of a cancer in the midst of his other troubles—it left little harshness in his soul.

So much for my Philadelphia relatives. My California relatives, especially my cousin Taza Grollman and her mother, Aunt Theresa Jameson, were of an entirely different order; for in the relaxed air of California all the harsh Hannoverian qualities had been softened and sweetened. They were so different, in fact, from all my Manhattan relatives that one might think they belonged to a different race. What a brisk, bubbling, smiling, enthusiastic, outgoing woman my grandaunt Theresa was: she made one, in those prepollution days, feel there might be something to be said for the climate of California! On her visit East, when I was thirteen or fourteen—I met her then for the first time—her very presence brought out the depressing qualities of our New York family's routines. None of its members, not even my mother, abated a single game of poker or whist in order to do something for her entertainment; and deep down I felt shamed alike by their insensitive self-absorption and their neglect. From that time on I drew further apart from these elders, first in spirit, then by absenting myself from family parties.

This alienation produced an unfortunate temporary effect which was only confirmed by the popular mentors of the time, like George Bernard Shaw, in their clever satires on family life and in their adolescent iconoclasm: for a decade it made me underestimate family life itself and question the value of all its involuntary attachments and loyalties.

CHAPTER SIX

Sunlight
on Prison Walls

I

Of the two sides of my education, the spontaneous and the formal,
I am inclined to look back to and dwell upon only the first; for my
present sense of my school days, until I went to high school, is of
something sterile, dreary, tediously repetitious, as of a day under a
leaden sky with no air stirring and no prospect that the sun will
break through. But the greater part of my childhood was spent in
school, and I must try to measure its effects on me and my generation
before I deal with the more vivid moments of my early development.

Even when I draw my mind back to the daily routine of learning,
I find that it is the intervals of escape that come forward first, those
cloud-breaking moments when our class teacher was ill and some
male substitute, not quite sure of himself, would come in and 'keep
order' by reading stories to us, without any attempt to carry through
the regular program of teaching, though in fact every moment of
the day was so rigorously organized and accounted for that he should
have been able to intervene at any odd hour and give the correct
lesson. But I remember one or two rarer moments when, in the middle of the morning, the teacher might send me, as a reliable lad who
wouldn't dawdle or loiter, on an errand a few blocks away, and I
would find myself on an empty, childless street, its loneliness heightened by the cowbell tinkle of a ragman's cart, myself almost frightened by this sudden emancipation from the normal grind, protected
momentarily against truant officers by a pass, yet hastening on my

errand in order to get back more quickly to the inviolable routine that held me captive.

For some private reason of her own, perhaps no better one than that she wanted to keep me close to her as long as possible, my mother never sent me to kindergarten, so I didn't enter school till the autumn I turned seven, though I had already begun on my own account to read a little. The bigness of the first school I went to, Nunber 165 on West 108th Street, was an ordeal for a little boy who had never been let loose on the streets alone out of sight of his own doorway. The school building loomed as a large, lowering place, in which events happened in the detached, unchosen, embarrassing way that they do in dreams. These huge schoolhouses—already being designed for fifteen hundred pupils—were, I am convinced, entirely out of scale with a child's world, and if the private reactions of the children had been studied, I am sure that they would often have disclosed fears and bewilderments similar to my own.

There was, in fact, a sort of prison pall over the public schools of my day which even the most inspired teachers could hardly dispel, for they, too, were the victims of it as well as the accessories. The schools themselves, Number 165 and also Number 166 on Eighty-ninth Street between Amsterdam and Columbus Avenues, were barren places, although they had only lately been built, with slightly Gothic ornamentation of the window frames. Number 166 even pioneered in an air-conditioning system whose defects were more easily remedied than those in fashionable current examples, for the windows at least could be opened.

These schoolhouses were still being built on too small plots of ground; their outdoor yards were too narrow for games and, because of their paving, too dangerous for rough sports; while their darkened indoor yards, which occupied the ground floor, were equally poor for sports and served chiefly as a marshaling area for children who came to school too early to be admitted to the classroom. To me the classrooms were as dreary as the lessons given in them and were relieved only by an occasional potted plant, colored chalk landscapes on the blackboard, or a tank of goldfish.

One day lunch must have been served late at home, and when

75

I got back to school, the indoor yard on the ground floor where we usually assembled before class was empty. I did not know what to make of it, for I had never been late before. I wandered about in a void, disoriented. Someone found me there and took me in tears to the Principal, and she, reproving me for my lateness and castigating me for 'loitering,' put my name down in a black book. I could not have felt worse if the Recording Angel had entered my name in the final Book of Judgment. This little incident somehow sets the tone for the whole six years I spent in primary and grammar school: I was as it were a prisoner, sentenced for a crime I had not committed, though I might hope by good behavior to have my term shortened, or at least to escape further penalties.

Do not misunderstand me: my teachers were, almost without exception, kindly men and women—women in the elementary grades, men after I had reached 6–A; what is more, some of the teachers who were strictest in imposing discipline were often the kindliest as persons. As for myself, there was not a touch of the overt rebel in me; on the contrary, I was the image of docility and submission, concentrating on my work, never getting into mischief, always doing my homework fully and neatly, especially quick in abstract subjects like grammar and arithmetic. Nor did I take refuge from this grind in any physical malaise: I was never absent, my report cards show, for reasons of ill health. Before the disruptions of adolescence I was, in short, the Model Pupil. But I was always a duffer in any kind of manual art except drawing, for while I had plenty of blocks to play with, my mother and Nana had brought me up to be a 'little gentleman'—which meant someone who didn't get his clothes mussed and his hands soiled by rough play or grimy experiments.

School, as it was conducted in those days, was under a lock-step discipline, as if teaching had first been invented for punishment in prisons and then applied to pedagogical purposes. Learning involved endless drill and 'memory work,' as it was called. Now, not all of these exercises were wasted, as progressive educators with the backing of questionable scientific findings later mistakenly came to believe. But the cardinal fault of the system was that it didn't recognize that the pupil had any needs or impulses of his own. If a child

76

had dared to ask intelligent questions which would have called for discussion, our teachers would have regarded this not merely as an interruption but almost as a breach of discipline, for it would have obstructed the orderly progression of their timetables.

I never rebelled openly against this system by letting my attention wander, by playing with forbidden objects, like the wonderful fly cages of corks and pins (for bars) that more daring boys made, by surreptitiously chewing and stretching out great lengths of bubble-gum, or throwing blackboard erasers when the teacher's back was turned. My conduct was, in fact, odiously correct, and I can still remember, as testimony to this, the ache between my shoulder blades from sitting up with ramrod straightness, my hands behind my back. This, indeed, was the only permitted posture when we were not writing or reading.

The teacher was, in fact, a sort of drill sergeant, since almost every activity of the day was preceded by a formal direction—"Attention! Desks down! Hands on desks, place!"—and was usually carried out in perfect unison. The greatest virtue in teachers was their ability to 'keep order,' and their greatest humiliation came from a palpable lack of it, while the great achievement of my fellow pupils was the ability to break discipline without being caught at it: indeed, some of the more pugnacious boys almost made a career out of this defiance.

My docility, as I look back upon it, had in part a favorable explanation: I hated the thought of being kept after school as a punishment. I surrendered every freedom in the classroom so that I might not lose even five minutes after class, writing out 'I must not talk in class' fifty times. True, the naughtiest boys, as I was to realize all too late, sometimes enjoyed the special chores they had to perform, like washing the blackboards, and even got to know the teacher affectionately as a human being with a home, a family, a dog, a date—not just as a martinet. But it was not till I went to high school that a teacher was for me anything but an official person, wearing an almost visible uniform, whom one kept away from warily, as if he were a policeman.

As for my scholastic record, that had behind it not so much a love for the subjects I mastered as an unwillingness to take second place. All through my early school career I earned nothing but A's, with a quite rare B or B+ to confess that I was still perhaps human. I liked the process of learning well enough, for my quick head and prompt memory made up for my inept hands: but apart from the satisfaction that reading gave me, I can hardly remember a subject that was interesting in itself, unless one got from it, as in 'mental arithmetic' or a spelling bee, some of the excitement of a game. Occasionally, on Friday afternoons, we would be tentatively introduced to little textbooks dealing with subjects not treated then in the curriculum; one on Greek myths and another on astronomy fascinated me. But these subjects were never pursued: they seem to have represented either innovations that had never been sanctioned or experiments that were prematurely discarded.

If the business of education was to turn out people without imagination, without desire, without capacity for choice, without initiative or will, this educational environment was well conceived, and the routine it served was no less admirable.

2

I have given a picture of these infantine prisons, as I gave a picture of the domestic interiors of my youth, because the schools of my day explain the kind of revolt that was slowly gathering headway and at last burst forth under the banner of progressive education during the twenties in a series of experiments that were later to be standardized and stereotyped by the Teachers Colleges.

Some of the people who led this revolt, like Caroline Pratt, the founder of the City and Country School, were friends of mine and my wife's. We at first sent our children to progressive schools with unquestioning faith in what the new teachers were trying to accomplish. Our son, Geddes, went to Miss Pratt's school, our daughter, Alison, at the nursery stage, to the Bank Street School—and my wife helped to found an equally liberated school in Sunnyside.

Remembering our own caged youth, we gloried in the informal discipline, in the bold work done in paint and clay, in the sturdy independence of the children. All this went along with the movable seating in classrooms without fixed desks, and the free ranging around the city *during* school hours to find out what went on in the streets, the warehouses, the wholesale markets, the wharves and ships of the waterfront. The confident initiative of these youngsters—always incited, their mentors held, by interest, never dulled by harsh discipline, drill, empty routine—seemed to us entirely admirable, without qualification.

But as so often happens in sweeping reforms, the leaders who made the advance did not carry with them any of the virtues of the system they rejected. They abandoned the coercion of the teacher but fell back, when they at last needed a modicum of order, on the coercion of the peer group, a much more difficult kind of pressure to stand out against or to escape. In progressive education's readiness to follow the lead of the child, it forgot the child's limited knowledge of its own interests, its own possibilities, or the actualities of the world around it, likewise the child's limited sense of what its own future held forth and what its further development demanded. This method of education too often allowed the claims and interests of the moment or the year to take precedence over needs that stretch for a whole lifetime—though admittedly much preliminary education must be accomplished in the early years, as is the case in the preparatory maturation of the sexual organs years before reproduction is possible.

Above all, the progressive educators forgot that in the dialectic of growth, polar opposition is often as important in bringing out a student's energies as encouragement. To make everything that a child does in school as smooth, as easy, as immediately assimilable as possible, is to deprive education of the conditions necessary for even a pleasurable game. In a game we not merely define fixed rules but inflict penalties and accept losses and failure as a valuable and essential part of the ultimate reward.

Certainly the long days of prisonlike drill, the weeks and months and years spent in following the sterile routines of the old-fashioned school, inflicted a great waste of time, indeed, a wholesale misdirection of life. But to admit this and correct it was a far different matter from the kind of change introduced by the followers of William Kilpatrick, that genial, kindly man, the Saint Paul of the Progressive-education Movement, who helped to turn John Dewey's experimental rationalism into a cult of benign effortlessness and permissiveness.

One cannot blame John Dewey for this miscarriage, any more than one can blame Jesus for the sins and superstitions of the Christian Church. It was not Dewey's fault that the schools of education made a new formalism out of their informality, or that, despite their belief in educational experiments, they lacked the courage to confess to some of their own ghastly failures—as in their obstinate commitment to teaching reading by the 'block method,' without regard to either individual letters or the sequence of words. No feedback! Their nearest approach to admitting this error was to inaugurate a new profession—remedial reading! This lack of candor and open-mindedness and self-criticism, this unwavering sense of self-righteousness vitiated many of the genuine improvements that 'progressive' education brought in. Not for the first time did the progressives of one generation become the entrenched conservatives of the next.

Mind you, I would not put the blame upon 'progressive' education alone, any more than I would put the blame for my own youthful passivity and docility on the old-fashioned curriculum. But I regard these ailments as being reinforced respectively by each type of school, even though the school itself was but a reflection of a more general attitude in society.

In these matters progressive educators would have done well to have heeded the lesson on which Ernest Renan dwelt in his 'Memories of Youth.' His teachers, he recalled, while "without a trace of what nowadays we call pedagogy . . . observed the primary rule of all education: not to make too easy exercises designed to teach the pupil the value of difficulties to overcome." The object, above all others, should be "to mold the character, to make good men." Roxana Siloti, the daughter of the Russian concert pianist, once told me that her father, even when he was past the age of eighty, used to practice his finger exercises regularly for hours every morning, just to keep in trim: he called it "doing his washing." That element of drill, as in Dürer's practice of drawing a perfect circle freehand, is a prerequisite of perfection in every art.

My elementary education was, as I look back on it, needlessly meager: it ignored most of the resources the immediate environment offered, strained all experiences through textbooks and even more sterile dictated exercises, and provided us with second- and third-hand information that was never vivified by direct observation or verified by experiment. We were given geography lessons about remote parts of the world without having watchfully walked over any part of our own region or examined the activities of our own city; we were given botany lessons without having handled living or even dead plants; we were given literature lessons largely through meritorious poems like 'The Chambered Nautilus,' which no child could understand. We parsed, analyzed, dissected, copied, without being encouraged to put anything together in school in our own right. In short, we got good marks for echoes and imitations, not for any signs of active constructive ability.

But at least we knew how to "do our washing." When we were graduated from grammar school, most of us could at least read, write, and calculate without embarrassment. Most important of all, perhaps, we were allowed to have, through what might now be looked upon as callous neglect, something very important for a child's growth: we had a private life of our own, an area no grown-up ever intruded upon, where the roots of our being were nourished, without being dug up for repeated examination, psychological appraisal, and public report. That was no little gift.

Admittedly we all paid a price for the order achieved in the school system of my time—an unnecessarily heavy price, for there was no inherent reason for all this regimentation. There was no reason, that is, except the prevalence of oversized classes—or the fact that contemporary industry, business, and officialdom were based upon a similar suppression of the human personality. With a more generous allotment of public funds to education and with smaller classes, more teachers might have developed those qualifications that Louis Sullivan, in his 'Autobiography of an Idea,' admiringly discerned in his master, Moses Woolson: the ability to infuse a rigorous discipline with one's own passion and high purpose.

Yet when all the weaknesses of the old scholastic drill are fully reckoned up, a positive good remains to be noted. Peace reigned within the walls of the American school. Teachers established discipline by moral authority alone, with only occasional resort to physical punishment, and without undergoing the risk of being attacked by their students either inside or outside the classroom. No child was daily in danger of being robbed, beaten, or otherwise assaulted on his way to school or even while in school, or subject to coercion by blackmailers or drug pushers. Yes, there were already ominous pockets of violence and crime scattered about the city, but the school was still immune. And apart from sly, occasional thefts, crime of any sort within the school was, in my youth, unthinkable. An accepted law and order still provided not only external security but at least the minimum of that internal moral conformity essential for all human cooperation. At the moment I write, all these conditions for education have vanished from my native city—as they have from the world at large.

3

Happily, the strictures about my education hold true only for the first part of it, until I had turned thirteen and was ready for high school. Between skipping three grades, and being out for half a school year when I was eleven, I had managed to escape almost two school years of the allotted boredom. Had I been confined to my own age group for eight full years, I probably would have had an even more unpleasant report to make on the defects of the system.

Though I hardly knew my grammar-school teachers as human beings, I find that I have singularly warm and vivid images of many of them, from Miss Rittenberg, my first primary-school teacher, to Miss Lacey, a bosomy Victorian creature, who was my last woman teacher, in 5–B: above all, of my last two teachers, Mr. Palen and Mr. Chase, the latter a big, powerful bulldog of a man. Both these men gave me something, as men, that was more precious than any formal lesson. Palen endears himself to me still by his quiet modesty and self-respect: he was sure enough of himself to confess the difficulties he had had in mastering some of the subjects he taught us, like algebra. He was a soft-featured, bald-headed man, with those fine wrinkles at the corners of his eyes that testified to his sense of humor, and he treated us in a quaint, unheard-of fashion by prefixing 'Master' to our last names, making us feel somehow grown-up. His air of quiet authority never deserted him, and one day he gave us a memorable demonstration of what lay behind this authority.

Each month our Principal, Mr. Thomas Moore, would visit the classes to hand out our report cards, occasionally with a word of rebuke to some laggard or misbehaving pupil, more rarely with a dry smile of approval when he beheld a sequence of A's. He was a formidable figure, always erect as if on parade, always dressed in a Prince Albert coat with a stock instead of a necktie. With his ample white goatee, his head topped by a crisp pompadour, and his small, piercing gray eyes, he seemed a gentlemanly Uncle Sam. Like Mr. Chase, he was a Civil War veteran, and though we called him 'Pop' Moore behind his back, we knew him as a stickler for form, and at times somewhat irascible.

This particular morning in Palen's class something had put our Principal out of temper, and when he discovered on a report card that one luckless lad had received C in Deportment and B in Effort, he turned on Palen and said: "No boy deserves the mark of B in Effort if he has C in Deportment: that shows he didn't make the effort." I saw Palen flush and remove his spectacles; then very quietly he said: "Mr. Moore, you have every right to find fault with the way in which I conduct my class or give my marks; but if you wish to reprove me, I expect you to do that in privacy, and not before my own pupils." Silence followed. The Principal's face, always red, turned almost purple, and he rose slowly and left the classroom without another word. We felt like cheering, but the utter hush that followed was even more eloquent. When the door closed, Palen soberly explained to us why he had challenged lawful authority.

That lesson in civic courage, in unshakable firmness in the face of superior power, was not provided in the curriculum, but it has lasted longer than anything else I was taught.

As for my graduating class teacher, William Chase, he was exasperated with me, as only a big, manly man can be exasperated by a febrile youngster whose mind he admires and whose performance in boyish games, in running a race, say, was always hopelessly inferior, for I handicapped myself in sprinting by flinging back my head, in imitation of the photographs of runners I used to see in the newspapers—not knowing that their tilted heads and open mouths showed that the race was over. But Chase gave me confidence in myself: a decisive final fillip before we parted and my days as a Model Pupil were over.

Since my marks qualified me as Valedictorian of the class, as well as the recipient of the sole award given at the exercises—a five-dollar gold piece!—Chase had given me the standard valedictory speech to memorize. He himself, years before, had probably written this speech, whose opening words I still remember: "Ladies and Gentlemen: To me has been assigned the duty and the pleasure of bringing these exercises to a close." He rehearsed it with me during school hours in the little scientific-instrument room *cum* lending library, lighted only by a skylight, on the top floor; and after two or three ragged trials there was a look of utter dejection on his face when he stopped me halfway through, with his arms crossed in front of him and his big gray head sunk in despair. "No! No!" I looked timidly up at him. "You don't feel what you are saying. You are just saying words. Try the first few lines, this way," and he showed me. Again I tried, and again I was wooden. After a few more attempts he said: "It simply won't do. You don't even know the lines. Go home and study it some more."

I left the room in anguish, ashamed, not only because I coveted the honor but because I wanted to please him, as a good pupil always wants to please his teacher and seeks, as a way of doing this, to imitate his mentor. But there was such a gap between us! I, small, thin, peaked, white-faced, with a high voice that had not yet broken, beginning to be a little furtive under the first sexual strains of adolescence, with dark circles under my eyes; and he, the very picture of big-handed masculine competence and solidity.

Next day I came back, and he waited, with face averted, for me to begin. I had worked hard over the declamation, and this time he did not interrupt me from start to finish. Finally, as I closed, he turned around to face me, shaking his head from side to side in a fashion one might interpret as despair. "I never heard anything like it," he rumbled: "You wouldn't think it was the same boy who was here yesterday. Now you've got it; we'll only need a few more rehearsals." Then he looked me in the eye. "Mumford, you can do anything you have a mind to do," and for a moment his heavy hand lingered benignly on my shoulder.

CHAPTER SEVEN

Roots
in the Countryside

I

Though I have described myself as a child of the city, there was a hidden part of my personality that had roots in the summers I had spent, between 1903 and 1908, on a farm near Bethel, Vermont. Those summers, with their round of rural activities, left such a sharp imprint that I have drawn on them ever since.

The farm where my mother and I stayed was owned by a friend of the family, Mrs. Josephine French, a woman of unusual character, long a widow, with cosmopolitan interests and friends. In her bedroom was a great four-poster bed from Jefferson's Monticello, given her by T. Jefferson Levy, the last private occupant, I believe, of that estate. Though Mrs. French's speech was deeply tinged with the idioms and inflections of her region (she used to say 'wa'n't' for 'wasn't'), she was sufficiently emancipated from the local mores to wear white duck trousers in the summer on the farm and to smoke cigarettes at a time when this was regarded as the definite sign of a 'fast' woman. That characterization could not have been applied to her, for all her independence, except by the overcensorious. To a nine-year-old boy she seemed rather the embodiment of bosomy, motherly qualities, still a little strict about manners, but always kindly.

The farm itself, some hundred and sixty acres, lay on the eastern slope of the White River valley: the hills on either side of the river formed a wide 'V', with the shallow waters hidden in a wooded cleft at the bottom. The farmhouse, built too near the middle of the

Nineteenth Century to have the comely proportions of an earlier architecture, lay almost midway up the slope. Below stretched the cornfields and the hayfields, and conveniently, across the road, spread the fenced kitchen garden, backed by a solid hedge of Jerusalem artichokes.

Across the river, high up the treeless mountain, was the marble quarry from which Bethel got its chief living, and one could watch the little engine hauling marble along the switchback railroad every day. All the primitive occupations—quarryman, hunter, woodman, herdsman, farmer, fisherman—were carried on before my eyes, so that either by observation or by actual participation I made them mine.

I was too timid and too 'bookish' a child to make as full use of this environment by exploring it alone as my son did in our own Oblong Valley. At ten I was more ready to read about wildlife in Ernest Thompson Seton's 'Two Little Savages' than to investigate it by myself. Nevertheless, I accompanied my older cousin Herbert on his woodchuck and squirrel hunts, and under his careful instruction I learned to use a .22 caliber repeating rifle; I even became a fair shot. Though later I took second rank to our son, whom the Army rated as 'expert marksman,' I remained good enough, even at sixty, to be sure of killing a vagrant rabbit at the end of our garden with a single shot through the head.

This whole scene was for me pervaded by a mythical figure, that of Sam Day, Mrs. French's brother, who had been dead a year or two before I started my summer sojourns there. Sam Day's genial ghost still haunted this whole domain; for he apparently was a man of unusual force and acumen, with an experimental mind. Sam Day was, for example, the first to introduce an indoor flush toilet—a 'turd machine,' his neighbors called it; and he tried out new vegetables long before anyone else around. What he had said and done always served as guideposts both to Herbert and to Augie, the hairy, illiterate, almost half-witted German farmhand, with tobacco juice always drooling from the sides of his mouth to his unshaven chin, who ran the place up to the time I ceased going there.

So strongly did the image of Sam Day remain with me that he

became the principal character of the first novel I ever attempted, a novel that started out in this same setting, though at the time I wrote it, around 1917, I was still so ignorant of common plants that I did not know that tulip bulbs were not planted in the spring.

Sam Day's influence on me touched more than the outdoors: if anything, it made an even more powerful impression indoors, for the living room boasted a library of perhaps two or three hundred books, most of them far above my level of understanding or taste even at fourteen—the time of my last visit. But there was one set I remember dipping into: John Ruskin's 'Modern Painters.' Sam Day had also a writing room, always known as the office, just about the size of the eight-by-nine room in which I am now working; and in the shabby little apartment that Mrs. French conveniently maintained in Bethel itself, over a shop on the main street, there were still bound copies of the 'Illustrated London News,' which I used to read, to the humming of the sawmill in the gorge of the river below, on long afternoons when Herbert would go off to shoot pool with his older cronies.

How keenly I remember those pages of the 'Illustrated London News'! There must have been at least ten bound volumes of them, going back through the blazing moments of Britain's imperialistic enterprise and glory, often singularly well illustrated, mainly with wood engravings. Its editors had enough esthetic sense, before photoengraving became common, to get Gustave Doré to depict with masterly vividness the awful slums of industrial London. Those wood engravings I made use of in 1938 in 'The Culture of Cities.' Some of that British ichor must have seeped into my blood, though part of it may have come from the equally enigmatic pages of 'Chatterbox,' a book-sized annual that was a yearly Christmas gift in my early childhood.

It was from these rural contacts that books of a higher quality first came into my life; and perhaps—I admit this seems farfetched—I was not untouched by the fact that Bethel's only celebrity was a writer, Mrs. Mary Waller, the author of a locally famous novel, 'The Woodcarver of 'Lympus.' At that time she was still living in a gawky post-Civil War mansion at the foot of the hill leading down to the more suburban outskirts of Bethel. On a Saturday night, after the farmers had been to market and to the barber's for their weekly shave, one could find Mrs. Waller's rustic types at long tables in the Bascom House, eating their supper mid shoals of vegetable dishes and pickles and hot biscuits before the long drive home.

This was doubtless a very special introduction to rural American life, though it might have had a counterpart in the antebellum Virginia that Bronson Alcott used to visit as a peddler. But certainly it doesn't correspond to the memories of one of my younger friends, Wright Morris, in rural Nebraska even a generation ago, nor yet to those of another mid-American writer, Virgil Geddes, whom I met in the Navy. Geddes had first become acquainted with the drama as a literary form by reading at the age of fifteen an advertisement of the works of Shakespeare in a Sears Roebuck catalog. Though farming was always an unprosperous occupation in stony Vermont—most of the old barns had never been painted, and even some of the houses had changed their original coating for the dark char of the sun—I saw immediately around me, not such rural seediness but the graces of a well-kept farm whose inhabitants belonged not only to their neighborhood but to a wider world.

2

The charm of those Vermont summers has stayed with me, undiminished for more than seventy years. In fantasy it is always a sunlit world, innocent, fragrant, profuse in bodily pleasures: the endless doughnuts that Annie, our plump, comely mulatto cook fed into a stone crock that apparently had no bottom; the cool, shaded milk room, where the milk was set in pans for the cream to rise; and the big glasses of milk at table, so creamy that the residual milk took up only the last inch at the bottom; to say nothing of hot blueberry puddings with creamed, melted maple-sugar sauce, nutmeg-spiced—a delight that has never been duplicated for me—and the plenitude of fresh vegetables, only an hour or so out of the garden. As a progressive farmer, Sam Day had introduced the little round watermelon, much sweeter than the bigger variety used to be, just as he had introduced black Mexican corn. But we would often roast field corn for ourselves between meals. To top this, Herbert would for a treat occasionally filch a can of lobster from the pantry shelf.

This freedom to take from the abundance of nature, to search and choose and gather and eat without the embarrassing ritual of buying and selling according to one's limited means—is this not the quickest way of returning to the Garden of Eden—the Eden of early pre-Neolithic man, who must often have starved but who was not kept by law or economics from enjoying the fruits Nature in her capricious bounty might temptingly offer him? Perhaps one of the worst mischiefs of our inflated money economy today is its attempts to return by the devious route of mass production to the same original state, where one can have whatever one's eye lights on without counting the cost. What is now called 'impulse buying' is the tasteless final dilution of the impulse garnering and eating of our more adventurous forebears.

Perhaps the greatest benefit I got from my summers in Vermont was my experience of this wilder kind of environment, a more primitive way of life that American boys, right up to the beginning of this century, had enjoyed everywhere except in the biggest and foulest cities. To get the first whiff of a skunk in the distance, to follow a chicken hawk circling in the sky, to encounter a shrew on lifting a log in a woodpile, to whistle to a woodchuck to coax him out of his hole, to pick up the trail of deer from their droppings or their hoof marks in the abandoned apple orchard, to watch a doe and her fawns skim like swallows over a high fence, to spend an afternoon by the chuckling waters of the stone-bedded White River, fishing for river trout—all this deepened my sense of my native American roots.

But even better, this whole experience, it turned out, gave me, as nothing else could have done, a greater sympathy with our more robust and adventurous son, who took to the country with a passion that made all my youthful reactions seem bloodless; for in the seventeen brief years when the Amenia countryside dominated his waking life, and even more, probably, his dreams, he realized in his rural experience at every season what I had taken in by mere samplings in the summer months. Yet even that sketchy rural background of mine helped bring us together, as my equally meager experience of Navy life deepened our common understanding when he felt the need, on his last visit home, to tell us in detail of what he had been through in the Army.

Not the least happy of my rustic hours were those I spent by myself, alone with my daydreams. On cool summer days I would lie in the hammock slung between the maples in front of the house, cover myself with the fringed edging, and listen to the whispers of the leaves above me for hours at a time. But it is next to impossible to record in their fullness and their immediacy the varied pleasures, the endless subtle changes that each new day brings to even a half-awakened soul in the country. As our twelve-year-old Geddes once said, speaking of our Amenia landscape, "I could live here all my life, and from day to day no part of it would ever be the same."

Let me recall a single moment in my childhood which still comes back with some of its original vividness: a ride in a four-seater trap one starry July night, fragrant with drying hay in the cooling sun-baked fields. Herbert was driving the trap, and a young schoolmarm from the neighborhood was with us. What I remember is the stars themselves and the mystery of the immense sky; for until then they had played no part in my urban consciousness, and in summer, even in the country, I was usually in bed before it was quite dark. Yet in grammar school I had peeked into a book on astronomy and had been fascinated by its cosmic perspectives.

Encouraged by the young schoolmarm's warm response, I remember speaking with a childish sense of importance about space and distance and the meaning of all these other planets and stars; and she added to the wonder by pointing out, more than once, a shooting star falling through the sky. I spoke of these far-off things with the curiosity and awe that children, perhaps, not unlike our primitive ancestors, sometimes show about ultimate matters. But the "silence of the eternal spaces" did not frighten me, for the reassuring jog of Pedro's hooves and the warm, musty smell of his body were as comfortingly near as the schoolmarm's arm around my shoulder, protecting me from the cool night air.

I have never since studied astronomy even in the most casual way, and I still perhaps do not get the fullness of Robert Frost's poem about Sirius, the Dog Star. Yet only a little while ago, in chatting with a group of M.I.T. astrophysicists at their weekly luncheon, I found myself curiously exhilarated by the play of their disciplined but daring minds, and realized how much I had lost by my tardy awakening to the cosmos itself. But it was not our first moon landings and rocket explorations, still less hectic fantasies of colonizing outer space, that awakened me. It was rather Alexander Marshak's brilliant demonstration of Paleolithic moon calendars scratched on reindeer bones that revealed to me the part played by sky-watching in man's earliest development of both writing and abstract thought.

Every part of the Bethel farm is etched in my memory: so well that one morning in the early 1940s, when our Dartmouth friends, Artemas and Marjorie Packard, drove Sophia and me along the still unimproved dirt road from South Royalton, I recognized all the familiar landmarks from half a mile away. Nothing had changed except the distances; for all the spaces had queerly shrunken back from a little boy's scale to an adult's, and the barn was twice as close to the house as I had remembered. Even Mrs. French was still on hand, in her mid-eighties, to welcome Sophia and recognize me, though we'd not met for a quarter of a century. Our visit was brief, but it confirmed the accuracy of all my memories and made them more fragrant than ever, just as Proust had later eaten a real *madeleine* and found it still tasted the same.

CHAPTER EIGHT

Adolescent Influences

I

In brooding over the memories of my early schooling, I have left out the effect of my fellow pupils, and perhaps this is because within the context of school itself—that was not of course true after school hours—they had so little effect on one's life, except when by chance they stepped out of line, and caused the whole class to be punished for some private misdemeanor when the teacher was out of the room. Like Oscar Wilde's prisoners in Reading Gaol, we were aware of one another; only the rules of the prison did not permit closer intercourse.

But it is strange how vividly I remember the names and the faces of my early schoolmates, though we were never to meet again, most of us, not even in high school: Major and Conroy, Eckelman and Elmer Jacobs, Rossman, Dreier, Rouland, Maurice Walters, along with more identifiable personalities, Phillip Greer, a lame lad, in braces after infantile paralysis, and Carlos McCormick, a Spaniard by descent whom we called 'Beef Trust' because, like the figure in the political cartoons, he was so huge. (By accident I learned later that he became a lieutenant in the Marines in 1918 and was killed in the battle of Belleau Wood.) Paul Brown, who lived on my block and drew wonderful horses, was probably the same Brown who continued to draw horses and won a name for himself among sports people. Carleton Swasey, my deadly rival in the graduating class, with upturned nose and derisive down-turned lips, was just such another little prig, as I was. Yes! What became of him? I never heard.

These schoolmates, in sheer variety, were typical of my city. With a few of them I used to walk home regularly from school, sometimes with our arms fraternally slung over one another's shoulders, in a fashion that no longer seems common. In spite of my good marks, or even worse, the *eulogium* that my teachers would often append at the end of the term to my report card, I was never cut off from my schoolfellows or treated as a 'sissy.' Somehow I always remained sufficiently extroverted to be accepted as a tolerable if not an intimate member of the gang. If I played some of our games badly, still I played them with gusto, as I ate with equal gusto the potatoes we would sometimes swipe—we didn't class it as stealing!—from the corner grocer and bake in the vacant lot behind my house on Ninety-third Street.

This touch of the banal, this appetite for the immediate occasion, came out a few years ago when I underwent a Rorschach test for a group making a comparative study at Columbia University. In spite of various contrary indications, it seemed that extroversion weighed a little more heavily than introversion in the balance of my character, and there have been many moments when this saved me, I would guess, from the sense of being 'out of it' that the intellectual so often has in addition to the natural loneliness of his vocation. If I have gone my own way, or as some would doubtless put it, played the lone wolf, it has been more a matter of choice than of temperament. A person who is by nature a lone wolf would hardly have become a cheerleader at his high school games or been voted the most popular member of the class, as actually happened when I was graduated from high school. Even the fact that I was nominated tells something.

One final layer of my early life remains to be uncovered: the traditional games that were passed on from one generation of children to another, with great punctilio, without any coaching whatever from the adult world. There were no municipal playgrounds in my neighborhood, or anywhere else in the city for that matter, except on the Lower East Side, and it was accepted practice on the part of the Central Park police that they would chase any gang of boys out of the park on the theory, possibly sound, that a gang would probably be up to mischief. The street was our playground, and the sequence of our activities there was so closely regulated that an observer who knew the seasonal calendar could tell what month it was by whether it was tops or marbles or buttons we were playing. Between the ages of six and twelve we played all the old-fashioned games, red rover, spanish fly, and above all, one-a-cat, with a hard, hand-whittled wooden cat, not the molded rubber kind that supplanted it. The last two games were favorites, and red rover was the only one that included girls, whom we called Mollies in a more affectionate mood, or Crows when we were giving them their due.

We had our own signals and war cries, too: "Chikky (cheese it) the cop!" when we were alarmed at being caught by no matter whom in no matter what mischief, or "Get a horse" to express our highly ambivalent contempt for the new automobile. We took Halloween more seriously, that is, more mischievously, than children do now, belaboring one another so vigorously with chalk and stockings full of flour that every sensible boy turned his coat inside out when he went on the street that day.

Even if one side of my life as a child was a little lonely and self-contained, it was still incomparably more sociable and normal than, say, that of Dickens or Ruskin. And if I have some insight into the transmission of oral traditions in archaic societies, it is because I once lived in such a society, a tribe whose inviolable folkways were faithfully passed on from generation to generation by the children themselves.

2

From the age of twelve, when I bought my first tennis racket, I haunted the nearby Central Park tennis courts, and the game itself haunted me. Until I was almost seventeen, I recall incredulously, I managed to live through the winter buoyed up only by the prospect of the first day in spring when the courts would open.

The public tennis courts in the park, south of the Ninety-seventh Street transverse, were informally laid out in a meadow that had not been too carefully graded to further the game. They were then cov-

95

ered with grass, and the most popular court, half denuded by constant playing, was called the dirt court. This court had gained favor, probably, because a little rise above it furnished a grandstand for spectators, though the upward tilt of the court itself gave an unfair advantage to the server on that side.

An aged keeper, with a gray beard spattered with tobacco juice, had charge of the marking of the courts and the stowing away of the nets. He was probably one of those Civil War pensioners who were still favored on the public payrolls, and we called him Captain; he had a vile temper and carried on an uncivil war of his own with most of the people who played there. He was often drunk, and the white lines he marked with his sprinkler showed no disposition to follow the straight and narrow path, yet this crusty character gave the place a certain flavor. We had to supply our own nets and poles, but we couldn't start playing till the Captain raised the flag on a central flagpole.

It was an odd gang that hung around the courts those days: a few reporters on 'The New York American' and 'The New York Press'; a languid theatrical agent whom we called Ted; a swarthy hunchback with no visible occupation nicknamed Dirty Ferdie; a few semiprofessional loafers who played for stakes; and a handful of young women who were usually attached to the older men, ancients who might be at least thirty years old, as well as a few boys of my own age or thereabouts, who took tennis very seriously. Among the latter were two quiet, gentlemanly lads, somewhat younger than I, the brothers Pringle, whom I cultivated for a time because they happily owned a net. (One of them, Henry, eventually wrote a standard early biography of Theodore Roosevelt.) Day after day through the muggy summer we would lounge around on the hill behind the dirt court and play, and lounge, and play again till we could scarcely drag our feet around the court.

Among all the curious characters who dawdled and gossiped on the courts, one in particular still stands out: perhaps because he addressed his more esoteric reflections to me. He was a tall bent reed, always listlessly slouching, with a cigarette dangling from his mouth, a scooped-out, yellow-stained, trembly-fingered man whom I knew only as Jake. Rumor said he had been a brilliant young philosopher at Columbia and had been knocked out completely by an attack of brain fever following his graduation. His head, with its scant, cropped hair, now reminds me of that of a dissolute Roman emperor, but he knew philosophy thoroughly from Aristotle to Aquinas, and it was the one subject that could stiffen his drooping cynical lips or banish temporarily his self-punishing boredom. He used to preach the superiority of the scholastic philosophers, particularly John of Salisbury and Aquinas, two whole decades before Neo-Thomism became a momentary password among the fashionable intelligentsia.

This was a complete, self-contained world; even on a rainy day we would come over to the courts with our rackets, sprawling on benches under the trees toward the reservoir, speculating on the weather. When the males were alone, the conversation would descend to basement level, and I would go home with new words I couldn't find in my ten-volume 'Century Dictionary,' sometimes with lickerish hints about aspects of life I hadn't the faintest clue to till I came upon Freud and began to study abnormal psychology. On the whole, perhaps, it was a good thing we played so much tennis: but apart from that I was protected by an armor of innocence, fastened tight by sheer ignorance, which few boys and girls of the same age today, I find, seem to possess.

I don't know if I can convey the precise flavor of the city that one inhaled on those Central Park courts in my day. It was perhaps closest to what one feels on a clean, sunny beach onto which the ocean periodically washes stale watermelon rinds, mildewed oranges, and discarded paper boxes. Hints of meanness, sordidness, dishonesty, perversion seeped into this inncoent world and tainted my own innocence. By the time I was fifteen I had acquired a sophistication that would have honored the proverbial cub reporter, and my tennis coach in high school, Ernest Quimby, once exclaimed in justifiable horror: "You talk like a disillusioned man of sixty."

Yet with all my early knowingness, as the reader will soon see, I went through the first experience of being in love as if all my life had been spent in Arcadia. When I was a member of the Board of Higher Education in the 1930s, I officially attended a song festival given by the girls of Hunter College, a charming lot of hussies whose dance routines would have done credit to Broadway. In the very alluring performance they put on, in the songs they made up, I detected the same combination of virginity and cynicism, of chastity and shamelessness—the curious protective patina that so often forms over the Spirit of Youth in a big city. They were exquisitely young and fresh, yet they were already a little hardened, a little cheapened.

3

Stuyvesant, then an industrial and scientific high school, marked the beginning of my active scholastic education; and it was, all in all, a stimulating and rewarding experience. Many of my teachers were young men who brought into the place the contemporary flavor of their colleges, Cornell, Chicago, or Wisconsin, as well as nearer universities; people who were stirred up over their subjects and who would break into a routine demonstration in physics with hints of exciting scientific news that would not for a decade or two invade the textbooks, though I might already have read about it in Hugo Gernsback's 'Modern Electrics.' Einstein's first theory of relativity, for instance, or the electronic theory of matter—then called the corpuscular theory—were not unknown to some of us. This new view made the old-fashioned doctrine of the indivisible atom look silly, except as a convenience in writing chemical equations. Yes: it was in 1911, I remember, that my physics teacher held up his pencil and said: "If we knew how to unlock the energy in this carbon, a few pencils would be enough to run the subways of New York."

Our Principal, Dr. Ernest van Nardroff, a sweet, portly man with a gray vandyke beard and a bald head, was excited about science, too; he kept a class in physics for himself all through his principalship and would beam at us when he had presided over a good demonstration. Some of the more menial subjects in engineering, like mechanical drawing, seemed to attract only routineers, but to make up for it, there were teachers in patternmaking or metal-turning who had worked with the Yale and Towne Lock Company or in the Baldwin Locomotive Works, and who were not tethered to the profession of teaching out of mere ineptitude at worldly tasks. As for the man who taught us forging, he was a German blacksmith of the old school, and his iron roses and his scrolly leaves were our envy.

That a school so strenuously dedicated to science and the mechanical arts should have had a good English department was extremely fortunate for a lad whose mathematical aptitude waned shortly after he wrote his first love letter. My teacher in freshman English, a rapt, brooding young man named Thomas Bates, with a freckled face and a huge mop of carroty hair, encouraged a little group of us to write a play; and from his lips I first heard the name of Bernard Shaw, a name uttered only with bated breath in my mother's circle because of the scandal of 'Mrs. Warren's Profession.' Strangely enough, we not only wrote the play but painted the scenery for it and put it on, pathetic little hayseed farce that it was, before the whole school.

Dramatic production was, of course, an extracurricular activity; and it was another such activity, tennis, that brought me close to an English teacher, Ernest Quimby, a descendant of the Quimbys who migrated to Salem in 1683: a tense, sharp, exacting man, proud of his New England family and passionate about humane letters, who so intelligently introduced me to Milton that I never took seriously T. S. Eliot's callow disparagement of that poet. From Quimby's services in both English expression and tennis, I learned the value of style, not to be cultivated merely as a grace in itself but as the surest method of sending the ball where one wanted it to go.

While my high-school studies were varied and interesting, these personal encounters were the most essential parts of the educational process, whether they took place in or out of the classroom. How much I received from my really first-rate teacher, Arnold, who taught me plane geometry! He was the only mathematics teacher who gave us any insight into the philosophical foundations of this subject, making us see the difference between the actual world, where all our measurements, however carefully made, were inexact, approximate, faulty, and the ideal world of mathematics, where perfection was possible. Arnold freed our minds from the textbook by the simple device of constantly labeling the figures we studied with varying letters or by turning the figure itself in different positions from those in the textbook.

Then there was Herman Mantel, a handsome, dark-haired man, looking like an Italian, who came in fact from a South German Catholic family. He was too goodhumoredly indulgent to drill us effectively in French or German, for we could divert him easily into more interesting discussions; but it was from him that I learned about the study of philology and how elemental words like 'mother' and 'father' may have traveled from Sanskrit into all the Indo-European languages. Even the very existence of philosophy captivated me when he repeated Descartes' magical words: *Cogito, ergo sum.* Thanks to Mantel the first course I elected in college was that on the history of philosophy.

In my last term at Stuyvesant High School I had still another teacher who left a mark on me. James Fyffe Wilson, who taught us English history, contrived to bring into the classroom the fresh air of the contemporary American world. He was a gritty, upstanding, challenging man whose quick anger existed to serve the purposes of justice: a Californian by birth and education, one of those in whom the Jeffersonian hopes of the pioneer in the beneficent freedoms of the New World had been chastened though not extinguished by the rapacities of financial monopoly and political corruption. From him we first heard about the conflict between vested interests and public interests, between capital and labor, between the railroads and the farmers, and between electoral corruption under bossism and honest choice; for Wilson spoke for the new Progressivism that was then sweeping the country and was bringing these old themes back to life again. What he taught was not English History I—it was his side-references to current American affairs that gave life to the English story—and Wilson himself, shrewd, admonitory, full of passionate feeling, exemplifying a kind of American that was beginning to pass out of the picture even in California, was the best lesson of all.

The effect of all these people, educationally speaking, was out of all proportion to what they taught in class or the time I spent in their company. Not the lesson itself but the overflow was what mattered—a hint, a pat on the shoulder, the confession of a secret ambition, a fragment of unposed life as someone had actually lived it, and the marks that living itself had left on the quick face. There is no curriculum, no methodology that can provide for such illuminations, and yet the better part of education lies in waiting for such moments and seizing them when they come. "I and mine do not convince by arguments," says Whitman. "We convince by our presence." That is the essence of teaching; and heaven help the generation that thinks it has found a substitute in teaching machines, whether they are fabricated in a factory or in a Teachers College.

As you see, high school brought none of the interminable close-packed boredom that remains the chief impress of my earlier schooling. There was no lack of stimuli in this milieu. Even some of the subject matter in the curriculum, some of my actual contacts with tools and processes as well as personalities, have remained with me all my life; and without the kind of elementary scientific and technical training I received, I would never have dared later on to give at Columbia University perhaps the earliest courses offered anywhere on the Machine Age, nor could I have written 'Technics and Civilization' and 'The Myth of the Machine.' Not knowing the kind of writer I was to become, it was still fortunate that I went to Stuyvesant; for whether I was destined to become the playwright I once meant to be or the ungowned philosopher I have in the end become, my high-school background was broad enough to serve me.

The three and a half years I spent at Stuyvesant gave me a big chunk of life to absorb. Perhaps we were stretched a little too hard by our studies during a period when our bodies demanded a larger share of athletic exercise and idle relaxation than we gave them. That would be my only criticism, obviously expressing my own physical limitations. Not having enough energy to meet all life's demands, I ceased to be a Model Pupil after the first year, flunked a course in algebra once, and achieved such a mediocre record, apart from English, that today I would have had no chance to get into a good college, perhaps not even into a minor one.

No matter: this was no prison diet, and apart from my getting low marks I flourished on it. By the time I had practiced tennis on the Curtis High School courts on Staten Island, traveling two hours for the sake of playing one, had made humorous public announcements in the morning assembly, had taken the part of the villain, Defarge, in 'The Only Way' at the Little Carnegie Theater, had helped edit 'The Caliper,' our school monthly, and had dickered with one-horse job printers on John Street, I knew my way about the city and had made at least a cursory inspection of what life there had to offer.

But well before I left high school, one thing had been decided. Unlike most of the members of the graduating class, the note under my biography in the yearbook announced: Mumford will *not* be an engineer.

CHAPTER NINE

Eros
in Central Park

I

In many lives it is the beginnings that are most significant: the first steps, though seemingly effaced, leave their imprint on everything else that follows. In my case I can write the more freely because Beryl, my first sweetheart, has long been dead; and all I have to tell about our relations is so utterly innocent that I draw on my memories easily.

When I say Beryl Morse was the first girl I fell in love with, I am not speaking by the book. At the age of five I fell in love with Maisie, a jockey's daughter, who lived at the Saratoga hotel where my mother and I sometimes stayed: the ugliness of her pinched, white face, scarred by a horse's hoof, seemed to me enchanting, and it haunted me. Later, as I was on the verge of adolescence, I had, while staying in the Vermont farmhouse, the same vivid experience in a more heady form with the brown-haired lass of twelve who helped as hired girl in the kitchen. But Beryl came earlier than Bertha and stayed far later.

When we were ten, I had admired Beryl from a distance: she was one of our small mixed group who used to play simple games, tag and cops-and-robbers and high jumping, on the paths by the tennis courts in Central Park. Beryl was beautiful as a child and she soon went on the stage; indeed, she was Wendy in Maude Adams's 'Peter Pan' at this time, though, alas, I never saw her act in that part. She had a special combination of wildness and gravity, of tomboyish agility and ladylike grace; and her long legs helped her to be the second best high jumper in our group, only Paul Brown being, as I remember, a better one, because he had mastered the side approach to the bar—or rather string—over which we jumped. The other boys called her 'Beer Bottles' behind her back, because her legs were so shapely; but though I adored Beryl from a distance, 'my' girl then was a little Russian princess—at least everybody said she was a princess, and her parents certainly looked loftily foreign—who had taken possession of me in a decisive, inexorable way that I have found all my life quite dampening to love and eventually fatal to sexual passion.

When Beryl and I met again, we were fifteen, and she was pitching ball in a tan middy blouse with another Wadleigh High School girl over the grassy spaces near the tennis courts, with that loose, accurate, free arm swing which so few girls are capable of achieving because, I believe, of a slight difference in the anatomy of the shoulder. I recognized her, but I don't remember who broke the ice first; perhaps I did by returning the ball to her when her chum dropped it. But before long we were meeting at the tennis courts every day. We had so much to talk about, as it seemed then, that we often forgot to toss ball; and since she didn't boast a racket, I never thought of teaching her tennis—though she learned quickly to become a good player under other tutelage.

We used to walk home together as far as Ninety-third Street and Columbus Avenue, where we parted; and there was often, at the moment when we shook hands, a kind of honeyed gleam in her half-closed eyes that has always remained in my mind as a private symbol of passionate intimacy. Oh! we were in love for the better part of a spring and a summer, no doubt about that: she, waiting coyly for the next move, I, palpitant and adoring but timid, mistrustful, untutored, wanting everything and daring nothing, though I was thrilled even by the mere touch of her shoulder as we walked side by side.

That year was to be one of the most intense, the most emotionally absorbed, the most rewarding years of my life, though streaked with painful jealousy and adolescent despair. But all that was so rich and radiant in it went on under the surface, a mere possibility, a distant hope, never to be translated into a more palpable reality. So it was little wonder that Beryl, before even half a year had gone by, was already gaily enmeshed with various other wooers and adorers, and with an abandon whose cause I only dimly suspected and innocently misinterpreted, was soon to awaken to real passion in an intimacy with an undiscriminating rival whose erotic talents left a residual effect on the rest of her emotional life, in and out of marriage with three husbands.

Yet before I was thrust into the outer circle of Beryl's admirers, with a special orbit of my own that lasted almost until her first marriage in 1917, I had moments with her that I can still recall with more than a little of their original glow. The earliest was an afternoon we spent together in early September in a house off Riverside Drive in the West Seventies that she and her mother had temporarily inhabited that summer, before some family misfortune she never divulged to me threw them into a few cramped rooms in a dingy old tenement off Eighth Avenue and 113th Street. Beryl's mother was out that afternoon; a thunderstorm came up, and at some point when the air became sultry with the amorous tension between us, Beryl took me down to the kitchen, and we made fudge together, pouring the little potful—and how clumsy we both were!—onto a platter many times too big for it. All this somehow only emphasized our intimacy; it was the first time I had ever been quite alone with a girl in an empty house. I didn't know what to do about it; I certainly yearned to kiss her, but I didn't. When her mother suddenly entered the room, something snapped between us, and I felt as guilty as if we had been caught together naked.

The other moments I recall had the same quality of hot desire, extreme tension, and denial. One was when she began to teach me how to dance, an art I never acquired till the end of that decade. On Beryl's first attempt to teach me I found that the mere holding of her in my arms for a few minutes—I boorishly begged off in the middle of the lesson!—roused my penis to a point of exquisite erotic delight that almost became pain. But I have said enough. My response to our first light physical contacts warned me that we could not take to petting—it was not called that then, but heaven knows it was done!—because petting would be emotionally intolerable unless we were prepared to go much further. I recoiled from doing that, partly out of a sense of honor, but even more out of a sense of unreadiness. I had wits enough to realize that if she felt toward me the way I felt toward her, it would all too soon lead to marriage, and I was not prepared for that.

As Beryl and I drifted apart, we spent endless hours gravely analyzing how we felt and what was happening to us. These post-mortems were, at intervals all through our friendship, a bitter ritual each time a sudden gust of passion made the dead ashes glow again. There was something in me that held her and fulfilled a deep need, something that represented a part of her nature that was being sub-merged in the gay, irresponsible after-work life she found herself leading as the favored artist's model for a string of magazine illus-trators when she became the main support of her mother. We did a lot of clarifying vivisection on each other; but I don't think we ever put forward the simplest cause of our difficulties, namely, that we were of the same age, even to the month. In other words, that I was at least five years too young, emotionally speaking.

So we took refuge, almost from the beginning, in what we called a platonic friendship; and it was not till after I had read Plato and gotten to know something about the erotic life of Greece that I re-alized how accurate that description was, for there was always, even in our coldest moments, my delight in her beauty, her long, straight limbs, her lithe body and firm breasts, her half-parted lips with the characteristically short Greek upper lip, her gray-green eyes, which would sometimes be blue, and her long chestnut hair, which she promptly bobbed around 1914 in the fashion of Irene Castle.

The whole course of our friendship was sustained by the entic-ing possibility, if not the urgent promise, of more open love and erotic delight. All my friendships with women, even those that be-came more maturely intimate, have shown the same quality of inter-play: erotic desire quickened, if sometimes postponed, by the uninhibited responsiveness of our minds. And surely, homosexuality aside, that is what the word 'platonic' should convey to us, in the context of friendship.

In going over the things that kept Beryl and me apart, and yet together, in a running stream of quarrels and reconciliations, I mustn't overlook the great temperamental difference between us;

for I, from the age of fifteen on, became more shy and ingrown, deepening in these disabilities for the next half-dozen years, while she, both by temperament and reasoned conviction, was an outgoing person, a little like Browning's Last Duchess, "too soon made glad, too easily impressed." Beryl was ready to be friends with almost anyone who would rescue her for a few hours from her sordid surroundings, and even before she had begun to go out with the artists she posed for and the other amiable men she would meet in their studios, she had a wide choice of older suitors, all more experienced, more prosperous, more adventuresome—above all, less censorious and less lugubrious—than I was. Her own favorite adjective for the life she was disposed to lead was 'hectic.'

Quite early in our friendship, when we were nearing seventeen, we had a showdown; and the letter she wrote me then is perhaps worth quoting from, if only to show what a radical change had been taking place then (that is, around 1912) in the adolescent patterns of courtship. I had put it up to her to choose between me and the most serious candidate for her affections. "Why," she demanded, not quite frankly as it happened, "do you single out Joe?

> There are other boys that I see far oftener than Joe, and anyway you know perfectly well that he is just a jolly, good-natured, lovable fellow—here now, there next—surely he won't keep his piece of candy very long—he'll return it and try another brand. And again, Lewis, you know my weakness, I love to be popular and admired and to go everywhere and see everything. And how can I unless I have a lot of friends? And surely if I *show* them that I like only one boy, they won't like me and my good times will be spoilt. I like to have one fellow crazy over me after another. . . . One more point, my grandmother may have been expected to choose the fellow she liked best when *she* was sixteen, but I don't think it's exactly required by law for me to do so now.

In short, Beryl rejected with scorn what most girls would once have taken for granted. This was true not merely of Beryl, but of her whole group: the generation that was to invent the cut-in as a method of changing dancing partners and was soon to change them almost as rapidly in bed. Sexually speaking, this was an Age of Confidence; and my own attempt to establish a different relationship was either thirty years too late or forty too early, though it doubtless came from the same jealous sense of insecurity that in the fifties made 'going steady'—and as a consequence prematurely early marriages—the temporary pattern after the Second World War.

There was, I think, some fluctuating midpoint between Beryl's easy extroversion and my own puritanically restrictive introversion, with its premature shutdown on tentative adventures, that would have given us both greater happiness than either of us, in youth, managed to achieve. Certainly I was not prepared for an early marriage; and I managed to tell her that, I see now, as I look over my early one-act comedies, in a variety of ways; for my heroes were too often some variant of Shaw's frightened John Tanner, who manages to escape, full of brilliant self-congratulations, the trap of marriage.

"None but the brave deserves to escape the fair" was the overt motto of one of my skits. The fact that I repeated the theme so often shows how well I realized my danger. Though I occasionally gave Beryl a bad moment by telling her how shallow and hollow the life she was living had made her, my conscience should have been troubled over my own inadequacies, not hers. I might set marriage aside; but sex was not so easily put down. By the time I was nineteen or twenty, Beryl wrote out a prescription for my case, with her customary feminine archness: "You really," she said, "ought to get to know a nice chorus girl or two—*intimately.*"

All through this account, I am now aware, I have been looking at Beryl through the eyes of my youth, giving her appearance, her acts, her words the same value they had for me when I was an enraptured, indeed a lovesick adolescent. Was she indeed the rare creature I have pictured? As far as her physical beauty goes, yes: and there I would probably have all my older contemporaries on my side. But what do her letters tell now? Is there a sentence or a phrase that would indicate, even to a charitable mind, any touch of the originality that her early career as a 'prodigy' foreshadowed? I will be honest: I cannot find any. Yet if I had my own letters to go by— fortunately she spared me that embarrassment!—would I judge any differently of myself? Except for my original studiousness and my growing unwillingness to accept second bests, there would be nothing to show above Beryl's level.

Yet that cold judgment does not do justice to either of us. There was a potential in Beryl which finally, after many blocks and diversions, emerged in middle life; and it was perhaps this potential that for long teasingly lingered in both our memories.

2

In the early part of our friendship it was Beryl who was my intellectual superior, as well as my mentor in etiquette. Had she not won prizes for her verses and stories in 'St. Nicholas'—a sophisticated teenagers' magazine I had hardly even heard of? Against great inner resistance on my part, for my new Shavian heroes were strikingly ungallant and even rude, she finally browbeat me into offering her my hand when she descended from a streetcar, and it was she who corrected my sometimes plebeian grammar and was scornful when I tried to justify 'he don't' by pointing out that this locution was used sometimes by Dickens, for it showed, she said, that I didn't realize Dickens was vulgar, too. She knew Lewis Carroll by heart and found 'Jabberwocky' adjectives like 'uffish' very handy. I still have the copy of the 'Bab Ballads' she gave me in 1912 with 'Gentle Alice Brown' marked particularly for my attention—that and 'The Suicide's Grave.' Perhaps a prophetic hint, because the Gay Young Sorter and the lovesick Dicky-Bird both came to a bad end.

Her novel reading, even during her most frivolous period, was always years ahead of mine, for she was devouring Balzac, Maupassant, and Dostoevsky while I was content with Cooper, Dickens, and Thackeray; and it was she, with her actress's diction and her real love of Latin, who caused me imitatively to say 'more' instead of 'mawr.' Beryl even taught me, without words, subtle forms of politeness, like that of her never closing the door of her own apartment when saying good-bye until after the elevator had begun to take me down. It was Beryl, too, who introduced me to a circle of New York life then quite outside my own province, taking me when I was eighteen or nineteen to a tea at the studio of her uncle Will the portrait painter, on West Fifty-seventh Street: a musical tea, at which someone recited "Tyger! Tyger! Burning bright . . ." My first studio! My first tea! My first entry into the adult world!

There were a few brief weeks, once at nineteen, and again at twenty-one, when it seemed, after a sudden unexpected flare of passion between us, that she would take my education as a lover in hand, too. One time, when she inexplicably came down to the pier to see me off on the night boat to Boston, I had a wild, momentary dream that she might share my cabin, and I could tell by the faint smile with which she dismissed my unspoken suggestion that the idea had passed through her mind, too. But both of us knew that this was a game we couldn't finish.

The last time we seriously contemplated our fate as possible lovers was just a year or two before her first marriage. She used then to preface her strenuous days, modeling for illustrators, by playing tennis on some nearby courts on Morningside Heights, the recently smart but already shabby district in which she was living. I would get up at five in the morning to play with her, partly because I loved the game, too, but even more because I still loved Beryl. Again our relations grew warmer—this must have been another of her between-engagements periods—and one night they came again to a head.

The sense of that hot summer night has never left me. The street below was swarming with children and inundated by a hurdy-gurdy thumping out a tune from 'Cavalleria Rusticana,' when I told her I wanted to marry her—*eventually*. She was very self-possessed about that. She sent me down to the corner for some ice cream, which dealers then used to heap up in flimsy paper boxes, and then she took me up to the roof of her apartment house, a flight higher than the elevator went, so that we could talk matters over while we dipped, turn and turn, into the ice-cream box. The thick summer sky flared to the east with the lights of Harlem, and on this high roof one had a sense of separation from the rest of the world one doesn't usually achieve in Nature at a level lower than five thousand feet. But nobody ever succeeded in making love convincingly when his hands were all sticky from ice cream. Perhaps Beryl knew that when she complained about the heat.

"Always remember," she said, "in spite of what I do and what I seem to be and how circumstances may alter themselves, we'll always be the best of friends. Hunh?" I had not said the words I had planned to say, and this was not the response that Beryl was supposed to make; but I fear I was relieved. For I abruptly left her and went down to the steamy pavement, on which big raindrops were beginning to spatter, feeling dramatically solemn. The same tune, probably from the same hand organ, was still clanging in the middle distance. And I was already sketching in my mind the first act of a play to be called 'Love on Morningside Heights.'

3

If Beryl was long to remain for me the paragon of beauty, of elegant manners, and of a lovely feminine wile that was equally bewitching and exasperating, I too had a special niche in her life, not just because I was 'different' but because, until years of living with superficial and inferior people had dimmed her own capacities a little, she had a quick and questing mind, and kept me company in all my own activities.

During my first year at college we began collaborating on short stories and motion-picture scripts, though without any success in either genre but for a sentimental film based on Poe's poem, 'The Bells,' which was produced by the Edison Company in 1913, to our immense delight. But it promoted unwarranted hopes, for the other nine scripts we offered around were all treated as they deserved. Beryl's own life might already have served as background for a novel or two and a score of stories; but neither of us was mature enough to draw on that, and the earliest use I made of it was in a little sketch called 'The History of a Prodigy,' which was printed in 'The Smart Set Anthology': a wry portrait I am not proud of. By the time my first short story came out in 'The Forum,' in 1914, our collaboration had almost ceased, though I would often try out my latest play or story on her.

But Beryl shared my excitement over my courses at City College and for a while faithfully devoted one night a week to keeping her wits alive by getting me to lecture to her on what I had been studying and reading in my classes. This insured me regularly of at least one evening of her company; so I took on the job with unction, and got as much out of it, through our eager discussions, as she did. Though we might begin with ethics or the history of philosophy, two of my favorite subjects, we would range far, and often come back to home territory to light up our more private problems. She had a way of sometimes patting down a place on the sofa, to bring me nearer, that gave an underpinning of intimacy to our austerest dialectics.

As Beryl's flirtatious involvements grew more pressing, our academic sessions became intermittent, but they lasted off and on until 1915; and they helped give me, perhaps, a little of the facility that Fontenelle was to find through his attempt to make science comprehensible to the lovely bluestockings of his day, for, as he observed, there is no better way of clarifying one's thoughts than to observe how much of them passes without further disentanglement into a woman's mind—a *woman's* I echo boldly in the face of 'Fem Lib'— because there is a kind of aggressive masculine pride that spurns any simplification and boasts of the very knots that curb understanding.

Surprisingly enough, no reciprocal tutoring took place in art. For a while at fifteen I had harbored the vague notion of becoming a painter, but the nearest I ever got to art school was to wait for Beryl on the street, on damp November afternoons, in front of the American Academy School—then on West 109th Street near Amsterdam.

About the time we symbolically said good-bye to each other on the rooftop, Beryl's life was in a more than usual tangle; and I discover, not from memory but from a wooden one-act play, done in a preposterously clinical manner, that she had even appealed to me for help when she was trying finally to overcome her active erotic attachment to Joe sufficiently to marry the well-groomed young businessman who was, in fact, shortly to become her first husband. In the final lines, the heroine discards both of them for the young man (me) who unbares her real motivations and so steels her to break with Joe. But though I now wince at every line the hero speaks, it remains true that Beryl did appeal to me as a benevolent if not disinterested friend, then and later, particularly after my disparaging prophecies about George, her first husband, turned out to be justified. That marriage, I had smugly predicted, was Tennyson's bitter 'Locksley Hall' all over again.

As for my role, I was to be a perpetual reminder to Beryl of the talents she had repressed or flouted, at first under sheer pressure of economic necessity, and of her need for escape from the poverty-cramped domestic background that this pressure imposed. She had too good a mind not to know how much of herself she had not used. After five years of marriage, she began asking me to recommend books, to bring her back once more into the world of ideas, and after another five years in Hollywood, she turned to me again, more urgently than ever, for help. Despite the letters that reveal these demands, desperate gasps from a spirit on the point of suffocation, I might have doubts as to the part I played in Beryl's inner life had I not met her Vienna-bred psychiatrist at a party one night, half a dozen years after he had analyzed her. He had drunk a little too much, so he violated the confidences of the analyst's couch sufficiently to say, when we exchanged names, "Not Lewis Mumford! Ha! Ha! *I know you!* You're the Lewis who used to keep popping into one of my patient's dreams. Mrs. La Cava; you knew her once, yes? You meant a lot to her." Then he remembered his professional obligations; and with a knowing leer sealed his lips with his forefinger.

In a way, I suppose I served as a sort of pricking conscience, or superego, to Beryl: often, in both the Roman and the Freudian meanings, as a censor. But I had other uses, too; for when she got engaged to her first husband, I think she managed to cover up all her other sorties in love by concentrating her George's attention on the one person who, erotically speaking, meant least to her—that is, on me. (More than once, I discovered later, I was to be conveniently drafted to play this role by other wives, to draw attention away from unmentioned lovers.) At all events, she managed to make her husband so jealous of my special place in her life that he forbade us even to correspond, except, she added in her farewell letter, under provocation of some emergency—like a great change in my own life, such as my marriage.

George tried to turn Beryl into a suburban housewife, and she, being always an actress, made a show of being one. But though in time she became the mother of two children, her heart was not in suburbia, and she called Philadelphia the City of Brotherly Bores. Such a platonic friendship as ours might, if sanctioned, have served her marriage usefully as a counterweight to her boredom. As it turned out, it was a friend that George himself had introduced to her, Gregory La Cava, who, after her divorce, ran off with Beryl; though she hesitated to marry her new fiancé until she had first my tacit approval.

By that time I was married to Sophia; and though both these young women were beauties, they felt no rivalry and, indeed, rather admired each other. La Cava was then a minor motion-picture director, and by way of introduction to him they took us to a cheap uptown playhouse to see one of his early pictures, a comedy so tortuously obvious and dull that I feared for their marriage on that ground alone. Never was I more painfully at a loss for words than when that ordeal was over: but what could I do except cross my fingers and give her my blessing?

As it turned out, La Cava proved a better director than a husband: in the thirties, after they were divorced, he made a still memorable comedy, 'My Man Godfrey.' Beryl tried to act her part in Hollywood, too: a far more hectic part than she had ever played as an artist's model, she told me later, for her life was immersed in the sick-making bacchanals that had then become the stigma of Hollywood success. She was present earlier at the lewd party that resulted in the death of a young actress and brought the film career of the once-famous Fatty Arbuckle to an end. Her revulsion from that episode probably prompted her finally to make the break that brought her back to New York and put her under the care of a psychoanalyst.

My last glimpse of the girl I knew came in the early 1930s. She was still marvelously beautiful at thirty-six, and I was mature enough at last to have become a possible lover, even if not a husband. Her mother was again living with her in an apartment on Central Park West and Ninety-seventh Street, close to our old haunts; and even her mother looked much as she had always looked, with a round red face, an irritating cackle, and a tendency to self-righteously remind her daughter of the many times her mother's judgment had been right.

Since Mrs. Morse had always been rather favorably disposed toward me, she began to make the inquiries usual after a long separation. But Beryl peremptorily shooed her mother out of the room and then faced me with all her old charm. Before we knew it, we were rapidly comparing notes about our own lives. For some reason I had called in the morning, probably because she was having afternoon sessions with her analyst, and we didn't get as far in our self-revelations as we might have. But we made a brave beginning, and the more we talked the more we liked each other. At that particular moment I was insulated against her appeal, both by my old attachment in marriage and by a new relationship that had upset and animated me. But even in that brief hour we reached a warm kind of understanding, out of our common maturity, and we kissed on parting with the familiarity of old friends, doing what we had never done when we were young.

At that moment, three women I loved suddenly came together in my consciousness: Beryl, Sophia, and Catherine Bauer. And when I left Beryl, something very much like my 'Love on Morningside Heights' reaction took place in me: I found myself vividly sketching out a novel in which a whole lifetime involving three women would come to a climax in a single day. As I walked through Central Park, this fantasy took hold of me and elated me: yet some bitter sense of reality made me bring about the hero's death before the day was over, perhaps because I knew such a triple tension could not be maintained without undue suffering through any single lifetime. Beryl's kiss made me realize that life had caught up with us too late, or rather, we had caught up with each other, but only for a teasing moment; for we would both have to stay in our own orbits and inevitably draw apart.

But I must not let this conclusion seem more rational and prompt than it actually was. When I phoned a few times afterward, always in the morning, too, for the purpose of meeting Beryl again, I doubt if my intentions were as platonic as they had been through the long saga of our adolescence. The proof of my ambivalent feelings is that each time the maid told me she was out I was a little relieved, and the relief deepened when she herself made no effort by letter to bridge the gap, probably because she was too deeply involved in her self-analysis to welcome a new complication before she had come to grips with the source of her earlier marital mishaps. In this she was wise; and we both were lucky; for in her third marriage, if I can judge from the few reticent leads she gave me, she found at least the political comradeship and the intellectual self-respect she needed.

That was not our last meeting, but it was my last meeting with the girl I once knew. After that a strange new Beryl came into existence, and our correspondence lapsed, so that I became aware of her only after her new self was fully formed. Sometime in the late thirties, she passed through New York, and at a luncheon that turned into a sparring match I discovered this new woman. Beryl had emerged from her psychoanalysis with a chastened sense of her own failure as a wife and a mother, and had perhaps saved herself from complete deflation by attributing that failure, in some degree correctly, to the society around her.

At first she had espoused Communism, the religious salvation of those Depression days, with the desperation of a frustrated woman seeking to put meaning and purpose into a life that had become increasingly empty. When I met her, however, she had already been to Soviet Russia and had become totally disillusioned with the steely tyranny she found there. But even this last change did not bring us closer together; for though she rejected the Soviet remedy, she still kept her newly acquired faith in the Marxian analysis of capitalist activities as the automatic key to overcoming all our present evils. By 1938 she was disillusioned with me, too, because at the moment I was one of the few voices advocating a militant policy of democratic action against the totalitarian encirclement that was rapidly taking place: a movement that reached its climax with the rapprochement of Nazi Germany and Stalinist Russia in 1939. Beryl now saw exploitation and knavery everywhere; and her only goods were now negative ones, like preventing war at any cost. Though I was aware of the same evils, I never accepted the innocent notion that fascism was only the last stage of a decadent capitalism; and I counted on the survival of enough of our humanist hopes and our historic democratic practices to counteract the patent weaknesses of our society, committed as it then was and still is to profit and power alone. As political interpreters, neither of us impressed the other: perhaps neither even *heard* the other.

4

Once Beryl had come into my life, it was long before she entirely passed out of it. My wife and our daughter, Alison, can still bear witness, as they often used to do with loud mocking groans, to her continued existence. But I can say that equally of every other person who has closely entered my life; for even when natural changes of interest in maturity have alienated us and separated us, I have retained my sense of the earlier bond and what it meant to me.

I have told about my relations with Beryl in far greater detail than may seem justified; yet the reader sufficiently zealous to ponder what lies between the lines will see that I have given a clue to something that runs through my entire life and work and, purged of circumstances, has now come fully into my own consciousness as the background of my philosophy of life. All the characteristic traits are there in embryo: the fusion of the emotional and the intellectual, the equal awareness of past and future as essential components of the present they are both continually shaping and remolding—the unwillingness to put any part of life in a separate compartment detached from the whole; and not least, of course, my inability to enter lightly into an erotic relationship or to abandon it lightly, either, even later, when it threatened my marriage.

The pattern of my relations with Beryl, with all the inevitable tensions my own demands and purposes imposed, was repeated in my marriage with Sophia. Even during the decade when I strayed from marriage, that fact, openly acknowledged, faced, dwelt upon, became part of our marriage and so even in its most painful moments helped confirm its strength, as a vessel that has ridden out a storm has tested and confirmed its own seaworthiness.

By dwelling on Beryl, I have also accounted for the whole gallery of girls and women who in my youth I was fortunate enough to enjoy as friends, beginning with Agnes, the beautiful auburn-haired Agnes, a fellow painter to whom Beryl turned me over when she finally decided to marry George: Agnes with whom I used to walk over the Westchester Hills. Agnes then lived in a pre-Raphaelite world of Rossetti ladies and Burne-Jones knights and Maurice Hewlett adventurers, and—alas for my amorous education!—she was then quite as shy and chaste as I was: so my memories of those walks are chiefly of the autumn foliage, in its challenge to the rich dyes of Agnes's homemade clothes and the natural russet splendor of her hair. The truth is, neither of us awakened a quiver of erotic interest in the other: it was frigidity, not chastity, that kept us from even a tentative embrace.

Then there was Elsie, a schoolteacher I had met at Ogunquit, Maine, in 1915, somewhat older than I, rather dumpy, but smart, sporty, and sophisticated. She introduced me to the verses of John G. Neihardt, whose 'Song of Hugh Glass' had sounded a new note then; and I gave her Edwin Arlington Robinson. She must have been secretly amused at a young man who was so daring in words and so backward in deeds, never quite realizing what heroic scrimping was required on his part for the rare occasions when he took her out to dinner, even at one of those Italian restaurants, like Bertolotti's or Gonfarone's, where a dinner with a half-bottle of wine then cost sixty-five cents or so.

Not least, there was Sarita, another schoolteacher, of Eastern European extraction, who lived in the Bronx. Sarita was a combination of outspoken nihilist defiances and unspoken Jewish reserves, sweet, loquacious, coy, didactic. We used to spend hours together, wandering through Bronx Park on winter days, fiercely discussing Tolstoy, Nietzsche, Marx, William James, socialism versus anarchism. Again, it was not insensitiveness or absence of sensual pressure that kept us apart, but a fear, on my side, of being overwhelmed and carried away, combined with an unwillingness to be committed till I found the girl I was ready to marry. And Sarita? I can only guess; but her gesture of taking down her long hair and pretending to comb it was not lost on me; only it had the contrary effect of fortifying my resistance.

But stop! This threatens to turn into a derisory catalog of the girls I never went to bed with. Allowing for strong differences in personalities and circumstances, the pattern established with Beryl applied to these others, too. Perhaps I should apologize to them, belatedly, with a smile! "None but the brave deserves to escape the fair!" But my debt to them remains nonetheless. They rose to my company and my letters with unconcealed pleasure, and they had faith in my future work. During my early years of invalidism, isolation, and editorial rejection that faith helped keep me alive.

CHAPTER TEN

Our Metropolitan Pageants

I

The nonscholastic part of my education had actually begun with my childhood walks with my grandfather; and apart from the streets, the parks, the racetracks, and the cemetery I knew so well, two other aspects of the city captivated my early adolescence: the theater and the tennis courts. Between them they lifted the gray blight that would, without them, have crept over my youth.

Well before my college days I tapped a source of delight that penetrated even deeper than had tennis: the theater in all its forms, from the circus and the Wild West Show to vaudeville, from the parades on Fifth Avenue to the great naval pageants on the Hudson, and, later, the masques and musical festivals that became popular in the years before the First World War. Percy MacKaye's 'Caliban' at Lewisohn Stadium, and—even more wonderful—Claude Bragdon's 'Song and Light Festival' on the lower lake of Central Park stand out: the latter a kind of democratic opera with the audience as an active participant. In this communal drama Bragdon's faery geometry counted for as much as the choral music floating over the water. The enchantment of that scene has never quite faded from my mind.

Central to all these special experiences was the vaudeville show; for, like so many West Side boys of my age and background, I used even before adolescence to go occasionally, on Saturday afternoons, to Proctor's or Keith's, particularly to the old Colonial Theater on Broadway and Sixty-second Street.

Like the circus, the vaudeville show was then an international performance: a single program might offer, besides our American clog dancers and monologists, an Italian acrobatic team; a London music-hall performer, like Little Tich; a Scots comedian, like Harry Lauder; a French chanteuse, like Yvette Guilbert; a troupe of Japanese jugglers; and by turns one identified oneself with each of them and conceived a new role and a new life. How colorful, how suggestive of the world's own variety—and of its oneness, too—were these variety acts!

My youth coincided with the last great days of vaudeville. I saw Vesta Victoria and the swagger Vesta Tilley, and Anna Lloyd who sang 'There Was I, Waiting at the Church,' and some of the best of the old-time monologists and magicians. But it was all magic. One walked home under the sparkle of Broadway lights, with a lift of the heart and a gleam in the eye, imitating in fantasy the juggling and dancing, the pattering and drawling in a style that daily life had never presented.

All too soon the vaudeville theater and the music hall disappeared: but my taste for them did not, though this only heightened my distaste for the dull girlie shows that took their place. I count myself lucky to have seen the best of the classic English music-hall singers, not least Marie Lloyd at her farewell performance at the Holborn Empire in London in 1922, only a few weeks before her death. Yes, there she was in the very theater in which she had made her first appearance—singing some of the songs that had won her popularity: Marie Lloyd, with her violet eyes and her wicked wink, with her voluptuous, almost Flemish body, and her broad, earthy humor.

Like most of the best English singers and comedians of her day, she had begun her career in a pub, and she was part of that juicy comic tradition that reaches back through Smollett and Wycherley to Shakespeare and Chaucer: "I'm one of the wrecks that Cromwell knocked abaht a bit . . . one of the wrecks of the Cromwell Arms." The audience loved her, knew every song, sang with her, and clapped and called for more. And again more! From this experience I perhaps learned as much about the behavior of a living community with an oral tradition as I could have discovered on an expedition to New Guinea.

One other thing the theater gave me then: a sense of style. The actors and actresses of those days had style, and even the poorest ones at least caricatured it in their hamming: they presented an image, not of the banalities of life as they actually were, but of an ideal form that might, at least temporarily, be laid over them, not without leaving a subtle impress on everyday existence. These actors knew the difference between naturalist mimicry and art. At a low level, style would often descend into mere theatricality, falsity, rant: but at its highest level it could give even a mediocre play a touch of fresh life, just as good acting could prolong the youthful image of an old actor. When Arnold Daly tripped across the stage in 'Candida,' one forgot that he was too middle-aged and body-soft to play Marchbanks, the youthful poet, for the very movement of his legs was a poem, and every gesture was as delicately modulated as an effective metrical line.

Even minor actors had some of these virtues, plus the assurance and dignity that went with them. My mother's friend, Dorothy Rossmore, once a 'leading lady' to John Drew, would sweep into our parlor with the queenly air she had so often exhibited on the stage and talk with the same care in shading her vowels and sharpening her consonants. Certainly there was nothing in my gangly adolescent years to indicate by my physical appearance or gesture that I had absorbed this lesson of style. But I now realize that it has perhaps influenced every part of my life.

2

In the autobiographic chapters of the final volume of Arnold Toynbee's 'A Study of History,' he reveals the part that the great museums of London played in his own intellectual development, not least those in South Kensington, which adjoined his neighborhood to the north. My own youth was spent in precisely the equivalent area of New York, and to the extent that I was later cut off from formal academic studies, I made even fuller use of the two great museums of art and natural history that stand almost opposite each other, with Central Park coming between them.

These museums were old haunts of mine from childhood on, but now I went to them for solid food, not merely to get occasional refreshment. The American Museum of Natural History was, back in 1915, just on the point of turning from a showcase museum, full of detached specimens, into an ecologically ordered museum, dramatically presenting organisms functioning in their natural environments, in visible association with other species in a symbiotic, if necessarily static, relationship. All this was being done with the aid of artists like Charles Robert Knight, as well as naturalistic taxidermists, in a way that had never been attempted in the past. In the Hall of Evolution the curators had made the beginnings of a connected presentation of the whole course of evolution; they were not yet embarrassed by the confused wealth and muddled proliferation of the later decades, from which a semblance of order is only now beginning to emerge.

The Metropolitan Museum of Art had a more personal effect upon my life, in ways that those who are interested in art only as detached esthetic experience would not suspect: above all, by putting before me a personal ideal of bodily beauty. There was one particular figure that had, unaccountably, a special influence on me: a handsome Roman copy of, I think, a Greek athlete, a rather mature man with a beard, using a strygil to wipe the cleansing oil off his body. I wanted to look like him, though I stopped short of the beard! That statue used to stand near the old south entrance, and the museum never seemed quite the same to me when they removed it sometime in the twenties, probably to the cellar. But it played a part in my general physical rehabilitation during this period. Perhaps such noble nude statues produced a similar response in the ancient world: did not their gods serve as models?

3

I began to use the great central library on Fifth Avenue in 1912, shortly after it was opened, and I have memories of its original space and amplitude, its bright marbled freshness, the soul-filling silence that once pervaded its halls, the sense of a building lifted above the rush, the congestion, the pressures of the teeming city outside. If I may paraphrase the poet, the museums were but my visits: this was my home. With a lordly gesture of hospitality that great library invited me to use what was then and perhaps still is—despite the staggering difficulties of keeping it so—the best organized catalog in the world, and what was for long the quickest service of books. I have waited for the moment to sing the praises of this library, and now the moment has come.

The new building itself, designed by Thomas Hastings (Carrère and Hastings), was conceived primarily as a great classic monument,

The Brooklyn Bridge

in the same fashion as the Pennsylvania Station, done about the same time. But no sufficient allowance was made in that design for the continued expansion or alteration of the facilities of the library, for the need for internal flexibility, for the requirements of stack space and readers' space in the future years. So within a decade the special rooms of the library began to overflow into the corridors, and this process has kept on, through sheer inner pressure, until one of the greatest qualities of the building, its repose, its inviting emptiness, has disappeared, even in the two rooms that held out the longest:

the Catalog Hall and the great Main Reading Room, where now a second stack of books prevents one from reaching, without the help of an attendant, the volumes along the walls that used to be accessible at will. Here as elsewhere in our culture excessive quantity has eroded quality.

The spaciousness of this monumental building was not in itself an error on Hastings' part; quite the contrary, it had an immediate effect on the mind which favored all the proper offices of the library. If the decoration was a too sedulous mixture of classic motifs, with such atavistic features as lions' heads spouting water for a drinking fountain—a sanitary aberration soon to be absurdly corrected by triggered taps issuing from the same mouths—my reproaches even on this score would not be too heavy; for I can remember what a blessed relief it was, after an hour of close reading, to lean back in my chair and pick out some intricate figure on the ceiling, so much better than a blank space or a spot on the plaster, on which to rest my eyes: indeed, there was a nude girl, whose beautiful trunk tapered into a leafy scroll design, who became a sort of platonic mistress and sometimes served as the center of my still youthful erotic dreams. I even once wrote a sticky poem to her. But it was while waiting for the indicator to call me to the delivery desk that I first read Emerson's 'Journals' and James Legge's edition of the Chinese classics.

4

During this early period of manhood (1914–1919) I began to experience the waterfront of New York, by repeated rides on ferryboats, in a fashion that has now become impossible. Everywhere the wholesale commitment to bridges and tunnels across and under the rivers and bays, for the sake of speed alone, is depriving us of this primal source of recreation, causing us to go farther in search of enlivening change—and often to fare worse.

But surely the ferryboat was one of the great inventions of the Nineteenth Century: that great turtlelike creature—plodding through waters often iridescent with scum near the ferry slips, doggedly meeting the hazards of time and weather, sometimes serving as a summer excursion boat to Staten Island, sometimes bumping and cracking through the ice floes in the surly black water, so that the salt spray would tingle in one's nostrils.

What endless variations on the simple theme of 'passage' by water! Even the short trips to Jersey City from downtown New York provided a touch of uncertainty and adventure, allowing for the tide, dodging other boats and ships, all with a closeness to the sea and sky and the wide sweep of the city itself that no other form of locomotion could boast.

Ferryboats would have been worthwhile for their value as a source of recreation alone: no, I would go further, they were worth running if only to give sustenance to poets and lovers and lonely young people, from Walt Whitman to Edna St. Vincent Millay, from Alfred Stieglitz and John Sloan to myself. Ferries had uses beyond the ordinary needs for transportation, and their relative slowness was not the least part of their merit—though as to speed, it has often taken far more time to cross by motorcar from Manhattan to Brooklyn or from San Francisco to Oakland during the rush hour, amid poisonous fumes and irritating tensions, than it once did by ferry. Those who put speed above all other values are often cheated even of speed by their dedication to a single mode of mass locomotion.

No poet, hurtling by plane even as far as Cathay, has yet written a poem comparable to 'Crossing Brooklyn Ferry'; no painter has come back with a picture comparable to John Sloan's 'Ferryboat Ride,' which, for me, in its dun colors, recalls one of the moments I liked best on the North River: a lowery sky, a smoke-hung skyline, and the turbid waters of the river. When I read Whitman's poem now, I realize the special historic advantage of belonging to a generation that is "ebbing with the ebb-tide," for I am old enough to have felt every sensation he described, to have seen every sight—except the then-bowered heights of Hoboken—with a sense of identification that even the most active imagination could hardly evoke now.

Those wonderful long ferry rides! Alas for a later generation that cannot guess how they opened the city up, or how the change of pace and place, from swift to slow, from land to water, had a specially stimulating effect upon the mind. But if I loved the ferries, I loved the bridges, too; and one after another I walked over all the bridges that linked Manhattan to Long Island, even that least rewarding one, the Queensboro. But it was the Brooklyn Bridge that I loved best, partly because of its own somber perfection of form, with its spidery lacing of cables contrasting with the great stone piers through which they were suspended: stone masonry that seemed in its harmony of granite pier, classic coping, and ogive arch to crystallize the essence of Roman, Romanesque, and Gothic architecture; while its cables stretched like a bowstring to shoot a steel arrow into our own age.

Since we lived on Brooklyn Heights between 1922 and 1925, I took every possible occasion to walk back and forth across the Brooklyn Bridge; and I knew it in all weathers and at all times of the day and night; so it is no wonder that when I came to write 'Sticks and Stones' in 1924, I gave perhaps the first critical appreciation of that achievement since Montgomery Schuyler's contemporary essay, published in his 'American Architecture' in 1893.

At that period, as it happened, Hart Crane and I—then personally unknown to each other—were living on Brooklyn Heights, and he, in his poet's way, was engaged in a similar enterprise: indeed, some time later, after I had moved away, he consulted me about biographic materials on the Roeblings, the builders of the Bridge. Thousands of people must have felt the same as we in our different ways had felt, ever since the Bridge was opened; but no one had freshly expressed it until the twenties. Only then did the first formal biography of John Roebling appear, to be followed a decade later by David Steinman's detailed study of the building of the Brooklyn Bridge—a book that by happy chance passed under my favorable editorial eye before my own publishers decided to go ahead with it.

So deeply did the Bridge itself capture my imagination that before I had abandoned my aim of becoming a playwright (as late as 1927), I wrote the first draft of a long play on the theme of the Bridge: a play that I recognized, even while writing it, could be produced only when done over into a motion picture. Fragments of that play still haunt me: not least a love scene, at night, high up on one of the piers of the half-finished structure, with a sense of giddy isolation heightening the passion of the lovers—and the muted whistles and hoots from the river below, in the spreading fog, underscoring with the note of the city itself their private encounter.

That scene no one will of course find in any Roebling biography, but the stuff of it I was soon to encounter, if less exaltedly, in my own life; for many of my written fantasies have turned out to be gropings, forebodings, formative anticipations of unconscious urgings that were soon to take on outward shapes, all the more because of their contrast with the sober, neatly planned, dutiful routine, so close in its more workmanlike qualities to that of an engineer, that characterizes such a large part of my workaday existence.

There was a slightly older contemporary who, as it seemed in 1915, had caught the very beat of the city, a beat that had begun to pulsate with quickening consciousness in all of us. This was Ernest Poole, who in 'The Harbor,' through his choice of scenes, characters, social issues, said something for my generation that no one else had yet said, though he was never—that was perhaps his tragedy!—to say it so well again. Brooklyn Heights and 'The Harbor' took shape almost entirely in Poole's imagination. But he captured the contrast between the depths of Furman Street, on the level of the waterfront, rimmed by a jumble of warehouses and docks, and the top of the stone-walled escarpment, with its seemly rows of brick or serpentine houses which commanded the whole harbor. There on Furman Street in the middle of the afternoon I had already seen an aged, drunken slattern, foul with whiskey and fouler with words—exhibiting the destitution and squalor that the gardens and mansions above both actually and figuratively overlooked.

I hardly dare to look at 'The Harbor' to find out how the printed pages would compare now with the sensations I had in 1915, when I first read the book. Somehow that novel seethed with my own hopeful excitement over the contemporary world of factories and steamships, of employers and labor unions, of political strife and private ambition, giving me much the same reaction I had felt earlier when reading H. G. Wells's 'The New Machiavelli' or his 'Tono-Bungay'—both books that influenced my youth. 'The Harbor' satisfied my appetite for the concrete and the contemporary, which was a very real appetite in those quickening days. The fact that Poole saw the city in much the same way I was beginning to see it gave moral backing and political support to my own efforts.

Not that I needed much backing! We all had a sense that we were on the verge of translation into a new world, a quite magical translation, in which the best hopes of the American Revolution, the French Revolution, and the Industrial Revolution would all be simultaneously fulfilled. The First World War battered and shattered those hopes, but it took years before the messages received through our eyes or felt at our fingers' ends were effectively conveyed to our brains and could be decoded: for long those ominous messages simply did not make sense. Until well into the 1930s we could always see the bright side of the darkest cloud. We did not, while the spirit of our confident years worked in us, guess that the sun upon which we counted might soon be in eclipse.

5

Yes: I loved the great bridges and walked back and forth over them, year after year. But as often happens with repeated experiences, one memory stands out above all others: a twilight hour in early spring—it was March, I think—when, starting from the Brooklyn end, I faced into the west wind sweeping over the rivers from New Jersey. The ragged, slate-blue cumulus clouds that gathered over the horizon left open patches for the light of the waning sun to shine through, and finally, as I reached the middle of the Brooklyn Bridge, the sunlight spread across the sky, forming a halo around the jagged mountain of skyscrapers, with the darkened loft buildings and warehouses huddling below in the foreground. The towers, topped by the golden pinnacles of the new Woolworth Building, still caught the light even as it began to ebb away. Three-quarters of the way across the Bridge I saw the skyscrapers in the deepening darkness become slowly honeycombed with lights until, before I reached the Manhattan end, these buildings piled up in a dazzling mass against the indigo sky.

Here was my city, immense, overpowering, flooded with energy and light; there below lay the river and the harbor, catching the last flakes of gold on their waters, with the black tugs, free from their barges, plodding dockward, the ferryboats lumbering from pier to pier, the tramp steamers slowly crawling toward the sea, the Statue of Liberty erectly standing, little curls of steam coming out of boat whistles or towered chimneys, while the rumbling elevated trains and trolley cars just below me on the bridge moved in a relentless tide to carry tens of thousands homeward. And there was I, breasting the March wind, drinking in the city and the sky, both vast, yet both contained in me, transmitting through me the great mysterious will that had made them and the promise of the new day that was still to come.

The world, at that moment, opened before me, challenging me, beckoning me, demanding something of me that it would take more than a lifetime to give, but raising all my energies by its own vivid promise to a higher pitch. In that sudden revelation of power and beauty all the confusions of adolescence dropped from me, and I trod the narrow, resilient boards of the footway with a new confidence that came, not from my isolated self alone but from the collective energies I had confronted and risen to.

I cannot hope to bring back the exaltation of that moment: the wonder of it was like the wonder of an orgasm in the body of one's beloved, as if one's whole life had led up to that moment and had swiftly culminated there. And yet I have carried the sense of that occasion, along with two or three other similar moments, equally enveloping and pregnant, through my life: they remain, not as a constant presence, but as a momentary flash reminding me of heights approached and scaled, as a mountain climber might carry with him the memory of some daring ascent, never to be achieved again. Since then I have courted that moment more than once on the Brooklyn Bridge; but the exact conjunction of weather and light and mood and inner readiness has never come back. That experience remains alone: a fleeting glimpse of the utmost possibilities life may hold for man.

CHAPTER ELEVEN

Mannahatta, My University

I

On leaving high school in June 1912 I had ambitions that were both vague and indecently modest: there was nothing in my immediate environment to suggest that they should be otherwise. Our domestic finances had sunk so low that I was under considerable pressure, though certainly not from my mother, to look for a paying job, and by this time I had begun to think of newspaper reporting as a career more in line with my talents than engineering. But I dreamt of college to the extent of writing to Syracuse University for a catalog, for my high-school freshman English teacher, Thomas Bates, had loyally recommended his alma mater, which gave a bachelor's degree in belles-lettres. For a week that title charmed me.

Unthinkingly I had rejected the obvious choice of regular courses at City College, whose tuition was then entirely free. Yet by chance I read in a newspaper in September that the Evening Session of that college was about to begin its autumn semester, and I was tempted into registering there, since evening courses would not interfere with any job I might find. There was no required curriculum: so I began my college life in irregular fashion, by choosing courses in English poetry, politics, psychology, and philosophy.

With that began my first great awakening to a whole world I had never explored, hardly even suspected. Before a year was over, I had dropped my newspaper ambitions and was playing with the thought of embarking on an academic career as a professional philosopher. I have never regretted this choice of the Evening Session, or the informality of my curriculum, for the required courses of the Day Session—some, like chemistry, merely repeating a quite adequate introduction in high school—might have dampened my ardor and postponed my intellectual growth at a moment when I was ready for richer fare.

This superworld of the mind, I promptly discovered, was what I had been waiting for all my days. The magic of being able to open door after door of the great House of Knowledge to which I now had full access! To be at home, suddenly, in Plato's world, in Descartes' world, in Berkeley's world, in William James's world. What a release from academic tick-tock! This was real living. At any moment an idea planted ages ago might come to life in one's own mind and start to grow! The discovery then that every life-furthering intellectual experience is always tinged, sometimes deeply colored, with emotions and feelings kept me from accepting any more desiccated version of the mind's activities. "Intellectual passion," observed Leonardo da Vinci, "drives out sensuality." Yes: but every living thought is a divine orgasm.

In every way this was a remarkable experience. The trustees of City College had chosen a grand site, almost an Acropolis, for their new building when the college moved up from Twenty-third Street; and the architecture had a powerful effect when one climbed the hill past the Hebrew Orphan Asylum through the deepening October twilight and saw the college buildings, in their dark stone masses and white terra cotta quoins and moldings, rising like a collection of crystals above the formless rocks of the hill. Below, the plains of Harlem spread—a vapor of light beneath the twinkle and flood of a large beer sign. The Gothic architecture of the main building, which followed the curve of the escarpment and dominated it with the tower of the Great Hall, did magnificent justice to its setting. In the afterglow, or on a dark night, these buildings could awaken nostalgic tremors as easily as might those of Trinity or Magdalen.

For the next two years, the two best years of my college life, I spent every night except those of weekends in the monumental main building of the Old College on Convent Avenue, either in class or in the wonderful little library, all paneled in dark oak, with high, monkish desks—a room, long since turned into an office, which was under the apse of the Great Hall, at the end of the long corridor that bisected the arc of the rest of the building.

Once in a while we would walk with one of our professors to his nearby home, along Convent Avenue or Broadway, or sometimes a group of us, heady with the discussions started in the classroom, would stalk down Riverside Drive hilariously matching outrageous puns, taking sides fiercely in arguments about free will and determinism, or bursting into irrelevant song. This setting, particularly at night, made for the special closeness that a small college gives, combined with the intensity of stimulus that comes only in a great city, with its mixture of occupations and interests and beliefs. Even New York could offer this experience only once, for the college I knew, with some five hundred students and a close, intimate life, disappeared under mere pressure of numbers within half a dozen years of its inception. It was one of those important experiments that City College began before it went the way of other metropolitan institutions by succumbing to giantism.

The students in the Evening Session were mostly more or less mature men, and they spoiled me for any other kind of undergraduate: their maturity gave, in fact, the kind of incentive and stimulus that one never quite gets from people of one's own age when one is young. Among them was a well-established maritime lawyer, with an argumentative Scots tongue; another was a South American consul; and there were doctors, brokers, accountants, engineers, and advertising men, as well as people almost as infirmly established as myself. By comparison there was something amoeboid and unformed about the ordinary day student, as I found him later; but we night students had a shape, a backbone, a definite point of view. Our class discussions were sometimes battles; and though we often lived to change sides, there was nothing tentative or hesitating in our espousals: certainly we did not suffer from the academic paralysis of 'open-mindedness.'

Out of their maturer interests more than one of my fellow students enriched my private curriculum: it was a professional model

Morris Cohen

J. Salwyn Schapiro

John Pickett Turner

maker for the Metropolitan Museum, Dwight Franklin, whose passion for Emerson broke through my own indifference to him. A group of us whose literary interests overlapped used to go out for country walks on Sundays, and from this group came one of my most sustaining friendships, that with Jerome Lachenbruch, a man whose sober gifts as a human being outweighed his talents as a writer.

Of the dozen or so young men who passed in and out of that small group, at least half of them later had professional careers of distinction: Herbert Feis as an authority in American diplomacy, Norman Fenton as a humane psychological transformer of prison routines, Henry Hazlitt as an expert in finance. A fourth, Irwin Granich, who later became Michael Gold, as one of the most promising literary talents that was ever sacrificed to the petrified dogmas of Russian Communism. In his original anarchist phase, so much closer to his natural disposition, it was Gold who brought a copy of 'A Shropshire Lad' to read aloud on one of our walks, for we were all stirred by the 'new poetry.'

Our teachers, too, were men of character: people like Morris Cohen, who thought and taught out of a passion for things of the mind as pure as that of a Socrates or a Spinoza. But I knew Cohen then only through our Evening Session Smokers, where he obligingly entertained us by reciting Robert Burns in a quite personal Scots-Yiddish dialect. When in the Day Session I sought to take his course on the philosophy of science, he refused to admit me because of my inadequate preparation in mathematics. We both smiled over this when we met in later life.

Among my own teachers was Alfred Compton in Advanced Composition, a slim, sardonic gentleman, with a touch of Robert Louis Stevenson about him; and there was John Pickett Turner, a handsome man with a massive dark head, a wart on his cheek, and shoulders of Platonic dimensions; he spoke with a southern deliberation and enlivened his course on psychology with case histories drawn undisguised from his own life and marital experience. Even-handed and tolerant, he didn't quiver a hairsbreadth when in the ethics class a sharp little Rumanian, Jallyer, declared that the *summum bonum* would be to die at the height of an orgasm in the arms of a beautiful woman. Since Turner professed himself a pragmatist, for a while I loyally became one, too.

Not least, there was J. Salwyn Schapiro, one of James Harvey Robinson's brilliant disciples, who filled the air with epigrams and paradoxes. Under him I studied politics, constitutional law, and European history, and learned the value of a comprehensive yet selective bibliography and a Voltairean wit.

Our relations with our instructors were well symbolized by the fact that in imitation of monastic practice they substituted 'Brother' for 'Mister' in addressing us, and friendships developed so easily between teachers and students under these conditions that it was Schapiro who, in 1914, gave me a guest card to the Old Liberal Club on MacDougal Street, and indeed kept a benign eye on my whole literary career. At my last meeting with him, in the early fifties, he spent almost two hours delivering an exhaustive and helpful review, orally, of my book, 'The Conduct of Life.'

And then there was Earle Palmer, a little man with a drawn white face, hunched shoulders, and dark eyes that smoldered behind his glasses. He took us through Pancoast's anthology of English poetry, living and enacting the poems, with an acrid humor in commentary that sprang out of passion rather than bitterness—a frail but ageless figure, half pixie, half demon, with the sudden dark touch of one who had not lightly triumphed over terror and wrath and pain. My Harvard friends used to overfill me with tales of their famous Copey, but none of them has ever made me feel the least regretful that I missed that histrionic professor. One touch of Palmer's ruthless sincerity was at least half a college education.

With a few of my teachers, like Schapiro and Palmer, I kept in touch off and on through all the years that followed; while some of them, like Dr. Stephen Duggan, the first director of the Evening Session, or like Morris Cohen, I met under different circumstances later, with the foundations of understanding already laid. Perhaps the sweetest personal reward of my student days, my most valuable diploma, was my sense of my teachers' pride and pleasure in the work of my maturity: the fact that, though we had not met in forty years, Professor Turner attended my Bampton Lectures, on 'Art and

Technics,' at Columbia in 1951. When I tell later about the transformation effected by my contact with Patrick Geddes, I beg the reader not to minimize the importance and the range of this earlier immersion. These men and their teaching made me ready for him.

2

Once I had acquired the equivalent in credits of nearly two years of work, I decided, after consulting Professor Turner, to complete my preparation in the Day Session, with my eye on an early Ph.D. in philosophy. But when I transferred in the autumn of 1914, I found to my disgust that I was being entered as a freshman, since I had taken all my courses in the wrong order and had not yet fulfilled the then inescapable freshman requirements: even worse, I had already flunked my first term of Latin and had to take it a second time.

This was a stumbling block and a humiliation, and I did not take it with grace; I resisted all the more because my daytime companions, youths of my own age or less, seemed so palpably juvenile as compared to my fellow students in the Evening Session. Their college spirit bored me. With an exalted sense of my own maturity, I would cut classes in order to work on a play or finish a story I hoped to submit professionally for publication. On only one point did I outwit the system: since I had already passed a course in advanced English composition, the Dean's Office, however reluctantly, did not insist on my taking the required one in freshman English.

My disdain for college routines was reinforced at this period by the fact that I had already appeared in print in 'The Forum,' the lively intellectual monthly in a handsome format that Mitchell Kennerly was then publishing. So, somewhat prematurely, I considered myself a professional writer first, and a degree-seeking student only in a minor way.

As it turned out, the next four years were largely to be years of failure in both departments. The one exception came through my entering a contest, held by 'The Metropolitan' magazine, for a reply to Bernard Shaw's challenge, 'The Case for Equality'; though Lincoln Steffens got the sole prize of five hundred dollars, mine was the only other essay to be printed, and for that I received their regular rate of 7½¢ a word, or $87.50: a sum engraved on my memory because, as the equivalent of many times that amount today, it seemed to me a fortune.

But before these early tokens of my qualifications as a writer dropped into my lap, my resistance to the routines of the Day Session had gotten the better of me and endangered my status as a student. Upon being summoned to Dean Carleton Brownson's office, I learned that I was supposed, like anyone else, to keep up my attendance and do regular academic work, whether I had literary aspirations or not. Spurred as I was by my own inner life, and doubtless inflamed by pride, this seemed to me tick-tock all over again: the shades of the prison house were closing in once more. But I was no longer passive, no longer docile, no longer concerned with being—academically at least—the first in my class: in fact, I was in revolt against all conventions and conformities.

So except in the few studies that interested me—history, literature, and biology—I got far less from my daytime teachers, good men that they often were, then they were prepared to give me. Yet I must confess, in parenthesis, that many of them had such positive personalities that I can still hear the thunder of Burke's stentorian voice in Latin; recall popeyed Lafargue ('the Frog') graphically illustrating stories of his training as a cavalry lieutenant in the French army; and I can conjure up in detail a dramatic demonstration lecture by Charles Baskerville in chemistry, each phase of which was presented with theatrical adroitness. Then came his climactic conclusion, "And that which could not be done . . . *was* done!"

My rebellion against college took other forms besides loafing and absenteeism: it came out in a series of attempts to put down on paper an extensive but far from orderly criticism of what was the matter with education in general, and with my own education in particular. I still have the fumbling, painfully pretentious beginnings of more than one book on the subject: but unlike some of my less ambitious notes of the same date, they show only faint traces of intellectual independence and even fainter traces of coherent thinking.

In both content and style these experiments were smudged reproductions of the modern authors I then admired—Bernard Shaw, Gilbert Chesterton, and even more strangely, Allen Upward, a name long forgotten, who wrote 'The New Word.' I cottoned to Upward because he—following William Morris—had launched a wholesale attack on Latin and Greek as a source of spiritual corruption and made an atavistic effort to set things right by getting back to the original meanings of old Anglo-Saxon roots—an effort that stopped a good distance this side of 'Lady Chatterley's Lover.'

What was perhaps defensible in my wholesale rebellion was my sense that if one did all one's assigned college work thoroughly, one would never have time either to digest one's knowledge or to express one's own responses, both requirements that were then dear to me, and still are. The notion that an arbitrary bell, at the end of fifty minutes, could cut short a lively discussion or cause a thought not yet matured to miscarry seemed to me an affront to the needs and ways of the mind. Though even then I had learned to do my own work on a fairly regular time schedule, I think I was at least partly right, and I was confirmed in my own judgment by our daughter Alison's similar discontent and complaint some forty years later; though unlike me she was graduated from Radcliffe *magna cum laude*. Harvard had given her an ability to do sustained and exacting research that it took me a number of years, after my all-too-capricious academic preparation, to fully acquire.

While still in the Day Session, I aired these criticisms and contentions to anyone who would listen to me, particularly to a friendly little man named Schneider, already getting bald and full of more personal vexations, who used to walk home with me sometimes. What was I but an early version of Britain's postwar Angry Young Man attacking the Establishment—and determined to suppress even its virtues? Yet surely we had less reason for anger then than have the young today—conditioned to mass regimentation and groomed for mass destruction.

But I might never have had enough courage to leave college of my own volition. Mere pride might have made me recapture my grip and pass even trigonometry—the course in which I now floundered most helplessly. Fortunately, the decision was taken out of my hands.

If, to paraphrase Melville in 'Moby Dick,' I have in any degree departed from the pattern of my generation, if my work shows any qualities that I could not have achieved by climbing the academic ladder step by step, if in spite of my lifetime lack of a bare collegiate degree I nevertheless am a member of various learned societies whose stamp confers an honor on the recipient, I owe it probably to the fact that a vigilant physician at City College detected an active spot on my right lung—"slight dullness at apex of right clavicle with numerous subcrepitant râles"—which coincided with a recurrence of my earlier tubercular symptoms just before I was graduated from high school.

After consultation with Dr. Storey, the head of Physical Education, I was enjoined to quit college and advised to follow for the next few years a routine of sedulous invalidism—with warnings that I must not overtax my body or treat sore throats and colds carelessly. That prudent advice not only drew me back from a premature grave; it gave me time to think. And this new regimen coincided with my discovery of a new teacher, Patrick Geddes, who gave me something more to think about.

The break in my college career might have turned out to be more disruptive than it did had my mother's Park Avenue physician, who now looked after me, followed current practice and sent me off to a sanatorium. There my condition might have been aggravated by overconcentration on its symptoms, as if the disease were an independent entity, much as happened to Hans Castorp in Mann's 'The Magic Mountain.' Instead Dr. Snyder confined himself to checking my heart and lungs every month and advised me to stay at home and live at a slower pace. He even played with the notion—please note that this was in 1915!—that psychoanalytic treatment might improve not only my lungs but my erratic and over-rapid heart, which concerned him far more. That summer, as a first step toward full recovery, he sent me off to Ogunquit for a month, where I might be under the eye of a younger doctor, a budding psychiatrist, who shared his Park Avenue office. That month by the sea—basking on the lonely dunes, reading Plato and Whitman, reciting verses at the top of my voice, or racing along the hard sand for the pure joy of motion—shook me free of my cramped, dingy past, and irradiated the rest of my life.

How lucky I was to have fallen into the hands of such a subtle diagnostician, who was less interested in the depredations of the tubercle bacilli than in the disorders of adolescence, which might prove to be the source of a whole variety of quirky symptoms. Since, as it happened, I escaped both the sanatorium and the analyst's couch—instead I studied Bernard Hart's remarkable early Freudian primer, 'The Psychology of Insanity'!—the worst scar left by my peremptory exit from regular college routines was a lingering hypochondriac concern about 'keeping fit' which to my shame I did not throw off until middle age.

3

For the next four years I lived a restricted, valetudinarian, yet internally stimulating life. And since my body quickly responded to this treatment, I resumed my studies intermittently at New York University, at Columbia, and again, 1917, at the Evening Session of City College. In all, though I acquired enough miscellaneous credits for a B.A., I never sought the minimal support of an academic diploma. But note: rebellious though I was against the prescribed collegiate requirements, I was not a 'dropout' in the later 1960s sense, for I never rejected the genuine goods of higher education; and still regard with skepticism those who would completely dismantle the university instead of rebuilding it on broader foundations which would make it serviceable during every phase of one's lifetime development.

Happily, on this new regimen, I knew for the first time what leisure was, and how sustaining it is to the soul to have no obligations except those that spring from within—not upper-class leisure filled with all sorts of insistent duties disguised as gaiety, excitement, or social courtesy, but the leisure of a Thoreau or a Whitman, with hours too precious to be traded for anything that money can buy. On fair days, every afternoon, I would go wandering about the city, visiting parts of it that an ordinary New Yorker would never see, and even making rather faithful notes of my observations when I returned home: notes that I still have in my oldest files and even once or twice used half a century later in writing 'The City in History.' On weekends I would go farther afield, alone or with my Evening Session friends, exploring the Westchester Hills, the Palisades, the Ramapos, or the nearer areas of Long Island.

This was the sort of vivid open-air education that the youngster who grew up in fifth-century Athens had every day of his life: and one can tell from the many references Plato makes in his 'Dialogues'

Walker and Westchester Avenues

to the common trades and occupations of his city that this direct acquaintance with its working life, so much of it taking place even today in the open air, gave him indispensable firsthand impressions, to say nothing of the detailed knowledge and human insight no amount of reading would have achieved.

At this moment of my life Plato himself took possession of me: and anyone who would seek to appraise the effect of nearer thinkers upon my intellectual outlook would go widely astray if he did not also take account of my lifelong intercourse with both Plato and Aristotle: first in direct encounters, and later through the works of Gilbert Murray, Jane Harrison, and Sir Alfred Zimmern, whose 'Greek Commonwealth' helped free my Greek studies from the plaster-cast images of ancient Hellas.

Though I realized my involvement with Greek thought began early, I only recently discovered notes typed in 1915 that remind me of another almost forgotten influence, that of the educator Thomas Davidson—he who originally founded the Fabian Society, and became Morris Cohen's mentor. Davidson's treatise on Aristotle was the first to introduce me to the Greek way of life; and Davidson's interpretation of the Greek idea of balance (harmony, proportion) as essential for the full development of all the powers of a human being made a deep impression on me; indeed, it became my dominant guiding principle, long before I learned from Dr. Walter Cannon's works its biological basis. Davidson's study sank deep into my mind at this critical moment. If I quote a single passage, it will remove the need for other citations and explications.

"The men who fought at Marathon, Salamis, and Plataea," wrote Davidson,

> were puritans, trained in a hard school to fear the Gods, to respect the laws, their neighbors, and themselves, to reverence the wisdom of experience, to despise comfort and vice, and to do honest work. They were not enfeebled by esthetic culture, paralyzed by abstract thinking, or hardened by professional training. They were educated to be men, friends, and citizens, not to be mere thinkers, critics, soldiers, or money makers.

However I might fall short of this ideal, it was by its standard I henceforth sought to live.

CHAPTER TWELVE

Enter P.G.

I

Though Mannahatta in all its richness and variety was my university, my true Alma Mater, I have still to single out the distant teacher who helped to bring all the diverse parts of my education and my environment together and transform them into an increasingly intelligible and workable—though never complete or final—whole.

In the autumn of 1914 this new voice spoke to me, a voice that singled itself out from the many stirring contemporary voices then clamoring for my attention: William James, Bernard Shaw, H. G. Wells, Samuel Butler, Gilbert Chesterton, Graham Wallas, Leo Tolstoy, George Russell (A.E.), Henri Bergson, Peter Kropotkin, Thorstein Veblen. This voice came from Patrick Geddes, and it called me, not because it was more high-pitched or penetrating but because its rustic Scots burr roused something in my soul that no one else had yet touched.

That day in the Biology Department's library at City College when I first dipped into Geddes and J. Arthur Thomson's 'Evolution,' a little volume in Holt's admirable Home University Series, was surely one of the decisive days of my life. From this time on, in my new explorations of the city, the shadowy figure of this new teacher accompanied me, and the sound of his voice steadily became louder and clearer, though almost nine years passed before we actually met.

Up till then my mind had opened out in many directions: but it was still unfocused, and every prudent counsel urged that I settle down to the mastery of some single field of thought, some recognized discipline or vocation, on which all my distracting energies could converge, even if this meant an immediate sacrifice of some equally promising aptitude or interest. At that moment, indeed, I had in effect deliberately committed myself to working for an academic degree in philosophy, although even before I came upon Geddes's thought, the study of life in all its forms—including my own life—had already begun to claim me.

What Geddes's voice did was to lead me away from the well-paved avenue to professional success: his was the Song of the Open Road. By his own example he revealed a different approach: one full of pitfalls I could not anticipate, even had I known his life story better than I then did, but also full of generous rewards, equally unpredictable.

As soon as I searched the Fifth Avenue Public Library's great catalog to find out what books had been published separately by Geddes and by Thomson, I identified without difficulty the writer whose voice had called me: for whereas Thomson wrote in a supple English style that earned for his popular biological papers a regular place in the English weekly, 'The New Statesman,' Geddes wrote in a more crabbed and cryptic prose, with a dash of Meredith's brilliant ellipses or of Carlyle's explosive epithets. In his best moments Geddes was likewise a master of the memorable epigram, for it was he who first defined specialization as "knowing more and more about less and less." Above all, his was the audacity of an original mind, never content blindly to follow established conventions, still less the fashions of the moment. Geddes not only made old ideas come alive again but applied insights derived from biology to traditional forms long considered effete, as when he arranged the Gods and Goddesses of the Greek pantheon in two facing ellipses, so as to disclose them as ideal representations of the Seven Ages of Man, following the curve of life, from infancy to senescence, from Eros to Zeus, from Hebe to Hera.

Geddes believed that abstract thinking must be enriched by wider experience, clarified by reflective criticism, and completed by communal action. The role of ideas for him was not merely to illumine the mind but to overcome fixations, regressions, or hallucinations.

In a little while, the outline of Geddes's own career spread before me. He had begun as a biologist, at home with both animals and plants, and remained one to the end of his days, for his final opus was not his long-dreamed-of 'Synthesis of Sociology' but the two-volume study, 'Life; Outlines of Biology,' written with his old collaborator, J. A. Thomson, and published in 1931.

For lack of systematic research and publication by Geddes after the 1880s, his fellow biologists tended to undervalue his ecological approach. Still, it was he who had discovered that certain animal organisms produce chlorophyll, like plants, and thus broke down the barrier that once existed between these two kingdoms: a discovery that evoked the admiration of the great French chemist, Chevreul. So it was natural for Geddes, in the midst of his final town-planning career in India, to do an expository biography of the Indian physicist, Sir Jagadis Chandra Bose, who experimentally revealed not only unsuspected sensitivity in plants but even the beginnings of tropism in metals!

For Geddes, the world of biology included all human phenomena: cities were as much a natural structure as anthills or beaver colonies; and when a disconcerting attack of blindness in Mexico limited his capacities for microscopic biological research, he turned increasingly to economics, sociology, history, and civics, and from the eighties on produced a series of path-breaking papers and encyclopedia articles in all these fields. Though his search for knowledge was insatiable and his range of reading wide, he had an equal capacity, plus a persistent inner need, for constructive activities, such as organizing museums, zoos, town-planning exhibitions, even World Fairs. It was Geddes who conceived the Rue des Nations, built for the Paris Exhibition of 1900 as a world symbol of national individuality and international cultural unity. Though the original buildings were not preserved, the idea strangely came to life again—at least outwardly—in the later Cité Universitaire in Paris.

Geddes's reach, if not his immediate influence, extended far beyond the provinces usually assigned to him. In many cases he paid the penalty of the pioneer: by being thirty years too early he was forgotten, or rather, never even discovered. The now fundamental doctrine of energetics in physics did not become familiar until Wilhelm Ostwald (1908) and Frederick Soddy (1909) had given it public exposition. But Geddes in 1881 had already taken in this shift in focus from supposedly solid matter to energy, visible or invisible, latent or active, as the basis of all existence. He applied this concept to the analysis of economic and social phenomena in two early published papers, 'The Classification of Statistics' (1881) and 'The Principles of Economics' (1885).

Geddes's philosophic structure had taken form before the publication of Freud's 'Interpretation of Dreams': for Geddes dreams, myths, and esthetic symbols were as real as atoms or Roentgen rays. He refused to set psychology apart from biology. Geddes in fact practiced 'Holism' long before Jan Smuts coined that term: he taught that no aspect of the living organism could be interpreted except in terms of the dynamic interacting, interpenetrating, all-enveloping whole in which it functioned. For Geddes, as for Darwin, ecological thinking had become second nature, well before the discipline had been defined or even named. Geddes's special endeavor was to apply ecological principles to the simplest and the most complex social phenomena alike.

The other side of Geddes that drew me close comes out plainly in his discussion of evolution theories. His emphasis was not merely on the natural setting itself but upon rural occupations and rustic life-values as a necessary counterpart in thought to the more sophisticated and specialized interests of the city dweller. Without knowing it, I had been mentally starving for fresh country food. Geddes himself, though not strictly a country boy, had as a child helped his father in the garden and had mastered the rural arts. So he brought into my mainly metropolitan background the very interests and proposals I most needed to enrich my mental diet and fortify my own energies. Geddes's appreciation of the city carried with it no such contempt for country ways and rural personalities as Karl Marx and H. G. Wells habitually expressed. In this Geddes was close to his friend and colleague, Peter Kropotkin, the author of that seminal work, 'Fields, Factories and Workshops.' Thus Geddes not only saved me from becoming 'just another specialist,' but he delivered me from the smug isolationism of the metropolitan world.

I hadn't read more than a few pages of Geddes before I found myself almost choking with excitement over his way of looking at things, as when he contrasted the two main traditions in biology as reflections of the urban and the rustic background. The first is abstract, departmentalized, sterilized, given mainly to the refined analysis of lifeless organisms—"we murder to dissect," as Wordsworth

Patrick Geddes

put it. The second is concrete, intuitive, undisturbed by its inability to conceptualize complex living processes and inner transformations, but never needing to deny the significance of those manifestations of organic creativity which do not lend themselves to the accepted methods of scientific investigation or precise abstract statement.

For Geddes, these two traditions were summed up in the two early teachers who had made a deep impression on him. One was Thomas Henry Huxley, an incomparable lecturer and demonstrator, never messy, never vague. He could take an organism apart, Geddes said, as swiftly and neatly as an engineer dismantling a machine he himself had designed: and indeed Huxley confessed once to this assistant—who inwardly agreed with him!—that he should have been an engineer. "From him," said Geddes, "I understood the organizing powers of the mind, which has created all the great mechanical achievements of civilization, from the Pyramids to the Firth of Forth Bridge." As for the other teacher, Henry Bastian, a lesser man, dimly known now only for his abortive experiments with 'spontaneous generation,' Geddes said he could never approach Huxley in clarity: Bastian would always reach a point where he would admit bafflement or try to put his understanding into words even more obscure than the process he was trying to describe. But from Bastian, Geddes would add, "I learned something that Huxley had never discovered—the mystery and wonder of life itself far exceeds in its range and depth and multifold richness anything that the best minds could encompass and express in a hundred lifetimes."

Here, then, was a man who sought to embrace every aspect of existence; and who, if he had not taken all knowledge as his province, at least had something challenging to say in almost every sphere of human activity, even in literature, where he was especially at home among the French writers of his generation, from Hugo to Henri de Régnier, from Renan to Bergson. Far from bidding me stop at any one point in my studies and dig in there, Geddes's writings rather urged me to further adventures, even if—he wrote me once—I had to mortgage my future in order to gain freedom for my own development. While Geddes remained a lifelong professor, first with a specially provided niche of his own as a botanist in Edinburgh, then as full professor during the summer term at University College in Dundee, he felt that a new kind of education was needed, which would provide passageways and meeting places for all active minds in every field.

3

Now let me go back to the beginning. After I had identified Geddes, the biologist, the next book of his that I read was 'City Development,' a report to the Carnegie Dunfermline Trust published in 1904. This was an extensive presentation, elaborately illustrated, with a succession of detailed proposals for the embellishment of the town-scape and the improvement of the social and cultural life of Andrew Carnegie's birthplace.

Geddes had trained himself as a planner, not by going to a planning school—none in fact existed independently at this time—but by pushing through a series of concrete demonstrations, renovating old tenements, turning waste spaces into small public gardens, and soliciting private funds to build much-needed student hostels in the Old Town of Edinburgh. The Dunfermline report, drawing on his Edinburgh experience, teemed with fresh ideas in both city planning and education, expressed in far-reaching designs and presented with a remarkable mastery of detail. Yet despite Carnegie's admonition to the trustees of his foundation that they launch out boldly on new paths and dare even to make mistakes, the timid, unimaginative burghers rejected Geddes's ambitious proposals *in toto*.

The effect of 'City Development' on me was decisive. It brought fully into consciousness my own growing interest in the city, for which my strolls with my grandfather had long ago prepared me. Up to this time only a handful of books about the nature of the city, and the more specific problems of the American city, existed. Lincoln Steffens had written 'The Shame of Our Cities,' and Charles Zueblin in 1915 published his report, 'American Municipal Progress,' and there was a vast guidebookish literature on historic cities, but it was largely political and architectural, with little insight into the nature of the city itself as the organic shell of a living community.

In 'City Development' I got my first glimpse of the city as an age-old instrument of human culture, essential to its further development. Though none of Geddes's fitfully published writings ever did full justice to his conception of the city's origin, its nature, its drama, and its destiny, 'City Development' at least opened up this wider urban landscape.

Soon after, the publication of Geddes's 'Cities in Evolution'—which I promptly imported from England—enabled me to become familiar with the growing literature of urban planning in Europe, particularly that of Britain, France, and Germany.

No one who today reads one of the many recent editions of

'Cities in Evolution' can possibly guess the exciting effect of that book on me, though it was, to speak soberly, only an uneven collection of scattered papers which Geddes, reluctant writer that he was, had brought together without any attempt at rewriting or reorganization. By now even I marvel a little at my own excitement over these intermittent flashes of Geddes's mind. Perhaps what explains it is the fact that he indicated a new approach, more direct and more comprehensive, for dealing with the complex activities of the urban community of which I was a part.

For a century, the architectural and social disorders of contemporary urban civilization had been depicted graphically in the novels of Balzac, Hugo, Dickens, Dostoevsky, Zola, Gissing, and H. G. Wells; and there were even massive journalistic studies, like Mayhew's classic 'London Labor and the London Poor.' But Geddes was the first practicing physician to put the whole clinical picture together, exposing the crude empirical remedies that had been applied to urban affairs without anyone's bothering to take the patient's history or to examine all his organs and identify their poisonous waste products.

Until then the city had been virtually unrecognized as the essential core of man's higher culture. Meanwhile in Europe other scholars had begun to work in the same area: notably Max Weber, Marcel Poëte, Pierre Lavedan, and Paul Schultze-Naumburg; but Geddes was almost alone in translating this new urban knowledge into action, or at least concrete proposals for action. For him civics—he never used the term 'urbanism,' still less 'urbanology'!—was applied sociology.

By the time I encountered Geddes's ideas, he had not merely rehabilitated some of the worst slums in Edinburgh but had built up a new kind of laboratory-museum, the Outlook Tower, and in 1911 had written and staged an encyclopedic 'Masque of Learning' which was successfully performed by amateurs under his direction in Edinburgh and London in 1912.

In the year 1914, when I read 'City Development,' Geddes had just embarked on a full-time career as a city planner in India. During the next ten years he made surveys and set forth proposals and plans for some fifty towns there. Among these, his two-volume report on the replanning of the capital of Indore perhaps comes nearest to giving the full measure of his mind—for he was always at his flashing best when dealing in detail with actual situations.

Once I was on Geddes's trail, I pursued the scent further and, eager to find out more about the Outlook Tower as well as its creator, I corresponded with the secretary, who as it happened was Geddes's son-in-law and architectural collaborator, Frank Mears. With an elation equal only to that upon the publication of my own first book, I imported in 1915 a little packet of pamphlets and books which included Geddes's London University Extension Lectures and some of his early graphs. I even made plans, which I now recall incredulously, for studying at the Outlook Tower the following year, 1916—or at least *'when the war ended.'* But the bloody First World War didn't end then, and I did not yet realize that no one was left to study with, and that, in fact, the Tower, *sans* Geddes, was but a hollow shell.

<h1 style="text-align:center">4</h1>

Naturally I dreamed of coming closer to the Master himself: and by 1917 I had succeeded, despite wartime ship sinkings, in reaching him by letter in India. Like so many people of stature I encountered when young, he readily gave me his time and his attention. In this he behaved like Bernard Shaw, George Russell (A.E.), or Miguel de Unamuno, men whose letters have always remained before me as models, in their promptness and amplitude, for my own intercourse with the young. By 1919 Geddes was already talking of my joining him the next summer in Jerusalem, to act as his 'assistant' and to pick up what I could of his thought at first hand.

Had I done so, I am afraid that the results would have turned out just as rueful for me as Rainer Maria Rilke's 'secretaryship' with Auguste Rodin had proved a little earlier; for Geddes and Rodin were both Jovian personalities who could not help wielding thunderbolts in their personal encounters, never even suspecting the point at which their passionate absorption in their own work might lead to their committing spiritual violence on those around them. But Rodin was either wiser or luckier than Geddes; for almost every distinguished sculptor of the next generation—Lehmbruck, Despiau, Maillol, Bourdelle, Meštrović, Brancusi, to name only enough to indicate their extraordinary variety—passed under his tutelage unlamed, and emerged a highly individualized artist, with a style entirely his own. Not a single little Rodin could be found among them.

With Geddes it was—alas!—otherwise; and the reason for this was explained to me by a friend I made in England in 1920, Gladys Mayer, a West Country girl, level-headed but warily adventurous, blithely indifferent to any merely genteel conventions, who had not yet come fully under the supersensible spell of Rudolf Steiner's Anthroposophy and who was still open to the more positivist influence of Geddes. Her early judgment of P.G. anticipated and confirmed my own experience.

> Professor Geddes [she wrote me] talks about my helping him to write up some of his notes. If I have time, I shall do it very gladly. [Yes: *"If I have time!"* But nobody, once within Geddes's orbit, somehow ever found it possible to break into his endless soliloquy and get down to work: his time and other people's time rarely coincided.] I have a very deep confidence in him, Lewis, not as a man who will not make mistakes—overfly his mark sometimes and over-colour some of his pictures. . . . He's an intense person, and I should say, will sometimes err on the side of intensity. He says things very vividly—as an artist or poet. But my confidence is in his essential inside rightness—his integrity, and his bigness of soul. There's nothing little in him, and nothing flamboyant or showy. All his intensity and his picturesque expression is real and earnest, none of it for effect. And between whiles he takes you into his confidence in the simplest way, as one child to another. And he's possessed of the most delightful humour—which enjoys the jokes against himself equally, if not more than the others. You would like him very much. He is too integral for the specialists to understand, I think. They have to dub him a little mad—or else think that of themselves.

This sums Geddes up, almost as Pallas Athene might have summed up the qualities of Father Zeus: noting his weaknesses without being put off by them, since they were manifestly linked in the flesh with his strength. Integrity and bigness of soul Geddes had to an exceptional degree, as illustrated in the quiet sentence in his preface to 'Cities in Evolution' where he mentions the sinking of his great Cities Exhibition—the product of half a lifetime's collection— "by the enterprising and indefatigable German cruiser, Emden." No hint of his personal loss or any show of outrage against 'German barbarism'—though none understood better than Geddes the menacing arrogance of feudal-industrial-militarist Prussia.

Throughout his life one part of Geddes exemplified the scientific tradition at its purest, honoring the example of his master, Huxley, who, when Geddes, working under his direction, found it necessary to correct one of Huxley's observations on the physiological mechanism of the odontophores, warmly congratulated his pupil on his success and took pains to see that the paper was published. Geddes felt it a point of honor to acknowledge his own sources, whenever possible, instead of concealing them for the sake of claiming personal credit. But, as Goethe explained to Eckermann, he knew that if anyone fully acknowledged his sources, the world might foolishly think he never had had an original thought.

When people took over his ideas without acknowledgment, as many did, Geddes only chuckled with pleasure at his success; for, he used to say, he was a cuckoo bird who laid eggs in other birds' nests and then flew off, giving them the trouble of—and the credit for— hatching them! Claims of priority seemed to him vulgar and meretricious, for scientific thought was a cooperative process, and sometimes an insignificant worker in a remote laboratory might add the necessary link that would make possible some experimental discovery or some unifying generalization.

By the same token, Geddes had no use whatever for the brawl and glitter of publicity: he wanted to give his full energies to his work. And he was impatient of all the time-wasting forms of polite social intercourse, though the very soul of old-fashioned courtesy in direct personal relations with people, however ready he might be to jump down their throats over intellectual differences. Untidy, careless of dress, as scholars so often used to be, he would forget the impression he made on people in high political or military offices, whose life was one long dress parade. Once, in Jerusalem, after an unwelcome lecture from Geddes, the official victim said: "Don't let that dirty old beggar in my office again." But the essence of Geddes was his reverence for life, and his passionate commitment to thinking itself, along with sex and art and love, as the highest manifestations of life. These aspects of Geddes's personality made the deepest impression on me—and still do.

5

Years before I met Geddes in person, he taught me how to take in the life of cities, both from inside and from outside, both in time and in space: not as a mere spectator or as a collector of statistics or a maker of abstract models, but, to begin with, as a citizen and a worker, participating in the total life of a community, past, present, and prospective.

From the moment I grasped Geddes's message and method, I began exploring the streets and neighborhoods of New York and tramping over the surrounding countryside with a new sense of both personal direction and public purpose. Geddes had already given names to this approach: the Civic Survey and Regional Development. And between 1916 and 1920 I made fairly systematic explorations of my native environment and recorded my experiences in a series of factual notes, quite 'unliterary,' which ranged from geology to slum buildings. These surveys laid a firm basis for all my further studies in architecture and urbanism. Even now when I travel or tramp, the old habits I formed then of seeing, appraising, sketching, and looking ahead spontaneously go into play and vivify even chance impressions.

But it was not only by his civic doctrines and activities that Geddes actively affected my life. The peculiar influence that he had on me in my early years was no doubt in part due to the fact that Geddes was what would now be called an educational activist: indeed, he characterized the kind of renovated university he favored as a 'University Militant,' a catchword he borrowed from a now forgotten

American writer early in this century, Charles Ferguson. Such a university, Geddes believed, would leave the liberating imprint of scientific and historic thinking on all the activities of a community, as the Church had once imprinted its theological and esthetic visions on the medieval city. And the city in turn became for him, as it did for me, what now has come to be called an open university.

At the time I happened upon Geddes's writings, I myself was, as the reader already knows, a somewhat premature student 'activist,' full of rebellion against the formal requirements of a fixed curriculum, critical of bureaucratic routines, contemptuous of working for credits and passing examinations. To be honest, I seethed with many of the same inner hostilities that broke out collectively during the widespread student rebellions of the 1960s—and was not without my own share of their willfulness, their sweeping rejections, their arrogantly egoistic demands, their too innocent utopian expectations.

Geddes's example freed me from any sense of guilt over my own heretical departures. But possibly my youthful dissidence gave me a certain independence in picking and choosing among the mixed intellectual wares that Geddes set before me. Some of these are precious gifts, which I have conserved through a whole lifetime: some show marked flaws, which I discovered after giving them patient trials, even before we met. My correspondence with Geddes from 1920 on, precisely when his intellectual influence on me was at its height, shows that even at this early moment I expressed my doubts or reservations on points of Geddesian doctrine or methods. But by this time Geddes's fixations were so deeply embedded in the whole graphic structure of his thought that they were no longer open to free discussion, still less to challenge or contradiction. So it was Geddes the insurgent thinker, the academic activist and 'advocate,' rather than Geddes the system-maker, the insistent follower of Auguste Comte and Frédéric Le Play, who permanently influenced me.

As the years went by and Geddes's physical energies waned, his pleas became the more pressing that I devote myself to translating into words the now almost chimerical Opus he could never bring himself to assemble in readable form. I find from a copy of a letter

I wrote him as early as 1920 that I openly expressed my doubts about my ability to transform the articles, lectures, notes, and diagrams, the unsortable and often indecipherable debris of his whole life, into a coherent and intelligible book. What Geddes urgently demanded of me was an impossible lifetime of devotion as Collaborator (read docile filing clerk!), as Editor (read literary secretary!), or as Secretary (read handy drudge!). In short, the perfect disciple: his alter ego.

What young man would not be flattered by such a premature expression of confidence? But fortunately I knew my limitations better than Geddes recognized the pathos of his inordinate demands. Except for J. Arthur Thomson and Victor Branford, who had known a younger burgeoning Geddes, he drove off potential students and disciples, who, like myself, were not ready to take over his now dusty shop of intellectual wares, lock, stock, and barrel.

The gap between Geddes and me had opened visibly in 1920, when his sociological colleague, Victor Branford, first introduced me to Geddes's most comprehensive graph, the skeleton of his 'Opus Syntheticum,' or 'Chart of Life.' This was, in effect, an effort to replace Herbert Spencer's 'Synthetic Philosophy,' an audacious work in many volumes, by a condensed version, a graph of thirty-six squares: a laborsaving device which P.G. called a 'thinking machine.' This graphic mechanism might now be taken as an unconscious Victorian caricature of the most original achievement of today's microtechnics: the miniaturization of an entire book on a single card of microfilm.

But alas for Geddes's thinking machine! This turned out to be the invisible wall that separated us. When at last we met in 1923, the intellectual distance between us did not lessen, but widened. A year later, in a letter I have quoted in full in 'Findings and Keepings,' I made a detailed criticism of his static categories and his graphic manipulation of them, pointing out that when one substituted other equally plausible values or meanings for the same terms Geddes arbitrarily fixed and clung to, one got quite different results. People were not convinced of the impersonality or universality of his logical method. "It seems neutral," I said, *"but what comes out of it is Geddes!"*

All these qualms and doubts and resistances took time to develop, and still more time for me to acknowledge fully. But certainly it was not for lack of either effort or gratitude on my part that the Geddesian system *in toto* never held me fast. For it was Geddes himself, in person, who taught me to beware of all self-enclosed systems—not least his own. That debt I expressed at length in the section of 'The Conduct of Life' called 'The Fallacy of Systems.'

Part of my recalcitrance was no doubt due to the fact that I had already been absorbing no small number of Geddes's freshest sociological insights from other contemporary sources, not least Charles Horton Cooley: for Cooley's treatise 'Social Organization,' with its organic view of history, showed that "no single factor or set of factors is more ultimate than others." Indeed, Cooley denied that "the so-called factors—such as the mind, the various institutions, the physical environment, and so on—had any real existence apart from the total life in which all share in the same way that the members of the body share in the life of the animal organism: It looks upon mind and matter, soil, climate, flora, fauna, thought, language, and institutions as aspects of a single rounded whole, one total growth." Yes: that was basic!

I copied that note before 1918. Had I studied under Cooley—I had had a good talk with him at Ann Arbor, but alas! only once, shortly before he died—my own sociological views probably would not have been essentially different, though it might have taken me longer to assemble and organize them into a coherent whole.

For all that, my early debt to Geddes remains. In the formative period between 1915 and 1925 Geddes's ideas, but still more his audacious insurgency, left their mark on my whole life. Geddes's greatest gift to me was to deepen and reinforce the foundations that other minds had already laid, while he gave me courage to build an original structure with new materials in a different style: radically different, necessarily, from his own. Those critics who can find in my work only what I have taught them first to find in Geddes have little insight into either of us. What Nietzsche wrote about his master, Schopenhauer, applies to my intercourse with Geddes: "What he *taught* is put aside: what he *lived*, that will abide."

CHAPTER THIRTEEN

Youthful Explorations

I

"Vivendo discimus"—"We learn by living"—was Patrick Geddes's favorite motto. That truth I tested for myself during the next decade of my life.

Well before I had encountered Geddes, in my last year of high school in fact, I used to spend Saturday mornings threading my way through the brokers' offices of the Wall Street district, picking up and delivering the loose-leaf books of my uncle Herman's 'monthly statistical analyses.' The physical demands of that job horrify me in retrospect, for it involved toting two very heavily loaded suitcases at least half a mile, and up and down the two long flights of the Sixth Avenue Elevated stairs: no load for a growing sixteen-year-old who weighed only a hundred and five pounds. But it gave me a passing kinship in drudgery and overwork with the longshoremen I had watched on the waterfront.

So, too, I count it as a timely educational advantage that I had spent two months in 1913 as a copyboy on the old 'Evening Telegram': another typical metropolitan enterprise. I worked on the early morning shift, called the 'lobster trick,' and reported for duty at four A.M. My humiliation at taking such a lowly position at the advanced age of eighteen was covered by the promise that in a short time I would be made a cub reporter; but the wound to my vanity bit so deep that I never had any difficulty in understanding why Melville, in 'Redburn,' made himself out to be a couple of years younger when he shipped as a cabin boy.

The job forced me to get up at two-fifty A.M., make my own breakfast, and catch a Sixth Avenue El to Herald Square; and I could tell, by leaning out of the kitchen window and noting whether the train then passing had green or yellow lights—even at that hour they ran at *ten minute intervals!*—how much time I had left for finishing my cocoa. The darkness and loneliness gave a dramatic touch to this journey. It made one feel slightly superior to be abroad alone in the city at that hour, before even the milkman had started on his rounds. The cold white flare of the arc-lights intensified one's feeling of aloofness, and an occasional light in the bedroom of an otherwise darkened tenement house might add a touch of mystery, hinting of someone in pain, someone quarreling, someone dying or being born.

But often I would be oblivious to the sleeping city because I was reading, with an indescribable priggish elation, a few pages in Plato or William James. Reading 'A Pluralistic Universe' at three-twenty-five in the morning almost counteracted the indignity of sweeping the floor and setting out the 'flimsy' (copy paper) in the stale air of the City Room half an hour later.

The 'Telegram' was, even in 1913, a pretty seedy sheet; but James Gordon Bennett, the original owner, was still alive, and some faint, ridiculous spark of his vindictive energy would cause an editor or a reporter suddenly to jump out of his skin. Bennett was the same insolent devil who had coolly offered to give Stanley back his old job on 'The Herald' after he had found Livingstone and made himself world famous. At this time the name Roosevelt was taboo on both 'The Morning Herald' and the 'Evening Telegram'; he could be referred to only as 'The Third Termer.' Among other examples of Bennett's crotchets was an ice chest in one corner of the City Room, which was duly filled with ice every day, supposedly because the Old Boy himself might suddenly appear and want ice for his champagne. Bennett's alpaca coat, too, hung on a hook in his private office, waiting.

As for me, my first task was to rush the beer and sandwiches and coffee from the corner saloon on Sixth Avenue, while the night city editor was marking up the sheaf of morning papers for the re-write men. Even at that hour the saloon would still have a few stragglers in it. The rewrite men, who averaged thirty-five dollars a week then—the night city editor got only fifty!—used to tip me, too, even if I did read William James and sometimes do a stick or two of rewrite myself when one of the men came in late. If any small story broke in the neighborhood, I would be sent out to cover it; but a sewer explosion or a burning mattress was about all that came my way, and my pride suffered as my boredom grew: so I chucked the job after a couple of months. This brief dip taught me not to look for 'life' in newspaper offices; and thenceforward I read newspapers with a scorn and skepticism born of intimacy. Had I not, when a freighter without a wireless sank near Halifax, seen a big front-page story manufactured in three-quarters of an hour out of a rewrite man's stinking clay pipe and his otherwise unaided imagination?

Yet who could have asked for a swifter and more illuminating induction into one of the central activities of the modern city—not greatly changed in essence today, though radio and television now have far more sophisticated ways of doctoring the news and dramatically distracting the public from the otherwise unbearable daily grind or the frightening future?

Perhaps the most stimulating of my work experiences, at least for its effect on my urban studies, was the six weeks or so I spent as an investigator for the Joint Arbitration Board of the Dress and Waist Industry, originally like the other garment industries of New York, cut-throat in competition and dependent on sweated immigrant labor, but now, thanks to the remarkable intellectual leadership of such men as Sidney Hillman and Jacob Potofsky, passing on to the stage of responsible organization, looking not only to higher wages but to more sanitary working conditions, better distribution of seasonal work, and eventually to paid vacations and a more active social role in every field from politics to the theater.

In 1916 the New York garment industry was in a state of transition from its old ramshackle quarters below Washington Square (on Wooster, Greene, and Mercer Streets) to the new loft buildings on Seventh Avenue in the Thirties. The investigation of the Dress and Waist Industry was mainly for the purpose of finding out how faithfully earlier agreements about wages and hours had been kept by both sides, for there were many union complaints against arbitrary, unfair, or cheating employers. This survey was headed by Ordway Tead and his young wife, Clara, a handsome team who then seemed destined to become American equivalents of Sidney and Beatrice Webb, despite their smart country-club air. My merry but acutely intelligent friend, Herbert Feis, still studying at Harvard, had been chosen as economics expert; and it was he who invited me to become an investigator.

Now for the first time I lunched, with my fellow investigators, and occasionally with Feis, in the restaurants and tearooms of the central district, no longer eating by myself in Automats and drugstores; and I came face to face with the sharp, truculent factory owners and managers, who were reluctant to have their books opened and their payrolls examined; likewise I met suspicious but uneasy union delegates, who didn't want their personal authority challenged or their union's claims compromised. The abstractions of Capital and Labor now turned into flesh and blood people, and between them I had distant glimpses of a third force, a political one, represented by Mrs. Belle Moskowitz, she who later became Governor Alfred Smith's policy shaper, whose formidable abilities both sides already respected (and feared!).

My first task, though limited to copying out payrolls, gave me vivid contacts with every aspect of this industry. I visited dubious shops in buildings that were firetraps—this was before the ghastly Triangle fire—and was at home in elegant modern quarters in the new loft buildings, supposedly fireproof, where delectable models calmly walked about the salesrooms in their gauzy silken underclothes—exciting creatures toward whom I feigned indifference. I was so stirred by all these new metropolitan sights and experiences, despite the boring nature of the actual bookkeeping, that for my own satisfaction I decided, before I chucked the job, to write a neat monograph, 'The Geographical Distribution of the Dress and Waist Industry,' hoping secretly that, when it was finished, my superiors would be sufficiently impressed to recall me, or at least make further use of my constructive suggestions.

I dwelt on the fact that our investigations showed there was a growing tendency among the manufacturers to escape from the higher wage scale established in the central district by moving to outlying areas, like Passaic and Newark, where cheap unorganized labor was still available. This threatened the whole New York industry with serious economic competition. So I pointed out that the labor unions, no less than the employers, would have to cope with these efforts to escape high rents, high taxes, and high wages by organizing and unionizing on a regional scale, and not confining their efforts to the convenient Manhattan enclave. Since I actually did write this essay, it proves that my commitment to regionalism, as a key to effecting a more rational distribution of population, industry, and educational advantages, goes back at least to 1916; and this idea— though still ignored or belittled—was perhaps my earliest contribution to the urban planning movement.

Naturally my presumptuous and obviously callow monograph never got further than the office wastebasket; and doubtless I didn't help it any because, having sampled as much as I needed for my education, I threw the job over before the investigation was finished, to return to my playwriting.

2

This whole period was for me one of uneasy probings, interrupted beginnings, and quick endings; and until I entered the Navy in 1918 I pursued my further education. Two courses left their imprint on my thinking: one entitled the Modern World, under Dr. Edwin Emery Slosson, at Columbia, and another on geology, at the Evening Session of City College.

Fortunately for me, Butler, the man who introduced me to geology, though still in the lowly rank of a tutor through lack of a Ph.D., had such real gifts as a teacher that he laid a foundation in geology which prepared me for further independent study in geography. On solitary field trips about the region I became acquainted with the rich outcrops of local rocks: Manhattan schist and granite, Inwood limestone, Tuckahoe 'marble'—visible in St. Patrick's Cathedral—to say nothing of the igneous traprock of the Palisades and the Belleville red sandstone of New Jersey, sometimes used on Brooklyn Heights. Soon I could identify the micaceous schist that composed the original City College buildings, or the chocolate-colored sandstone, from deposits near Hartford, which began to cover the façades of new residences just before the Civil War.

Whatever blank spots might remain in my knowledge of the region, there was nothing superficial in this approach. And thanks to Geddes's influence, I was from the beginning familiar with the human and regional geographers of France and Germany before their

Manhattan, from the top of the Palisades

American colleagues had even recognized their existence. (In 1917, if I remember correctly, the words 'region' and 'regional' did not yet appear in the card catalog of the Library of the American Geographical Society: the first learned society I joined.)

Dr. Slosson, who had been a professor of chemistry, provided a special underlayer of emerging scientific thought to my sociological studies: for even before I came upon Geddes's early (1881) replacement of 'matter' by 'energy,' Slosson had introduced me to Wilhelm Ostwald's *'Energetische Grundlagen der Sozialwissenschaften.'* In his course I did a paper on sugar in all its forms as a fundamental source of human energy; and for a term paper I made a study of the Scandinavian countries, particularly Finland, as a locus of contemporary advances in the arts, especially architecture. Thus it was that Eliel Saarinen's new railroad station of Helsingfors first introduced me to modern architecture, before I had even heard of Louis Sullivan or Frank Lloyd Wright. If I hadn't chosen a Scandinavian country, I should have turned to New Zealand, for the social experiments in these two countries made it seem to many people that there, if anywhere, a new age was dawning! Slosson's influence neatly dovetailed with Geddes's!

3

For a decade after my Vermont visits had ceased, virtually my only contacts with the countryside were on weekend walks, but I never lost a sense of its pervading influence. One of the courses I took at Columbia in 1916 was Agricultural Economics! I chose this course under the influence of the Irish poet, A.E. (George Russell), whose weekly paper, where he preached argricultural cooperation as well as Irish nationalism, kept me in touch with rural realities. A.E.'s social proposals were enlivened by an imagination somewhat like Blake's, in which mystical cosmic intuitions were seasoned with a firm practical sense, often more hardheaded than that which 'practical men' pride themselves on.

This down-to-earth interest was later fostered by A.E. himself in a correspondence that began with my sending him my first book, 'The Story of Utopias,' and lasted until his death—although we were only once to lay eyes on each other. Molded by A.E.'s example, no less than by Geddes's, I was convinced that it was perilous for a writer to be concerned only with literary affairs; on the contrary, it was essential to live out my ideas in everyday practice, like Dante or Goethe—at least once my energies were equal to these heavier demands and this wider outlook.

A.E.'s poetry never, alas! attracted me, much as I wished to like it; not because it was 'mystical,' but because it was misty, in the sense that it drew heavily on colorful but nebulous abstractions. But A.E.'s thoughts in 'The National Being,' to say nothing of his often penetrating estimates of other writers, literary leaders, and politicians, from Yeats to Sir Horace Plunkett, were apt and discerning; and he kept rural interests constantly before my eyes all through a period when my own habits of life and the dominant activities of the metropolitan scene might have limited my outlook.

Even before I had firmed my roots in the country, I had become acquainted with the work and thought of Liberty Hyde Bailey, the American horticulturist, one of a long line of passionate observers and experimenters beginning with John Bartram, whose vision of living nature, in both its wild and its domesticated state, in some degree offset the depredations of the reckless land-skinners and timber-miners and subdivision-exploiters who had scarred the land, neglecting or obliterating many of its organic potentialities. But the progressive minds of the twenties were so remote from such rural interests that the editors of 'The New Republic' turned down my suggestion for an article on the significance of Bailey as a rural philosopher.

4

Though these varied activities showed no immediate results, it would hardly be fair to call them false starts; for they all in one way or another enlarged my view of the wider territory that I would later explore further or take possession of. Far from abandoning my involvement with the life and fate of cities because I was now directing my energies toward the theater, I pursued these opening interests in other places: notably on visits to Philadelphia, where my favorite relatives lived; to Boston, where my friend Irwin Granich had momentarily settled as a special student at Harvard; and finally to Pittsburgh, where I had my first intimate acquaintance as a *worker* with a classic paleotechnic (smoke and steel) town. As a *worker*, I emphasize, for I already was at home in dingy industrial Camden, Walt Whitman's final domicile.

Boston captured my heart: not the present Boston, butchered

and eviscerated by throughways, parking lots, and embarrassingly impotent bureaucratic erections—a city now doing its best to look like Chicago or Los Angeles, going in for modes of 'contemporary design' already half a century old; buildings disreputably obsolete by the light of any trustworthy scientific, social, or esthetic standard, even before they were built! The older Boston I beheld in 1915 still gave, even in its most sordid areas behind the State House or Scollay Square, more hints of a genial life, despite its palpable corruption and decay, than the sterile fantasies of pseudomodern design one finds today.

That Boston was still cut to the human measure; and even the name of the street on Beacon Hill where I lodged for a few days—10 Joy Street was the house—intensified my own pleasure in the comely red brick front itself. My first venture there—and in the very area where Henry Adams had once lived! The sound of leather-heeled shoes clacking on the brick pavement, filtering through sleep into my basement room in the morning as people went to work, was so much music. This was indeed Joy Street. But there were other Boston landmarks whose names and visible presence gave equal joy: the Common, Louisburg Square, Beacon Street, and above all Mount Vernon Street, then as now, despite later raw intrusions, perhaps the most beautiful enclosed urban neighborhood in the United States.

As late as 1915 Boston was still a genuine metropolis, in the literal sense of the word: a true Mother City, the attractive nucleus of a whole ring of communities, more nearly country towns than suburbs, which reached out as far as Concord and were easily accessible by frequent trains from the North Station or by electric trolley. These small towns, like the original boroughs of London, had their own local governments and were insulated from one another by agricultural green belts maintained independently by market gardeners and farmers. In addition they were fortified and further protected by Frederick Law Olmsted, Sr., and Charles Eliot, Jr.'s equally green girdle of metropolitan parks. While this pattern was in formation, Boston needed only a little further political remodeling to turn into a truly modern metropolis, a regional city, in which the smaller units would maintain an autonomous life of their own while participating in all the diversified activities of a larger city—and without paying the price in population congestion, environmental degradation, or suburban sprawl.

Unfortunately, the great economic collapse of 1893 caused the old New England leaders in finance and public works to lose their nerve. So they never carried through Sylvester Baxter's crowning program for a metropolitan government. By the time I first visited Boston, its political vitality had oozed away through the migration of the more prosperous families to the suburbs. But both the old pro-

L.M., 1917

vincial Boston of the three hills (Tremont) and the new Boston of the Back Bay and beyond were still in good working order; and the serene view from across the Charles, topped by the gold State House dome and punctuated only by church spires, was as highly individualized as that of San Francisco Bay once was. Saloons were still called taverns or ale houses in 1915; indeed ale was then as common as beer; and though it was mere coincidence, that older Boston was closer, I found later, to Dublin—with the Common and the Public Garden taking the place of St. Stephen's Green—than to any American city.

Boston opened my eyes to what a great metropolis, reorganized to take full advantage of all our intermeshing facilities for rapid transportation, instant communication, and social cooperation, might actually be. And though the whole metropolitan area of 1915 has now been defaced and in large measure obliterated, the image of what it was and still more of what it might have become remains in my mind's eye, and has given a concrete foundation in my thinking to even bolder urban designs. When a few years ago I was asked to write an introduction for the Museum of Fine Arts Back Bay Exhibition, I readily recaptured and confirmed my original admiration for Boston's early urban leadership.

5

I have still to say something about my later efforts to explore an American city through having work to do in it. This brought me face to face with a typical industrial city, Pittsburgh: the original center, if one includes outlying company towns like Homestead, of the steel industry and its allied mines and limestone quarries.

My initiation in Pittsburgh came through my somewhat older friend, John Tucker, who had been trained as a civil engineer at the Stevens Institute in Hoboken: a long-faced, red-haired, white-skinned, shortsighted young man, angular in build and in mind, who like me had once been threatened with TB. As with Beryl, we first met at the Central Park tennis courts: that informal community center for the West Side young. Tucker was a queer one: precisely dogmatic, coldly enamored of mathematics and the physical sciences, but like many other physicists from Einstein down, with a passion for music. Though I was three or four years younger than Tucker, he valued me, I suppose, because I was by temperament his precise opposite; so that we were bound to have delightfully endless arguments about everything under the sun.

Tucker took Karl Pearson's 'Grammar of Science' as his bible, swore by Ernst Mach, and explained Einstein's first theory of relativity to me years before the great managing editor of the 'The New York Times,' Van Anda, blazoned Einstein's later elaboration on its front page. There was a streak of obstinate independence in Tucker:

he refused, for example, to memorize a string of formulas necessary for passing a physics examination, and instead, with his grasp of the fundamental equations, would derive a particular formula as needed. That streak of independence never matured, I regret to admit, into originality; but perhaps it made him more ready to react to my own streakiness, sometimes with a loud, appreciative guffaw. Yes, we were both queer fish, and 'fish,' it happens, was our common masculine epithet for each other: "You poor fish!" "You crazy fish!"

We planned in 1915 to go for a walking trip in Germany "when the war was over," imagining in our hopeful impatience that this would be next year and that the Germany an older generation of American students had glowed over would still be there—if indeed the romantic Germany they had encountered as mere visitors would ever have borne a closer examination of its realities.

After being graduated from Stevens, Tucker took construction jobs in various places, and we kept up our friendship through correspondence; once he wrote asking me to send him some sea water, for the Maryland girl he was going with had never had a taste of the sea, and I complied with an elaborate and realistically obscene formula for making a synthetic substitute for a Coney Island sample. Finally in 1917 Tucker left construction work for a post as Assistant Physicist in the cement testing laboratory of the Bureau of Standards in Pittsburgh; and he suggested to me that I might get a military deferment if I accepted an appointment as laboratory helper: a job so menial that it did not call for a civil-service examination. I had already studied Paul Kellogg's pioneering 'Pittsburgh Survey,' and I needed no special persuasion to seize that opportunity.

Our rooming house was at 343 North Craig Street, directly under Squirrel Hill, which was still wild enough to harbor frisky cottontails. Every morning, after pancakes and coffee alone at a dingy hash house across the street—Tucker, poor fish, started his day in his bedroom on a pint of milk and a raw egg—I'd join him for the walk under the hillside and over the Bloomfield Viaduct to Arsenal Park in Lawrenceville, a group of Civil War buildings where the local laboratories of the Bureau of Standards were then located. My daily task was to mix cement, make batches of briquettes, and when they dried, test their breaking point on a machine, to see if they met specifications.

Though I kept at this job little more than two months, I am surprised now to find how deep an impression the whole experience made on me. Through my fellow workers in the lab I got a view of the vulgar sexual experiences of young Pittsburghers—not so puritanic as you might guess!—in that Presbyterian stronghold where motion-picture houses were still closed on Sundays. They were far more free in talking about sex than my New York friends. One laboratory worker was sufficiently expert to advise that the quickest approach to a girl was to fondle her 'boobies'; while another, a Filipino, reputed to have a visible tail sticking forth from his rear, said that he had found the quickest way was simply to ask: "Do you like fucking?" for it was surprising how many girls without blinking an eye would answer "Yes," especially the married ones. This exemplary advice was lost on me; but, as you see, the impression has remained, to remind me that there is only a quantitative difference, not a qualitative one, between the mores of that older America and those that now prevail.

Even if I had not been held back by puritanic timidities, to so much as make advances over an ice-cream soda would have presented difficulties for me, subsisting as I did on eleven dollars a week, a regimen that was, even in those days, pretty constricting; Pittsburgh, at least for food, was an expensive town. But I have memories of being a guest of the director at the Kaufmann Settlement House on the Hump, of dining once or twice with a visiting friend on the roof of the William Penn Hotel, and of brooding over the war, in the darkening summer twilight, on the viaduct over to Schenley Park, after reading one of Randolph Bourne's antiwar essays in 'The Seven Arts.'

I remember no less keenly evenings of concentrated reading in the Carnegie Library nearby. At the end of some notes I made on my Pittsburgh visit I now find that I had been reading: Aristotle, Plato, F. S. Marvin, J. L. Myres, Ruskin, William Morris, Dewey, Bertrand Russell, James Joyce, Romain Rolland, Meredith, W. H. Hudson, Chekhov, and, not least, Jane Addams's account of her Hull

House experiences. Yes: and heard Max Eastman cagily denounce the war at an antiwar meeting in Homestead; and on another Sunday ramble, brought back a fossil pebble with the imprint of a scallop—fossils were easy to find in that oily shale—which still lies on my desk. These odds and ends are what fall out of my pockets as I turn them inside out.

6

All this was to come back to me vividly when in 1950 the Mellon Educational Cultural Trust, through their director, Philip Broughton, a onetime Dartmouth friend, invited me to come to Pittsburgh to give them an outsider's view of what was going on in their still disordered urban milieu. This involved meeting college presidents, museum directors, city officials, even the mayor, to evaluate what had been done, what was contemplated, and what needed—or so at least I understood my mission.

Robert Frost had attempted a similar task in his own characteristic way a little while before. Without my earlier background I would hardly have been drawn into such a hasty survey, still less willing to frame even quite tentative conclusions. Superficially Pittsburgh had become quite a different place from what it had been in 1917, and in some ways, as in the lessening of smoke pollution, it had become better. But as so often has happened in the process of modernization, what it gained in cleanliness it had somewhat lost in character.

Naturally it took more than one visit before I came to grips with the city and had any concrete proposals to make. On my third and last visit plans were being discussed for turning the old Hump, once a dingy, dilapidated slum, now called Lower Hill, into a high-class residential center on the dreary bureaucratic pattern first glowingly publicized by Le Corbusier as *la ville radieuse*. Another of the projects that the Mellon Trust was excited about was the removal of the Summer Light Opera, a very popular series once held in the open in Schenley Park, to a bang-up modern auditorium. I caustically criticized the proposed high-rise apartments, which made no esthetic use whatever of their hilly site; and I took even greater pains to demonstrate the absurdity of taking the opera out of the park and the open air and putting it into a closed-in auditorium.

Fortunately, during my 1917 summer in Pittsburgh I had had many opportunities to observe how storms would thunder over the valley, dramatically blackening the sky and suddenly drenching the whole landscape: so I knew that there was reason to provide for shelter. But I also realized that even if the retractable roof the architects prided themselves on designing could be drawn closed in time, the metallic patter of the rain, mingling with the thunder, would make it impossible to hear the music. Besides, these outdoor concerts had been immensely popular partly because of the special pleasure of hearing music in the open in such idyllic surroundings, so different from a crowded air-conditioned hall; and even the sudden scramble for shelter from the rain gave the whole occasion a tingle of adventure which no watertight auditorium could offer.

My criticism of these technological monkeyshines should have made the sponsors think twice, not only about providing the retractable roof but also about their proposed abandonment of the park site. But if any of the responsible administrators had read my criticism, there is no evidence that they took any part of it seriously. The architects, the engineers, the businessmen were all, for their own dubious reasons, committed to the gigantic concert hall—doubly enamored of it, doubtless, because of the mechanical magic that was to operate the supposedly retractable roof.

Though the original plans for the rebuilding of this whole area, I was told, eventually lapsed, the auditorium was nevertheless built; and everything turned out even worse than I had anticipated, especially the absurd roof; for it could not be closed quickly, and indeed, without hiring a prohibitively expensive crew to stand by and operate the machinery, the roof could not be opened or closed at all. So it had to remain permanently shut—a metal shell, storing bake-oven summer heat by day and adding extraneous sound effects to the music during storms. If some of my sharpest pages in 'The Pentagon of Power' have to deal with the mischiefs of pecuniary pressures and superfluous technological trickery, they had the support of experiences like this.

Almost needless to say, I received no further invitations to visit Pittsburgh as a consultant. But these visits served my purpose well by giving me an opportunity at last to examine the handsome Hillside Housing Estate, in whose planning my friends Clarence Stein and Henry Wright, especially Wright, had played so effective a part. Though this still is one of the best examples of modern neighborhood planning and housing middle-income groups anywhere—and from the beginning was *economically* successful—neither the Buhl Foundation, which built it, or any speculative builder has ever thought it worthwhile to repeat it or imitate it.

7

I cannot leave Pittsburgh without recalling a session at the Duquesne Club at the end of my next visit in 1950—a whole day with the Director and the Chairman of the Mellon Trust, a youngish executive named Adolph Schmidt. Schmidt had served in the Second World War; and instead of discussing this or that detail about Pittsburgh's possible improvement, he told me how shabby and sordid Pittsburgh had suddenly seemed to him and his fellow officers after the war, when they had come back from the handsome old cities of Europe; for this contrast had awakened in his group of young Pittsburghers a keen interest in rehabilitating their environment. But first he wanted to know my opinion (he had been reading Spengler!): What prospect did this civilization have of lasting long enough to benefit by all the costly improvements that might be made?

The questions, the problems, the doubts we discussed were fundamental ones; and we ranged freely over the entire world situation, not least our own country's ominous commitment to nuclear weapons of extermination, and their equally hideous bacterial and chemical adjuncts. It was such a talk as I had had with Alexander Farquharson one memorable weekend in the Chilterns a quarter of a century before. For a while it gave me fresh hope that a social-minded ruling group might possibly be rising from within the old system, now sufficiently sated with money and power and sufficiently liberated to think more responsibly and adventurously about mankind's future than their predecessors had done—not to mention the old-fashioned working-class reformers and revolutionaries.

That day in the Duquesne Club with Schmidt and Broughton, canvassing in a detached mood the fate of our whole civilization, threw a light on both the actualities of Pittsburgh and its latent potentialities. The Duquesne Club is the club on whose steps Alexander Berkman, an active ideological anarchist, had attempted to assassinate Henry Frick, the steel magnate, back in the eighties; and in the great dining room at lunch I beheld in cross section the industrial-financial hierarchy that still ruled Pittsburgh: a perfect model of the "pentagon of power" that now effectually rules and increasingly wrecks our civilization.

There they were: at one long table, United States Steel; at another, Jones-Laughlin; at another, the Mellon Bank; and so on: each a self-contained estate if not a biological caste. Such social insulation, such ideological armor could fend off any stray ideological bullets! And yet somehow, where two or three people gathered together, liberating thoughts sometimes secretly scatter and penetrate—as they seemed to be doing that day, to my surprise, in our prolonged dialogue. The fact that such young Pittsburghers as the Heinzes and the Mellons had embarked on this exploration might prove more significant than any conclusions we came to.

Unfortunately, few things that have happened since, in Pittsburgh or the United States, have fortified this first hopeful impression. The mental deep freeze of the Cold War hardened during the next two decades; and only the obstinately blind could harbor the illusion that the skies were brightening.

If the reader will pardon my use of a time machine to travel backward to 1917, I will now return to my private life and my native territory. Though I had registered for the draft in Pittsburgh, my desire to get back to my writing, abetted by the realization that even my slim chance of military deferment did not offset the waste of time on this blind-alley job of cement testing, sent me home to Manhattan in midsummer. By the middle of the following frigid winter the war was beginning to congeal my own life, too.

Yet before the First World War brought these extracurricular activities to a halt, I made a premature effort to pull them together and salvage all I had so far learned. I presented to Appleton's, a publishing house that had brought out a series on American municipal affairs, the synopsis of a book, a kind of sociological Tale of Four Cities: Boston, Philadelphia, Pittsburgh, and New York. At twenty-two this was a preposterous undertaking, and I shudder to think what a mess I might have made of the job before I acknowledged my inadequate preparation. Still, there must have been something plausible about my outline, for old Appleton himself invited me to discuss the proposal with him, and said then that if I could get academic support for such a work, he would consider its publication.

That interview throws an even more revealing light upon publishing in those days than it does on the young author. My sole credential was the pure idea of the book. When I contrast this easy access by letter and personal talk with the responsible head of the house—and without any friendly intercessor, any institutional sponsor, still less an author's agent—I realize how fortunate I was to begin my career as a professional writer at such a favorable moment.

CHAPTER FOURTEEN

A Writer's Apprenticeship

I

My commitment to my vocation as a writer came gradually: early failure did not impede it, early success did not hasten it, despite my having a measure of both.

Though I might easily have been looked upon as a bookish child, the kind of books I read before I was twelve were as sedulously confined to my age group as if picked for me by a 'progressive' educator: on a low level almost all of Horatio Alger, likewise of George Henty, still the two great boys' writers of my childhood; and if I did, for a year or two, have a subscription to 'The Youth's Campanion,' I certainly didn't enjoy it as much as I did 'The American Boy,' though it had greater pretensions to being 'literature.' Cooper, Dumas, Scott, and Dickens followed; yet books did not greatly count in my life, and except for one brief period, I never took out a library card until I was sixteen.

My first awakening to literature came, as I have told, through falling in love; and trying in my letters to please Beryl by being clever or witty or drippingly sentimental—and how sentimental I hardly dare remember!—I found myself caring for words and seeking to use them more effectively. How low my tastes were I can perhaps best describe, at least to my surviving contemporaries, by saying that until I was eighteen I read 'The Philistine' and enjoyed that unctuous long-haired fraud, Elbert Hubbard—a curious combination of the glib advertising writer, the patent-medicine seller, and the provincial wiseacre, who managed to give even the puritanic sobrieties of the Arts and Crafts Movement an unmistakable touch of charlatanism. My embarrassment now is a little relieved by the discovery that a more toughminded youth than I, Stephen Crane, for a passing moment fell for him, too.

In High School, English was always my best subject; but when I look back on my other marks, that wasn't saying much. In my junior year I was appointed to the board of editors of our school monthly, 'The Caliper'; but it was as a sports writer, giving slangy accounts of football and basketball games, that I first took office, before moving over into my natural post as literary editor. In the imitative stories and verses I wrote for 'The Caliper,' I achieved levels of banality that even in memory make me wince; for if some stray copy of those issues might still be dug up, they would establish the fact that I had not even a chemical trace of literary talent—unless the desire to write and to put one's achievement to public test be all that is needed to start with.

If I had any talent at that time, the only evidence of it was what our faculty advisor, Dr. Frederick Law, found in my comments on other students' submitted manuscripts: a knack for summing up a judgment in a few sharp words. So it was little wonder that my highest ambition, when I left Stuyvesant, was to become at least temporarily a newspaper reporter and though it seemed audacious, I added a little later the hope of being a short-story writer, on the basis, of course, of all that I would get to know about 'life' through newspaper work. As for being a novelist, that was something I put off to the remotest future, until at nineteen I began work on a novel that I never pushed beyond the opening chapters. Later, however, my friend David Liebovitz, no lenient critic, found them promising.

But I needed money, since until I received my meager inheritance, I had to borrow a few hundred dollars from my Philadelphia uncle, George Ebeling, to cover extradomestic needs, like doctors' bills and travel. Sheer necessity drove me to explore one dodge after another to scrape up the crumbs of an income. My first snippet of an article, written for 'Modern Electrics' at fifteen, was partly prompted by this need for money, and my first check was for twenty-five cents! But my mother fondly kept the check as a private memento.

In those days there were two or three writers' magazines in existence, giving advice and encouragement of a commercial kind, canvassing the publishing markets, and furnishing at least the addresses and names of magazines in every field. As it happened, the Assistant Editor of one of these little sheets, a man named Edward Wickes, was in one of my classes at City College. He was at least fifteen years older than I and in ordinary conversation was almost an illiterate. In appearance, he resembled a tall cigar-store Indian—those wooden figures had not yet found sanctuary in our present museums of folk art—if one can conceive such a creature with square, stooping shoulders, dressed in shabby black clothes. Wickes had black lanky locks, too, a saturnine complexion, and a wide, wrinkled grin that disclosed a gold tooth in the front of his mouth. He had the habit of taking vile-tasting potassium pills for his habitual indigestion, though a little decent food was probably all the medicine he needed. His favorite exclamation was 'Wow!'

Wickes had begun as a song writer (in fact, he had written a once almost popular song, 'He Laid Away a Suit of Gray to Don the Union Blue'), and it was he who introduced me to what he called the writing game. Thus my first mentor in literature had nothing to do with the art as such: he was a dedicated hack writer. We edited the Evening Sessions section of the City College yearbook in 1914; so we saw much of each other, and occasionally I'd even call for him at his office on Union Square and have a quick lunch with him over a glass of beer. In order to become a writer, after knocking about, he had to begin at the beginning and learn grammar; and I remember how humiliated I was once when he detected two errors in grammar in my copy and made it worse by suggesting that I dig into Wooley's 'Handbook of Composition.'

Wickes's chief duty on 'The Writer's Monthly' was as motion-picture editor, conducting a correspondence course for the benefit of those who needed criticism. When 'The Bells' was accepted by the Edison Company with a formal contract and the promise of twenty-five dollars when it was signed, I was elated; but feeling that I needed practical counsel, I showed the contract to Wickes to find out if it was 'all right.' He read it intently and returned it with one of his broad, sheepish grins. "Hell, yes: I guess it's all right," he said. "It's the first time I ever seen one of them damn things. You know I ain't ever had a script of mine taken, though I think I'm on a hot trail now."

Never was an authority more suddenly deflated: perhaps this was the insidious beginning of my lifelong disrespect for inexperienced 'experts.' But Wickes was not to be daunted by his lack of success; the man had a Grant-like doggedness. When I saw him a few years later, he had a cubicle of his own in an office just off Broadway in the Forties; and, as he put it to me, he was "in the money"; for he was writing ghost autobiographies for second-string motion-picture stars. What heights or depths he finally reached I never learned.

2

The white sail of literary success appeared above the horizon for a few hours in 1914, when I was eighteen; for 'The Forum' had accepted an article of mine on community cooking, fomented by my experience in keeping house alone with my uncle Charley whilst my mother recovered from an operation; and a little later the editor took a story, imitative of Galsworthy, called 'Fruit.' The editor even put in type another sketch in the same pseudobiographic vein, but it was never used. And that sail vanished into a cloudbank that never lifted for four long years: years I devoted to exploring with patience and persistence every possible medium of writing and publication.

That false dawn had the mission of confirming me for good and all in the choice of writing as a career, perhaps in the same way that difficulties and obstructions in the conjunction of lovers may transform a mere effervescence of erotic desire into the more complex state of being 'in love,' with its possible involvement of much larger areas of the two personalities and a more enduring relationship. All this happened after I was exiled from City College because of my health, when my other ambition, that of becoming a Ph.D. in philosophy, faded away. Writing seemed to conform, even better than teaching, to the limitations imposed by my invalidism: it did not impose regularity, and it could be done anywhere, free from external pressure, even at home.

As for regularity, I was to discover that this was for me the condition of any kind of sustained productivity: so, on the advice of an older writer, I set myself to writing at least a thousand words a day. If I never, at any time of my life, followed that advice with mechanical punctuality, I at least formed the habit of regularity: to such good effect that if I find I cannot, within an hour of sitting down to my typewriter, write at least the first few pages, I take it as a sign that I am either over-fatigued from the day before, or coming down with an illness, and desist. So my standard advice to students on methods of literary work respects the principle of complementarity: first, to write regularly every day, whether they feel like it or not; second, never to write until they have something that urgently demands to be expressed! The second part calls for a readiness to break into routines at any moment in order to wing an image, an idea, or even a happy phrase. As with all life's other polarities, both methods must be kept in operation together.

Apart from these favoring conditions, I realized that if I was prepared to live a life of spartan rigor and renunciation, writing would give me a freedom that no other profession promised. I might have made better use of this freedom; but it was always there, and the sense that it might be used is one of those conditions that makes me even today accept more easily my self-imposed restrictions.

But if I was lured by my early trifling successes into treating writing as my permanent vocation, I will not say that I took on the chin the rebuffs that followed without sometimes wondering whether the next blow might not lead to my being carried out of the ring. I got to know every variety of refusal, from the printed rejection slip to the noncommittal letter, from polite interest to the desperate confession, "We'd like to print your fine work, but we're going under, too!" Toward the end of this long period of nonacceptance I hung on to my hopes grimly, but felt increasingly groggy; so that I could not forgive, and still haven't forgotten, the remark of a younger

friend during this period, who once referred to my being a writer—
"at least a *would-be* writer." I didn't openly show my resentment then
and there, but my coldness became glacial and remained permanent.

On the other hand, I never felt otherwise than grateful for the
kindness of Mitchell Kennerley when he sent back my third contribution to 'The Forum,' since the new owners had no use for it: for
he went out of his way to speak a word in my favor at 'The New
Republic,' a door on which I had repeatedly knocked in vain until
Francis Hackett, as literary editor, opened it a crack in 1920. I didn't
realize at that time that Kennerley's supposed friendship with Walter
Lippmann, whose first book he had published in 1914, was already
as ambivalent as his with me was to become. Yet the faith that Kennerley had shown in my abilities when no one else was impressed
sustained me over the next few years, for all their long subterranean
passages of doubt.

One other encounter that took place during this period had a
formative effect on both my literary career and the economic conduct of my life. It must have been in 1915, just after the new Pulitzer
School of Journalism had opened at Columbia, that I decided to
invest in a college education with the bonds and preferred stock that
had been turned over to me a year in advance of the original trust
date. Meanwhile my health had improved; so I went to consult the
director of the school, that seasoned newspaperman Talcott Williams, who dressed in the black clothes of a scholar, with a scholarly
stoop and a drooping gray mustache that marked him as the product of an earlier day. Williams was not only accessible but generous
of his time. I told him I wanted to become a philosopher; but not
just an academic philosopher teaching out of books alone, for I was
a pragmatist, as I proudly called myself then—today my counterpart
would probably say existentialist—and I wanted to come to philosophy by firsthand observation of life as it was lived. How better, I
innocently thought then, than as a newspaperman?

I laid all my cards on the table, including the four thousand,
five hundred dollars left of my inheritance; and my situation seemed
to touch Talcott Williams, for it recalled his own plight as a young
man and his own career. "When I was your age," he told me, "I

wanted to become a philosopher too: but I had a family to support, so instead I've spent all my life as a newspaperman and never fulfilled my deepest ambition. I wouldn't advise you to come to this school, though we'd be glad to have you. Instead, if I were you, I'd hang on to that four thousand dollars as long as I could. It's your margin of freedom: while you have it, you need never be driven to do work that goes against your conscience or offers you no inner reward; it will protect you from drudgery and give you the time you need to get started on your proper work. Spend that capital, if you have to spend it at all, like a miser. I envy you for being able to begin your life with that sum in reserve. Remember: *it's your freedom*."

I made no record of Williams's actual words, but this was close to their substance, for they remained graven on my memory. There have been only two or three other times when I got advice at the right moment as sound, as experienced, as decisive as this was to prove. If I have had any better fortune than many others in choosing the work I wanted to do, and in rejecting distasteful or meretricious or blind-alley jobs, it has been due, not just to having come by that nest egg, but to my having heeded Talcott Williams's advice. For this money kept me going for the next six or eight years, until I could at last stand on my feet; and instead of a degree in journalism, it gave me what turned out to be something better: a 'postgraduate' period in Europe.

For all this, my inner misery during a great part of this time was acute. Since I was hoarding my capital, my income did not permit me to blow money away on flirtatious dinners or theaters or sprees of any kind; and this greatly increased my natural diffidence in my relations with young women and so brought on a period of emotional repression that contrasted with the seething springtime fantasies deep within: a sort of hibernation in reverse.

On this matter the psychologist Erik Erikson, in his 'Young Man Luther,' has made a penetrating observation: "Potentially," he notes,

> creative men . . . build the personal fundament of their work during a self-decreed moratorium, during which they

often starve themselves socially, erotically, and last but not least nutritionally, in order to let the grosser needs die out, and make way for the growth of their inner garden. Often, when the weeds are dead, so is the garden. At decisive moments, however, some make contact with the nutriment specific for their gifts.

All this applied in full measure to my own case. And so, though these self-imposed measures were not without danger, that four-year interlude of withdrawal, rejection, and inner toughening proved invaluable to me. I have seen many more young writers crippled by premature success than by starvation and showers of rejection slips.

The ten months I spent in the Navy, from April 1918 to February 1919, terminated, without my knowing it, the hardest part of my literary apprenticeship. I was to have lean days, certainly, for many years afterward; but never any doubts as to the career I had chosen, and never any uncertainty as to the final outcome, thanks partly to my own inner adaptability, but still more to the fact that Sophia Wittenberg, the girl I married in 1921, was more ready to make spartan sacrifices for a worthy cause than I was, and even less ready to rebel against an overload of macaroni and baked beans when my earnings were meager, as they were for the first two years of our parenthood.

Almost as soon as I was mustered out of the Navy, the fortnightly 'Dial' took me on as a writer of book reviews; and after I had done a few, Robert Morss Lovett, then the Editor-in-Chief, offered me a post as Associate Editor. This was far better than any of my dreams. More than once in the brief period that followed I said to myself: "This is the happiest time of my life! I could not hope to have better days." I never uttered truer words.

My apprenticeship as a writer, nevertheless, was not over when I became a 'Dial' editor in 1919: for as in the old guilds, I now had a tour of duty to serve as journeyman before I was ready to execute the 'masterpiece' that would entitle me, in the eyes of the Masters sitting in judgment, to enter their ranks. I shall not attempt to fix on the particular book that served eventually to establish my scholarly rank. In architecture and social history, it was perhaps 'Sticks and

Stones' (1924), in literature and American culture, 'The Golden Day' (1926). In any case I had a hard five years to serve as journeyman; and it was curiously appropriate that one of the columns of 'The Freeman' I frequently contributed to was signed, whoever wrote it, 'Journeyman.'

During these early years I put forth feelers in many directions, hoping to achieve an early success. Unfortunately, in terms of getting a living, my nagging need from week to week, to cash in quickly on my writings, too often kept me from doing the exploratory delving and the consecutive thinking that would have made my work even more worthy of acceptance.

On this need for preparation and concentration, the earnest counsels of my 'Dial' colleague Geroid Robinson, in his early days on 'The Freeman,' to restrict my field were well advised. And yet, I am not altogether sorry I did not immediately heed them, for in view of my widening span of interests and of the use I was finally to make of them in giving a more rounded view of human development, this dabbling here and there, often floundering in water then beyond my depth, was a more adequate preparation than a restricted but academically orthodox approach would have been. All too easily in our segmented and regimented society one gets ticketed as being fit for only one task; and though I have spent my life in avoiding just such pigeonholing, even now I find that it is hard to avoid that fate in other people's minds.

Fortunately for me, acting on Van Wyck Brooks's advice, I ventured in 1922 to write my first book, 'The Story of Utopias': a pure *tour de force* I have gleefully described in all its scandalous details in the introduction to the Viking paperback edition. That book was conceived in February of 1922; and I turned in the finished manuscript in June, in time to read proofs before sailing for Europe with Sophia toward the end of July! Ah, youth! Ah, halcyon publishing days!

'The Story of Utopias,' and the two books that followed it, gave my journeyman years a kind of coherence and continuity they would otherwise have lacked; and though neither of my first two books sold much over a thousand copies the first year, they were reviewed widely enough and favorably enough to establish my reputation and have somehow remained in print almost to this day. When one remembers that nowadays a young writer or, rather, his literary agent must try to persuade a publishing house that his book will sell at least ten thousand copies the first year, one sees under what favorable conditions the literary life was then pursued.

The turning point in my career as a writer, at all events the economic turning point, came in 1925, the year our first child was born. From then on I realized that my essential problem was to earn

L.M., 1921

enough money during autumn and winter, when we lived in the city, to have long spacious days in the countryside in which to devote myself to larger literary tasks. Except for a demi-Guggenheim fellowship in 1932, I managed to write my first six books without any outside financial aid. Meanwhile writing for immediate publication in periodicals had the benefit of providing in some degree an objective standard of clarity and intelligibility and kept me in touch with an audience, even when I wrote strictly to satisfy my own curiosities and interests. Until the Great Depression of the 1930s there was a sufficiently wide variety of weeklies and monthlies, some, like 'The

Dial' and 'The American Mercury,' paying a modest two cents a word, some, like 'Harper's' and 'Scribner's,' paying more, so that I never was compelled to undertake a subject that did not, in some way, further my own purposes.

By 1927 I had reached a point where I no longer vainly sought a permanent editorial job, even though I never, until 1942, could see more than a few months ahead for my income: my sole security consisted in my willingness to remain insecure. This is perhaps one of the qualities that underlaid my friendship with Robert Frost, which began about this time, though he, in fact, had lived through even greater hardships for a much longer period than I.

In a note written at the beginning of 1928 I found that in the previous year I had turned down the following invitations: to become a Community Editor of Paul Kellogg's weekly, 'The Survey'; to write a book on St. John's Cathedral; to write a book on Frank Lloyd Wright; to write a book on the Rockefeller Foundation and similar respectable outlets for idle money; to edit a book of selections from American history; to become an editor of 'The American Architect'; to become American Correspondent to 'The Studio'; to become an editorial writer under Walter Lippmann on 'The World'; to become part-time Art Advisor to the Du Pont de Nemours Corporation.

Without more than a day's hesitation I turned down all these jobs, even the last two, and look back on all my refusals without a twinge of regret. The last offer, which came through the advertising agency that handled the Du Pont account, occasioned a flutter of debate in our household; for Sophia was a little piqued over the fact that I refused even to confer with the agency and find out what the scope of the work and the salary would be. I told her I simply didn't want to be tempted. Such a job, with such a well-established corporation, might offer an income triple our present one, and once it came as a definite offer, might be hard to resist. What was worse, if I got absorbed in the work, I would not be able to keep it at half-time. No matter what we resolved, I pointed out, our standard of expenditure would go up; and once it did, my chances of coming through as a writer would be gone. I never said No with a better conscience—nor, Sophia would now add, with greater shrewdness.

This necessity to finance my own freedom had its difficulties, for by 1926, the year after our first baby was born, we had exhausted my minuscule inheritance and Sophia's maternity savings. So as a safeguard against accidents or illnesses, I accepted a commission from Mrs. Helen Resor, of the J. Walter Thompson Advertising Agency, the same outfit that had seduced a behaviorist psychologist into putting his talents as an animal conditioner to commercial use— as in his nonsense slogan, "Not a Cough in a Carload," which increased the sales of a popular cigarette.

My scholarly Amenia neighbor and friend, J. E. Spingarn, had recommended me for the job of selecting a few thousand volumes with which Mrs. Resor proposed to line the walls of the reception room in their new office; and Spingarn had suggested that, instead of decorating the room with economic, financial, and practical administrative treatises, she might pleasantly amaze the waiting visitor with such a collection of books as one might find in the library of an educated gentleman of wide tastes. But I treated that suggestion in my own way, and doubtless disconcerted Spingarn a little by some of my own ungentlemanly interests in sociology, psychoanalysis, and the more heretical economists like Veblen and J. A. Hobson.

Nothing could have served me better, in showing up the vacant spaces of my own scholarship or in guiding me into new areas where fortunately I had the brashness to draw on the expert counsel of my growing circle of professional friends. But I shocked Spingarn by selecting the World's Classics or Everyman editions of standard works, with good introductions, cheap enough to be in my own still meager library, instead of more expensive and better-printed volumes. What is worse, I became conscious of my limited reading in esthetics and religion: for I had not listed even a single volume on atheism! By Spingarn's higher standards I was obviously neither a scholar nor a gentleman!

But Helen Resor, from first to last, behaved like a lady, as well as a keen businesswoman. She made no effort whatever to extract kudos for this novel scheme of wall decoration, and I was never called upon to justify a single choice. As far as I know, this singular library remained an office decoration. With what consummate tact and forbearance this able executive treated me! Yet she was the same ruthless innovator who confessed to me once that she longed to have a big publisher's account, with authority to reduce the yearly output of titles drastically—and then concentrate on exploiting profitably the dozen volumes that might remain. Such thinking as hers was in due time to sound the death knell of those publishers who still believed that the importance of books cannot, in less than a century, be judged by the profits from their sales.

That singular commission came through no effort of mine, and it proved unexpectedly profitable to me as a scholarly exercise, doubtless helping to account for the quality of my later bibliographies. Happily, having named at the outset an immodest price for my services, I emerged from this immersion in the business world with two thousand untainted and untouched dollars, most of which Sophia and I promptly banked in a postal savings account, which yielded only 2 percent interest. Yet how well that prudent investment paid off! For the next year, 1929, terminated in the Depression, and when in October all the commercial banks temporarily closed, our postal savings tided us over until the royalties on my 'Herman Melville' fell due. .

It would be foolish for me to underrate the drawbacks of my independence. All my books, up to 'The City in History' (1961), had to be done on a limited budget of time: at best I could devote five months in the spring and summer to them, during which time I did a minimum of reviewing, lecturing, writing articles, or teaching. Always my major books had to be executed under pressure, with utmost concentration; and since the books themselves made a vital contribution to our income, sometimes they went to the printer as soon as they were finished, without the extra time one should have for reconsidering the work as a whole and for achieving greater grace or economy in the presentation. Compared to the leisure for research and writing that foundation grants now give to scholarly writers connected with an institution, this was writing under disadvantageous conditions. But on the other hand, the outside pressures were all impersonal, and one never had to court official approval or academic good will. Best of all, one felt free to explore neglected areas or unorthodox approaches without current academic sanction.

My books might occasionally show the effects of haste; but since the better half of them are still in print, some after half a century, that turned out to be no crippling disability.

I have written this account chiefly for the benefit of talented younger writers today. True: their burdens are heavier, their temptations more seductive, their chances of hewing close to their own line dimmer; in short, all their prospects are murkier. But let them remember Robinson Jeffers's words: "Corruption never was compulsory."

3

I would not minimize the difficulties, inner and outer, that a young author faced in the twenties, but the fact is that the period from 1914 to 1929 turned out to be the Golden Age for coming American writers: so much so that it would seem almost sadistic to give the present generation of writers an account of the liberated state of publishing then in almost every field, magazines as well as books. Even those men of letters who, like T. S. Eliot, remained more soberly orthodox in their literary criteria nevertheless were carried along by the same venturesome spirit, which in a quite unprecedented way then favorably stimulated the business judgment of chronically cautious publishers.

Strange though this must sound now, the initiative in the brief renascence of American literary culture during the twenties was taken by a group of courageous young publishers who, on the proverbial shoestring, dared to compete with the staid veteran houses, like Macmillan, Holt, and Scribner's, by venturing to open their doors to quite unknown young writers who were dealing with aspects of life both in the United States and in England that stuffy middle-class minds had never willingly confronted. This generous open-mindedness was accompanied by an equally generous openhandedness with higher royalty rates and liberal advance payments.

The fact is, however, that these new publishers, men like Kennerley, Knopf, Huebsch, Liveright, and the Boni brothers, were as ready to defy orthodox taste and stale publishing conventions as the

new poets and novelists were to break through the provincial esthetic restrictions and moralist smugness of the middle classes.

For the first time since the germinal period between 1830 and
1860—the period that reached a creative climax in Emerson, Whitman, and Melville—mental adventures as audacious as the activities
of the western settlers and pathfinders seized the minds of a whole
generation of writers and publishers.

Not only did the new publishers offer to support young writers
of substantial promise, but they made themselves personally accessible, not just to discuss a new manuscript, but even for a casual chat.
As was true in many of the older houses like Harper's, publishers still
thought of books in terms of their literary quality, not just of their
immediate financial profit; or, as my English publisher Fredric War-
burg put it neatly in the title of his autobiography, publishing was
still considered "an occupation for gentlemen."

Writers who know only the book-publishing practices of today
will think I'm telling a fairy tale if I go any further. From 1920 on,
my initial business arrangements were always with the heads of firms:
what is more, I had such relations even with a half-dozen other important houses, from Scribner's down, that did not publish me, or
even wish to seduce me. Still more fabulously, my earliest contracts
were equally informal: a dozen lines on a sheet of letter paper sufficed to define the terms of my first three books with Boni & Liveright! A lawyer or an agent seemed then as superfluous as a policeman
would have been. Were these careless practices? Sloppy? Unbusinesslike? Yes, of course: but look at the quality of the books that
were ventured and sold under those very conditions! And some of
that easy informality endured even into the forties in the handling
of the flock of authors that had by then emerged.

Though my first three books, despite their modest sale, had established my reputation in more than one field thanks to favorable
English as well as American critics, my work was not quite spectacular enough to hold the congenital gambler in Horace Liveright: nor
were the working habits of his associates quite sober enough to assure me that Horace's increasing distraction with drink, women, and
the theater would promise a safe haven for my later books. At my

final luncheon with Liveright, his halfhearted interest in my work was obvious, though he resented my saying I was glad to learn that he was not yet wholly committed to the theater. But I already could see in Horace's face, which had become more and more like that of a dissolute Roman emperor, that he was losing his grip on himself as well as on his publishing affairs. I was sad yet relieved that our parting had become, for both of us, inevitable.

So in 1928 I outlined a program for three new books and offered it, not only to Liveright but to four other publishers whose president or editor-in-chief already was personally acquainted with me. Alfred Harcourt astutely outbid the others by saying, "With your architectural interests, you might possibly do better by going to Scribner's, but with the books you have outlined, beginning with your new biography of Herman Melville, we'd be pleased to publish you." The contract was no longer as brief as Liveright's had been; but in the new fashion of publishing, it assured me a straight 15 percent royalty no matter how few copies were at first sold.

CHAPTER FIFTEEN

Almost
in the War

I

From 1914 to 1918, while all these events were taking place, the ominous boom of the war drum, whose muffled beat we had first heard—and how incredulously!—in 1914, became steadily louder. Since I was still following a tubercular invalid's regimen, I heard that sound as a mere auditor, not suspecting even after the United States entered the war in April 1917 that it would soon issue a peremptory summons to me.

Like most Americans at first, I was inclined to take a lofty, detached view of this unseemly outbreak. Was it not a travesty on civilization, and even worse, a heretical denial of all the increasingly visible signs of progress? Though my sympathies were with the French, the British, and the Belgians, my youthful veneration for Bernard Shaw made me take as more or less trustworthy his 'Common Sense About the War,' for its apparent candor toward the malpractices of the British Establishment was refreshing. There was mischief and guilt on both sides, we saw: above all the terrible guilt of not having worked night and day to keep this monstrous eruption from ever occurring. But the more loudly the Germans sought to justify their position, the more palpable became their arrogance, their studied brutality, their insolent conviction that Germany's cultural superiority gave them the right to conquer and if necessary destroy those who stood in her way.

In 1914 I did not realize how deeply these militarist assumptions had penetrated the whole German population. Years later I was profoundly shocked to find that perhaps the greatest of contemporary German writers, a European of the Europeans—Thomas Mann, in fact—had without blushing made the same insufferably juvenile claims for *deutsche Kultur*. And did not our young friend and temporary household helper, Hildegarde, brought up under the Weimar Republic, tell us as late as 1936: "But we were taught in school that war is necessary for the health of a nation!"

Yet even in my most responsive moments of sympathy for the peoples threatened by Germany, I did not feel personally involved; and I was so lacking in both physical hardihood and martial courage that, unlike such gallant young Americans as Ernest Hemingway and E. E. Cummings, I did not seek to enlist in the ambulance service, still less to take a more active military part. Yet much as I loathed all the violence of war, eager though I was to see this conflict terminate in rational political proposals that would lay permanent foundations for worldwide cooperation, deeply as I valued peacetime activities, I was not at heart a pacifist.

Theoretically, at least, I knew that there were ideal causes worth fighting for and, if necessary, dying for. And though I had been troubled by Randolph Bourne's dire anticipations and sympathetically impressed by his antiwar sentiments, I didn't accept his isolationist stand. Plainly I could not honestly become a conscientious objector, and indeed had no impulse to become one, even if some of my friends at Columbia and elsewhere were in militant opposition to the war, and still more to America's adoption of conscription. I nevertheless honored the few who remained steadfast and uncompromising conscientious objectors, like Roderick Seidenberg, for they needed both moral and physical courage of the highest order; and the deliberately harsh mistreatment they met at Fort Leavenworth was one of the many degrading incidents in our national war record, to be counted as morally one with the earlier use of torture on Philippine rebels by our 'water cure' treatment, and with our later atrocities of calculated ecocide and genocide in Vietnam.

My own assent to the war was never, as it turned out, to be validated in combat or in facing death at sea. Though I wasn't 'above the battle,' I remained an outsider, increasingly alienated from the war by the palpable failure of the leaders of the democracies, despite Woodrow Wilson's morally stirring original pronouncements, to confirm their supposedly high aims with proposals inclusive enough to make sense in good time to both their enemies and their own fighting men, and not least to their subject peoples. Wilson's own later demand for "force without stint or limit" as the key to victory showed me that he had mislaid the ultimate key to victory; and from that moment on I viewed the whole conflict and the ensuing bargaining with mounting misgivings and with an increasingly intransigent utopianism.

Behind all this was one personal premise I must not conceal: until I underwent physical examination by my local draft board, I hadn't the faintest premonition that I was in a sufficiently healthy state to be accepted for military duty. So I was shocked to find the draft board doctor passing me, despite my tubercular record, and it was even more of a shock to find that the lung specialist at Roosevelt Hospital, to whom I had been sent when I appealed for a further checkup, confirmed the soundness of my lungs and, despite his finding an unusually rapid and erratic heart, qualified me for military service.

This verdict should have made me rejoice, as it was in effect an unconditional release from invalidism; but it had no such immediate result, for it took me years to break entirely away from the protective and restrictive routine whose importance the City College physicians had all too successfullly impressed on me. My first response indeed was still self-serving rather than patriotic. Following the example of my friend Lachenbruch, I used the last opportunity open for enlisting in the Navy for training as a radio operator before my number turned up for induction into the now man-hungry Army. Fortunately, though the Navy had stopped taking enlistments in the Naval Reserve, they were still accepting 'regular Navy' volunteers for the 'duration of war.' Even so, in April 1918 that seemed a somewhat ominous condition: the way the war was going then, after Ludendorff's near breakthrough in March, it seemed as if it might last another four years, if not longer.

This was not a decision I can now morally justify, still less be proud of: I would prefer to dwell on my son's contrasting decision at a later juncture to get into the action early, confirmed by other similar acts right on to his death in combat. But leaving aside my lukewarm patriotic impulses and my egoistic reluctance to abandon my writing, I couldn't have made a better choice than this enlistment in the Navy as a 'rating.' Though I went through the usual grilling and drilling, my Navy service gave me as great a sense of detachment, as much personal freedom, as one could hope for under war conditions. Not the least valuable contribution under the increasingly throaty anti-German emotionalism of the civilian population, abetted by the police, was the greater license it gave me to express my opinions openly in conversation: a freedom I would not long have enjoyed as a civilian. The old Navy regulars in the lower ranks actually scorned the 'Limeys' and openly admired the technical efficiency of the German Navy's radio in the Jutland encounter.

From the beginning, then, I was in the Navy but not of it: my mind remained elsewhere. Somehow this enabled me to endure the many unpleasant aspects of Navy life: the loss of privacy, the indignities of belly inspection and short-arm (penis) inspection, the misery of being awakened from deep sleep to stand watch on the cold breakwater or do guard duty in the 'head' (latrine), the always predictable and sometimes unpalatable food (except the fresh-baked rolls and butter, which were always excellent), the systematic bullying and browbeating that were meant to break our spirits and ensure our obedience.

But there were unexpected compensations, too, from the time that our batch of enlisted men, Landsmen for Radio, stepped aboard the Fall River liner that took us to the Island of the Newport Naval Training Station. How happy was that lingering, sidelong glimpse of New York at sunset, going up the Sound; and in spite of all the dreary, harried days we were to spend in learning to accept the unacceptable, I still count as precious the hours of sentry duty at the water's edge, overlooking Narragansett Bay, whether at midnight or at sunrise. Just to the degree of our deprivation from any common touch of beauty or intellectual stimulus or love, each slight taste of these things nourished one for days. One of the lasting friendships of my life, with David Liebovitz, the novelist who wrote 'Youth Dares All' and 'The Canvas Sky,' began on that first trip to Newport.

I have no wish to underplay or palliate my inner resistance to the whole routine of Navy life; for this resistance caused me to lose much that I might have gained if I had been more willing to identify myself with my shipmates and absorb all that this life, so different from that which I had known before and was to live later, had to offer me. I can now see that some of the things I detested were what I most needed for my own maturation: the severe physical training, the insistent discipline, the experience of hardship, the necessity to submit to distasteful conditions and arbitrary regulations and commands! All this toughened me up for real life, though in my willful way, once I was out of the Navy, it was years before I would stand in line even for a theater ticket.

But how stupidly I turned my back upon the opportunities so many of my shipmates sought—visiting submarines, destroyers, battleships, looking over the equipment used, and talking with their crews. Such inspections might have enriched my later studies in technology! And though I knew what to do when one stepped aboard ship—one saluted the flag and reported to the officer of the deck— the only naval vessel I ever actually climbed onto was the whaleboat on which I pulled stroke oar. I used to think this funny: but now I am disconcerted to find how lacking I was at twenty-three in any appetite for the raw realities of everyday existence: how impervious I was to both opportunities and temptations! By the same token I have never, even under the guise of pursuing my urban studies, visited a house of prostitution or come nearer to a professional whore than to say a distant good evening to the two 'call girls' who in 1950 rented the apartment below ours in Manhattan.

Though by and large the whole routine of life on the Island was repulsive to me—for this training station prided itself on its hardboiled masculinity, and the pat sailor's term for Newport was 'the arsehole of the universe'—I find that the good moments all come back now finely sharpened and intensified. Actually I enjoyed marching to the mess hall for chow to the sound of the bugle, and again at the end of an exhausting day the dying sound of taps became a tender benediction, all the more because I was always too sleepy to hear the last notes.

We had a trim, tense young Greek, a Chief Petty Officer, for battalion commander; and my company soon gained the reputation for being a 'bad' company, like the 'bad' Russian table in 'The Magic Mountain.' So Axiotis—yes, I remember his name!—was always on the point of disciplining us, if shouting didn't bring us around. Axiotis was doubly tense the morning he took us out for the first time in a whaleboat; and with good reason, for most of the crew, miners, midwestern farmers, or cowboys, had never been on salt water or pulled an oar.

That first spring morning on the choppy waters of Narragansett Bay was, contrariwise, sheer delight to me—heightened of course by the fact that in this exercise I was sufficiently expert to escape the Chief's tongue whipping. And what verbal lacings he used to give us! One morning the company was so sloppy in its uniform, so disorderly in formation, so incorrigibly perverse in executing commands that Axiotis had exhausted not merely his patience but the conventional stream of Navy curses; and he paused finally to muster his ultimate in polite contempt: "I don't know what's the matter with you people! You are all a lot of—*masturbators!*" Worse he couldn't say about us.

After three weeks of confinement to the Island we were at last given overnight shore leave; and though I certainly spent some of the time at the 'Y' with a chosen few of my shipmates, eating food not on the Navy bill of fare, what I remember best are the hours I spent by myself, wandering around Newport, then still a well-preserved relic of its two earlier selves, the fishing and sailing village of William James's youth, with its narrow, almost medieval streets, and the post-Civil War sprawling residential villa district by the bay, where the leading talents in architecture had exercised their taste for either luxury or gawky experiment.

On one of these rare weekend leaves, I spent a few blissfully indrawn hours in the Redwood Library; and when after sunset I walked back under the slowly deepening violet sky by a roundabout route to the bridge that joined the mainland to the Island, I had for the second and last time an indescribable but exalted sense of my whole future life spreading out before me. Perhaps this is what religious people have meant when they speak of communing with God. To me the experience said that the world had meaning: and life itself even at its worst was more wonderful than anyone had been able to say in words. What I was later to find personally in the swift moments of love and joy and sorrow, and again in the greatest works of art, was the exaltation of pure being—the ultimate reality for which all visible bodies and passing experiences were only a preparation. In that breathless moment past and future, my past and the world's past, my future and the world's future came together. Yes: a glimpse of eternity. That vision vanished even before I was challenged at the gate by the sentry. But like my earlier experience on the Brooklyn Bridge, it has never left me.

Part of my training, once the first weeks of hardening and drilling were over, consisted of mastering the Morse code; and though I had never even attempted this as a young wireless experimenter, I proved so adept that I ran the risk of being shipped right out to sea, to get the rest of my technical training while on sea duty. By good luck I escaped this, first by coming down with measles on the very morning of shipping out, then by staying behind to spend a relaxing week of fever and a week or ten days of convalescence between sheets—real sheets, not just blankets!—in the Naval Hospital. Finally, with the help of the Roman Catholic chaplain (who outranked the head of our Newport Radio School), I got shipped off to the new Radio School at Harvard, even though my record should have sent me straight out to a battleship.

What marvelous luck that was! And what a fine, intelligent, educated man Father Gleason was, too! Never once did he ask me which church call I attended. And how right Nana was : "Never be backward in putting yourself forward!" For once I had followed her advice. When I left Newport, I knew that I was escaping hell, at least what for me would have been hell! And as soon as I spent the first night in Cambridge at Winthrop House, I knew that I had arrived in heaven.

During my compulsory sojourn at Newport I had many flighty dreams about my future; but none of them ever envisaged the possibility of my revisiting the Island in any capacity. Every night, when 'colors' was sounded, we were all obliged to stop in our tracks, face the Hill dominated by the Naval War College, and stand at salute before the lowering of the flag. That building was the emblem of the vast distance between us underdogs and the Brass. How could I have guessed that one day, in the early 1950s, I would be called for at Providence by a Navy car and conducted into the presence of the

L.M., 1919

Rear Admiral who was commandant at the college, where I was to lecture on the political consequences of our commitment to atomic weapons!

What would my younger self have said to my accepting this invitation, let alone the fact that his now rather elderly self would be talking as an equal to a group of officers in all the services, none below the rank of Lieutenant Commander or Colonel, many of them naval Captains, if not Admirals? Would he have been horrified by my consenting to have truck with his onetime overlords? Or would he have chortled over this reversal of a gob's fortunes? I can't answer for my younger self and rather fear his verdict. But I know that I chortled.

Suddenly all my old naval training had come back, too: I was proud that I had once had a place, however reluctantly and feebly, in that fine, battle-tested organization! I was even prouder that I instinctively realized that, though I was the Admiral's guest, he would pass out the door before me; and that I in turn would show what an old Navy man I was by always keeping a respectful half-pace behind him! This happened in the midst of the ugly McCarthy days, and the question of Alger Hiss's guilt or innocence was discussed at the official luncheon with a nonchalant skepticism on my part which possibly awakened a dire suspicion in the Admiral's mind that he had given a platform and hospitality to a covert Communist. During that lunch I probably felt more at ease in this company than the officers and their wives felt in mine.

Somehow this revisit to Newport had evened up old scores and canceled out, in a few swift hours, all the indignities I had once undergone. Whenever I chance to think of that reinduction, I find myself smiling.

2

Though I was still in the Navy when I began my serious Navy Radio School training in Cambridge, it seemed too good to be true—and so it was. For just a few days after I was assigned to permanent quarters—as I remember, in Adams House—the Navy had begun to build wooden huts on the Common for its enlarging school. Meanwhile, to ease its housing problem, the school permitted those who wished the privilege to live alone in nearby lodging houses, as Harvard students then did. I needed no persuasion; and I was lucky enough to find a room at 33 Kirkland Street, in a big white house with a wide lawn before it, later wiped out, I think, by the Lowell Auditorium.

Once the afternoon muster was over, the remaining time till chow was my own; and conveniently for me Memorial Hall, where university cooks still prepared our meals, was close by. My first act was to get my mother to send my typewriter up. That would be an almost impossible request today, now that the once so-efficient railway express service has been junked along with the railroads; but in 1918, and in wartime at that, the typewriter was promptly conveyed from door to door, unscathed. How people fool themselves in thinking that the private motorcar and continental trucking have made all transportation cheaper, swifter, and more convenient!

The area around Harvard was then still charmingly domestic, with a wide sampling of houses and styles, from dingy workmen's quarters on Mt. Auburn Street to the palatial dwellings of Brattle Street, beginning with the Longfellow House and the handsome Victorian Gothic of the Episcopal Seminary. But the names of the streets and landmarks were as exciting as 'Joy Street' had first been to me in Boston. Better still, the Washington Elm, where Washington had assumed command of the Revolutionary Army, was still at a far corner of the Common; and to walk along the Appian Way was almost as wonderful as to be in Rome itself.

Though I did not suspect it at the time—and could not have planned it so—the Navy's main contribution to my education was to open my mind to a neglected period of American architecture, which I was to treat in 'The Brown Decades': the period that came to a sudden splendid flowering in the work of Henry Hobson Richardson and his successors in the Chicago School. As it happened, I spent every morning in class in what had been the Law Library of Austin Hall, a building whose traditional Richardsonian masonry was enlivened by a free placement of windows that closely corresponded to the functional needs of the interior. In some ways this was a more innovative building than Richardson's Seaver Hall, and with better proportions, too: though the archaic masonry, for all its Romanesque color and texture, is hardly to be put alongside the subtle brickwork and molded panels of Seaver. And even before I had identified the building with Richardson, I loved the shingled Stoughton House on Brattle Street, as it was then—before it was hidden behind a high fence and defaced by an altered top story.

The fashion setters from the 1890s on had turned away from Richardson's final attempt in the eighties to find a fresh modern idiom, and after the manner of the *nouveaux riches* had dressed up their buildings in the style of other regions and periods: Medieval, Renaissance, Georgian, Federal, Greek, Roman, what not: so that after 1910, architecture, whether in cities or suburbs, had become a cemetery of dead forms, pretentious shams, at best vulgar imitations of a life that could no longer be lived. Such patrons, such critics could not 'see' Richardson: indeed, the last person to write about him appreciatively before 1924 was Montgomery Schuyler in 1892. Through no deliberate effort of my own, I became the first critic to look at Richardson's buildings again with keen eyes and an open mind—and to understand the creative vitality of his whole generation.

One of my fellow lodgers on Kirkland Street was a man named Bigelow—a rather jaunty old boy, with a scraggy beard and the air of a man who had in his younger days had money to squander in Paris; but whose life had now thinned out, so that he welcomed an occasional chat with the studious young sailor, clicking away at his typewriter. It turned out that he had been an architect and was in fact the Bigelow of the original firm of McKim, White, and Bigelow. From him I got, almost by osmosis, a fuller initiation into the ideas and architecture of the period; all the more because he had kept bound copies of 'The Century' and 'Scribner's Magazine,' to which Mrs. Schuyler van Rensselaer, the first biographer of Richardson, had contributed. Bigelow helpfully put these periodicals at my disposal and further vivified them by his own recollections. Unfortunately I made no notes of my conversations with him; and what is worse, I was too ignorant to ask him searching questions; so I failed to elicit the kind of firsthand impressions and explanations one can get only from the living relics of a period. Yet Bigelow opened a fresh path for me, in a way that no American book or university course on architecture then in existence could have done.

In the Boston area there were other important things I found out for myself, thanks to my established practice of making deliberate explorations of my environment. So, almost a decade before I appreciated Frederick Law Olmsted's great innovations like the superblock—independently used later in England by Sir Raymond Unwin and Barry Parker—I discovered for myself the prototype of this new form along Brattle Street and in some of the Boston suburbs like Longwood, dating back to the mid-Nineteenth Century. So, too, I appreciated Olmsted's new conception, the strip park, in the Back Bay Fens. With these fresh insights I eventually came back to New York with eyes already open to welcome such innovations in planning and neighborhood layout as my new friends Henry Wright and Clarence Stein were soon to make.

All in all, as it turned out, fate had chosen exactly the right branch of the armed services, at exactly the right moment, to give me the maximum opportunities to cultivate my own life, assiduously if not always wisely. As a radio amateur, with an excellent high-school course in physics under my belt, I sailed through the elementary classroom exercises in radio theory without any extra study. This left me free to spend my evenings either in Richardson's old Cambridge Library or in the new Widener Library in Harvard Yard. That time was not wasted. But I am not at all sure about the weekends I spent toiling earnestly over an essay I had committed myself to offer in a prize contest fostered by the 'Journal of the American Institute of Architects.' What possessed me to entertain that idea? The lure of badly needed money certainly played a part—was the prize a thousand dollars?—but just as urgent, or even more so, was my feeling that I wanted to make further use of my brief familiarity with the garment industry. I called the project—I blush!—'Garment Gardens.'

I flinch from examining my files now to see if I still have that essay; but, pretentious as it must have been, the plan provided for new house types in rows and new floor layouts with interchangeable or expansible rooms that at least testify to a certain self-confident readiness to break with conventions. Otherwise, I could hardly have dared to enter such a competition or entertain such a hope. Possibly somewhere in my paper there was a flash or two of more acute analysis, if not creative design, though I lacked even the shakiest vocational preparation as an architectural draftsman, still less as an architect. What an ass I was! Or to put it more gently, how insolently young! Fortunately I was unabashed by my failure to win even honorable mention; and if I had any pangs of regret over my wasted time, it is only now that I am conscious of them. Even after I had been recalled to quarters in September, I rented another room further along Kirkland Street, so that I might doggedly spend the bright October weekends finishing up this essay.

This account of my strictly personal 'war activities' is partly to correct the howler made gratuitously by a professor writing in 'The New England Quarterly' when he suggested that the "traumatic experience" of war turned me into a pacifist! What a traumatic experience! Pacifist reaction indeed! Many other young men of my generation were painfully crippled for life by their military experience, even if they could show no visible scars; but my half-year in Cambridge was sheer good fortune: for at least it gave me a back-door entry to Harvard; and that has sufficed me, I can say without teasing mockery, almost for a lifetime. But in the end another back door opened for me at Leverett House, where from 1965 on I spent five seasons as Visiting Scholar.

3

The time has come to dam this flood of 'Navy' memories, though the flood itself would probably raise interesting problems to a more aloof analyst. I stop all the more easily because I have touched other phases of this experience in that semibiographic novel in demi-verse I first published in 1928 in 'The Second American Caravan,' 'The Little Testament of Bernard Martin.' But there remains one large episode of the period that stands out: a scrape that might have had serious, possibly shattering consequences.

All through this Cambridge sojourn, I had been tramping around the countryside, with a sketch pad, a box of watercolors, and a U.S. topographic map, neatly cut up into sections in my middy blouse. One Sunday afternoon, on a hill above Belmont, a middle-aged civilian had come upon me and demanded to look at my fumbling impressionistic sketch. In my innocence it took me a little time to realize that this was not an admirer of art but a suspicious citizen who probably had a jittery vision of me as a German spy, despite my Navy uniform. How silly! I thought.

But there was no smile on my face when, standing on the bridge between Chelsea and Charlestown—I had gone by ferry to East Boston and was making the circuit—a policeman came up to me and asked me what I was doing. I pointed to the view with a ship in the foreground which I had been sketching. "Some dagos told me a spy was drawing plans here: so I'll have to take you to the station house." That was a chancy moment for me. As I started walking toward shore with the sketch pad still in my hand, I had a desperate impulse, since I was next to the railing, to let the pad drop into the water. In a flash all the nightmarish evidence against me had presented itself. Not only had I been found sketching the view of the Navy Yard, but worse, I had topographic maps with me! What innocent person would carry such maps in wartime?

If inquiry were made, it would turn out that I rarely went out on the town with my shipmates. I kept to myself! What was worse, I had rented outside quarters for weekend use, and my landlady could testify to my constant use of a typewriter in my periodic solitude. Had they made further search in New York, they would have found that I was partly of German extraction, and even worse, that in my bedroom at home was a whole stack of pro-German pamphlets which my uncle James Schleicher had sent me earlier in the war. My heart sank. Good heavens! Men had been hanged on frailer circumstantial evidence than this! If in my rising panic I had thrown my pad into the water, that act would have been the final clincher. No need to dredge up the evidence! If ever I needed a guardian angel it was at that moment. . . .

When we reached the station house, the Irish sergeant demanded to see the pad, and my heartbeats quickened as I turned it over to him, for the maps were still clipped under the sheets at the back! Happily even the sergeant could recognize that there was no useful information in my smudgy sketch. Without looking inside the pad he asked me where I was stationed and what my name was. I presented my dog tag. As a sensible man, that satisfied him. "I'll have to report this to your commanding officer," he said, returning the pad to me without—bless him!—turning up the maps.

Unbelievably I was free, though I still, after anxiously hastening back to Cambridge, had to confront the officer of the day and tell him what had happened. And there my luck continued to hold: the officer of the day was a seasoned Navy Lieutenant, Jerry Cronin: competent, unflappable, strict in discipline but never hasty or arbitrary: above all, sure to be loyal to his men in any run-in with the civil authorities.

After I had told my story and explained my private weekend tours of the region, he asked me if I had my sketch pad with me. Scarcely glancing at the sketches, he opened the clasp and turned to the topographic maps. Fortunately for me, I had not attempted to allay suspicion meanwhile by getting rid of them. My perfect innocence exonerated me. Not being a fool, Cronin at once recognized that no spy would expose his guilt in this fashion; so he blandly said: "If the police do anything about it, I'll set them right. Don't worry." With those reassuring words he banished my nightmare.

Yet how close I had been to marring, if not utterly ruining my life! Do I exaggerate? No: I have recalled that episode more than once, and each time I have inwardly blenched. As with people who later were falsely accused of being Communist traitors during the panicky Cold War investigations by the Un-American Activities Committee, the very fact that I could be suspected of being a spy brought on the guilty feeling that would almost have justified the accusation without a corroborating act.

4

One weekend late in September I got word that my mother was ill and wangled a weekend pass to run down to New York to see her. Nothing really alarming: it was 'just influenza.' But when I got back on Monday morning, utterly fagged by sitting up all night in the jerky train, I discovered that the whole Radio School had been quarantined for influenza, and all of us with rooms outside were recalled to barracks—in my case to the Harvard dorm on Mt. Auburn Street, hard by the car yards, where Alfred North Whitehead received me twenty years later.

Just influenza indeed! It had already reached plague proportions: all over the world people were coming down with this disease, and some tens of millions eventually died of it. We quickly realized how serious this outbreak was, because the naval authorities canceled all classes and even dispensed with drill: we spent a large part of the sunlit October days lolling on the grass of the stadium—though the tedium would be repeatedly punctuated by men keeling over and being carried off to the hospital.

Once more, quite incredibly, my luck held. Though my tuber-culosis had been arrested, I still had a sensitive throat, often sore enough to need treatment at Sick Bay; and I was chronically suscep-tible to colds. Plainly a proper candidate for influenza! My shipmate from Honolulu, who occupied the bunk below me, awoke shivering in the middle of one night: so I covered him with one of my blankets and the next morning supported him on his walk to the Sick Bay, with the same blanket over his shoulders. He had a ghastly time of it for a month and barely pulled through; but nothing whatever happened to me. By the time I saw him again, pale and weak, the war was nearly over, and we spent the early Armistice night together mid the crowds milling around the Common, until I elbowed a pas-sage for us down to the subway at Park Street Under.

Yes, the war was over: dismayingly, before I knew it, Harvard faded away before my eyes. But for nearly three tedious months more I was back in the old Navy—with no compensations except a little extra pay and weekend passes. As it happened, I was one of a handful in my class that emerged with a second-class rating, instead of a third, because I could take twenty-nine words a minute in Morse code, close to the required thirty for first class—though many of my slower comrades often had a skill in sending messages that I never bothered to acquire, since it wasn't part of the course. By any fair rating they were certainly more competent radio operators than I was.

None of the further details of the next three months, which now keep welling up in my memory, is worth recounting except for a theft I committed before leaving the Naval Station at Pelham, my final stopping place. In the library there I came upon an ancient volume, 'The American Cottage-Builder,' which some thrifty patriot had donated, ostensibly for our entertainment. Without a qualm I decided that this book belonged to only one person, myself; and I still have it. Without the slightest consciousness of commitment, it seems that I was already preparing myself for the further study of American architecture.

Until I found myself writing this account, I had never looked upon my ten-month tour of duty in the Navy as a rewarding period: quite the contrary. Certainly, if given the choice, I would have avoided it. But even the most boring parts of that life did not infringe on my inner freedom. Best of all, perhaps, my Navy stint gave me a vivid sense of my whole American background. My shipmates, coming from all parts of the country, from many different trades and callings, taught me far more about my own country than I could have discovered in a similar period of travel. Our son, a manlier sort of person than I was, fortified by some rough experiences in travel and wheat-ranching even before he became a soldier at eighteen, summed up this side of military life to perfection: "You could line up a thousand people in the Army in double file," he observed, "and each one of them would have something to say to the soldier facing him. That's more than would happen with civilians."

But I have yet to record my final debt to the Navy. Without this whole experience I would not have been so well prepared to get under Herman Melville's skin or write a competent critique of his work: one of my first mature literary achievements. Remote though I was from his main experiences at sea, the Navy I knew was still, in essentials, the same Navy that Melville knew when he returned from Hawaii in the naval frigate, 'United States'; and behind that Navy was the archetypal mode of military-bureaucratic organization that had been handed down, as I was later to trace, from century to century, from culture to culture, from government to government, beginning perhaps before the Pyramid Age, five thousand years ago. Even the small sample of this type of centralized, authoritarian control I had swallowed as a young man—hardly a sample, barely more than a sniff—gave me a fresh insight at long last into those formative forces that have both held the institutions of civilization together, and then, by insulating them from more life-conserving occupations and more humane modes of cooperation, brought about their destruction. That combination of method and madness, of fruitful rituals and demented sacrifices, eventually gave me a long-missing clue to war's ultimate massive arrest of civilization.

Not merely the 1918 Navy, but later 'Moby Dick' and 'White Jacket' were to give me essential insights into the miscarriages of life in our own time. And how could I, without the godlike imagination of a Shakespeare, have reached such a fullness of understanding without my service, grudging and brief though it was, in the United States Navy?

Naturally I made desperate efforts to speed my way out of the Navy at the earliest possible moment—all futile of course—but I was not a little uneasy early in 1919, when I eventually was released, as to what might happen to my literary ambitions. The minuscule income I drew from my 'estate' was barely enough to cover my board and lodging even at home; and on the basis of my previous earnings through writing the prospect for getting a living that way was bleak—and would long remain bleak. If a computer had been fed with the data on my qualifications, it would probably have advised me to give up writing as a career, just as it would have advised the British to surrender to the Nazis after Dunkirk. Occasionally, indeed, I was visited by a vagrant impulse to spend a year or two at sea as a radio operator—the one specialized occupation I was almost qualified to pursue—in order to 'see the world.'

This shadowy possibility remained in the background a few months, as a comforting guarantee against starvation. So it was with a measure of uneasiness that, one sharp February morning, I pocketed my discharge slip and, with my seabag on my shoulder, marched to the subway station, leaving behind as dimming shadows in memory my now scattering or scattered shipmates.

CHAPTER SIXTEEN

Time
on 'The Dial'

I

New York in 1919! The city never wore a brighter look than it wore that year. Partly, as with all other returning soldiers and sailors, even those who had not seen active duty, it was the contrast with the bleak training camps, the humiliating routines, the blind obedience, the appalling monotony and uniformity of the life we had been living; so that the first few weeks of wearing civilian clothes, making the little personal choices of a necktie or a suit, filled one with a sense of returning to an abandoned self that had somehow survived one's absence and was waiting to be reclaimed. One touched the old familiar objects—the desk, the shelf of books, the typewriter—and rubbed one's back against them, catlike, purring. They were still there: we were still there, too!

The brightness in the air of the whole city was doubtless chiefly the reflection of my own inner glow; yet it seems in retrospect almost palpable and quite independent of any private response. I remember striding up Fifth Avenue in the warm rain of an April afternoon, absorbing thirstily the brownstone houses, the fine flat facade of old St. Bartholomew's, sandwiched between other buildings, the wet pavements, the new buses, the lingering clop of a surviving hansom-cab horse, above all the smart young women and the handsome young men: even that smiling young fellow who accompanied me in the plate-glass shop fronts! How often one would encounter a friend in that drifting stream of people!—as if we were all part of an intimate circle.

At last I was not merely in New York but of it: the city was mine and I embraced it. A thousand years had passed since that February morning in 1919 when I had dropped my seabag in the hall of our West Ninety-fourth Street flat, and Nana, greeting me, had said: "Welcome home! Everything is different now. We eat toast instead of rolls in the morning."

Yes, everything was different, different but so much better: that was my first impression of postwar Manhattan. The winter of my adolescent discontent was over: there was burgeoning everywhere, and it would have been strange if a bud or two had not opened in me. Why, there was even a new subway! Well before Prohibition had closed the saloons, coffeehouses had begun to spring up all over the city in true Viennese style, sometimes connected with an elegant bakery, as they had been in Van Wyck Brooks's earlier day, when writers frequented Fleischmann's Bakery near Union Square. In addition, a new feminine influence had made itself felt in a scattering of bright little tearooms, though the old masculine chop houses, like Broad's, with their sawdust-sprinkled floors, were slowly passing away.

Oh! there were many other signs of life, too. The Rand School of Social Science on Fifteenth Street was in its hopeful heyday. Was not the Socialist Commonwealth just around the corner?—or so at least many people thought until in 1919 the New York legislature staged a Star Chamber inquisition of suspected radicals, and in the name of democracy deprived the handful of duly elected Socialist members of their seats. More intellectually promising than the Rand School was the New School for Social Research, headed by Dr. James Harvey Robinson: a true *école libre* on the French model, with no prescribed courses, no examinations for credits, no degrees—and to be quite honest, no social research either: though it attracted students, young and old, who sought to supplement or continue further their higher education.

So in a little while another private dream of mine came true; for that spring I took a course in modern economic development under the scholar I had already admired at a distance, Thorstein Veblen, with his 'The Theory of the Leisure Class' and his sardonic, deliberately baffling style, couched in a jargon that mockingly reflected that of his academic colleagues; for in the university world this ruthless iconoclast needed protective coloration. At the New School, too, I would hear Graham Wallas—the Willersley of H. G. Wells's 'The New Machiavelli'—lecturing in his tense, inimitable sputtery fashion, as if struggling with new thoughts for the first time.

Well before the First World War the long-fermenting ideas of the Nineteenth Century had reached a sufficiently heady state, promoted by the belief that a swift and radical transformation of human society was imminent. This notion had become widespread: even the most reactionary minds, like those of the Action Française or the later German Nazis, conceived that it was possible to effect a wholesale revolutionary transformation by forceful leadership and ruthless suppression alone. All this was disguised as a popular demand for a more meaningful life than our pragmatic profit-oriented economy had been able to produce. Change and novelty were considered in themselves as sufficient guarantees of improvement: 'new,' 'progressive,' 'advanced,' 'modern,' and 'revolutionary' were interchangeable words of beatification.

In Greenwich Village century-old ideas for a better life were now swarming like midges on a summer's night: not merely socialism, communism, syndicalism, anarchism, Ibsenism, Nietzscheanism, Shavianism, New Republicanism, progressivism, liberalism; but feminism, vegetarianism, free-loveism, nudism—indeed, every conceivable mode of monocular utopianism. There were even pious souls who thought that the Single Tax or the Initiative, Referendum, and Recall would rectify most public abuses and usher in a truly democratic and therefore permanently better society. That majestic feminist, Henrietta Rodman, as chaste as the Statue of Liberty, practiced nudism, at least at home, as did Maurice Parmelee, the City College sociologist; while at the Liberal Club the militant I.W.W. leader, Bill Haywood, confidently preached revolution through "One Big Union" and the General Strike; or Dr. A. A. Brill, the translator of Freud, would explain the incestuous Oedipus Complex with shockproof Teutonic deliberation.

Greenwich Village, with all its bohemianism, had become a genuine cultural center, providing in its experimental audacities sundry precious qualities that the University, the Church, and the Business World had in their prudent officialism excluded. Naturally the Village had its share of charlatans and fakes: witness Joe Gould, New England's grimy, cast-off child. Though quite innocent of literary talent, Gould was supposedly writing an interminable *omnium gatherum* of contemporary history, which happily vanished entirely save for one boring published fragment. And there was J.C. (John Coffey), the gentlemanly thief who, under the guise of redressing social injustices—the earliest of such morally pretentious looters—had perfected the art of filching expensive clothes by secreting himself in a department store overnight.

For all that, the Village with its cheap rents had been attracting genuine writers and artists from the days of Albert Pinkham Ryder on: such a concentration as it can no longer in its frightened opulence afford. By taking a turn around Washington Square, or by lingering in one of half a dozen restaurants from Bertolotti's or Three Steps Down to Romany Marie's and The Brevoort—yes! The Brevoort—one would rub shoulders with the new intelligentsia, a term, if not a group, that came in with the new Russian novelists and revolutionaries, whom everyone read.

Anything might happen in this lively milieu; for no hard and fast lines had yet been drawn, and our intellectual differences did not keep us from enjoying each other's company. Thus Irwin Granich—later a grimly vehement party Communist—arranged my very first public lecture in 1917 at the *anarchist* Ferrer Society, uptown in Harlem; in his Boston days Granich was coeditor of a short-lived magazine, 'The Flame,' which, as its name perhaps suggests, was a soon-extinguished anarchist sheet. At the Ferrer Society I talked to a small and openly suspicious audience on Kropotkin and Regionalism—it was the Regionalism that was suspect!—and next day one of the members collared me at the library and accused me of being a capitalist hireling. Still, they had listened!

Before the war I had hovered near the entrance to this Bohemian community, just close enough to smell what was cooking and to feel my mouth watering. Suddenly, here I was, an Associate Editor of 'The Dial,' with a desk facing Clarence Britten's in the front room on the second floor; and now every day I touched intimately all those aspects of New York I had known chiefly as a hesitant intruder before 1919. Now I, too, belonged to the Younger Generation; rebellious, defiant of conventions, but not yet wholly disillusioned; and Greenwich Village was our rallying ground. The immense easy sociability of literary New York, as one knew it half a century ago, before Prohibition and the speakeasy had corroded our decencies, found its home in the range of restaurants and cuisines, which reflected every taste and allowed for every pocketbook: even the menu at the Lafayette was modestly priced by present standards.

Part of the quality of this life was due to our willingness to ac-

L.M., 1920

cept something close to poverty as the normal condition of people dedicated to art and letters. Most of us did not try to live or dress or spend like stockbrokers, film stars, or 'sports.' With a few 'uptown' exceptions, we did not dream of "a diamond as big as the Ritz." Certainly the words 'status,' 'security,' 'affluence,' 'prestige,' 'publicity' and 'clout' had no place in our vocabulary, still less in our lives. Our most expensive taste was a taste for conversation; and I can recall our scorn when, on a weekend by the sea, our more affluent hosts cut short an exciting conversation by inviting their guests to go to a motion-picture show. What sort of person would leave off a good talk for a movie—least of all a 1923 movie!

For a brief period during the second decade of the century it looked as if Chicago, with its dynamic university, full of challenging minds, and its emerging novelists and poets—Robert Herrick, Sherwood Anderson, and Carl Sandburg—would contend successfully with New York and Boston as a literary center, and that San Francisco at least would make a fourth. Indeed, H. L. Mencken, in an article in 1919 for the London 'Nation,' had with some reason hailed the Chicago literary scene as a focus for a new mid-American culture. But the very migration of the fortnightly 'Dial' from Chicago to New York in 1918 was an unfortunate sign that New York's financial ascendancy and ever-widening cosmopolitan interests would in the end prevail, as Boston had prevailed after the Civil War. And it is only now, half a century later, that minor cultural centers are belatedly beginning to exhibit self-sustaining communal activities of their own.

2

The accounts of the origins of 'The Dial,' its migration, and its transformation that one finds in the now-current standard histories of American literature, and in an equally standard encyclopedia, are so liberally spattered with misinformation that, for the sake of the public record, I should perhaps, as a lonely survivor of the old 'Dial,' set down a few forgotten facts.

This little independent review of books had been revived as a fortnightly in Chicago back in the eighties, with the memory and name of Emerson's transcendentalist quarterly for a blessing; and its chief owners were the redoubtable Paul Carus family, who also supported two quarterlies, 'The Monist' and 'The Open Court,' in whose pages Charles Peirce's challenging philosophic contributions had been hospitably received. In 1917 Scofield Thayer, a young provincial New Englander (Worcester and Harvard), had joined the editorial board for a while, and presumably contributed financially to 'The Dial.' The following year, Martyn Johnson, an intellectual entrepreneur—

slightly monied, slightly radical—took over the responsibilities as publisher and moved the review to West Thirteenth Street in New York.

The migration of 'The Dial' brought with it a change in policy: the old fortnightly 'Dial,' once devoted to book reviews aimed at both professors and booksellers, sought to enlarge its scope and influence by serving as an organ of Reconstruction, sympathetic to radical movements in the many forms they then took. A new board of editors had been chosen with this aim in view, headed by John Dewey, who was then in China, by Thorstein Veblen, and by Helen Marot, an old 'Masses' editor, who had been a crusading women's rights radical and a women's trade-union organizer; while the active work of writing editorials and editing copy, once Robert Morss Lovett had abandoned his editorial chair, fell to the Associate Editors: Clarence Britten, myself, and slightly later, Geroid Robinson. What would now be called our 'activism' was what specially distinguished us from 'The New Republic' and 'The Nation.' 'Reconstruction' was our watchword.

There was half a year of hopeful suspense after the November 1918 Armistice when it seemed, not just to a few liberals and radicals but to millions of people all over the world, that the wholesale mutilations and destructions of the First World War might be redeemed by some massive outburst of peaceful creativity. Though H. G. Wells's slogan "The war that will end war" quickly proved only an empty catchword, the desire—if not the patience—to lay down permanent foundations for peace between the nations was hopefully widespread: so that Woodrow Wilson, in his evangelical postwar tour of Europe, was spontaneously hailed as a living Savior by the crowds that greeted him everywhere.

Wilson's early addresses had identified victory over the Germanic powers with the achievement of justice, liberty, and rational political cooperation: he promised release from sordid imperial ambitions, national arrogance, and class exploitation. This hope for an immediate rectification of ancient evils and injustices was, it is easy to see now, both exorbitant and naïve. Yet it is only in the light of these expectations that one can understand the shocked disillusion, the corrosive cynicism, the bitter sense of betrayal that followed the publication of the Treaty of Versailles. What happened to 'The Dial' and its editors encompasses both the elation and the deflation that took place during this fateful year.

The term Reconstruction has become unintelligible now, in the sense it was used in 1919; and even then it could not have the same meaning in the United States as it had in the war-shattered areas of Europe. For us, Reconstruction had a far broader significance than that of restoring the blasted factories and flooded mines with which the defeated German armies had vengefully punctuated their retreat. Reconstruction here carried the hopeful notion that the war had given each country such a jolt that every institution, shaken off its ancient base, would be searchingly re-examined and reshaped on a more humane pattern—as if the invisible structure of men's minds were as accessible and as open to reorganization or replacement as shell-pocked fields or broken-down bridges. It now seems strange to think that when Reconstruction was finally set forth in more specific terms, it could for even a short while have seemed so full of promise.

When the editors of 'The Dial' talked of Reconstruction in industry, they meant shop committees and industrial councils and democratic participation; perhaps national guilds to control the major industries and ultimately their government ownership. When they talked of Reconstruction in education, they meant Dewey's "learning by doing," along with greater activity by the students, and a loosening of formal requirements, abetted by a willingness to experiment in new modes of teaching and learning.

And actually, to be just, not all the hopes and expectations for the 'Reconstruction period' were hollow or without consequence. If few of our immediate plans could be realized, in more than one field sounder foundations had been laid. Through Helen Marot I came into contact with one of Dewey's most animated followers, Caroline Pratt, a tart spinster whose original City and Country School sought to make every part of the visible environment open to the young, in both winter and summer. At Columbia University the students, among them our young friend Dorothy Swaine Thomas, proposed drastic revisions of the curriculum and got the faculty to introduce a new orientation course in history that would cover, not just this or that country but world civilization from its beginnings. An overdue innovation.

And so, too, in housing and urban planning, the group of architects and community planners Charles Harris Whitaker brought together in 'The Journal of The American Institute of Architects' sought to apply the experiments made in wartime housing for factory workers to the eradication of slums and the regeneration of cities. It was through Whitaker, whom I met the same year I joined 'The Dial,' that I myself, for the next decade, took an active part in this effort.

Doubtless Reconstruction was not the right word for describing these varied initiatives; but the war, by demanding the impossible of both men in combat and the civilians who lived under the constant threat of invasion or subjugation, had made many people ready to face more robust measures for the improvement of their daily lives. Given the incentive and the will to cooperate, people had seen throughout the war how much that had seemed beyond human reach could be accomplished. Unfortunately these robust demands did not reckon with the negative by-products of war: the exhaustion and the letdown that follow any overstrained effort, and the disappointment over the disproportionately small positive results.

All too soon the bright dreams faded out: our country sank into the deepest slough of 'normalcy,' as that blandly corrupt nonentity, Warren Harding, who became our postwar President, called it. It was not till a decade later, with Franklin D. Roosevelt's New Deal, that many of the major proposals of Reconstruction were at last carried through—sometimes, as with public housing, on a scale and with a swiftness that surprised even those of us who believed in them.

3

Not the least attraction of my new post on 'The Dial,' as I first envisaged it, was the opportunity it would give me to get nearer to Veblen—if indeed any human being could ever get near to Veblen. Still he had a motley band of faithful disciples, and by report exercised a strong amorous attraction over women. Veblen was a strange combination of the austere, seemingly superobjective scholar and a passionate, wilful human being. Physically, as he himself might have said, he was a typical Norse hybrid, long-headed, but broad of brow, with sandy brown hair and eyes, and a close vandyke beard: almost the image of a medieval saint, pale with fasting. In keeping, his voice barely rose above a whisper.

Veblen, in short, was the kind of man who rouses great love or great hostility; and though David Riesman's study of him wickedly overstresses his sadism, that trait was the obverse of his tenderness for the underdog. Jacques Loeb, who knew my relation to Veblen, completely misinterpreted Veblen's impassiveness and aloofness; for I remember Loeb—that professedly objective materialist, that cold detached scientist!—denouncing Veblen's lack of *feeling* in an argument!

Before meeting Veblen, I had read all his books and had been stirred by them in much the same fashion as I had been by those of Geddes—and for the same reason. Veblen's original studies, from 'The Theory of the Leisure Class' on, left an even clearer impression than Geddes's scattered papers and reports. Both men refused to recognize the no-trespass signs that smaller minds erected around their chosen fields of specialization; except for Max Weber and Werner Sombart, no other contemporary economist or historian had anything like Veblen's cultural range. No wonder his work attracted me!

As an economist well-grounded in technics and anthropology, Veblen was as much a suspected heretic in the academic world as Patrick Geddes was; and those who were not able to cope with his immense scholarship covered their embarrassment by not paying sufficient attention to his ideas. Even in one of the best of his students, the economist Wesley Clare Mitchell, it was hard to detect any direct influence of Veblen, either in outlook or method. Not strangely the very traits that drew me to Veblen gave a special excuse to more pedestrian scholars to ignore him. When Veblen's first book came out, William Dean Howells had, with the critical acuteness of a novelist, hailed its special merits as satire. But Veblen's unconventional approach, his insidious criticisms of the business establishment, doubtless helped to dampen his reception in the academic world, almost as much as did his readiness to speculate on matters where more positive evidence was absent or just—with Veblen's help!—being discovered! Our coming together on 'The Dial' gave me some further claim to Veblen's attention: but as with Patrick Geddes, his influence on my thinking had been greatest before we met.

Veblen had made two cogent analyses of the current political situation: one was 'Imperial Germany' and the other, one of his masterpieces, was 'The Nature of Peace' and dealt with the terms for its perpetuation. But how little effect they had on our day-to-day thinking—or even on Veblen's! Neither of these fundamental treatises prevented the editors of 'The Dial' from looking impatiently to a decisive solution—Marxist or utopian—for dissolving with a few magic passes the long-embedded institutions of war and class enslavement. Untutored by his own massive scholarship, Veblen himself, who had gone back to Neolithic culture to understand the 'instinct of workmanship' and expose the violence done to it by orthodox business enterprise, pinned his faith on a chimerical "soviet of engineers" as holding the key to both economic productivity and social justice. How youthfully quixotic was his smoldering impatience, for these expectations were unballasted by either his historic scholarship or his lifetime's experience. In the end he covered up his disappointment by translating the 'Laexdala Saga' from the Icelandic.

For all this, the essential Veblen, who was both a redoubtable sociologist and a man of letters, never quite lost his hold on me; for his literary aptitudes brought him closer to me in some ways than was Geddes. Not only did I later write an admiring obituary of Veblen for 'The New Republic'; but in a canvass of the important writers of the preceding two decades that I contributed to in the literary section of the 'New York Herald-Tribune' in 1931, I concluded my final essay with an appreciation of Veblen as the mordant satirist he was. Even now, despite the many changes in my critical judgments that maturity brings, I would not withdraw that praise.

In editorial policy Martyn Johnson leaned heavily on Helen Marot; and it was possibly her respect for Veblen that led to his becoming one of the senior editors, though he functioned only as a contributor, except when he offered our editorial meetings his gift of impassive silence. Helen Marot was a courageous, militant woman, whose spinsterly feminism was partly activated, I have reason to believe, by an unfortunate love affair. Red-haired, scrawny in the flesh, with a voice that sometimes rose to an hysterical falsetto, she was a strange combination of hardheaded realism and guileless romanticism, whose most sensible thoughts had a way of becoming scrambled in the act of her setting them in written order.

Like so many generous spirits of her period, Helen Marot was heart and soul for the Revolution, not out of any formal loyalty to Marx or Marxism but in direct reaction to injustices and inhumanities she had personally witnessed. Sophia, who had earlier come on 'The Dial' as secretary, remembers that when the October Revolution took place in Russia in 1918, Helen even led a group of 'Dial' employees to join a parade on Fifth Avenue in celebration of it; and she had squelched Martyn Johnson when he disdainfully inquired what that "bundle of red rags"—those defiant revolutionary flags!— was doing in the editorial office.

For a while Helen even insisted, in accord with 'democratic principles'—whether Russian Soviet or British guild socialist didn't matter!—that all the workers on 'The Dial,' down to the office boy, should be present at our editorial policy meetings. She called this a 'soviet'— then-blessed word!—though Helen could not hide from herself the fact that the staff's bashfulness about expressing themselves vocally was equaled only by their indifference: so, well before 'The Dial' changed owners, we had to abandon the practice, for the same reason that drove Emerson to give up his egalitarian innovation of having the cook and the housemaid sit down to meals with the family.

Apart from Veblen's articles, it was through Helen Marot that Veblen and Dewey most influenced 'The Dial,' more by her presence than by her literary skill, for, based on her personal experience, she often had a shrewd intuitive grasp of situations that came closer to the mark than the objective appraisals and precise statements of more equable people. Under Helen's guidance, literature took second place to Reconstruction and the labor movement; and trade-union leaders, production managers, and socially minded engineers like Walter Polakov were more at home with us that summer than were poets and critics; though we managed, thanks mainly to Clarence Britten, to keep open house for both.

For all of Helen Marot's tested experience and personal shrewdness, there was a vein of unabashed romanticism in her basic proposals: this vein ran through most of the forward-looking plans of the whole period. Helen's one book, published a few years before, was entitled 'The Creative Impulse in Industry'; and in it she had set herself the difficult, if not impossible, task of reconciling the narrow, repetitive, mind-depressing operations of machine industry with the need for personal involvement and human companionship that farming and handicraft and even petty business had once fostered, under all but the most servile conditions.

This belief that work should be evaluated as an educational experience was an insight that united the philosophies of both John Dewey and Patrick Geddes; and the need to appraise the productive process, not just in terms of profits, wages, and the physical output of goods, but in terms of the kind of human being it nourished, was a more radical idea than Marx's acceptance of the dominant system of production as the sole generator of truths and values. Had Helen known Frédéric Le Play's work, she would have appreciated his dictum that the most important product that comes out of the mine is the miner.

CHAPTER SEVENTEEN

Nike on Thirteenth Street

I

My brief career as Associate Editor of 'The Dial'—it lasted just seven months—gave me not only a new circle of friends and colleagues but professional experience in the jobs of proofreading and editing, fortnightly practice in writing to a set theme, and a sense that doors that I had never dreamed even of knocking at were actually ready to open for me.

But the best gift 'The Dial' gave me was the opportunity to become acquainted with the girl whom I was a few years later to marry, Sophia Wittenberg. And though that door opened more slowly to me than all the other doors, so that more than once I lost heart and was ready to turn away, it became in fact the main entrance to every other part of my existence: so much so that to tell the story of my marriage in any fullness would be to tell, directly or indirectly, about the better part of my life.

Even before I knew that Sophia worked on 'The Dial,' I was conscious of her existence; for I had seen her in the company of two or three young men striding away from the Rand School on East Fifteenth Street, sandaled, with her long skirt flying in folds behind her, looking—and the image came to me at once—like the Nike of Samothrace, but better! for her head, now kindly restored by nature, had a kind of Greco-Oriental cast, with a straight, short nose, an almost Greek chin, and flashing dark-brown eyes. Other girls in Greenwich Village were wearing sandals, and even flowing skirts, in

1919; but none carried her head so high or walked with such a sense of sweeping the world before her.

Sophy—forgive me if I continually shift from an 'ia' to a 'y' ending, as I've always done in life—had come to 'The Dial' just a little while before I began dropping around for books to review; and I was pleasantly startled, a week or so after first beholding her that gusty March day, to find that my new goddess was Robert Morss Lovett's secretary. Though this creature had promptly captivated me, we still tease each other occasionally over the memory that I failed to make any such impression on her; for, a month or two after I'd been coming regularly to 'The Dial,' she reported to Lovett vaguely after one of my visits that a reviewer, whose name she had forgotten, but it began with an 'M,' either 'Munson' or 'Mumford,' had been in to see him. "Was it," he asked, "the one with the bald head or the one with the happy smile?" My hair and my smile were all that then identified me.

Once I was ensconced in my editorial chair at 'The Dial,' not the least charm of the job was the fact that every day I could look at this beautiful young woman, and could even try to attract her attention by means other than the dictating of letters; though the means I chose, like our going out to lunch together, were so much part of the general camaraderie of the office, and so often included a third or a fourth person—like the other secretary, Eleanor Minné, or my part-time fellow editor, Geroid Robinson—that she was hardly aware of my attention: indeed, since Robinson and Sophy worked together in the final job of 'putting the magazine to bed,' he saw far more of her than I did.

Sophy remembers being more than a little excited the first time I talked to her in the office library in a purely personal way; but even after I'd summoned up enough courage to ask her to have dinner with me, probably at Three Steps Down on West Eighth Street, she baffled me by her aloofness or irresponsiveness: she seemed to have reserves that my sallies could not penetrate—or was it just her carapace of indifference that kept me off? At that time she was so untrustful of the effect of her charms that she absurdly supposed I favored mousey Eleanor; and when one noon, returning from lunch, Eleanor and I did a mock Greek dance along Thirteenth Street in the mode of Isadora Duncan, she resented us both because we were so damned uninhibited, while she was too self-conscious to attempt such display—though *she* was the real Greek.

For all that, my amorous temperature was rising rapidly; and by the time October came, I even visited her at her home in further Flatbush, on Avenue N, reached by a subway station located between two avenues that boasted my own initials: L and M. Was that an augury? It was a two-family house, set in the midst of open fields,

Sophia

surrounded by the remains of a war garden; and in our walks along Ocean Parkway, during the next few years, we might have been in the forest of Fontainebleau for any sense we had then of motor traffic. It was on the porch of this house, on a hot summer night, that I was to feel for the first time the thrilling rondure of her breast from under her loosened silk blouse; but that intimacy still lay a few years ahead, for she long remained impassive to my all-too-hesitant touch. At this unawakened moment of her life, she was absorbed in secret dreams that kept us at a distance. She seemed, indeed, so passive that I foolishly applied to her the epithet 'cushiony'—the most maladroit adjective possible for that withdrawn but vehement soul.

But there was no doubting her outward serenity, which gave her an air of both self-confidence and sophistication. I hold to the memory of one November night, when I waited for her in the doorway of the old Majestic Theater on Columbus Circle—she would not break an earlier dinner engagement with someone else—where we were to listen to 'Ruddigore,' an operetta then rarely performed. Sophy knew Gilbert and Sullivan from end to end, for her family had sung almost every operetta together, during those days when pianos were fixtures in most middle-class homes and the capacity to produce music was not left to paid professionals. Big flakes of snow were falling, and suddenly out of the white haze came this handsome creature, in a new fawn-brown toque and a heavy brown tweed overcoat, striding along as fresh as the snowflakes themselves, majestically self-sufficient: far too fresh in her femininity to need makeup or perfume.

Is all this a lover's exaggeration? If it seems so, let me add the early testimony of Salwyn Schapiro, my City College professor:

> About a year ago I happened to drop into the Civic Club when a dance was in progress. I do not enjoy the spectacle of Reformers dancing, so I hovered on the outside. Suddenly I noticed a girl on the floor that made me stare and stare. What could she be doing in this nest of Reformers? She was beautiful to a degree and in a way that sets a man thinking of Life and Destiny and writing articles about Truth and Beauty. I asked her to dance and the way she danced convinced me that she was destined to marry one who could write but not dance. Were he to dance, he would spend all his time dancing with her and desert his pen.

On top of these charms, I suppose the fact that Sophia was linked in my mind with Beryl, through their devotion to Gilbert's ballads, may have played a secret part in my own response to her, as it did later, in curious little linkages, with other girls who crossed my erotic horizon. But that night, somehow, remains a landmark: the first sure premonition of the deeper bond that would finally bring us and keep us together.

2

Before I go deeper into Sophy's quandaries, I must interrupt my courtship for a moment to give a brief picture of her background; for if one part of her belonged to Greenwich Village, the fact is that Martyn Johnson took her on at 'The Dial' only after she had confessed that she still lived with her parents—in Flatbush!—which sat-isfied his need for a secretary who could be counted on for sober fidelity to the job.

Her parents were Russian Jews who, when threatened with a long separation by conscript service, fled in desperation to America. Almost penniless, they found that the Promised Land, in the midst of the depression of 1893, was almost equally penniless. By their intelligence and dogged courage they survived that harsh initiation: yet not without carrying, however hidden, the scars it left. Sophy's father, William Wittenberg (Volodya in Russia, Wolf to the immigra-tion officials), was born in a little village in White Russia, and re-tained the memory of a primeval oneness with nature, with the wide sky and the lazy river and the companionable clouds, the songs of the loggers floating the logs to market in the spring, and the rough, wily peasants who still tolerated a Jewish settlement or two in their midst, for trading. None of Father William's later memories, of life in a small country town, Sirotyna, or of an illicit residence in Moscow in order to undergo a surgical operation, always in dread of a police visitation, were as deep as his sense of an aboriginal unity with na-ture. When he was in his nineties, he would still sit for hours at a time, at the end of the bush-lined alley where our home acres then opened up, gazing into the clouds and imagining for himself a better world than the one he had found.

That inner serenity, maintained through a hundred trials, hard-ships, disappointments, and defeats, Father William imparted to all who came near him. With his fluffy white hair, his pointed beard, his wide Tartar cheekbones, he seemed to our friend Naum Gabo, the sculptor, when he first met him, the very picture of an intellec-tual Russian noble of the old school; and a noble man he was; but not in the sense Gabo first meant.

Father William's wife, Elizabeth (Elisaveta Mironovna)—a grand-aunt of the Russian Prima Ballerina, Maya Plisetskaya—must have had, from the beginning, some of the high spirits and strong will that might, under a happier sky, have rounded out her husband's qualities. As a young seamstress in Chernigov she had practiced her sewing skills in the houses of upper-class families, and observantly took on their ways. Being a ravishing beauty, she had attracted the attentions of a Gentile officer, whose wooing, I suspect, made her flee the more quickly to her Volodya's arms for safety.

Even in her sixties, the remains of Elisaveta's beauty and her fine singing voice were still manifest: these gifts, coupled with an irrepressible but quite natural vanity, incited her to dreams that life left unfulfilled: dreams of triumphs as a concert singer that she could hardly bear to relinquish even when her mirror and her ear told her that they would never be fulfilled. Her memories of her life in Chernigov were of a warmer, gayer Russia: dancing and singing, mid the vernal fragrance of the acacia, which she declared was sweeter and stronger than that of our American honey locusts.

The brute realities of New York in the nineties put an end to the sanguine expectations of this couple: but as a Socialist working for the improvement of his fellow workers, even when in time he became the owner of a small garment shop, Father William was less frustrated than was his wife, for his occupation made use of his extraordinary mechanical ingenuity, just as it revealed his sweet lack of a practical business sense. He gave to the Singer Sewing Machine Company, gratis, in return for their cooperation in manufacturing his model, the valuable device for making buttonholes he had invented but was too innocent to either patent or sell.

Caught in a round of childbirths, forced to watch every penny, working desperately from morning to night, Elizabeth became worn and old long before her dreams retreated. But the money that would release her never came, as frequently it did to harsher natures than Father William's, more intent on financial success. Slowly, but never securely, their position improved, largely thanks to her foresight, her skill, her scrimping. Each move of their household represented a further measure of ease and security: from the Lower East Side to part of a house in Williamsburg, from Williamsburg to a brownstone house on Lafayette Avenue, finally from Lafayette Avenue to a suburban house in Flatbush. But never was there enough money to free this ambitious spirit, until all hope was gone except that which she had invested in her children and grandchildren. Among her own family of four daughters and a son, Sophy, though she had always made her own decisions even when they did not agree with her mother's, had been closest to her in temperament and the most sympathetic in her responses.

But, alas! all her positive qualities—her fierce maternal devotion, her social conscience, her instinctual sympathy with all forms of life, all of which made her notable in the care of both young babies and gardens—were too often obscured to the casual eye, including the all-too-casual eyes of her children, by her self-absorption and her self-admiration. Some deep residue of bitterness, of vain sacrifice and unfulfilled life, remained; remained and deepened, I fear, during her final years; all the more because Father William's unconsciously ingratiating disposition made everyone overlook or depreciate Elizabeth's real virtues.

All that I have been telling of this background I learned in dribbles over the years: and if I were a novelist, I would be tempted to put it in a novel, for there was much rich material that this sketch must leave out. But what I saw and felt immediately in this Flatbush house was a warm, close-knit family, which, if ruffled by temperamental conflicts, was sustained by kindness and deep loyalties. A Jew, but completely unorthodox, Father William, on principle, never stepped across the threshold of a synagogue; but neither did Sophy's mother ever serve bacon or ham. In short, a family close to their Old World roots, and all through Sophy's early youth still, despite their own poverty, offering hospitality to newcomers from Russia.

In this household only English was spoken, but English so well mastered by the parents that all their children spoke it without a trace of an accent and without that stilted purity that often comes from an attempt to abolish the last traces of a foreign tongue. True, they delighted in Russian food—borsch and piroshki—and Yiddish jokes; as did my own family in German food and 'Fliegende Blätter' humor. Apart from these distinctions, they were, by temperament and habit, all that my mother's family were not; and Sophy had a training in family discipline that I never had: though she also had had to contend, as I did not, with the overconfident superego of her elder siblings, laying down the law—*their* law—about American manners, taste, fashion, morals.

Sophy's mother had bridled at the thought of her marrying a Gentile, and a poor one at that, who wore a winter overcoat he didn't even recognize as being shabby. When we finally approached marriage, the possibility that I had Jewish blood in my veins may have softened her opposition, but she and I were never, I regret to admit, to achieve an intimate relationship. For all that, my frequent visits to Flatbush made me feel part of the family long before the relation was formally established, though my jokes and sallies were sometimes misunderstood, as when once I excused myself from remaining in the company of the three sisters who had been discussing clothes by saying—as I supposed teasingly—that I had had enough of their "inane conversation."

When, earlier, Sophy lived on Lafayette Avenue, I might well have passed her on the street near Tompkins Park on her way to the library, while I was going to the Siebrechts': but I should not have looked twice at the round, placid little girl, nor could I have guessed how, while still a child, she used to ask herself, as children sometimes do, those ultimate philosophical questions about the meaning of life, that in the fullness of our later days we put too quickly aside. Just as our daughter, Alison, at five, wanted to know how she could be sure that the hill before her was still there when she closed her eyes or turned away from it, so Sophia had wondered how man could say that he was more important than the insects in the world's purpose: did he not perhaps exist to serve *them*? Further, she felt a deep resentment—again such as many children feel—over having to obey adult commands. These commands, she reasoned, came from one individual only, not from tribal authority. Communal injunctions she felt she could have accepted, and life as lived among the American Indians would have suited her needs.

There was a free, wild, passionate spirit enclosed within this seemingly complaisant and dutiful child; and that spirit received its most grievous blow later, when, following her completion of a three-year commercial course in the Eastern District High School, she was obliged, before she was sixteen, to take on an office job. She had no natural talent for stenography and still less for bookkeeping; and she felt her parents had 'thrown her to the wolves' when, immediately after her graduation, they permitted her to take a job in Manhattan: a place she had never before traveled to unless accompanied by an older relative, a job that would keep her *alone in a room with a strange man!*—a thing she had been enjoined never on any account to permit. And what was still more dismaying, Sophy saw no reason to believe that this stultifying routine might not continue for a whole lifetime, with no prospect of release, except a one- or two-week vacation every year. The shock of this prospect remained with her; she never adapted herself to the idea. In short, Sophy never took for granted that callous wholesale sacrifice of life upon which so much of our civilization for five thousand years has been based. How healthy she was! How salutary was that rebellion! And how much of that child still remains!

Like many people in her circle, she was a Socialist—Sophy confessed that she had never met a professing Republican till she moved up to Dutchess County!—and she spent her adolescent energies working for socialism at the Rand School, marching in peace demonstrations and suffrage parades. Her conscience was nevertheless so revolted at the suffragettes' plan during a national rally for burning an effigy of President Woodrow Wilson that, though she had been transported to Washington to take part in the protest, she absented herself, even though she knew she would be called on the carpet later. Happily 'The Dial' opened up for her a larger world and rescued her for good from the blank commercial routines against which she had rebelled. Had she had a touch of her mother's ambition, this would have given her a lifetime's career. Instead she had another destiny; and I now come back to it.

3

That autumn of 1919 I had all the symptoms of malaise that mark a young man falling in love. But though Sophy and I went on walks over the Westchester Hills together and roasted frankfurters by the lapping waters of the Hudson, under the Palisades, we both had immense reserves to overcome, immense distances to leap, before so much as a kiss was possible.

Oh, yes: I was in love with Sophia, seriously in love: so truly in love that marriage was for me the inevitable next step; but I was held back, too, by the fact that my editorship at 'The Dial' came to an end when the magazine changed hands in November 1919, and I had no immediate prospects of work, except such meager pickings as reviews and occasional articles. This economic drought caused me gingerly to place one foot, then the other, into the shallow waters of marriage, prospectively, as one might probe the cold wavelets on a Maine beach before plunging in—or retreating.

Prudence, like pity, plays the devil with erotic energy; and by training and necessity I already had a larger share of prudence than a passionate lover should have. So even when I was on the brink of sailing for England, in April 1920, Sophia and I had not gone beyond a kind of warm but wary comradeship—and at that point, for more than a year, Sophia was content to leave it.

Still, we had had one faint glimpse of something beyond. One February evening in 1920 we walked the length of Park Avenue through a windless, downy fall of snow that made halos of the streetlamps and left a pleasant sting on the lips: that empty avenue, that enveloping whiteness gave us, as we strode along holding hands, the sense of solitary communion lovers crave. For the moment we didn't need many words; and that made it all the easier for me to tell her that I loved her, and so we airily discussed the possibility of her coming to join me in England, even if she wasn't sufficiently sure she loved me enough to risk marriage. We ended our walk at the apartment of a friend of hers who lived on West Fourth Street, and who had thoughtfully retired into her bedroom for the evening, leaving the living room free for us. Here, for the first time, we kissed and embraced, with a tentativeness that could hardly be called abandon; for the deliciousness of that hour was muffled for both of us by a lifetime of inhibitions.

Theoretically we two were as free as any young ones of that period could have been; but the freedom was entirely of a cerebral order, the kind that Bernard Shaw had made fashionable. Though neither of us cared a fig for convention, so that it seemed quite natural that we might travel around the world together without any further commitment, the very quality of our kisses—and our sedate drawing apart to recover our breaths and begin talking about our astonished states of mind—showed what a long way we had to go.

Even at that moment I sensed our mutual difficulties; for the very night this happened, on the long subway ride back from Flatbush, I wrote, as a mere scrap of paper still reminds me, "I feel as though we'd broken open a cocoon before the butterfly was ready to fly." That said much more than I realized. In the weeks that followed, our snowy passion melted into a slush of blue doubts. My departure for England only emphasized a psychal separation that had already taken place. On our last Sunday together, picnicking at a friend's empty hut in the Westchester Hills, we quarreled over finding ourselves still so far apart!

Yet for me all seemed clear sailing: I was in love with Sophy, and ready to risk everything to become her mate. Everything, that is, *except*—to be honest—*my future as a writer!* I realize, when I look at the situation squarely now, that my sudden readiness to face marriage, a wild proposal for a young man who had never supported himself for more than a few months at a time, was based partly on my reliance on Sophia's own upstandingness and self-supportingness. The fact that she was that sort of person was hardly less important than her beauty, her erotic promise, her sense of absolute integrity, her pure Sophyness. But had she been of the clinging sort, or had she expected me to give up my hopes and drives as a writer in order forthwith to provide for her, I surely would have retreated before letting myself fall so deeply in love. For, to speak honestly, her independence was then for me an integral part of her appealing charm. We emphasized that fact by preferring the word 'comrade' to 'lover.'

But with Sophia the situation was different. That summer, in the very act of making and remaking plans for our being together— one went so far as to take us both to Bombay, where Geddes had asked me to serve for a year as his 'assistant'—she found herself developing in a different fashion, more expressive of her budding femininity, which attracted her to a quite different sort of life than that I held out to her. Before any rival intimacies had developed, she was apprehensive of the possibility of my being drawn back to America by my love for her, since she still felt so lukewarm and so uncertain.

Sophia's remoteness and irresponsiveness baffled me, all the more because in the midst of it she would still soberly discuss the possibility of joining me in England, or even the prospect of going off with me on my return for a week's vacation in North Carolina! It baffled me, too, because I was too deeply stung by unsatisfied desire to think of such a flight together in any form but a nuptial flight, or at least a liaison. I did not suspect that what in another girl would have indicated either sexual ardor or shameless audacity was at that time in her only a confession of dream-ridden ignorance: such abysmal ignorance as one would hardly have guessed possible at that period.

I have paused here to cross-question Sophy as to what she *did* mean when she entertained the notion of such adventures with me. Did she, for example, picture us sharing a room without my making any further advances? At this she is now almost as puzzled as I was then. What was to follow was to her a blank. She was in fact simply too ignorant of sex to know how ignorant she was. Just a year or so earlier she had danced one night at the Rand School with a young man—*Negro* as it happened—and he had held her so tightly, navel to navel, that she was afraid then that she might have conceived!

Though Sophy had, a year before this point, carried on with her mother a vigorous discussion on the advisability of sterilizing hardened criminals—a discussion prompted by a series of articles in 'The New York Globe'—she had not acquired even a dictionary acquaintance with the mechanics of sexual intercourse. And while books on sex and marriage had been in circulation in America for more than a century—did not Whitman's phrenologists, Fowler and Wells, put one out?—she had never, even by accident, seen a penis or known that one existed. For Sophy a monumental fig leaf covered the entire realm of sex, even her own.

After making this admission of her early ignorance, Sophia reminded me that the newspapers had lately reported a case that had come before a marriage counselor: two young people who had been married a whole year, deeply in love, wanting children, came to the counselor for advice, because the wife had not yet conceived. On close questioning it turned out that they had never even guessed that sexual intercourse was the happy prelude to this event: they had lain fondly side by side in bed, naked, delighting in each other, eagerly looking for conception to happen in much the same way that Sophy had feared it might, despite the contraceptive of clothes, at a dance. Possibly they had taken the biblical phrase "Abraham had lain with Sarah" too literally! But during the period of our youth, I must add, girls at Barnard used often to faint, during their first academic lessons on sex, as medical students sometimes faint at the first sight of an opened cadaver.

4

These hopes and torments were the other side of my first visit to England; and they came to a head in a June letter whose opening lines I read at the breakfast table in Le Play House, only to thrust the letter into my pocket and bid my fellow resident Farquharson go on talking as if I were not present—though my heart was thumping wildly under my jacket and I was to feel, not for the last time, that jealousy that Milton calls the "injured lover's hell."

This letter was nothing less than a grand confession that Sophia had been shocked out of her dreamlike sexual impassiveness by an artist she had recently met at a stadium concert: a youngish man who had suddenly revealed to her, by his imperious advances, inner stirrings and ardors she had not yet been aware of, still less tested. "The long and short of the whole matter," Sophia explained to me, "was the meeting with an Italian sculptor who proved to be so much more passionate than any man I ever met that he somewhat upset my equilibrium . . ." (He was a fast worker; but perhaps a little too fast for the task before him, that of melting a proud iceberg.) "When I had been with him a bare hour or two he proceeded to ask all manner of personal questions. When I objected, he explained his method of getting acquainted, which is to ask every question that comes into his head." But she had baffled him, too: he could not explain her continued resistance, despite her theoretical freedom as a feminist, except on the basis that she was already in love with me. That, actually, was the least of her blocks.

The letter that Sophia tore up before writing this substitute probably contained more intimate details in the same spirit of candor as his questions; but even the censored account was painful enough. That his seduction was not successful was hardly a consolation to me: even when it was coupled with the fact that she had withdrawn her consent to pose for him when she discovered that it was not her beautiful head but her naked body that he wanted to model. From this point on, Sophia's sexuality could no longer be purely cerebral.

Though rebuffed at their first meeting, Ruotolo, the sculptor, his passion perhaps inflamed by denial, resumed his pursuit; and Sophia, who was at that time not at all sure she wanted a permanent relationship with anyone, ironically had the virtuous woman's ambivalent reward for denying easy access to her body: in a little while Ruotolo proposed marriage as the only way left for attaining his goal. If she had been ready for any closer relation then, he might have been successful: but he made the mistake of taking her to a great Italian dinner in Brooklyn, presided over by the famous Italian anarchist, Carlo Tresca, to honor the longshoremen who had refused to load munitions to be used against the Communist armies of Soviet Russia. She noted with surprise that so few women were present and asked, naïvely, where the wives were: "Wives? An Italian wife stays at home." That settled for Sophia even his more honorable efforts. She had no intention of becoming an Italian wife.

Through this first ruffling of her sexual feathers, Sophia gained self-consciousness; and now she took a new look at herself. "When I was very young," she wrote me,

> mothering and teaching, always bound up one in the other, seemed to me the only goal. Then social service, in a broader way than teaching. That preceded and included my Rand School period. Now where? I don't know. Very slowly, but surely, the realization that I am not the fine glorious creature I used to think I was has come to me. It hurts, but it's

so, and I suppose I ought to go about trying to plan my life with that realization. When one lacks a keen sense of humor, when one's mental abilities are proved to be nothing more than ordinary, when one's emotions have never been tried, there seem to be but two courses open. Either to acknowledge mediocrity, or to live gloriously in a dream world and ignore the real world. I hate mediocrity, and so I have chosen the latter course. But I know it won't do indefinitely. I realize that I must shake it off. But then what?

That first disturbance by a maturer man's passion was the beginning of a profound change in Sophia: a change that worked slowly, tortuously, often blindly through a number of years. This change raised the problem of what her true nature and her true destiny were, and what attitude she should have toward the beauty that commanded men's eyes, sometimes beckoning their hearts, if not always, as with the sculptor, pricking their genitals. During my long absence Sophia suddenly came to realize what it was to be beautiful and to be a woman: the passionate Italian had, for the first time, given a tinge of realism to the covert eroticism of more maidenly dreams.

Though Ruotolo's advances may have routed Sophy's peripheral early suitors, who were perhaps even less ready for amatory exploration than I was, the remaining months in London gave me time to recover from the shock of finding Sophy so swiftly stirred by a possible liaison. I realized that her disturbance over this challenge revealed how downright callow my own timid knocks on the door had been, how tentatively I had beckoned her, how little I had succeeded in intruding on her own sexual reserves even to the extent her sculptor had succeeded in doing.

The new turn that Sophy's life was now taking obviously lessened my chances of winning her, and it took time for me to overcome my blind envy and jealousy. By September happily I had recovered my balance sufficiently to write a sympathetic, seemingly objective letter: the kind of letter that only an older and far more experienced man might have written to a girl already ignited and ready to blaze. At the time I wrote that letter, the prig in me overrated my rationality; for, looking back on it, I see that I transferred to Sophy my own smoldering passion.

"I don't see why we shouldn't talk unreservedly about sexual matters, since if we are going to be mates (and even if we aren't) it is only by knowing the ins and outs of ourselves that we shall be able to get through life without hurting each other and everyone around us. Thank Heaven you didn't tear up your last letter in order to write about what you call 'politer matters.'

"Do you know, Soph, what the thought was which kept on sobering me and forcing me to see straight each time I read over your disturbing letter? Knowing how persistent my own sexual desires are, in spite of the fact that my conduct would pass for A-I in a YMCA secretary, and guessing that those of a normal girl may be even deeper and more overwhelming, I wondered what chance I could have of remaining in a state of virginity if someone had been wooing *me*. Precious little!

"My outward impeccability is simply a reflex of the sheltered and solitary life I have so long been leading, and though this has carved deep channels of habit which in a sense 'protect' me, I simply wouldn't give tuppence for the sort of chastity and purity this signifies . . . Think of all the crippled neurotic people in the world: people who have made all manner of mess and meanness out of their lives because they would not face the facts of their sex or because they would not act in terms of their deepest desires and loyalties, but preferred money or security or fame or whatnot to success in terms of a fuller life."

Today, at eighty-four, I would stand by those words; though the young man who wrote them was not yet sufficiently qualified by experience to utter them. But another letter in the same vein might nevertheless serve with apologies as the key to this whole autobiography. Writing Sophy in October 1920 for her birthday on the eighth, I said:

"The usual wishes for happiness are always a little banal, because people usually do not know what they mean when they talk about happiness: they think it is pleasure or comfort or 'having all you want in the world.' And they are disappointed when they find that these things have as much capacity for producing misery as for creating anything else. When I say that I wish you happiness, I mean that I hope as you grow older you will become more intensely alive."

That one birthday wish was in time to be fulfilled for both of us, through the ultimate alchemy of the spirit that Emerson celebrated in 'Uriel' and 'Brahma.'

CHAPTER EIGHTEEN

The Collapse
of Tomorrow

I

The summer of 1919, when the Communist regime in Russia was menaced both by the White Guards and by the invading armies of the wartime Allies, including our own armies in Siberia, Soviet Russia—still romantically identified as a hopeful symbol of liberty, social justice, and humanity!—was uppermost in our thoughts.

For the next few years, even beyond the twenties, the fate of the world seemed bound up with the outcome of the Bolshevik Revolution; for by its sentimental association with older revolutions in England, in America, in France, in Latin America, the Russian Revolution seemed a climactic event in a progressive movement that was bound to sweep over the world. This aura of historic authenticity—the inevitability of the inevitable!—for long remained proof against the evidence of our senses. Meanwhile the forces of the counterrevolution, in Russia itself at first, then in Italy and Germany, were quite as openly hostile as the Soviet government was later to be to the genuine democratic gains that had been made during the Nineteenth Century. Even Stalin's servile alliance with Hitler in 1939 did not for many ideologically blinded souls completely break that spell.

As late as 1932, the year Waldo Frank wrote 'Dawn in Russia,' I found myself deeply impressed with one of the first new Russian films, 'The Road to Life,' and felt wistfully that the leader in the camp devoted to the redemption of 'Wild Boys' gave one a fresh sense of the New Man who would eventually emerge. But he was only a good actor, playing a part Tolstoy might have written.

'The Dial' was especially eager for firsthand information about the Revolution from every reputable source: so it was at 'The Dial' that I first met Dr. Gregory Zilboorg, lately arrived from Russia, where he had been secretary to the Minister of Labor under Kerensky. Zilboorg was, of course, no Communist, but he did confess that the Leninist leaders of the Revolution were capable of leading a more abstemious and spartan existence than he himself or his own liberal associates. With the same concentration on power, the same unflinching disregard of personal ties, the same contempt for bourgeois precedents, Kerensky's party, he felt, might have won out.

Passionate to the point of inarticulateness in his half-mastered English, magnificently energetic, always presenting a debonair front in his impeccably tailored gray suit, Zilboorg might casually confess on sitting down to lunch with us that he had had nothing to eat during the last two days. Before becoming a practicing psychoanalyst, Zilboorg had acquired a philosophic background; he had a literary flair, and in 1920 he hastily put together a manuscript, 'The Passing of the Old Order in Europe.' The duty of turning Zilboorg's eloquently incoherent prose into English and giving his personal observations and reflections some continuity was turned over to me by Thomas Seltzer, his publisher; and there is more than one page in that forgotten book for which I might claim doubtful credit. It was not, heaven knows, a scholarly work; but it had some good passages of on-the-spot reporting, for Zilboorg had served as a physician near the front, and had seen the grass-roots revolution of the Muzhiks— the revolution that had made the Bolshevik take-over possible—exploding in Kerensky's face well before Lenin had arrived on the scene.

My new 'Dial' colleague, Geroid Robinson, was already committed to his lifelong dedication to Russian history and politics; and in the office library, where we kept the files of other magazines, he used to follow on a map, with pins, the shifting battles between the Whites and the Reds. Robinson had earnestly applied for a post on 'The Dial,' even at half time, a few months before I, without knowing about his first rejected advances, had innocently walked away with a full-time appointment. But presently, when Helen Marot decided that our fortnightly needed a special Labor Editor, I readily consented to dividing my functions and my salary with Robinson, since this would give me more time for my own writing: so we never became rivals. Instead, we soon became warm friends; and we were drawn closer by forming a little soviet of our own to give the magazine's editorial policy a little more consistency, and to offset Helen Marot's flying off the handle. In time we both, happily, developed an affectionate relation with Helen, too.

My editorials and reviews at this time shared the naïve hopes we all had for both a radical labor movement and a triumphant Revolution: so they exhibited the same well-grounded distrust of the American Army's Siberian expedition and the same unwillingness to sanction our joining a League of Nations that might commit us willy-nilly to similar interventions. In this I was guilelessly repeating the opinions that my presumably more seasoned elders expressed; and I regard with contrition my own unfeeling reaction to Woodrow Wilson's moral plight and sudden physical deterioration. We deserted the trans-national common cause when we turned, as William Bullitt had, against Wilson, just as we betrayed justice when, following the cocky lead of John Maynard Keynes, we were more indignant over the actual terms of the Treaty of Versailles than we were earlier over the far harsher terms that the Germans had begun to impose upon the defeated peoples. Forgetting all that the French and Belgians had endured at the hands of the Germans, we pitied only the starving Germans and reprimanded the French for not immediately embracing their still arrogant and vengeful enemies.

This attitude, so far from being impeccably rational and emotionally neutral, supposedly in the interests of justice, has remained characteristic of the morally undiscriminating code of current 'civil liberties' liberalism, which still lingers on, in those who are more tenderly concerned to protect the vicious criminal than they are to safeguard the victim he has mugged or murdered or the prospective victims he may attack again.

By some obscure link my own life in 1919 mirrored that of the world at large; so that in attempting to chart the swirling currents of this period, or even to describe my personal life, I shall find it difficult to do justice to one aspect without seeming to underplay the other. The sense of relief we all felt when the war was over reflected not only a natural release of tension but also a sudden buoyancy, a rising to the surface as in a delivery from drowning. Unfortunately we succumbed to the illusion that no further effort would be necessary to keep afloat.

What we forgot was the millions of young people whose hopes had been destroyed: in effect, a whole generation. Unless we who survived were prepared to take over, and make sacrifices as great as the dead had made doing their duty, their efforts would become meaningless. We were alive, we survivors; but suddenly we were less alive, because we had progressively lost both our old illusions and our new hopes. It was the counterforces to human development that now took the lead and dominated the scene, sometimes by power and cunning contrivance, but too often, perhaps, through our personal failure to overcome our mental inertia and moral insensitiveness.

I still remember, almost as if I were looking at the thermometer, the chilling of the air that took place in the summer of 1919. How different it was from February! Did not the Department of Justice, under Wilson's government, stage illegal raids against the socialists, while nearer to home Helen Marot and Martyn Johnson were summoned to inquisitorial State hearings and bound under some undisclosed threat not to reveal what questions were asked? These inquisitions had begun during the war, and even now have not abated after more than half a century. That proved but the beginning of a larger debacle.

Although 1919 was the year when the Age of Confidence visibly collapsed, it was actually the earthquake shock of the First World War that had brought about this change. The very fact that the war had broken out, that no effective efforts to forestall it had been made, was what in time undermined the youthful confidence of my generation. Not that a general relapse into barbarism had not long been anticipated by a few prescient earlier observers. Anyone familiar with the letters of Jacob Burkhardt, the aphorisms of Nietzsche, or the historical analyses of Henry Adams would know that, under the surface, more penetrating eyes had, generations before, discovered ominous cracks and tremors in the whole structure of Western civilization. But the 1920s was the decade when all the liberated spirits of the Nineteenth Century became ghosts, and when its supposedly suppressed demons again became monsters of flesh and blood. Those demons had always been present, intermittently visible over five thousand years, often powerful enough to take over the very institutions of law, justice, and religion that had been built up to restrain them, if not to eliminate them. The new name for these anti-idealisms was Fascism, Nazism, Hitlerism, Stalinism.

How quickly reorientation and transformation took place! One suspects now that some of the change had long been in preparation and was not entirely attributable to the war or the more sordid realities of the immediate postwar period. The very solidity of our Western institutions and organizations, their seeming rationality, their growing humaneness, their constant scientific discoveries and technological improvements, and their prospects of steadily spreading over the entire world—all this was to prove a tricky illusion, not entirely baseless, but not nearly as firmly founded as we had believed. It is in the nature of illusions that they come from nowhere and may vanish without warning into nothing. And this was what was in fact happening, though for the next half-century perhaps only a sensitive minority dared to realize how much had already disappeared.

Before we editors knew it, our 'Dial' became as much a ghost as Emerson's 'Dial.' In its minuscule way, this was a symbol of a more insidious general collapse. In November 1919 'The Dial' changed hands almost overnight, and the politically radical fortnightly was replaced by Scofield Thayer and James Sibley Watson's esthetically oriented monthly. Except for the secretaries, Clarence Britten—who stayed on to tide over the editorial transition—and Sophy, Britten's associate for production, all members of the old 'Dial' staff found themselves out of a job. We were doubly desolate because a whole world on whose solidity we had counted was beginning to crumble away.

Even the personal change was abrupt: a sort of transvestiture. Martyn Johnson, who had kept 'The Dial' alive for a while by forays into Wall Street—an amusing scandal for a magazine that swore by Dewey and Veblen and castigated the aims and sins of capitalism—slipped out of his erratic publishing orbit into the world of motion pictures. During the next decade in Hollywood he was to appear at intervals on film, usually in evening togs, as the urbane gentleman he was, mostly in background roles: with his gray hair whitening at the forehead, his little gray mustache, his expressive pug-dog eyes, his imperviousness to any kind of female charm.

My own departure from 'The Dial' was as sudden as my joining it had been. Economically the bottom dropped out of my life, and it took me half a dozen years to rebuild it partly, for though I tried persistently to secure a sustaining editorial post, first on 'The Freeman,' then on 'The New Republic,' and finally as a last resort on 'The Nation,' I was blocked at every turn. Never again could I count on a secure yearly salary until I became a full professor at Stanford in 1942. This failure to find a regular post proved in fact to be my good fortune; but it took a decade before I could appreciate its many benefits.

That oozing deflation, as if a great balloon had been punctured, was registered in individual persons, as well as in collective activities. But the most startling transformation was that which took place in Helen Marot. One afternoon in December 1919, when I visited her in her apartment near Columbia to discuss the possibility of launching a new magazine that would be close in spirit to our old 'Dial,' she announced that she had turned her back on the Revolution and even on Reconstruction, and had buried her old hopes for the labor movement.

At this impasse in her life Helen Marot turned from the indignant exhortation and 'advocacy' of her past to scientific research. At first she even tried to get a foundation grant that would enable a group of biologists, psychologists, and anthropologists to work to-

gether on a common basis: a proposal at least a whole generation
ahead of the academic world. Indeed, as I wrote to Geddes in the
letter from which I cull these facts, "Helen Marot plus Thorstein
Veblen would make a mathematically complete sociologist." But not
finding any collaborators—still less foundation money—she was
compelled to work by herself; and almost nothing she put on paper
over the next twenty-odd years was ever published.

Seeking a more fundamental insight into the human condition,
Helen turned to the study of psychology, in search of a firmer basis
than that provided by the dominant behaviorists or the stimulus-
response school. Her brain remained active to the end; but it needed
for the development of her thought what only unreserved intercourse with other keen minds can bring about. Even had Helen been
more at home in the academic world than she actually was, I doubt
if she would have found, except by luck, the intelligent support she
needed; for those who might ideally have collaborated, like George
Mead of Chicago or Charles Horton Cooley of Michigan, were by
then too old and self-absorbed to respond. Her proposals, as I look
back on them now—with their implicit critique of her own past—
were timely and penetrating; but she fumbled over the means, for
she sought this knowledge mainly through Sherrington, whose classic work on the integrative action of the sympathetic nervous system
for a time became her bible.

Overnight the Helen Marot I had known on 'The Dial' dropped
the preoccupations of a whole lifetime, as if they were so many soiled
garments. When she arrived in London a year later the new novel
that she excitedly presented to me then and there was no radical
tract: it was 'This Side of Paradise'! That is where our whole spiritual
generation, old and young, suddenly found themselves.

3

Though I was not a typical member of the younger generation, before I knew it I was dragged along in the same powerful currents,
sharing the sense of desolation, feeling bitter and scornful over the
betrayal of our hopes by the politicians, the businessmen, the mili-

tary leaders; but more ready then to leave the field to them than to try to repair the damage. One of my editorials in 'The Freeman' in 1922, reprinted later in 'The Freeman Book,' was a defense of the younger generation in all their gaily irresponsible assaults on traditional social duties and sexual conformities: a defense against the rebukes of an older generation whose grim sense of 'national duty' had sanctioned such meaningless slaughter for such humanly irrelevant and often covertly sinister goals.

But more than a year earlier I had published an even better diagnosis of our condition in an editorial entitled 'The Collapse of Tomorrow.' What can one expect, I asked, of the young people whose lives and habits of work have been disrupted by the war, "except that they will seek out whatever promises to give them immediate enjoyment and satisfaction? Scarcely anyone will take the trouble to be an artist or scientist when he may so speedily cease to be even a man. Does this not account a little for the lassitude, the febrility, the spurious gaiety that a good many observers have noted in Europe today? What we call the future is in a sense always an illusion, and the greatest disillusion that Europe possibly suffers from is the loss of something that never existed outside the minds of those who molded their activities in terms of it—the loss of a tomorrow.

"Civilization is the magic instrument by which men live in a world of time that has three dimensions: the past, the present, and the future. When neither security of life nor continuity of works is maintained, civilization must necessarily collapse. It has done so before; and it has taken hundreds of years to weave a new fabric; and it may do so again. A pretty prospect for the encouragement and discipline of adolescents!"

Though I would not now use the term 'civilization,' except in an ironic sense, I might have made the same diagnosis half a century later with even greater acerbity, since, to use Melville's words in 'Pierre,' in comparison with our present hell, that of the 1920s would seem like heaven. As with the young in the 1960s, the First World War had alienated us in some inexplicably decisive way from the older generation.

Though in my 1921 editorial I drew all my evidence from Europe, a year later, when I wrote 'Abandoned Roads,' the same malady was already rife in the United States, despite the fact that as a nation we had experienced no comparable physical losses or mental disruptions.

By temperament as well as by memory I carried more of the Age of Confidence into my work than many others of my generation. Yet I too felt alienated. Only part of me was then left. Increasingly I became conscious of being caught between the incoming tide and the undertow of the past, though not altogether lost like those who fled to the South Seas, sought hideouts in a decadent Paris, wallowed in George Grosz's Berlin, surrendered their souls to the grim Marxist dogmas of Lenin, Trotsky, or Stalin, or, more overtly, committed suicide. But without a secure professional niche, a stable marriage, and durable personal and social goals, I was not yet safely established on more solid ground.

Everything I have told here was summed up with a poet's swiftness by William Butler Yeats in his poem 'Nineteen Hundred and Nineteen.' The second stanza, beginning "We too had many pretty toys when young," makes the more reflective portions of this chapter almost superfluous. "O what find thought we had because we thought that the worst rogues and rascals had died out. All teeth were drawn, all ancient tricks unlearned." That bitter lesson took a long time in the learning, all the more because the worst rascals too often turned out to be ourselves: particularly in those parts of our personality we had never dared to examine, still less to correct or cultivate.

But what right had we to be so disheartened? Why did our natural disappointment turn so quickly into despair, and why did we cover our despair with cynicism and irresponsibility, whether in politics or in sexual relations? Anticipating a similar reaction after the Second World War, but being myself more fortified to face the threatening irrationalities of our time, I tried to forestall that response by a fresh examination, in a whole series of urgent writings, beginning with my 'Faith for Living.'

Still, the fact that our outrage over the aftermath of the 1914 war was so excessive gives the measure of our original innocence. We had thought that war, on any scale, was not only a monstrous

betrayal of the future but '*a thing of the past.*' We were to discover—
some of us at least—that our very belief in the inevitability of progress had helped resurrect a past we had never dared look at without
putting on rose-tinted glasses. Augustine and Machiavelli and Mon-
taigne would have been better guides than most of our own present
mentors: they might have prepared us to face the actual condition
of man in our time.

Oh! we had a right to be frightened: *but not to run away*! A new
smell of violence hung in the air, as if an earthquake had opened a
sewer whose very existence we had not suspected. That smell was far
from imaginary; but the stench was not of recent origin: it was rather
like the nauseating odor that the Roman archeologist Lanciani confronted when his workmen opened up the ancient Carnarium, a
trench where the bodies of dead animals and human victims, slaughtered for public pleasure in the Colosseum, had lain putrefying since
the days of the Caesars. We had yet to face the black side of human
experience, as Homer and Sophocles and Shakespeare and Dostoevsky had faced it. The past century, though it had been the first in
which mankind had been able to uncover with any fullness the mottled record of human development, had made us oblivious to the
fact that the worst savageries and irrationalities of history had never
been completely extruded, still less left behind. Evil had lived on,
colossal masses of evil: indeed in Russia, Turkey, Italy, Germany the
official cultivation of evil had been elevated into a profession.

My account of this deflation and despondency may seem exag-
gerated, or at least fall under suspicion of my transferring back to the
twenties a judgment based on the aberrations of the present period.
Fortunately by some quirk of memory I have preserved a flash of
corroboration: a conversation that took place on a bleak motor ride
in November 1919, with Geroid Robinson, Caroline Pratt, and Hel-
en Marot, for a weekend visit to the farm near Fishkill which had
till recently housed the summer home of the City and Country School.
We discussed the possibility that the militant General Leonard Wood,
a protégé of Theodore Roosevelt, known for his intransigence and
efficient ruthlessness, might actually be aiming at a dictatorship—for
the age of dictators was already visibly setting in. After surveying all

the dismal possibilities that our disruptive civilization presented, one of us said: "Perhaps we are at the beginning of a new Dark Age."

Before 1914 that notion would have been unthinkable, hardly acceptable even as a cynical jest. Now the image of a Dark Age had for a moment become a frightening reality. Gravely we canvassed the prospects for survival and looked around for a religion, a church, a chain of monasteries, in short a line of retreat that would ensure continuity and eventual recovery. We did not return to the subject that weekend, and I don't suppose any one of us brooded frequently over this possibility during the next decade. But when I was preparing to write 'The Condition of Man,' with its opening study of the disintegration of the Hellenic-Latin world from the Fourth Century B.C. on, that conversation came back to me. As happens sometimes in nightmares, our unconscious proved closer to reality than our more plausible and more comforting daylight perceptions.

By now it should be plain that our most sinister anticipations erred on the side of complacency, for we clung to an unjustifiable faith in the progressive powers of 'science' and 'democracy' to bring about a happy ending—*in the long run*! As if there were any guarantee that the run would be long enough to do the preliminary job of reconstructing 'science,' 'democracy,' and 'education'!

CHAPTER NINETEEN

London
and Victor Branford

I

With 1920 my 'Dial' days were over—those radiant days!—and the next move, it turned out, though I could not guess it then, was to mold the rest of my life. My first entry into the world of letters had ended all too abruptly, and a baffling period of exploration began, when, to avoid the financial uncertainties of journalism, I hovered on the outskirts of a subacademic literary career. This anxious transitional stage lasted for the better part of the decade; and some of the uncertainties and tensions it produced lingered even longer. Sometimes I wonder how, in the midst of this uneasy turmoil, I got the inner peace needed to write the first four books which, more than anything else, were to establish my position as a writer.

While I was still an editor of 'The Dial,' my correspondence with Patrick Geddes had evoked a new possibility. He and Victor Branford, well before the end of the First World War, had begun a series of books under the ambitious general title: 'The Making of the Future.' I had sent Branford my 'Dial' review of one of these books, 'The Coming Polity,' and this brought about a friendly exchange with him. When Branford learned that I had lost my 'Dial' post, he offered me, quixotically yet shrewdly, the acting editorship of 'The Sociological Review,' the revamped organ of the Sociological Society in London. Branford's invitation came shortly after a quite independent bid from Geddes to join him the coming summer in Jerusalem, where he was beginning to plan the new University of Jerusalem. I was then to follow him to Bombay as his 'assistant.'

Since Geddes's offer was somewhat vague as to both duties and pay, while Branford's was more definite, I decided to go through with the latter, at least temporarily. Both of my major decisions in 1920—that of going to England and then that of coming back to America in the hope of marrying Sophia instead of going by a P. & O. ship to India—turned out to be among the most fateful of my whole life. And though Branford's offer caused me to gamble part of my fast-dwindling inheritance on this venture, I have never regretted it. Not its smallest benefit was that it gave me something more lasting than a tourist's introduction to London.

At the end of April 1920 I set forth for England in an old White Star liner, the 'Adriatic,' in second class. My first crossing was a miserable one, partly because I was then a bad sailor, partly because I was cooped up with three older men—a grim-faced Methodist clergyman, a drunken Irishman who snored like a foghorn, and some now faceless other—in a cabin so small that it would not a decade later have been offered to a couple. Some of my misery came from the fact that the 'Adriatic' was a strange sea-creature that both dipped and rolled, and when her stern rose out of the water, a violent shudder would run down her spine, so that one might easily believe the rumor that a nautical engineer had prophesied she would break in two someday in a storm. (She didn't.)

I mention the defects of this old ship because its meager accommodations remind one how much the physical standard of life has risen, all along the line, during the last fifty years. What distinguished the old vessels, what made one seasick almost the moment one went below, was the lack of circulating air in the cabins and the passageways: the stale, sour smell was revolting, enriched as it was by the carbolic germicides that were then used in lavatories: so that I attribute my relative freedom from seasickness in later days more to air-conditioning and stabilizers than to any gain in seaworthiness on my part. I have said many harsh things about the total commitment to air-conditioning on land by fashion-blinded architects, but on the sea the fine blasts of ocean air that come into every cabin, not tainted, as they would have been on land, by recirculation, took half the curse off ocean travel, in the halcyon days between 1930 and 1970.

2

Cities have some of the human attributes of personality. That they show character, moods, visible gestures of welcoming or rejecting is something that men have known almost since they began to live in cities. This personification once brought forth municipal gods and goddesses, and if that is, psychologically speaking, only a projection, it remains true that each city induces in those that dwell in it a curiously similar response, whose likeness its citizens recognize and share as easily as they recognize an ancestral face.

London, though in all my visits I have lived in it for a total of little more than two years, has had a deep influence over my life; and my going to London gave me a sort of postgraduate education that rounded off all I had learned, formally and informally, in my native city. Did not Emerson say that the essence of a university was to have a room of one's own, with an open fire, in a strange city? That was what London offered me, though my little bedroom, on the top floor of 65 Belgrave Road in Pimlico, doubtless meant for a servant originally, boasted only a gas grate.

In preparation for this immersion in London I had my early saturation in Dickens: the Dickens of 'The Pickwick Papers,' 'Nicholas Nickleby,' 'Great Expectations,' and 'David Copperfield,' and not least the young Dickens, avidly picking up material in the byways and dark alleys of London for his 'Sketches by Boz.' As a member by adoption of the Sociological Society—somewhat of an upstart among learned societies, unwilling on principle to accept the domination of temporal authority through incorporation by royal charter—perhaps it was as well that I also had under my belt the memory of Dickens's farcical papers depicting the meeting of the Mudfog Association for the Advancement of Everything. Besides Dickens, I had H. G. Wells, who was once the observant novelist who wrote 'Tono-Bungay' and 'The New Machiavelli'; for both those books took one close to twentieth-century London. Yet I was to find, in the postwar London of 1920, much of Dickens's London still left in the very heart of the city, while the suburbs and South Kensington were much as Wells had described them.

The first sight of England, the first lilt of the English voice at the dock in Southampton, sent a happy shiver of recognition through me, not least because John Cowper Powys, a fellow passenger in second class, introduced me at the dock to his brother, Llewelyn, an even more handsome Englishman, bronzed, ruddy, freshly home from Africa, the epitome of lazy, confident masculinity, whose idea of coming to America to settle down as a writer I sympathetically encouraged. And then came the fields and the gardens of southern England, with its "sportive hedgerows, little woods run wild," all trim and tidy, as if lovingly carved in wood and colored by some patient craftsman. Finally, the rich grime of Waterloo Station and a high, sensible old taxi taking me deviously through Westminster to Pimlico, with glimpses of the green Embankment, the playing field of the Westminster School, the helmeted policemen with chin straps, the black-uniformed, bemedaled messengers, the towers of the Abbey and the Houses of Parliament, till, after turning through Churton Street, with its dreary little shops, we finally halted in Belgrave Road at the headquarters of the Sociological Society, Le Play House.

In effect Le Play House was a New York brownstone with an English basement, newly done over with a coat of muddy stucco. The reek of soft coal fires, still omnipresent then, hung in the air: an odor I used to find as pleasantly haunting as the dim rural aroma of a skunk—when inhaled from a sufficient distance. There were two rooms to a floor, except at the top, where the narrowness of my room allowed three. However austere the furnishings of my cell were, it was bright and cheerful, for it faced west, and there was a glass of flowers—five narcissus and a tulip!—with a note on the mantel shelf. The young woman who had left them, Branford's part-time secretary, Dorothy Cecilia Loch, began with that gesture our life-long friendship.

I spent many lonely evening hours in this room that summer, dreaming, hoping, planning, yearning: my thoughts mainly centering on the aloofly beautiful girl I had left behind in New York, who was still sealed in dreams of her own, still impervious to what I could offer in friendship and love. I was then in the thrall of adolescent sexual megrims: it surely could not be called chastity, for 'chastity' and 'healthy young males' are almost contradictory terms. Abstention from sexual activity, as the hermits of Alexandria long ago demonstrated, may make sex far more obsessive and pervasive than almost any amount of actual intercourse. I mention this side of my life with due Augustinian frankness because it perhaps explains why I only half-used the opportunities that spread before me on this first visit, and why, so often in the midst of them, I felt dull, baffled, unreasonably depressed.

Certainly there were many times when London itself lay heavy on one's chest, the very 'City of Dreadful Night' that James Thomson called it. In 1920 the poverty of London was still corrosive, abject, and inescapable, as it had been all through the Nineteenth Century: it left such bad odors that jokes about smelly feet were still good for a laugh in the music halls; it poisoned the stale food, even in seemingly respectable restaurants on Oxford Street; it still left a trail of scrofulous heads and rickety bones in every poor quarter one visited—though no amount of debasement, seemingly, could ever quite down the jaunty confidence and resilience of the barrows men who would turn Churton Street at Pimlico's Saturday-night market into a little local fair. Dickens's London and my own London of 1920 were blessed by the same cockney vitality: slatternly, but not yet diluted or pedagogically 'refined.'

Looking back through the letters I wrote during this period to Sophia, I am amused to find how full they are of righteous American indignation over English ways: how horrified I was to discover that our Scots housekeeper, Mrs. Long, a lovely, buxom woman from Inverness, would not merely climb five flights every morning to bring me my can of shaving water, but would swoop under my bed for my shoes, so that she might take them down for polishing, and would seek them out even if I had shyly hidden them. She had me in such awe that I abandoned, while at Le Play House, my Tolstoyan practice of making my own bed. But I cottoned to the English way of serving fried tomatoes, the small hothouse Dutch kind, with eggs, along with bacon-fried bread—though the heavy English breakfast, which began with porridge, unsalted, used often to make me feel logy for a whole morning.

This was a world different in every gesture and accent from my

American one; and I would have been far more ill at ease in it than I actually was, had I not had the good fortune to come under the tutelage of Dorothy Loch, the young woman who had left the flowers on my mantel. Before long I came to call her Delilah because, in gently pressing me to conform to English ways, she was behaving as a post-biblical Delilah, shearing the rough locks of her young American Samson. She was six or seven years older than I was, short and slender, with her brown hair tightly twisted in a bun: but the lovely impression made by her sensitive, animated face, especially her brown eyes and her full mouth, was lost on me because I had been spoiled by having three almost overpowering beauties in succession for close friends, and I was too young to know that there is only a conventional connection between erotic animation and formal bodily beauty.

Delilah, like me, had been hopelessly in love, recently enough to show an almost visible scar; for she had had the ill luck to be drawn to a young man whose Jewish ancestry made him unacceptable to her family. To make matters worse, he was killed in the war. But she was fortunately not quite so innocent in the ways of love as I was: so she treated me with just the right combination of motherly solicitude, familiar sisterly tartness and humorous feminine charm I needed, without evoking any skittishness on my part. She came of the sort of family that had peopled the Empire with colonels and civil servants of the upper grades: and her family's flat in Harcourt Terrace, South Kensington, was a late Victorian museum piece, whatnots and all, filled with Indian hangings and carved knickknacks.

Under Delilah's watchful tutelage I learned what topics might safely be discussed at tea with a retired Indian civil servant—the Labor question and postwar British policy toward Russia were taboo!—indeed, I even learned how an American barbarian with no dinner jacket might spend the weekend at a Country House without being embarrassed by lack of dinner clothes. (One arrived on a late train on Saturday night, after dinner, and remained till the morning train on Monday; for happily, in the country no one dressed in the evening on Sunday. This information, alas! proved superfluous. Unlike Herman Melville, in all my visits to Britain I have never been invited to *that* kind of Country House.)

Delilah also introduced me at Richmond to its celebrated Maidsof-Honor Tarts, which I detested, and she schooled me, with firmness, in the importance and utter inescapability of tea at four o'clock, a British custom that I held to, with lapses, for many years; though I felt cheated when I discovered much later that, like many seemingly venerable customs in England, it had not become fashionable till the 1870s. This is the reverse of the other English habit of calling 'new'—as in 'New Forest' or 'New College'—something that had been laid out or built in the Thirteenth Century.

Delilah still lived in London on my subsequent visits in 1922 and 1925, and our friendship, which by then included Sophia, kept deepening. Her letters to me during that period are not merely vivid human documents on the decline and fall of the Sociological Society, but they are the expressions of a mature, independent spirit, seeking beauty, love, and fellowship in a routine-ridden society. When I came back later to a city empty of her, I felt as if someone had stolen an essential piece of England and London away from me. To have had someone like Delilah waiting for me, so to speak, on my first visit was not merely my blessed good fortune—it played an essential part in my later education. The tone of this friendship I happily caught in a few stanzas of 'The Little Testament of Bernard Martin.'

I still treasure Delilah's letters—especially those written in the frugal period that in England followed the First World War. I find them even more fascinating now than they could have been when originally received; for apart from all Delilah reveals about the recurrent personal tensions in Le Play House, her own fiercely honest thoughts were often written on the reverse side of letters drawn from correspondence files dating back to around 1906, the Sociological Society's high period of activity. So one of her best letters begins on the back of a note to Branford from his friend, Lady Victoria Welby, that extraordinary woman who founded the science of semantics— she called it more intelligibly 'significs'—a generation before Ogden and Richards wrote 'The Meaning of Meaning.' It amuses me to picture a biographer and an autograph collector pitted against each other in an auction room for the possession of these letters: one seeking a rare holograph and the other an even rarer insight into life's tragic dilemmas.

3

What Delilah did for me in getting me used to British ways, Victor
Branford did, quite as thoughtfully, in introducing me to his friends
and associates, from Lord Bryce down. I have described my first
encounter with Branford in fictional guise in 'The Little Testament,'
but I there combined in one setting some of the personality of Geddes
and the temporary London-cum-New Forest background of Branford. Like Randolph Bourne, I had been attracted to Branford's
'Interpretations and Forecasts,' which Mitchell Kennerley had brought
out in America, at about the same time I stumbled on Geddes.
Though the Geddesian imperatives in that book now seem stale,
Branford's allusions as well as his illusions belong to a vanished world.
I recall the impression they then gave of opening up new intellectual
and social horizons. What fares worst in all of Branford's writings is
his rhetoric, for he struggled in vain to find the right verbal equivalents for his original insights. Too often he would get lost in woolly
comparisons, decorated by brummagem metaphors which in Elizabethan times might have been made of gold and precious stones.
(Am I perhaps falling into the same vice in the very effort to pin it
down?)

Yet Branford's early interpretation of the significance of religion as the binding force in all human societies enabled him to anticipate by two or three decades a change of philosophic orientation
that is still going on. Actually, the first premonitions of this point of
view were those of the Scots sociologist, J. Stuart-Glennie, who
pointed out long before Karl Jaspers the significance of the emer-
gence of the great Axial religions and philosophies in the Sixth Century B.C. And it was Benjamin Kidd, who, in his 'Social Evolution,'
had indicated that no purely rationalist ideology could cope with the
deep-seated irrationalities and mysteries of actual existence, or sum-
mon up sufficient readiness for collective sacrifice to ensure even the
biological survival of any group or community. Without that ultimate "faith for living," man's cold intelligence would repeatedly have
counseled surrender or suicide. Branford was acquainted with the
work of these scholars, and in various essays and books, mainly 'Liv-

ing Religions' and 'Science and Sanctity,' he made his own contribution.

None of Branford's books, admittedly, did him or his subject justice, because too often he felt impelled to lay out the whole Geddesian system before getting down to his own vital contributions. So it is mainly in his pamphlets, where he had no space for these preliminaries, that his ideas fared best: 'The Modern Midas,' 'Hell or Eutopia,' 'The Drift to Revolution.' These summations had an incisiveness that was lost in his other works; and single phrases that he or Geddes coined—"the resorption of government," "the socialization of credit," "the third alternative" (as between reaction and revolution)—almost have the impact of a whole book.

While my first meeting with Geddes was to be in the purlieus of New York's Lower West Side, an environment depressing to both of us, my first meeting with Branford took place at a Victorian brick farmhouse on the edge of a moor a few miles from the station at New Milton. This was in the New Forest of Hampshire, whose yeomen had stoutly defended their footpaths and commons from high-handed seizure by the gentry. A little donkey cart had fetched me from the station, but halfway over, the donkey refused to budge, so the governess and the children and I walked part of the last mile.

Branford was waiting in the garden for me, a slim man, with a sharp face and a pointed beard, in ragged—this is not a misprint for 'rugged'—old tweeds, tense and nervously voluble, bowing me into the hall of his house with a courtliness he maintained on all occasions for all persons. My host showed me to my room and pointed out the very limited toilet facilities. "Perhaps you will do as I do," he said with a swift twinkle. "We have no neighbors for half a mile, and the gorse is thick and beautiful. You can see it from this window. You will understand why Linnaeus knelt down and worshiped it when he first came to England. It must have been about this time of the year."

I saw the textured spread of prickly green stems and golden gorse flowers, and over the moor I heard the call of the cuckoo, that round, mellow note, slow as a church bell and so different from a frantic cuckoo clock. The elation of that moment! I knew I had come to the right place, not least because I was enveloped, on this and every other visit, with a hospitality so tactful, so permissive of individual departures, so undemanding of forced responses, so understanding of the need for privacy and isolation—if living under a common roof is not to be a nagging duty—that it has served me as a criterion of hospitality, as both a receiver and a giver, ever since.

Branford's second wife, Sybella—an ample, buttery sort of woman, gracious but fuzzy, High Church and antipuritanic as concerned art and games and dances—was one of the early products of

Victor Branford

Oxford's women's colleges. Branford, who adored the whole Oxford milieu but castigated the archaic Renaissance education that was still carried on there, was in a constant intellectual feud with his wife; but he was scrupulously polite, nay punctilious, especially when he was most clearly in a state of smothered exasperation, baffled by the tattered rags of moth-eaten ideas which Sybella would pull out from time to time, as from an untidy drawer. But Sybella's goodness, her little acts of thoughtfulness and kindness, were constant; and until she was stricken with cancer, only a few years later, she gave Branford exactly the sort of environment that should have met his every need—except his wild Elizabethan need for passionate adventure and romance.

This lack of erotic stimulus and fulfillment, I am inclined to believe, multiplied Branford's ailments, and brought a certain edginess into his other personal relationships. Being a shockable young man, I was sometimes amazed in London by Branford's openly turning around to look at a passing girl with a beautiful figure or a trim ankle: he would even, with an appreciative gleam in his eye, give voice to his admiration. But being no longer shockable now, indeed ten years older than Branford was then, I feel rather a certain sympathy toward his responsiveness: and I like to remember that only the winter before he died, he won a prize in figure skating in Switzerland with a handsome young woman as his partner. That he should have excelled in this courtly art and that the pair should have won a prize seems completely in character.

Branford devoted our first weekend together to canvassing the affairs of Le Play House and making me acquainted with his plans and hopes for the Sociological Society. But in characteristic English fashion, he first probed my own background, trying to account by my 'family connections' for my having chosen to become a writer, and even more remarkably, to be concerned with sociology. Since nothing in my familiy's intellectually dingy past had any plausible English equivalent, Branford was particularly struck by my account of my almost daily walks through Central Park on the way to the great Forty-second Street Library: he felt this gave an important clue to my all-round development.

From Branford I got a personal concern and sympathetic understanding in greater measure than I was ever to get from Geddes. If the barriers of age and national custom sometimes kept us apart, our minds still met freely in genuine conversation quite different, I found later, from Geddes's self-absorbed insistent monologues; and it was only in the territory pre-empted by Geddes's graphs that I found any lack of resilience in Branford's approach. Unfortunately, it took me time to discover that what I regarded with misgiving as Branford's arbitrary graphic categories were in fact Geddes's. Paradoxically, not the least service that Branford performed for me was unintentionally putting me on guard against Geddes's increasing imprisonment in his 'thinking machines'; particularly his 'Opus Syntheticum.'

Victor Branford was, I found, a unique combination of the man of affairs and the speculative thinker: a type England has so often produced from the time of Sir Walter Raleigh and Sir Francis Bacon. By profession he belonged to the abstemious guild of certified public accountants, the medical diagnosticians, he used to say, of business; but by interest and attainment he was a sociologist, a historian, and a philosopher. Though in practical matters he was thoroughly at home in the modern world, by feature and disposition he always seemed to me a man of the Elizabethan Age. It was easy to imagine Branford in a multicolored doublet and a ruff, alertly sweeping off his cape to protect the Queen's feet even before Sir Walter would have noticed that there was a puddle in her path. He looked Elizabethan, too, with his long narrow head, his pointed beard, his trim body, his high forehead and thin nervous lips. Back in London, it was almost impossible for me to accept as real the conventional costume he affected when he went into the city: the striped trousers, the black jacket, and the top hat seemed only quaint fancy dress.

There was no place in the drab, business-bound London of Branford's day for his particular combination of gallantry, adventure, wit, and—remember that Cervantes too was a product of the same Elizabethan period!—*quixoticism.* If Branford could be called a financier, the right name for him was still Merchant Adventurer; though he played for social gains, not for a merely private fortune. Like my uncle James, he still held the old-fashioned economic notion that Capital had a social obligation and should be willing to take risks by developing backward countries; indeed, Branford's executor told me later that the assets that should have supported the Institute of Sociology, as the Society was later called, had seeped away in the stocks and bonds of a bankrupt railway in Paraguay.

By daily association and, up to a point, by interest, Branford lived in a more sophisticated upper-class London world than

Geddes's: it had a class consciousness, a sense of shades and distinctions of rank and breeding that Geddes, whose good father's highest rank in the regular army was that of Sergeant Major, never accepted. Geddes recognized only the aristocracy of talent and character; and he would have been as much at home talking with a trade-union leader or a common laborer as Branford would have been talking to a financier or a lord, for Branford would have met the worker only by an effort whose very courtesy would have established the distance between them. In this respect, Geddes's down-to-earth democracy, so much nearer to my own defiantly American heritage, made me feel closer to him. Yet it was Branford's tactful initiative or responsiveness in little daily acts that set a lasting standard of courtesy for me.

4

In describing my relations with Victor Branford I purposely emphasize those aspects that served to prepare me for my eventual encounters with Geddes—which turned out to be so much less fruitful than both of us had hoped. But in doing so, I am afraid I may smudge some of the quality of my days with Branford: for the experience of living under the same roof with him proved, too, a major incitement to my education. Branford had in Le Play House what he called a shakedown, that is to say, a room (on the floor below mine) with a table and the barest and hardest and narrowest of cots, which he occupied during his dashes to London.

That a man of ample financial means, with no lack of appreciation for the delicacies and refinements of life, should have done no better for himself than this monkish cell was not the least of the lessons I got directly from Branford, and by observation from so many of my other intellectual friends in England. Some of them might be agnostics or atheists, but they still lived the same kind of restricted, abstemious life by which the monastic orders had kept the spirit of Europe alive during the Dark Ages. If their poverty was not wholly monastic, it was re-enforced, as I am sure it was in Branford's case, by a noble contempt for the kind of material comfort or display sought by mere moneygrubbers. If one *had* money, it was for love and adventure and art and charity, not for expensive upholstery. This acceptance of the physical restrictions of poverty went in England, as it used to go in the rest of Europe, with a firm sense of the dignity of all intellectual and spiritual activities. This in turn produced the inner assurance that made it possible for a man like Branford to enter the dining room of a good hotel or club in the shabbiest of clothes without the faintest sense of embarrassment. He was at home anywhere.

After a day in the City, Branford would come back to Le Play House at four or five o'clock and throw himself down on his hard cot, completely exhausted: for he was a frail man, as tense as a terrier, and though I think that, with his sense of adventure, he got a somewhat perverse satisfaction in matching his wits with other financiers, he paid for that excitement when the day was over. But before half an hour was past, he would call me into his room, and, still lying down, he would begin to discuss the affairs of the Sociological Society, only to branch off quickly to some more rewarding general topic in sociology or philosophy. Once he had started on that track, his tired eyes would light up, and before one knew it, he would be pacing the room, animated, indeed exalted, by the glimpse of some fresh idea.

I remember how once, in one of these moments, he restated the whole theory of laissez-faire individualism, as found in Herbert Spencer, and showed how much more profoundly it acknowledged the complex realities of the social process than the conceptions of those who thought it was possible to impose, on the intricate system of cooperations men had built up spontaneously over many centuries, a structure that could be governed solely by Napoleonic dictate, parliamentary law, or bureaucratic overseership. "Only God is wise enough to do all these things, at the right time, in the right order; and God was so wise that he left it to individual men and groups."

Then, having raised the great doctrine to its old eminence, Branford would savagely turn on Herbert Spencer and the whole breed of laissez-faire theorists, and point out all they had smugly overlooked. Their liberal creed had simply issued a license to the

Devil to look after his own, giving countenance to the powerful to rob the weak, to the privileged to grind the faces of the poor. The first principle of all social life, Branford went on, was embodied in the family, and without the love and succor and mutual aid generated in the family, the results of laissez-faire become as monstrous as those of any autocratic centralization—indeed these results had brought on the very demand for that centralized control which Liberals and Tories, Imperialists and Socialists now all agreed on, each in terms of their own sacred ideology.

I never made notes on our talks; and except in representing Branford's spirit, these words are only approximations. But his penetration, his ability to approach a subject from many sides, the sheer joy he showed in bringing to light an unsuspected relationship, all left on me an impression that remains vivid to this day. "The joy of elevated thoughts," as Wordsworth put it, was written all over Branford's face at those moments. (This, incidentally, is the image I return to when I want some concrete equivalent for the quality of illumination Hindu philosophy calls sattva.)

Though I had had more than one good teacher before I came to Branford, none except Graham Wallas had yet left me with such an image of passionate intellectual intensity. Does not our formalized academic routine tend to tamp down such a full engagment of the personality, swaddling with qualifications and timidities the newborn idea? Academic scholarship, in its efforts to be scrupulously correct, to be faithful to the text, to pass on only certified truths, too often keeps remote from the student the process of thinking itself, and defrauds the beginner of one of the great incentives to creativity: his bearing witness to the birth cry of an idea in another mind.

I have given not a few lectures in my time, but the poorest of them were those in which I have used stale notes and have gone with safety over ground I had painstakingly prepared, whereas my best lectures were often those that were only half-formulated, lectures that therefore imposed on me the necessity for fresh probing in the act of bringing them forth. They might be ragged, as William James's classroom talks were reputed to be, but they were alive; and like both Geddes's and Branford's example, they perhaps taught my students the most important lesson of all—*what it means to be fully alive*! Those who have learned that lesson will never be content for long with a low-keyed existence or a sham life disguised by wealth and fashion.

5

Our morning breakfasts in the little back room on the ground floor of Le Play House—with its musty Victorian furniture—originally an office or a music room, I suppose—contributed as much to my education as my evening talks with Branford. Coffee and cigarettes with him, later with Alexander Farquharson (the sharp-witted Scot whom Branford had taken on when he saw that I would not remain as Editor) as a third participant, had a savor I can never recall without a nostalgic pang. If only I had been apt enough to reproduce Branford's Table Talk! Some of his observations were as astute as Martin Luther's. But out of them all I remember only one conversation, which incidentally illustrates the point about education I have been making.

We somehow had started talking about Egypt and began speculating on all that Flinders Petrie and his colleagues had been discovering about that still enigmatic civilization. "By Jove," Branford at length exclaimed, "that would be a fine place to spend a winter's vacation: it's strange one hasn't thought of looking around there before." At that moment Farquharson shook with silent but irrepressible mirth. When at last he found breath, he said admiringly, "There, my dear Branford, is the difference between us! When you think of Egypt, you think immediately of seeing it for yourself; whereas, while you were talking, I was saying to myself—you see the effects of my Scots education!—how nice it would be to spend a whole winter at the British Museum *reading* about Egypt." Yes, that was the difference, although Branford, once he started on his surveys, never forgot that records and documents and books, along with studious meditation, would often bring to light much that does not meet the eye, or yield its secrets to patient digging alone.

If I seem to linger unduly over Branford's personality and thought, it is partly because a close discipleship, like Branford's to Geddes, often reveals undeveloped or defective patches which the mind of the Master by its sheer exuberance conceals. I have to make clear, at least to myself, why they both exerted such a strong influence over me, and yet why I was never disposed to take over their thinking in block, or to give myself unreservedly to Geddes's ideological short-cuts—even to the extent of writing a single paper, still less a book, under his direct tutelage or with his 'collaboration.' None of the obstacles to a closer relationship with Geddes became visible at once, though I am surprised on looking over my lately discovered correspondence with him—now in the National Library of Scotland—how early I did become aware of them, and sought to make him understand my own different potentialities.

In both Branford and Geddes I came to recognize—and was somewhat appalled by!—a certain willfulness that kings alone dared once to exercise. That willfulness not only made gratuitous enmities but created unnecessary muddles, too. For all Branford's fine sense of punctilio in the little affairs of life, in more public relations his tact and even his firm core of common sense would often desert him. Did he not once ruefully confess to me, like a naughty boy caught gorging the jam, that he had had to do over his long 'Britannica' article on sociology because the first draft had been rejected by the editor on the ground that it was almost wholly about the sociology of Geddes and Branford! Here, not less than in other places, neither he nor Geddes was willing to 'play the game'; for they rejected the rules as futile and despised the prizes as unrewarding. Unfortunately, they did not realize that if one is going to improvise a new game, it is mere prudence to break as few of the old rules as possible until people have accepted the new game and learned to play it themselves.

Branford, though so much more intimately aware of the wiles of men than Geddes, indeed a mordant observer of all the varieties of human perversity and corruption—many of his City associates, he confessed, kept double books to reduce their income tax!—somehow never applied his knowledge to his own affairs. That is an old story, of course, but it reached a peak of self-betrayal, almost of self-mockery, in his proposal—in a codicil to his will—to spread the sociological doctrines he favored by offering an annual prize to university students for the best essay submitted on the sociology of Geddes and Branford. How he would have chortled over that folly of seeking to prolong the life-span of their ideas by thus embalming them—if someone else had committed it!

Though Branford's own writings about the city had influenced me before we met, our walks together around Westminster and South Kensington vivified and enriched these contributions; for Branford's reading of London's buildings and monuments was much more imaginative and many-sided than mine had been in New York. Not that I fell in too easily with his methods. When it came to helping him that summer to gather together a graphic survey of Westminster, to be demonstrated at the Summer School of Civics in High Wycombe where I was lecturing, I sometimes found Branford capricious or arbitrary in his choice of illustrations. For all that, my own use of pictures in 'Technics and Civilization' and later volumes owes not a little to all that I took in, against my original academic limitations, from Branford.

His direct influence culminated in the week I spent with him in August, first at his rented summer home in the New Forest, then on a motor trip he arranged partly for my benefit across southern England via Shaftesbury to Glastonbury, for a dance festival and a Regional Education Meeting. Those days with Branford, with their steady flow of scenic images and fresh ideas and contrasting personalities, still linger in my mind with a dawnlike vividness.

Not a few of Branford's penetrating ideas I assimilated unconsciously. Yet the ultimate effect of both his and Geddes's thinking upon me was to increase my receptivity to the adventurous sallies of many other minds, not just to their own; and in my very transmogrification of their ideas I was in fact more faithful to their essential originality than I would have been as a more uncritical disciple.

CHAPTER TWENTY

Le Play House
Galaxy

I

All this while I have been talking mainly about London, Victor Branford, and my new friends, and not about the Sociological Society and Le Play House. If an institution can be said to be "the lengthened shadow of a man," that Society ended by becoming the attenuated shadow of two men, Patrick Geddes and Victor Branford, for the shadow never found a single body that actively conformed to its ideal outline.

Their original intention was a disinterested one: to give academic status and influence to sociology, an area of science whose right to exist was still questioned at Oxford, on the lofty ground that its very name was a barbarous miscegenation of a Greek and a Latin root! Auguste Comte had indeed regarded sociology as the crowning mistress of the positive sciences, and the founders of Le Play House hoped to provide a common habitation for anthropologists, psychologists, economists, geographers, and workers in many other fields.

In theory, the new Sociological Society sought to reconcile diverse schools and break down partisanships and private idiosyncrasies, trusting that the extension and unification of the 'preliminary sciences' would make them as available for social and civic application as the physical and biological sciences had proved to be in the realms of engineering and medicine. (All too whimsically, the headquarters was named after the French mining engineer, Frédéric Le Play, whose detailed investigation of workers' family budgets seemed to Geddes and Branford models of social analysis.)

Beneath this impersonal aim were, unfortunately, more conflicting personal counterclaims: views of society that overweighted the role to be played by the postulates and methods and demonstrations of Comte and Le Play—which meant ultimately Branford and Geddes! And in turn they sought, without rallying further support, to project their ideas into an immediate program of action. So in time the Sociological Society became, without their fully realizing what this implied, *our* Sociological Society; and that led at the end of the twenties to the fission of the original society into Farquharson's Institute of Sociology (academic) and Margaret Tatton's Le Play Society (Geddesian).

Though Branford and Geddes preached 'synthesis,' and prided themselves that they could find a place for every kind of valid truth at some point in Geddes's supposedly comprehensive graphs, they were none too charitable to ideas and methods that differed from their own. Indeed, they found curious reasons for putting some of their potentially useful allies, like Professor Leonard Hobhouse, into limbo. (Hobhouse had, unfortunately, been given the chair at the University of London that Sir Martin White had set up specifically as a permanent post for Geddes!) Even within the circle of more acceptable scholars there remained a good many probationers whose worst fault was that they had not openly enrolled in the Geddesian ranks. This meant, in the end, that the 'true' disciples, like Amelia Defries, Geddes's first biographer, and William Mann, were in effect those who had no minds of their own.

Yet back in 1904 the Sociological Society had been founded under seemingly auspicious circumstances: it had the blessing of such venerable Victorians as Herbert Spencer and Francis Galton, and its honorary presidents were people like Lord Bryce and Lord Balfour; indeed, there was no lack of lustrous names among those who attended the Society's first meetings and contributed to the three challenging volumes of 'Sociological Papers' (1904–1906) or later sustained 'the Sociological Review.' But the first push that established the Society as a reputable scientific organization had lost its momentum even before the 1914 war caused it to vacate its original headquarters in the Strand.

In 1919 Branford took steps toward reviving the Society. The end of the war had, though only briefly, rekindled everyone's hopes; and it gave Branford fresh encouragement to provide sociological guidance on Geddesian lines for ultimately renovating the whole social order and releasing the potentialities that this power-obsessed civilization had repressed.

With a view to this revival, and without adequately taking into account his limited financial means, Branford had invited me over to serve as a catalyst in this transformation. Were not all Americans energetic and hopeful? Would not a young American like Mumford, already so sympathetic to the Geddesian outlook, be even more hopeful and helpful than most? That generous expectation proved too frail and wishful to survive, on more than one count. Branford did not realize that an American youth, alien to the British scene, could not serve even as a symbolic substitute for the younger generation in Britain that had been slaughtered en masse at Ypres, Verdun, and on the Seven Seas. It was they who were needed for this revival. What was lacking in England's postwar milieu, and so what was lacking in the Sociological Society, was the new generation itself. That human emptiness could not soon be replenished. Nobody can begin to understand the history of the last half-century in Europe who does not take in what this breach in the generations meant. An organic link, a link that can be formed only by living personalities, was missing.

Branford had chosen Pimlico as the Society's new home not only because one could lease a house cheaply in that backwater but because it was halfway between political and religious Westminster on one hand and the great university and museum center in South Kensington on the other, with an artists' quarter in Chelsea to complete the balance of cultural activities. He explained the dingy mediocrity of the Victorian buildings as due partly to the fact that an army clothing factory had been established in Pimlico near the Thames in Victorian days, and this had set the tone for the nearby subhousing of the workers, and somewhat sullied the neighboring elegance of even Eaton and Eccleston Squares. Between the army and the speculative builder, the barracks had left its mark everywhere. I think it also gave Branford some special pleasure to remember that Pimlico was in fact built over the marsh where the medieval Abbot of Westminister Abbey used to go fowling for snipe.

Some of the dinginess almost inevitably haunted our headquarters. Its lower floors were occupied by an old fraud of a phrenologist, now disguised as a vocational counselor; a Society of Railway Engineers, which held beery evening meetings at which the chief business, to judge by the odor in the hallway, was beer; and—how archly or how uproariously my American friends always took this item in the wall directory!—a Society of Assistant Mistresses. But the great social defect of this Pimlico location was not the Society's distance from the center of London, for where, pray, *is* the center? The real handicap of this rim of Belgravia was a dearth of intimate restaurants and tearooms: there wasn't one in half a mile. And I shouldn't be surprised if the Society forfeited a big donation from Sir Martin White—that old *bon vivant,* Geddes's generous Scots friend and main financial sponsor—the first time he tasted the desiccated sliver of brown roast beef that the nearby Belgravia Restaurant served up.

Yet it was around this decent but meager board that I had my first opportunity to talk with town planners like S. D. Adshead and Raymond Unwin—the latter promptly invited me to tea at his Hampstead cottage—with that fine old sociological positivist, S. H. Swinny, with his long, pointed nose, his long, pointed white beard, and his pertinacious memory, who could always be counted on to say a few words at the end of a discussion to correct any seeming neglect or disparagement of Comte.

Not least stirring, it was at a meeting of the Sociological Society that I met Frederick Soddy, the physicist, who had been one of Rutherford's assistants in atomic research in Manchester, and had written 'The Interpretation of Radium' (1909). As it happens, the first work on science I ever bought was Soddy's 'Matter and Energy' (1912) in the new Home University Library series: an outstanding contribution to that admirable series, still in my possession. By 1919 Rutherford's work had gone far enough to suggest the possibility of breaking up the atom and utilizing its energy. This came about two years after Henry Adams's prescient earlier prediction of a 'change of phase' by 1917.

Unlike the majority of physicists before 1940, Soddy, in the fourth edition of his 'The Interpretation of Radium' (1921), had accepted the need for establishing a firm moral and social control of these potentially devastating cosmic energies. Regrettably, his sociological insight centered on a quite peripheral program for national control of money and credit toward the redistribution of income: whereas nothing less than a release of exact science itself from its limited 'objective' premises and goals could cope with the irrational historic factors that the possession of absolute power by any limited human group magnifies.

Unfortunately for me, Soddy and I never formed any personal ties, even by correspondence. Still more unfortunately, when I wrote 'Technics and Civilization' in 1934, I neglected to take note of Soddy's early projection of the imminent need for a deep-seated change in the whole structure of civilization. My own failure, while I was canvassing contemporary sources of energy, to pay attention to the threatening negative potentialities of atomic energy, I regard as a grave lapse, for I had earlier absorbed Henry Adams's 1905 prediction and H. G. Wells's alarmingly graphic picture in 1913 of the destruction of a whole city by a single atomic bomb. (Ironically, Wells's book was entitled 'The World Set Free!') Both subjective intuitions were close to objective realities. Perhaps my failure then to entertain such a likely outcome partly accounts for my swift awakening to action after Hiroshima.

2

Quite early on in my stay at Le Play House I realized that, apart from the routines of editing, I had neither the professional zeal nor the personal inclination to further Branford's working program for the Sociological Society, no matter how readily one part of me responded to the man himself. So the arrangement fell apart almost before it could be said to have come together, and I did not stay on the job long enough to do more than the preliminary assemblage of the new 'The Sociological Review.'

This, incidentally, was typical of almost all the other attempts I made thereafter to take on a 'permanent' job other than writing.

Even as a full professor, my participation has been limited (except at Stanford) to a single semester a year, and deliberately subordinated to my own needs as an independent writer and scholar. Yet by the same token, each tentative venture has helped give me an inside view of the way our society operates. Besides all that London gave me directly of Branford's mind, and indirectly of Geddes's varied career, it offered me the immense stimulus of Westminster itself, even as viewed through the back door of Pimlico. At the same time it provided me with a growing circle of personal friends and a cast of diverse professional characters that I might not have otherwise acquired at all in any single university.

Not that I made the most of my Le Play House opportunities! Looking back, I realize how many promising openings I lost through inertia or bashfulness, as when I failed to identify John Burns, already an 'historic figure'—he had led the great Dockworkers' Strike back in the eighties!—on his dropping in one morning when no one else was around. What was worse, I did not take advantage of his invitation to visit him at home and inspect his collection of Utopias, of which he was justifiably proud. And, what was even more inept, I didn't even have enough sense to send him a copy of my own first book, 'The Story of Utopias,' when it came out two years later. Yet without such lapses perhaps I would not have had the leisure to absorb so much as I did.

Some of the most lasting of the benefits I owe to Le Play House were personal ones, like the chance to meet Edward Westermarck, the anthropologist who wrote what was in its day the classic 'History of Human Marriage.' This bluff, genial Finn, with none of the usual English reserves, promptly invited me to lunch with him at his favorite little restaurant in New Oxford Street, whose cellar pleased him. At the time I was wrestling with all the vexations and frustrations that my own erotic urges and my desire to live permanently with Sophia had conjured up. Every time I lingered for a few furtive moments before a contraceptive shop, or caught the eye of a pretty girl pausing to scan the street before entering her house door, my heart beat quicker.

Westermarck must have sensed what was going on beneath the

surface of his young guest: and I am sure it was not by accident that he called my attention to Marie Stopes's new book, 'Ideal Marriage,' one of the first to dwell in some detail on the choice of contraceptives and the desirability of simultaneous orgasms—though on the latter subject her advice was all too delicately allusive. (Her audacious but spinsterly suggestion to "smack the vulva" still lingers comically in my mind.) As a result of our talk I went back to America supposedly equipped for any theoretic erotic encounter, however impromptu, though I was far from being fortified for a real one, and even less ready to cope with marriage itself. Though I would have profited far more from reading Ovid than Marie Stopes, I remain grateful for Westermarck's shrewd human insight.

3

As early as July, when, after a series of discussions, it became plain to Branford that he could not meet my minimum financial needs for remaining in England, he transferred his hopes for the revival of the Sociological Society to Alexander Farquharson, an older and more experienced man, who had helped organize the Civic Education League. Yet in different ways both Branford and I were disappointed, though he took the disappointment gracefully because he still felt I might not be altogether lost, since Geddes's offer to make me his assistant in Jerusalem or Bombay was still open. As for me, though my experience in Le Play House and in London was ultimately to serve me beyond all expectations, I must have dimly realized that it would take half a lifetime for me to make full use of it: and that any further time I spent in work extraneous to my own vocation as a writer would be time lost for my essential life work— although I had yet to discover more specifically what that many-sided life work would be. Some inner conviction, however, already told me it would not be through any direct alliance with Geddes, still less through a permanent addiction to his diagrammatic ideological 'synthesis.' When, later in the summer, Branford learned that I had decided not to accept Geddes's offer, he still, out of loyalty to both Geddes and me, thought that I was missing the opportunity of a lifetime. (But what a lucky escape that was!)

And yet the word 'decision' seems to imply far more conscious intention on my part than the mixture of almost imperceptible hunches, impulses, and accidents would honestly allow. I was so near to accepting Geddes's invitation to Bombay that I went to the P. & O. offices one morning in August to find out about the cost of passage and sailing schedules. After waiting around for half an hour without evoking even a quiver of attention from a seemingly idle clerk, I suddenly decided that my die was cast. Heaven had spoken! *I would not go to India.* I defy any computer to handle the medley of invisible data that suddenly 'printed out' that last step!

Happily, London itself remained a large mouthful to swallow, and even had I spent all my days there, I should still never have finished that meal. But through being identified with Le Play House and its older members I had access to a much wider circle in many different areas: I got a glimpse of the newspaper world through Lapworth, a hearty Labor man, unmistakably Yorkshire, who wrote for 'The New York Daily Herald'; and I lunched on Fleet Street with the warden of Toynbee Hall; while as an observer for the 'Journal of the American Institute of Architects' I attended the first postwar Inter-Allied Conference of Town Planners—somehow I never got around to writing the article I had promised Whitaker, the editor— and likewise I shook hands with my first authentic British industrial workers at a weekend conference at Morley College in the South End!

Although I failed to write a promised article for 'The Freeman' on the Labor Party Conference I attended at Scarborough, I at least saw and heard the great luminaries of the labor movement, beginning with that down-to-earth miners' leader, Bob Smillie, to say nothing of Ramsay MacDonald, then the seemingly resolute, clear-headed dominie of pacifism—not yet the deflated windbag he finally turned out to be. Sidney and Beatrice Webb used to sit only a few tables away from me in the hotel dining room; and I had a good eyeful of her: a handsome, majestic woman, who never had any use for her outwardly inviting femininity. That glimpse still mingles in my mind with H. G. Wells's wicked picture of the Webbs in 'The New Machiavelli.'

It was at Scarborough, too, that I was invited for lunch at the home of one of the Rowntrees, my earliest contact with that fine old Quaker industrial aristocracy, which includes the Frys and the Cadburys, all makers of cocoa products and exponents of civic enterprise. In 1946 my visit to Birmingham would bring me close to Paul Cadbury and the model industrial village of Bournville.

4

Some of the colorful personalities I became acquainted with on my first visit must be left out, while more significant ones will enter my narrative later. But this sketch of the influence of London and Le Play House would be incomplete if I left out Alexander Farquharson, who, early and late, did more to introduce me to Britain than anyone besides Branford and Delilah Loch. The respect Alick and I had for each other, almost from the moment we met, survived sundry disconcerting moments, beginning with the first hour we took a walk together through Pimlico, when I said something disparaging about theosophy, only to have him say quietly that he had long been a theosophist. After this *faux pas* we never mentioned theosophy again: and as he came more fully under the sway of the Geddes-and-Branford philosophy, and thus became more 'socialized' and extroverted, his esoteric projections and fantasies seem to have either faded away or been pushed deeper into his unconscious.

Alick and I got on famously together, for both of us, not inept pupils of our masters, had a similar way of noting the wry or grimly comic twist in everything we dealt with, pleased by our own observations, smiling ironically over human weaknesses rather than being discouraged or rebuffed by them. Farquharson's Scots courtesy was as attentive and quite as ceremonious as Branford's.

We spent a memorable weekend at High Wycombe Inn outlining a series of lectures on Social Reconstruction, and the only thing that put a strain on me that weekend together was the very intensity of Farquharson's concentration: for I had never batted ideas about for seven unrelieved hours with anyone in America, not even with Herbert Feis. I was in the last throes of mental exhaustion by the

Clarence Stein and Benton MacKaye

Henry Wright

Catherine Bauer

Josephine Strongin

Paul Rosenfeld by Alfred Stieglitz

Van Wyck Brooks

Frank Lloyd Wright

Aline MacMahon

L.M. and Geddes, 1926

Geddes and Sophia at Martha's Vineyard, 1927

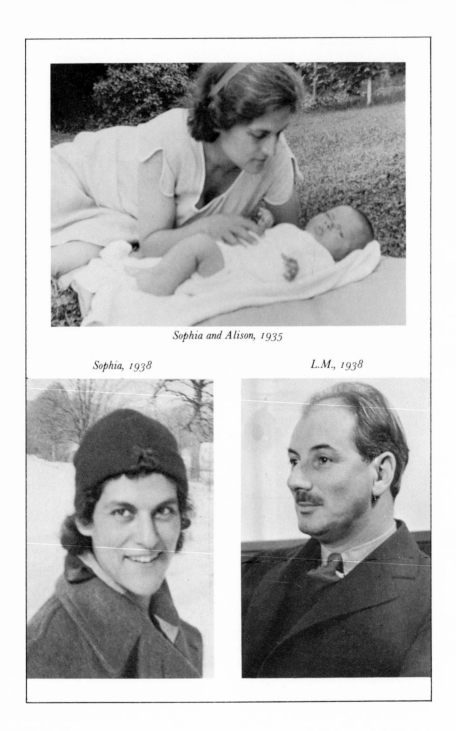

Sophia and Alison, 1935

Sophia, 1938

L.M., 1938

J. E. Spingarn at Troutbeck

Amy Spingarn

Alison, 1937

Geddes, 1938

The house we bought in 1929

time we had finished tea and taken a turn around the town before catching the train to London.

But those hours sealed and solidified our intellectual friendship; and they gave me an astringent sense of what a slack, half-awakened life I had been living up to then. Then in August we gave the lectures. For a still unseasoned young man nearing twenty-five, self-conscious, often halting in his exposition, with none of the experience that a lecturer needs before he acquires a sense of his audience and gives it only a little more than it is prepared to take, I perhaps deserved a passing mark. At all events, the students, usually much older people—teachers, a clergyman, a retired businessman or two—kept up a lively discussion and appreciated my grasp of economics. In those days, I should perhaps explain, everyone regarded economics as the main road to further social progress—unless one was ready for Freudian psychology! For a passing moment Farquharson and I talked of doing a book together based on our lectures. But the idea quickly faded; for it soon became plain that, outside the war-devastated areas, there was no strong impulse to 'reconstruct,' still less to create.

By themselves these lectures and these varied personal contacts would not have been so stimulating to me had not High Wycombe, with its ancient beech forests and its country houses and small villages, not also revealed so many bedrock strata of Old England. Fortunately, though High Wycombe had become a thriving industrial town, famous for manufacturing the Windsor chair, it had escaped the worst ravages of Victorian industrialism, and retained, side by side with commercialized mass production, many of the basic traditions of the handicrafts. In the hills, I saw chair legs still being turned on the aboriginal lathe, whose motive power was a bent sapling, released by a treadle.

Here was a living residue of medieval England, from the Sixteenth Century on, with a nearby veritable Anglo-Saxon church to carry us further back in time. The detailed notes I still have of my visits to a furniture factory, a paper mill, a wood-turner's shack have remained as solid early supports for my later studies in technics and human culture. Probably I learned more in that fortnight than a year of systematic reading might have given me. All these explorations were indeed in the best style of Geddes, Branford, and Le Play House.

5

Though my first stay in England covered little more than five months, it left me with impressions that have lasted a lifetime, deepened as many of them were by further visits, modified as others were by further changes that took place in the English themselves. Not all of these first impressions were favorable: quite the contrary, for the dank, depressing ugliness of Victorian England had left a grim mark on everything it touched—buildings, streets, shops, men, women, infants—and though I already knew by direct observation the squalor and poverty of New York and Boston, of Philadelphia and Pittsburgh, there were even more massive accretions in London, thanks to the fact that ever since Elizabethan times a vast human muck pile had been a-building.

Shaw's 'Pygmalion' happily provides the essential clue to the stratification of British society. As soon as anyone opens his mouth, he can be identified, and assigned to his proper social place. So each Englishman is a sort of Higgins, listening to and secretly cataloging those he meets, mentally 'placing' them, either respectfully or condescendingly (U. C. or L. C.!). Some of my most genial friends in England were crippled all their lives by cockney accents; and when I was with them in England, myself resonating to the social environment about me, I used to find that, against my loyal intentions, their speech made me self-conscious on their behalf. Often the local accent stood as a barrier against vocational advancement for many who were talented.

Back in 1920 these distinctions were even more abrading because they were still accompanied by the enormous economic inequities that separated the classes. But behind the barriers of money and privilege were still older separations that went back to the late Middle Ages, like the distinction between the physician and the surgeon—which reduced the lowest surgical skill, that of the operative dentist, to a status little higher than that of the barber—or the unbridgeable social distance between retail and wholesale trades.

Even talent and education could not vault over these barriers. To the end of his days John Ruskin, son of a well-to-do wine merchant, always felt that members of the aristocracy were his natural superiors: and when Carlyle or Matthew Arnold were invited to the great country houses of the nobility, they gladly went alone, without taking umbrage over the fact that their wives were usually not included in the weekend invitation. All this seemed odious to me then—and still does!

On the eve of my first visit to England, Walter Fuller had admonished me to repeat these words every night before going to sleep: *"The English don't mean to be rude. The English don't mean to be rude!"* Excellent advice for a newcomer! What seemed rudeness often turned out to be merely a mark of social insulation, a dodge to conceal a possible flaw in class status, or on another level, a protective shyness, an unwillingness to open up to a casual acquaintance, with no assurance that the new relationship would be sufficiently solid to last a lifetime. How different from my America, where a new acquaintance calls you by your given name in the first five minutes and forgets even your last name the next week. In Britain I found, once this oysterlike shell did in fact open, it would not lightly shut again. Still, to be honest, when I look back over the people I got close to quickly without cagey probing or fencing, it turned out they were either Scots, Welsh, Irish, or Cornish!

But there also remained, far more visible in 1920 than forty years later, another kind of rudeness: the deliberate barrier erected by the upper classes, protecting themselves from any infringement or invasion, indeed any acknowledgment of the existence of those with whom they did not wish to be acquainted. The glacial "Oeuooh" that congealed Emerson was then still as formidable as ever: an icicle that froze easy conversation.

All that as an American I was to discover about England, Emerson had in fact long before put in his 'English Traits,' a book I did not read until long after my first visit. But the very likeness underlying our two countries at the beginning has tended to sharpen our jealous sense of growing differences, which comes out in even minor matters of spelling, as well as grosser differences of idiom. Yet it remained for a Pole, Joseph Conrad, to say the last word about traditional England at the point where some of its singular characteristics, like our own aboriginal traits, were on the point of vanishing. Conrad, inwardly proud of his early submersion for twenty years in Old England's Merchant Service, summed up the ultimate British achievement in three laconic essays: 'Tradition,' 'Confidence,' and 'Well Done.' In singling out "well done"—the Royal Navy's high tribute to a victorious fleet—Conrad gave an ultimate accolade, as expressive as the muted words of Captain MacWhirr emerging from the typhoon. Those words remind us of sea-tested qualities that have repeatedly made England greater in defeat and disaster than in the insolence of victory.

6

Though this dip into the intellectual life of London gave me an even wider span of social experience (except in literary circles) than I had yet achieved in my own country, I had no lurking desire to be transplanted. Even had I been dedicated to widening the influence of Geddesian Sociology, I still had no thought of making this field my own specialty, and even less did I think of England as a place I wanted to settle in and make a fresh start. After all, 'making fresh starts' was an American specialty, and my own fresh start as it was beginning to shape up in my own mind lay outside the conventional boundaries of the established arts and professions.

Once I realized all that taking on a permanent post in England would mean, I saw how impossible it would be for me, despite the many ways and scenes and people that stimulated and nourished me, to accept the unspoken assumptions that the English still took so easily for granted: the deep chasm Disraeli recognized between the Two Nations, the rich and the poor; the presumptuous world dominion of the Empire; the stratified social order; in short, what has only recently become identified as The Establishment. I knew in my bones I could not fit into this society without forfeiting something I valued in my own American past.

My feelings about my own country were close to those Henry James held at the same age, though I never shared his later desire to finger the faded tapestry of upper-class English society, or to poke my head into family vaults and secret closets whose souvenirs of corruption awakened his keenest sensibilities. For me it is in the very novels and stories that penetrate this corruption—'The Portrait of a Lady,' 'What Maisie Knew,' 'The Princess Casamassima,' 'The Turn of the Screw'—that he seems to me to show his most original gifts as a novelist.

True: the actual conduct of the United States had increasingly mocked our constitutional professions in behalf of freedom and equality: for, by the insulation of the defeated south, the Civil War had in fact prolonged the institution of slavery rather than displaced it; and our continued robbery and butchery of the original Amerindian inhabitants was mirrored in our equally barbarous treatment of the land itself under rapacious exploitation. I was not blind to the fact that the American Dream was already fast becoming an American Nightmare.

For all that, my own country, by its very polyglot disorder, still gave me the sense of its being ready, responsive, and in some degree malleable, more open to favorable human pressures and plans and self-transformations. With Randolph Bourne, Waldo Frank, and Van Wyck Brooks, my part of the younger generation was still hopefully confident of reclaiming 'Our America.' Despite the disillusion that set in after the First World War, we believed that we might give a more humane shape to American culture before our molten desires had cooled. These latent hopes tempered even our postwar cynicism. In confirming my resolution to return to New York, the essays Van Wyck Brooks published in 'The Freeman' in the summer of 1920 intensified my own earlier and deeper allegiances.

But—need I confess?—much of the reasoning that drew me back to America was quickened by purely personal concerns, mainly that I was still in love with Sophia and realized from her increasingly dubious letters that other people in her growing circle had already begun to break through her adolescent armor of sexual impassiveness. If I stayed away longer, they might awaken in her stirrings for a more relaxed emotional life: a life more satisfying to her ego than any I was either temperamentally or financially prepared to offer. Yet even during this period when Sophia and I felt farther apart than ever, I never regretted the decision that severed my career from the potential destiny that Le Play House had once practically opened up for me, whether in London, Edinburgh, Bombay, or Montpellier.

CHAPTER TWENTY-ONE

The Long Courtship

I

Back from London in mid-October! Almost from the moment Sophia greeted me at the pier I realized sharply that during our half-year separation the change that had been taking place in her had by now spread much further than even her recent letters had indicated. This transformation reflected the social opportunities and personal responses she drew from those around her on the monthly 'Dial': a different crew altogether from the previous fortnightly 'Dial' contributors.

Sophy's duties as Editorial Assistant in charge of proofreading and seeing the final copy through the press no longer claimed her undivided attention or filled all her days. The new 'Dial' introduced her to a more varied, personally colored, lighthearted world, which evoked her latent femininity as no other would-be suitors had so far done. If she did not at first feel she could hold her own in quick repartee or knowledgeable esthetic gossip, her beauty nonetheless commanded attention and homage. Her relaxing visible presence was alone enough to charm her male companions, whether they took her to tea or dinner or the theater, or just boating of a Saturday afternoon on Sheepshead Bay.

In this galaxy there was no place whatever for me, as Sophia recognized. By the time I came back, she had already pigeonholed me as a mere sociologist, obviously a dull fellow, far too serious and single-minded when put beside her new group of artists and writers.

At the center of her life now was not only the coterie 'The Dial' attracted, but its owners, Scofield Thayer and James Sibley Watson. Until 1925 Thayer played the more active part in modeling 'The Dial' as an international review of literature and the arts, enlisting new authors, whether famous or merely promising, and zealously collecting varied works of modern art which could also be used as 'Dial' illustrations. Underwritten by their inherited family fortunes, both young men showed a flair for innovative expression in all the arts: witness their early publication of T. S. Eliot's 'The Waste Land,' Thomas Mann's 'Death in Venice,' and Eric Mendelsohn's dynamic black-and-white architectural sketches, which almost overnight turned into visible contemporary buildings. Under this literary leadership— to say nothing of Bruce Rogers' elegant typography—the 'Dial' at once put to shame the older, stodgier monthlies.

From the first, Sophy responded to the new esthetic, literary, and personal standards that the younger generation was now creating or absorbing; and though her curtailed early education had left empty places in her cultural background, to offset this, no moldy orthodox values stood in the way of her embracing modern forms and personal ventures in the Seven Lively Arts—as the recently added editor, Gilbert Seldes, would soon characterize them.

Even more rewardingly, Sophy's job brought her into increasingly close contact with Thayer himself; and she sometimes fell into heated arguments with her tense, exacting superior because of the differences in their reactions. By themselves these office flare-ups subtly turned into tokens of intimacy rather than alienation. Sophy remembers how, at the end of a contentious afternoon the two of them, still hotly quarreling, might leave the office together for tea in Thayer's nearby apartment on Washington Square East. But the moment the front door of 'The Dial' closed behind them, they became host and guest, all contentions left behind—until they met next day at the office.

The nature and extent of their burgeoning intimacy was known to me then only through its patent result in cooling further Sophia's already cool response to me. Though I did not learn from her any of the details of these extra-editorial encounters until half a century

286

later, she did not conceal her enjoyment over her new status as a desirable, self-assured, and physically attractive young woman. Sophy's letters to me in London had amply prepared me to face this change, yet when I came back, I was not sufficiently fortified against her detachment and remoteness: it was no longer the Atlantic Ocean but an Arctic Sea that now separated us. In more than one sense, we had suddenly reached a dead end.

All I could salvage from this wreck of my romantic hopes was—I noted early in November—"the moral honesty of Sophy." "I vow," I noted then, "this makes up for all the bitterness and sadness of my role in our relationship. Last night was, I think, the most painful evening I ever spent in her company," and the pain was not relieved by her surgical swiftness in opening the wound. Sophy made it plain now that she wanted freedom and opportunity to explore a quite different kind of life.

Even the brief sorties she had already had with comradely males in her circle had made her "a good deal happier," Sophy wrote. And if this proved truer to her nature, she added, she was "bound to develop further in that direction," rather than forgo this promising exploration for the prospect of an all-too-sober lifetime of marriage with me. "I am inclined," she concluded, "to let things take their course and see how they will turn out." Even marriage itself had become, at that point in her new life, something she was reluctant to consider, in view of her dissatisfaction with the state of most of the family relationships she had experienced or observed.

These forthright sentiments were, of course, not confined to Sophia alone. They had become common to the liberated young women of the twenties who called themselves Feminists, and who, with the widening availability of contraceptives, were ready for sex if not for love, and eager for the wild taste of love if not for marriage. The odds seemed heavily stacked against my prosaic proposals and my even less glamorous devotion to my career as a writer. I was now as much of an outsider to Sophy's newly awakened self as I was to the indifferent new editors of 'The Dial,' who had no use for such writings as I had published during the previous five years: that uneven medley of themes, a few brilliant, some promising, but too many—

like my 'History of a Prodigy' in 'The Smart Set'—just scattered left-overs from a younger self.

All that winter I hovered on the periphery of Sophy's conscious-ness, like a remote but monstrous superego: much the same role I had once played with Beryl. Sophia resented, naturally resented and rejected, my demands on her, perhaps expecting that her now emerging self, by developing further, would release erotic potentials she had so far suppressed even in her own consciousness, and would provide a conclusive answer for both of us.

Looking back on that bleak period between April 1920 and April 1921, I still find it almost too painful to put into words. The only self-respecting course that now seemed open to me was to re-sign myself to a quick exit, if not oblivion. So presently I withdrew with an unmistakable ultimatum: the weakest kind of revenge open to a rejected lover!

I told her that if she should change her mind, she would have to propose to me!

When I said this, I felt we had come to the end of the road together, and I steeled myself to go the next stage alone. That win-ter, despite sociable meetings with close friends, like Clarence Brit-ten, I felt lonelier in New York than I had ever felt in my gloomiest hours in gloomy London. Almost in a medical sense I was utterly sick at heart. Perhaps the surest sign of my mental stasis was that, during the first five months of 1921, just a single essay of mine, 'Toward a Humanist Synthesis,' was published: it came out in 'The Freeman.'

2

But how little had I fathomed the heart of that young woman! When spring came, something prompted Sophy to go off to a farm board-inghouse in New Jersey for a week's vacation: and without any pre-liminary overtures she invited me by letter to spend the coming weekend there—sleeping alone, of course, in a little detached cabin.

Commonplace though the boardinghouse and the nearby woods were, the scene still remains in my memory as a quite idyllic setting, for there Sophy disclosed her changed feelings about me and her still rather shaky hopes about our future together. I was so unprepared for this emotional turnabout that I recall the jutting rock where we sat and the scampering squirrels even more sharply than I can now remember any of our shy gestures of lovemaking. As for Sophy, what remains with her is that the night I arrived she could not go to sleep easily for being vaguely apprehensive over my sleeping all alone in the cabin—and wondering to herself if this concern was really a sign of actually being 'in love.'

Before this brief encounter was ended by our going back to the city on Sunday, we agreed on Sophy's circumspect proposal that we start living together openly for, say, six months, to see if such a tentative alliance was worthy of being more formally sealed, or might possibly be indefinitely prolonged, as had happened with some of her father's distant anarchist relatives. This seemed a tolerable halfway measure, if not a final solution, though I still favored the firmer alliance of marriage, if only to balance and somewhat equalize my earlier one-sided commitment to my vocation as a writer.

On the very day of our return to New York our sudden capitulation underwent its first test. In the subway car we found ourselves facing Sophy's Italian sculptor, too obviously 'there' not to be introduced before we got off at the next station. Was this chance encounter a jeering reminder that our future was still precarious?

Actually, something more obstructive to our brave plans lay in store for us. Quite unexpectedly, shortly after our return, on the recommendation of my new friend Paul Rosenfeld, now the animated music critic of 'The Dial,' I received an invitation to take over Padraic Colum's post, teaching literature to a mixed group of children at a small, informal school on the estate of a wealthy couple, the Arthur Johnsons, near Peterboro, New Hampshire. Joanne Johnson, as Lady of this Manor, had founded the school to give their two girls, aged five and eleven, stimulating companions during the vacant days of summer.

Whatever the pay promised me—characteristically we've both quite forgotten that impelling item!—Sophy agreed that this was an opportunity I could hardly say No to, and so we were to be separated again! Our first surface ripple of lovemaking was to be given no time to stir closer intimacies.

But at least, I felt, we could make a beginning! So, on our next Sunday afternoon in Flatbush, we quietly withdrew to an unoccupied room in the rear of the house, and for a few all-too-swift minutes, Sophy stripped off her clothes, undies and all, to let me breathlessly behold and embrace her naked body! This was a one-sided revelation, for it did not occur to her to suggest that I follow her example, nor, to tell the truth, did it occur to me then either! But it has remained for me one of the most precious overtures of our lifetime of strippings, and I even celebrated it in a stanza of 'The Little Testament.'

> *Blow hot! blow cold! blow warm breezes of spring:*
> *Blow through the leaf-dimmed windows:*
> *Blow away dress, camisole and shift:*
> *Blow against the dusky reticence of pink marble.*
> *Blow orange fragrance from that Hymettus*
> *Where no flower has withered,*
> *Where no bee has sipped:*
> *Blow twilight on the shadowy kiss*
> *That hovered hawklike over Venusberg!* . . .

That hasty snatch at lovemaking did not make our parting easier; indeed our prospective separation now seemed intolerable. So before I left for Peterboro, we vaguely canvassed the possibility of Sophy's spending the remaining week of her allotted vacation with me. Almost from the moment I arrived there, I began plotting in my mind a way to bring her up to this Headlong Hall, not guessing it might turn at first for us both into Heartbreak House. Unfortunately, so secluded was this estate that the only place where Sophy might have boarded was six pedestrian miles away—an impossible distance for casual meetings.

But once I had settled into my quarters, the simplest possible solution occurred to me and made my heart expectantly quicken. With Sophia's connivance I planned a move that only a far more adventurous fellow than I would normally have dared to entertain. Finding myself on pleasant, easy terms with the handsome, somewhat willful Mrs. Johnson, I was audacious enough to ask her if my 'wife,' who worked on 'The Dial,' might join me as a guest of the school for a week in July. When with gracious readiness she consented, Sophia lost no time in arranging her affairs for our reunion, based on her putative status as a Promissory Wife.

Still undauntedly innocent, Sophy not merely accepted that nonfeminist status, but consented to buy a Woolworth wedding ring to confirm it visibly: and still more woefully ignorant, on the very evening before her journey, after having canvassed various birth-control authorities, she visited the favored gynecologist in our circle, Dr. Mary Halton, to be fitted with the then fashionable (now obsolete) wishbone pessary. Neither of us had enough experience or enough imagination to realize how blighting that cold surgical rupture of the hymen would be next day to our first tantalizing essay at full-blown lovemaking.

3

While waiting impatiently for Sophy to join me at the Johnsons, I was able to explore the generously laid out estate which separated the Big House by a mile or more from the cottage by the small lake where we teachers lived and loafed. This gave me my first immersion in latter-day country-house culture—naturally, on a purely New England model, which supplemented my earlier, more rustic view near the White River in Vermont. That fresh experience, brief though it was, added a tinge of color to my picture of the Utopia of the Country House in my 'Story of Utopias'—the book I wrote in 1922.

This sub-aristocratic setting indeed seemed to promise much for our illicit honeymoon. We ate all our meals in mixed company at the Big House, and were even waited on by an English butler, appropriately named Jones. On the surface the whole stage seemed perfectly designed for Sophy and me as actors in our own improvised comedy. The only flaw, it turned out, was that we two had yet to learn our parts.

Was this opportunity to spend a week together in such a setting not indeed precisely what our first (and only) honeymoon deserved to be? Alas, no! For both of us that week proved an all too sudden plunge into depths and shallows neither of us had yet ventured to explore. My classes occupied only the morning, and except for meals, there was no formal sociability. Our adventure began ominously with Sophy's almost drowning, in fact almost drowning us both, in the one deep spot in an otherwise shallow lake where we teachers used to swim. Fortunately our floundering caught the eye of Cowell, the athletics instructor, who rescued Sophy more adroitly than I could. I am sure that an ancient Roman would have thought twice about any marriage begun on that note! What was worse, however, was that despite Sophy's surgical deflowering our repeated but baffled stabs at sexual intercourse left us both up in the air. All too soon that frustrating initiation was over, and Sophy went back to the city. My first letter to her recorded the beginning of melancholy days: "Back again in a lonesome room. An empty bed. No flimsy under-things lying around . . . the typewriter my only inspiration and work my only amusement. Morning. Alone. No heavy-lidded eyes to greet me with a teasing smile, no breasts to fondle. . . . Oh, Hell!"

Naturally, this abortive nuptial trial did not ease Sophia's doubts about venturing on a permanent tie with me: quite the contrary, of course. Yet when she was back in New York, no shyness or disappointment kept her from telling our friends and colleagues in the Village that we were, in fact, married. The tone of her announcement was so casual that no one questioned its validity: indeed, it called forth affectionate congratulations to us both in dozens of letters. Outwardly, at least, our new alliance already had the look of permanence; and it was only the two culprits who still had reason to remain dubious.

That fact led Sophy to repeat immediately on her return the reasons for her earlier uncertainties in a letter that closely echoed and even amplified the messages she had sent to me in England the year before.

I *am* uncertain. I never will be otherwise until I find something satisfying to do, or until I resign myself to being a female whose sole aim in life is to attract and charm. The one seems out of my reach, the other unattractive. I'm between the devil and the deep blue sea, now, which is one reason why I can't be as sure of myself as you are. You have your work, and you figure that I won't interfere with it— not to an appreciable extent, at least . . . For you marriage, while it may mean forgoing some experiences, will undoubtedly supply others quite as essential. That is where the trouble lies: you hit it in that sentence in your letter. 'I have my work cut out for me . . .'

It's exactly that: *You have your work cut out for you!* And I?

Nevertheless, soon after that Sophia wrote: "I can't escape the feeling that we're going to emerge triumphantly: also I can't believe it's going to be smooth sailing. But I don't want it to be. I can't seem to imagine us in eternal agreement—but we'll have a jolly time of it."

4

And now for the mocking outcome of our shivery, ankle-deep advance into connubiality! Sophy's frank announcement to her family that we intended to live together without any approved ceremony had repercussions that she naïvely had not anticipated. Her mother almost went into hysterics. Though the notion of a 'trial marriage' before accepting a lifetime union had long before been advocated by no less a writer than George Meredith, this was too much of a trial for her mother's feelings.

The case against a looser arrangement was backed up learnedly by Sophy's brother Philip, already an able young lawyer. He supported parental authority by confronting Sophia with the fact that she was willy-nilly committing herself to a common-law marriage, which was just as binding legally as a more ceremonious one, and even harder to get out of. This impasse was something that Sophy could not flatly ignore, or wish to prolong. So, hardly had we had time to settle into the dingy menage on West Fourth Street, which Sophy herself had found and spent a month scouring, furnishing it with the aid of cast-off pieces our families had supplied, when with unbecoming levity we took on the more final commitment.

One morning late in September, before she went off to 'The Dial' office, we appeared together, supported only by Sophy's older

293

sister, Edith, at the Brooklyn Borough Hall. There, behind a counter, an unceremonious clerk with an unceremonious patter of syllables bound us—despite our sense of esthetic outrage—in the bonds of legalized though certainly not yet Holy Matrimony. No bleaker or more offhand prologue to marriage could have been contrived; I shrink even now at its crudity. At the time, this sanctifying ceremony had so little meaning to either of us that we could never remember the date, and have never celebrated it. We agreed a bit later that it must have been the *thirty-first* of September!

Yet in spite of this dubious initiation, ours turned out to have the makings of a true marriage, even in the purest religious sense. According to the great doctor of the Medieval Church, Saint Thomas Aquinas, a valid marriage between a man and a woman requires neither legal nor priestly sanction, nor yet any public ceremony or celebration. Unique among the Christian sacraments, a true marriage is performed solely "in the sight of God" by the "twain who become one flesh." By this criterion, that first careless confirmation of ours before the clerk in Borough Hall was more defiantly sacrilegious than living openly in sin would have been. Yet who could have forecast that this sin would be expunged in the purgatory of daily life, and redeemed by unexpected and unpredictable glimpses of Heaven throughout our lengthening years together?

5

Sophia and I set up our first household in a grim top-floor rear apartment on West Fourth Street, number 143, an ancient tenement infested by cockroaches, with a dark, evil-smelling public hall that caused my mother to weep on her first visit. "To think," she sobbed, trying to catch her breath after the exhausting climb, "that I've lived to see my own son sink to this." We were none too delighted over the place ourselves; but for the sixty dollars a month we could barely afford, we couldn't, during that postwar housing shortage, find better quarters. The roominess—four rooms—and its open outlook to the north from our living-bedrooms were its chief virtues.

Since we lacked an icebox, one of my irksome duties, when the weather was warm, was to go down, before coffee was made, to the delicatessen almost below to fetch a quarter-pound of butter and the day's milk. The flat boasted a high, old-fashioned enclosed toilet, of a type that I remembered from my Philadelphia aunt's house; the dented tin bathtub hardly suggested or invited cleanliness; and because of horsy odors from the next-door stable, still in use, we chose to keep the small room that faced it as a storeroom, and as an occasional guest room.

Oh! we had separate beds, I in my study, Sophy in the living room, for I was still full of hygienic, post-tubercular qualms about sleeping together, while Sophy, who had almost all her life shared a bed with a sister, was still too bashful about flaunting our intimacy to think of suggesting that she sleep with me when her sister Edith came for an overnight visit. The private bed, that last refinement of privacy—once a prerogative of the French aristocracy—had been promoted, with a virtuously rational air, by Bernard Shaw. Still under his spell, I was one of those who cloaked my own sexual uncertainties in Shaw's sterilizing dicta on sex and marriage—the wisdom of a lifelong bachelor who had never had any genuine experience of marriage, since his prudent middle-aged marital contract with his Charlotte provided for complete abstention from sexual relations.

But these qualms were not all of Shaw's doing: they pointed to the lingering sexual anemia of the whole period among the more respectable classes, even in marriage itself. For almost half a century in the United States, the twin bed, too narrow for unconstricted lovemaking or still more for sleeping together, in pairs separated by the night table, became standard middle-class bedroom equipment; and as far as effective sex play went, this was made even more difficult by the introduction of the soft innerspring mattress. To make matters worse, prolonged rituals of oral and genital prophylaxis that left the female impeccably antiseptic and dryly unapproachable often delayed or frustrated the male response that the first striptease of undressing might have awakened. Sophia and I never entirely succumbed to these fashionable criteria, but we didn't entirely defy them either. Her bed was always three-quarter size; and long before slipping discs brought in bedboards and hard mattresses our mattresses were of the hard, horsehair kind: perfect for erotic acrobatics.

Separate beds were, however, the least of our hurdles. At the beginnng, I undertook to do the cooking: not only because I already had some practice as a cook, but because I had the free time to market and prepare lunch or dinner. This unfortunately only made more galling to me Sophia's personal freedom, and her easy companionship with the various editors, writers, and artists on and around 'the Dial,' who were not constrained by poverty to eat at home. With my commitment to the kitchen she even had the privilege of lingering on past five o'clock in the office, and on occasion my preparations might be nullified by her accepting spontaneously an invitation to dine out with someone else. Theoretically I had the same freedom; but in this critical early period it did not work out that way.

Sophia's older sister, Miriam, under similar constraint, had announced to her husband, on his return from the office one night, that they were going out for dinner: she wanted to be a Free Woman! That gave me my cue. One evening I met Sophia at the door of our flat with a towel over my arm, like a waiter, and an apron around my middle, like a cook. Throwing down the towel and tearing off the apron, I announced that henceforth we would go out for dinner at night: I was determined to be a Free Man! If woman was not ordained to be a kitchen slave, neither was I. Sophia, of course, caught the familiar echoes of Miriam's harangue and with a shout of laughter complied. Until she became pregnant, we rarely deviated from this regime except on weekends and holidays.

This underlayer of gaiety and high spirits was what helped us survive the dismal or harassing moments of our early marriage: with our misunderstandings and our unconscious cruelties and callousnesses—to say nothing of our honest but irreconcilable differences, a few of which have remained to this day, as unalterable as our bony structures. The cardinal mischief of such an account as this is that it too often deals with individual selves as if they reacted to each other in a vacuum: such selves as only dreams are made of. But even during the bleakest moments of our marriage, Sophia and I were in the midst of a lively multitude of other people, with other activities and other interests that enriched and rounded out our days.

Apart from our seedy tenement, we were just where we wanted to be, in the heart of Greenwich Village, among people we wanted

296

to be near. Across the street, in a cellar, Hendrik van Loon's second wife—and his fourth, too!—Jimmy, was then running a restaurant; Walter Fuller, the managing editor of 'The Freeman,' and his wife, Crystal Eastman, were in a new cooperative housing row nearby on MacDougal Street; Alyse Gregory and Llewelyn Powys were on Patchin Place; Harold Stearns and Clarence Britten were 'just around the corner'; my 'Freeman' friend, Helen Black, was living with Genevieve Taggard and another young woman in a basement in St. Luke's Place; Walter and Magda Pach were in a cold-water flat in an old brownstone on West 14th Street; while my new friend, Van Wyck Brooks, held forth at the 'Freeman' office on Thirteenth Street three times a week, though he and his handsome wife, Eleanor, were already living in Westport.

Sophy and I not merely had each other; even better, we had New York: the New York of the eye-opening art exhibitions, from 1920 on, with Van Gogh and Brancusi leading the procession, and Stieglitz's retrospective exhibitions, along with his intimate photographs, revealing to both of us his life-sensitive but demonic personality. The New York of the Provincetown Players, and the Washington Square Players, and the Neighborhood Theater, and also the New York of Eugene O'Neill's 'Desire Under the Elms,' and Shaw's 'Back to Methuselah.' Likewise, the New York of our Sunday walks, alone or with friends, along the Palisades or cutting across the Westchester Hills, halting only for frankfurter lunches broiled over an open fire.

No small part of this enrichment came from what Emerson called the 'escort of friends' that accompanied us, with the endless hot dialogues on art and literature and politics and sex and marriage—yes, of course sex and marriage!—that marked our social meetings and our country tramps. If our marital tiffs and depressions were real, our recurrent exhilaration over all that art or nature were offering us, close at hand, was no less genuine—and far more lasting.

These were the halcyon days of Greenwich Village, when artists and writers had not yet been displaced by tourists, sightseers, hangers-on, opulent arrivistes, and bedraggled hippies. There was still more of Montparnasse and the Rue des Beaux Arts in it than of either villainous Montmartre or the swagger quarters of the Faubourg St. Germain. Almost everything one needed for a good life in the city was within walking distance: so that to stroll home from a concert at Carnegie Hall or from a Broadway show was to prolong, in conversation, or later over hotcakes at Child's, the main pleasures of the evening.

True, the balls we eagerly went to at Webster Hall were never as nudely abandoned as the Students' Quatz Arts Ball in Paris, but the Independents' Ball at the old Waldorf-Astoria—where the Empire State Building now stands—was always relaxed, gay, dazzling; and Sophia, in an Oriental costume she had devised, with silken trousers and a filmy upper garment, was so voluptuously bewitching that I always marveled, at the end of those evenings, that she had not been carried off and ravished: she might, in the mood her body evoked then, have been one of Ingres' odalisques.

The fact that we had the best of New York during this probationary period helped offset the equally indubitable fact that we sometimes had the worst of each other. And yet, Sophia smilingly reminds me, this worst was far from being constant. Often we awoke in the morning relaxed and amorous, for musical comedy's 'But in the Morning, No,' had not yet been added to public advice for too-eager lovers. And not seldom, on those occasions when Sophy would unexpectedly come home to lunch with me, we might find ourselves full of high spirits and horseplay. Yet Sophy had only to call off a luncheon date or postpone her homecoming in the evening to awaken all my jealous torments: the marital sky would become overcast, the air cool, and by bedtime, if she came home late, we might both sink into the depths of recriminating despair, punctuated by a loud, savage 'Yah' from me which in itself, I hasten to admit, was almost a valid ground for her divorcing me. That's the way I remember part of our first winter together, though none of our subsequent winters was quite as dark as that.

6

Admittedly, from the outset our marriage labored under serious handicaps. But let me turn, rather, to its intrinsic foundations; for these have stood solid through the years, and upon them, indeed, a

298

fresh superstructure was erected: so that our later years made up in various quite unanticipated ways, even in erotic fulfillments, for what was lacking in our youth. Those original foundations held solid against the natural settling of the superstructure, against fire and earthquake and time's slow dilapidation.

And first, to offset what was originally the weakest part of our marriage, we always, once my adolescent acne had vanished, enjoyed the sight and the touch and daily use of our bodies; and this delight was not soon over. Even when she was past fifty, Sophia repeatedly had dreams of living in a familiar house, yet to her surprise discovering in it a new room, more beautifully furnished than she had ever suspected possible. This symbolism applied to much of our marriage. Our bodily intimacy and mutual admiration had a super base in our moral unanimity. At the beginning, when Sophia strayed furthest from me in her fantasies, and even when in the middle of our marriage, I strayed equally far from her in my acts, we shared the same human concerns and worked toward similar—or at least complementary—goals. If either of us diverged—as I did more than once—we were flouting our own deepest selves, no less than the other partner, and eventually paid a price for this freedom.

Our moral consensus applied to the small decisions of daily life no less than to ultimate questions of good and bad, right and wrong. Neither of us was concerned with money, beyond what was necessary for health and bare decency: the abstemious practices we followed out of necessity the first ten years of our marriage—but often making a game of it!—we continued to follow with sundry relaxations even at times when our income rose. Happily Sophia, not unconscious of her natural beauty, had no need to make herself more ravishing with expensive clothes: it was enough that they were distinctive; and when she was young, she even dared to defy fashion by wearing sweeping long dresses rather than the gawky knee-length skirts then in the mode.

And what freedom we gained by these practices—freedom from debt, freedom from anxiety, freedom from my having to take unwelcome jobs merely to underpin a rising standard of expenditure. Not for us elegant silverware, fine china, expensive furniture, vintage wines, a new car every other year—or any car at all, for that

299

matter, till we had been married sixteen years. Yet if Sophia had not taken these fundamental values for granted, she surely would have felt deprived, if not embittered, by this limited, impecunious life.

Yet from the beginning we spent freely on the things we cared for: particularly on travel and books; and as early as possible, in 1929 in fact, we bought a battered ten-room house in the hamlet of Leedsville, in addition to our little dwelling in Sunnyside Gardens, Long Island. Even during our leanest days we had four relaxed months in Europe; and since that time, long before cheap jet tours, we have shared repeated trips there: so Sophy has had compensations for what Van Wyck Brooks (bless his name!) called our "ascetic household." We still smile at that adjective, for we have our own kind of luxuries: not only wine at table nightly, which Emerson took to be the most valid reason for being a rich man, but even during our meagerest times we have spare cash on hand for other occasions and demands, occasions when "the gift is to the giver and comes back most to him."

These were solid foundations. Without them our marriage might not have survived the first tense uncertain years, nor would it have stood up against either the sudden erotic jars or the insidious erosions that later seemed to threaten the whole fabric. If, however, as with any other work of art, our marriage was a labor of love, the accent during the early years must fall for me on the labor rather than the love; and one must not forget that, again as in a work of art, there were moments when the work itself, on the very brink of taking form, seemed so confused, so far from our differing original conceptions, that one or the other of us was almost ready to abandon it. At that moment the experienced artist knows that he must not listen to such desperate counsel, but must either pause for a while until he recovers his original impulse or go on doggedly with the day's task till suddenly the disparate parts beautifully fit together.

And since I have emphasized our bodily fondness for each other, let me qualify that by admitting our essential difference, a difference that reached into every part of our anatomy and colored our minds, too. All our responses to life, and along with this of course our sexual responses, were in contrast: I swift, Sophia slow. Sexually, at the beginning, I was hair-trigger sensitive; while she had an extra safety catch that sometimes turned into a jam. To make matters worse, we started our marriage under a special if not peculiar handicap: we were both virgins.

A century before, if one is to trust Emerson's testimony in his 'Journals,' where he records his dismay over the fact that literary confreres like Dickens took for granted sexual promiscuity in young English males, and even fostered it, virginity before marriage was not an uncommon condition in America in young people of his class. But there is no doubt that this is an impediment, almost a built-in provision against facile sexual fulfillment; since the sexual act, the most involved, the most delicately rhythmic of dances, needs at least as much practice as a waltz if it is to be performed with the kind of poised abandon that will culminate in timely common orgasms.

But where was one to go to school? I don't envy anyone who has to begin his sexual experience in the arms of a prostitute: so I feel no embarrassment over the fact that I never had an impulse to visit a brothel, if only because I valued bodily health too highly to gain my knowledge at the cost of syphilis: a disease whose dangers were at last being openly discussed in the press during my adolescence. Student of cities that I am, I still know their red-light quarters only from the outside. A British writer, George Buchanan, has played in more than one book with the fantasy that there should be a dedicated caste of ladylike prostitutes—sexual priestesses, if you will— free from the coarser vices of the trade, who would initiate young males into the rites of love. In the case of D. H. Lawrence, evidence seems to show that an older married woman played this role with him. But her description of the event—"I gave him sex"—almost robs the gift of its value.

During my youth only unscrupulous young men seduced girls of their own class, and only rarely did even ardent young women 'go all the way' without some hint or prospect of marriage. But where was one to turn for sexual experience, if not formal instruction? At best, there must always be a first time: but doubtless that moment becomes more difficult if it is too long postponed.

At all events, I was a virgin, and uncircumcised: so there were a few fretful and frustrating months before, on my family doctor's advice, I surrendered my foreskin, and was sufficiently desensitized by the operation to give Sophy eventually a truer if not always adequate taste of married love.

Taking all things together, this was not an auspicious beginning for two young people, one of whom was not yet passionately in love with her partner and not at all sure that this was to become a permanent marriage. During those first months, Sophia sometimes had a wild sense that she had let herself be trapped, and in her shy private fantasies, at least, for not a few years she struggled to break out.

With such a beginning, one might be tempted to head the next chapter 'They Lived Unhappily Ever After.' But that would be almost as false as the opposite sentiment that used to close the commonplace Victorian novel. With rare exceptions, even the best marriages have their ups and downs, their unions and their separations, their strayings in fantasy if not in bed, and their cold fidelities. Yet I distrust the kind of marriage counseling that has become so popular nowadays, on the sound pedagogical grounds that there are some things one should learn by doing, though it might perhaps serve a purpose if it inculcated no more than the notion that thorns grow on the same stem as roses; and that marriage itself, once well rooted, is an all-season rose that may last into winter if properly nurtured and protected.

Yes, ours was to be a turbulent marriage, sometimes tense, sometimes stormy, sometimes dull and sluggish, sometimes ecstatic and radiant, sometimes opening on lazy placid stretches, when we drifted along with no need for a set destination, as we liked to drift in a punt under the willows of the Cherwell at Oxford: an experience that Sophia and I have gone back to again and again, since it is as close to a glimpse of a Theocritean heaven as we have ever come on. But we have had something better than bland happiness as our reward: we have had life itself in all its dimensions, with enough dramatic conflict, joy, antagonism, suspense—and alas! tragedy!—to induce us to stay through the intermissions.

CHAPTER TWENTY-TWO

Innocents
at Large

I

In 1921 a new turn of events was bringing back into focus the literary career I had almost lost sight of during my scrambling effort to pick up a few journalistic crumbs by random contributions to 'The Freeman' and 'The New Republic.' With youthful audacity and without any special preparation, I found myself approaching Horace Liveright, then perhaps the most venturesome of the newer publishers, with a proposal for a book on Utopias.

The suggestion for such a book had come to me recently from Van Wyck Brooks, who had once been tempted by this very theme. I rose to that bait readily, for when studying philosophy with Professor Turner at City College, I had chosen to do a term paper on Utopias. So I had read at least the classic Utopias of Plato, Thomas More, and—to descend from the sublime to the commonplace—Bellamy. Yet in introducing my project to Liveright, I told him I did not mean to restrict the canvas to the classic Utopias—I meant to take in the less obvious ones, like Rabelais's 'Abbey of Thelema'— and even more intangible collective Utopias, like that of industrial Coketown as depicted in the pages of Dickens and Samuel Smiles. Such an historic presentation, I pointed out, would be an examination, not of the actual deeds of men but of their underlying ambitions and wishes; and it seemed to me "that now is a particularly good time to strike this note; for wishes and dreams are about all that we can salvage from the wreck of the Great War. . . . In a rough way, we might divide our contemporaries into those who are feverishly trying to forget and those who are stirring uneasily once more and beginning to dream."

When Liveright returned from a brief vacation, he invited me around at once to discuss the proposal, and expressed his interest by volunteering an advance of three hundred dollars. The spirit in which this whole transaction was effected was so different from that of to-day's publishing that I am tempted to describe it in more general terms. As for the book itself, I don't know who was more foolhardy: the publisher or the author.

Though a taste for Utopias ranging from the sublime to the ridiculous has in recent years become fashionable, in the very act of appraising them I soon lost my own faith in Utopias as guides to future communities or to finer social conduct. Apart from my critical judgments on specific literary Utopias, it was only in my presentation of Coketown, Megalopolis, and the Country House that the fresh turn taken by my later thinking had already become visible.

Still, the most utopian aspect of my 'Story of Utopias' is the actual history of the book, from Horace Liveright's quick acceptance to my equally breathless writing and rewriting of the manuscript between the end of March and the beginning of June. This speedy sketch shows that American publishing itself was then, from the author's standpoint, almost an agent of Utopia! My manuscript was sent to the printer without any preliminary fingering or fudging by either editor or copyreader—though in those days the printer's proofreader was often less respectful!—and I had finished correcting final proofs by the twentieth of July, before Sophia and I sailed for Europe. Today this would be impossible unless a prospective sale of a million copies could be counted on!

Hendrik van Loon's delay in writing the introduction he had promised Liveright may have postponed publication a little, but the book came out in November, when Sophy and I had returned from England, less than six months after I had handed in the manuscript! At no point in this whole process had either the publisher's or the author's feet been entangled in today's sticky red tape. Yet the fact that this book, despite unusually favorable reviews, sold hardly more than a thousand copies the first year did not keep Liveright from publishing my next two books, 'Sticks and Stones' (1924) and 'The Golden Day' (1926). Unbelievable, *n'est-ce-pas*?

2

Fortunately, in 1922, I still had a little money left from my fast-waning inheritance; and we now found ourselves confident enough about my literary future—somewhat prematurely as it turned out!—to be ready to risk what cash remained on four carefree months in Europe. Sophia's status as Editorial Assistant at 'The Dial' made it easy to get such a long leave of absence, as Kenneth Burke eagerly took over her job.

In my book I had divided Utopias into those of 'Escape' and those of 'Reconstruction'—that blessed postwar slogan!—and both impulses proved restorative to our marriage. So much so that Van Wyck Brooks much later recalled in 'The Days of the Phoenix' his earliest impressions of us: "I thought of Lewis and Sophy Mumford as a new Adam and Eve, with whom the human race might well have started, for one could scarcely have imagined a handsomer pair. I always felt as if they had just stepped out of Utopia and were looking for some of their countrymen, astray on this planet, who were also waiting to get back home again."

'The Story of Utopias' served beyond expectation in my own domestic Utopia of Reconstruction; and at the same time my work made it possible to revive the hope we had nourished in 1920 of repeating together my own first private encounter with the Old World. It came about so naturally that neither of us can quite remember how or when—though the 'why' needed no extra support. What better plan for making a fresh start in a private Utopia of Escape? Instinctively we both were resorting to the ancient medical prescription for all pestering but undiagnosable ailments: *a long ocean voyage and a complete change of scene*! The new one-class 'President' steamers, ten-day liners, moderately priced, worked in with our plans, too, for we could afford an outside cabin for two on A deck.

Naturally in sailing on an American ship we did not leave America behind: but the advantage of a slow one-class passage was that we met a cross section of middle-class America, except for the top and bottom layers. Sophy enjoyed the novelty of just being on board a ship, of topping dinner with a Benedictine or a glass of port—our country being then in the transition stage from theoretic abstinence to barefaced bootlegging and boozing. Even when heavy seas sent most of the passengers cowering to their cabins, if not hanging over the rails, Sophy strode the decks like the all-weather Nike she was, and shamed me by her unfailing appetite at every meal.

Despite my unsailorlike upchucking, I must have enjoyed most of the passage, though it was years before I became quite so outrageously immune to the ship's rolling and dipping as Sophy. In the middle of the voyage I wrote to my mother this account of the impression we had made on the steamer-chair jury on deck: "The gossips are speculating eagerly—one of our acquaintances tells us— as to whether or not we are truly married; we seem to enjoy each other's company too much to be regularly and properly joined, unless we were on our honeymoon. And we have loudly and resolutely denounced that notion! It's great fun!"

3

We landed by tender in Cherbourg, then a rather quaint provincial seaport town, not the hive of industrial activity it has now become. We had to stay the night at one of those scrummy, once-fashionable waterfront hotels that never expect its overnight patrons to come again. Somehow the image of both of us naked in front of the old-fashioned full-length mirror in our room still remains in my memory, perhaps because I suddenly realized that I had become desperately thin, and that Sophy was more beautiful than ever, except for her new 'debutante slouch,' which contrived to reduce the rondure of breasts before they had become fashionable again. A brief walk along the waterfront, on cobbled streets, lined with gray stone houses and filled with the musty perfume left by many generations, remains central to all my other memories of Europe's ancient towns.

But our railroad ride to Paris lingers too: our first table d'hôte meal in a French dining car, with the then usual delicious omelet—a monster—served piping hot, and fresh almonds for desert, titillatingly exotic, if tasteless. And then Paris, crazy with noise but enchanting, despite our quite disenchanting hotel, the Hôtel de l'Univers et de Portugal. Sophy, whose untutored anticipations of staying at her first real hotel could only have been satisfied by the Ritz, was dismayed over the fusty furnishings of our bedroom, with its seedy blue velvet bedspread, its impossible bolster, its blatant chamber pots, its mysterious bidet. My new friend Walter Pach had recommended the place to us; but we didn't guess then that its chief virtue for him was that it was near the Louvre.

Our first impression of Paris was exciting, for we found that young people like ourselves kissed and embraced as unashamedly on the streets as did the English on their grassy Commons. Yet the population seemed unexpectedly drab. Though the 1914 war had been over for four years, there was a lack of young Frenchmen on the streets, and more conspicuously, the relatives of the dead were still dressed in deep mourning. And alas! few of the women, even the young ones, looked as delectable and chic as we had always believed French women to be.

Except for Dorothy Thomas, our steamer-mate, we were so lonely that we welcomed even the sight of other Americans at the American Express office when we went for our mail. But we had arranged to meet a group of my English friends in the Tyrol, and before we were sated with the Louvre and the boulevards and the Brasserie Universelle, we started off for Austria, a full day-and-night journey. By error we went past Jenbach, the junction town where we were to change for Mayrhofen, and found ourselves in the little village of Wörgl; a name which remains curiously unforgettable though we spent only one night there. Sitting in the garden of the mean little inn, eating a stew, drinking beer, we looked around us at the mountaineers in their leather knee pants and jaunty hats, the very picture of health and well-being, as contrasted with the *morne*, pale-faced Parisians. One of the drinkers in particular, a giant with a square red beard, might have popped out of a nineteenth-century Swiss painting.

Hotel Carnavalet

St.-Germain-des-Prés

Under the Café de la Paix, facing the Opéra

The Oratoire

The next morning we took the branch-line train to Mayrhofen, in the Zillertal, to join our friends; and without even having the sense to acquire alpenstocks we climbed the six miles to the little *Gasthütte*—was it the Alpenrosa?—where in a nearby field the hardy British had pitched camp. We two preferred a pine-walled bedroom at the *Hütte* to a cot in the open, for the nights were cold and the sun never reached this deep valley, surrounded as it was by high peaks on all sides, until nearly eleven in the morning. All the goods that came up here were transported on either donkey or human backs; and whether one passed a native mountaineer or a group of climbers on the road, one always exchanged a "Grüss Gott." As one approached the high slopes on the mountain, that salutation changed into a comradely "Heil!"

A swift glacial stream tumbled over the rocks below our encampment, and beside the rickety wooden bridges that crossed and recrossed the stream were votive shrines in gabled shelters on posts, or fastened to trees, to commemorate one who had been carried away in a flood: often the painted figure of an angel seemed to be pushing the victim back into the stream. I can still hear the bells of the goats on the Alps above us; I can see the leather-faced mountain women coming down with loads of hay on their backs and a sprig of edelweiss in their bosoms; I can hear the whine of a distant sawmill; I can smell the raw pine boards of our room; I can see the tops of the fir trees below on the slippery footpath that wound upward toward the snowy peak of the Alpenhorn.

By inclination, we would have climbed in the mornings and loafed the rest of the day, not too far from our bed in the *Gasthütte*. But under the guidance of Mabel Barker, our vigorously ascetic English friend, reputed to be one of the best Cumberland mountain climbers of her generation, we led a more strenuous life for a few days, climbing up beyond the tree line, ten thousand feet above sea level, where our treacherously smooth soles were a menace, and where we further risked our necks by climbing over the boulders, angular and gigantic, of a terminal moraine, alternating with a go on the slippery glacier. Perhaps our best moment was a brief venture into the gleaming green interior of an ice cave.

After a day and a night of this, we made our way back to the *Gasthütte* by ourselves: only to find on retracing our steps that the part of our journey we had taken in our stride, because a fog hid what lay below, was in fact a narrow, slippery path that wound between a wall of rock on one side and a sheer drop of some two thousand feet on the other. It made our stomachs momentarily churn and we walked that half-mile or so with our hearts in our mouths.

All in all this was an exhilarating experience; but it did not turn us into dedicated mountaineers. And though I have often dreamed of repeating such a modest climb again, just to compare notes with my youth, we have never done so: nor have we sought out similar adventures anywhere else. This memorable sample has sufficed for a lifetime.

4

While the first taste of the Tyrol was still keen, we decided to go on to Innsbruck, the baroque town we had glimpsed from the train, nestling beneath the snow-covered Alps. So we tramped down to Mayrhofen, the rail stop, only to spend five days waiting for the heavy rains to stop.

When, eventually, we reached Innsbruck we found it even more attractive than we had pictured: so I now find it hard to understand why, after just a few days of exploring its arcaded central streets, dominated by the glinting Goldenes Dachl which terminated a vista, we decided to catch the overnight train to Paris, though we had no engagements there to draw us back. But there had been a serious rail washout on the line above which had broken down the regular train service, and we had, indeed, to stay on an extra day. Late the next afternoon, we squeezed into the belated, tightly packed express whose coaches were so overfull that we spent half the journey sitting on our bags in the aisle before we found seats in a third-class compartment—only to be dumped out at the Central Station in Zurich at three the next morning for customs inspection.

Almost as soon as the scattered passengers had settled here and there in the spacious waiting room, we noted an unmistakably British bishop and his entourage already firmly established, pre-empting more than their share of available chairs, in a circle around an improvised tea table, where a kettle was already beginning to boil over a spirit lamp! How much that told us about the British character before we put foot in England!

Perhaps the most shocking, but salutary, experience of our brief sojourn in Austria was the lesson we got in the value of money. To me it had seemed sensible before leaving New York to acquire for convenience on arrival fifteen dollars in Austrian currency. In 1922 Americans were still speculating in German marks and Austrian kronen, expecting a windfall from an early return to 'normal' prewar values. We could not guess that the very Wall Street bankers from whom we bought these kronen, Zimmerman and Forshay, would eventually go bankrupt through making the same mistake. By the time we reached Austria, a few weeks later, our fifteen dollars were worth only three. That caused us furiously to think.

In Austria galloping inflation had knocked all money values into a cocked hat: a bar of Swiss chocolate and a night's lodging at our Bahnhofplatz Hotel in Innsbruck cost the same amount: ten cents in American money. This was a financial bonanza for people who had American or English money. Indeed, a rumor got around in Mayrhofen that those pale-faced English were people on the dole, sent to Austria at government expense to effect a saving and to restore flesh to their bones.

The real economy of the Tyrol was practically on a barter basis; for nominal values disappeared so quickly that services were practically given free, since by the time one's maid or one's waiter could get near a shop, the tip could buy little—if indeed there was anything to buy. So free were these folk then from the obsessions of money that it was almost like living in the blessed Thomas More's Utopia, where gold was used only for chamber pots.

People told stories about the Good and the Bad Nephew. When their rich uncle died, he left them equal shares in his estate. The Good Nephew invested his money prudently in gilt-edged bonds and life insurance; the Bad Nephew spent his inheritance in riotous living, and lazily left the bottles from beer and wine to heap up in his cellar. When inflation overtook them, the thrifty nephew went stone-broke; but the drunkard and wastrel not only sold off his bottles but was able to sell even the paper of the labels to be made into new currency! He was in clover.

We needed no financial expert to draw the proper moral: we resolved thenceforth to put any extra money we might ever have into tangible goods like books, or vivid experiences like travel. We have followed this plan faithfully all through life, and until our second child was born in 1935, I had only my minimal Navy insurance of six thousand dollars to cover Sophia's possible widowhood: indeed, until a pensionless old age loomed before us, we kept a barely sufficient backlog of savings bonds to tide us over a not-too-prolonged illness. When in 1929 my 'Herman Melville' had the good luck to be taken by the Literary Guild Book Club, we resisted all the gratuitous advice of our more knowing friends for investing it, with a sure 15—or was it 20?—percent return, in this rising stock or that usurious second mortgage. The Bad Nephew had taught us a good lesson.

5

Coming back to London and more especially to Pimlico was for me like coming home; and to make it more of a fulfillment of our earlier dream of being together there, we spent the first couple of nights in Le Play House, deserted in August but for Mrs. Long, who would have been happy to keep us there indefinitely if Farquharson, whose room we occupied, were not soon coming back. But Delilah Loch was at hand, and at first sight she and Sophy became friends.

Before we got comfortably settled in a very decent rooming house in Upper Bedford Place, we touched the abysmal bottom of London in a musty room on Doughty Street, not far from the house where Dickens had once lived; and it would have taken Dickens to describe the shabby furnishings of that room, with its mantel shelf cluttered with indescribably atrocious bric-a-brac, every piece of which was, in addition, broken; and the soiled bed cover, over torn gray sheets, damply odorous: with a perfectly Dickensian housemaid, slat-

313

ternly but red-cheeked, to bring us up our breakfast of scarcely edible fried eggs, almost as antique and broken as the bric-a-brac, and not quite rancid bacon. (But Sophy only remembers that the toast was marvelous. How much that tells about both of us!) The London of the poor, Dickens's London, Melville's London, Mayhew's London, Gissing's London, the London of James's 'Princess Casamassima,' I had already come upon before by myself in villainous eating houses. I knew its disheartening smells and tastes by penurious sampling. But a few nights of this place, in the drab, hopeless degradation that lurked behind its still respectable front, solidified all my earlier knowledge.

Our young friend Dorothy Thomas, slender, blue-eyed, twenty-two—already, alas! caught by academic birdlime—despite her curly blond hair and full lips, soon found an apartment for herself in Mecklenburgh Square, convenient enough to the London School of Economics, where she enrolled for an advanced degree. We settled down for the next few months almost as inhabitants rather than tourists, for we had the run of Dorothy's apartment and made it a second home. There I would occasionally unbend from the principle of manly emancipation sufficiently to go marketing in Pimlico for a steak to broil.

In 'The Little Testament' I transposed Dorothy into a big, buxom female, even as I turned Delilah, with fewer changes, into Charlotte: but apart from the charm of a slender feminine body and a tough masculine mind, what author could escape the attraction of a young woman whom he had found on the steamer eagerly reading his own chapter on the city in 'Civilization in the United States'? We had even, at sea, exchanged French lessons from an exercise book, and we had both broken into self-conscious giggles when I read her the sentence: "Show the gentleman what you have."

Far from being jealous of this attraction, Sophy rather encouraged it, and soon I in turn widened Dorothy's circle by adding the people I had met on my first trip. At last Sophy and I had a mixed group of friends.

The months we spent in England might have been more intensely occupied than they were. Foolishly, without having any serious project in view, I took to spending my mornings in the British Museum, vaguely looking into the works of obscure authors. Though 'The Story of Utopias' lay behind me, I still had no firm sense of where I was going, or what I should write next, so that my time was ill spent; and I might better have used it in Sophy's company in the exploration of London. She was, poor girl! wasting her mornings equally, sitting for a time-consuming and quite unrewarding portrait by my all-too-insistent friend Gladys, so that she missed, to her dismay, the only pea-soup fog that happened during our stay.

But there were other moments that were more rewarding. As when Gerald O'Donovan, an Irish novelist, one of Liveright's authors, took us in tow and presented us at one of Rose Macaulay's literary evening parties. In this period everyone still wore dinner clothes at such affairs, and Americans without them, as Sophy and I were, stuck out like weeds in a well-tended flower garden. Miss Macaulay, nothing daunted, piloted us across the room to the only other person not in evening dress and said brightly, "Let me introduce you to Mr. Brown; he's an American too." O'Donovan was much more tactful. When he took us to the theater, in a box, and the same dilemma presented itself, he quietly placed us at the rear, where the audience need not be shocked by our impropriety. Though O'Donovan's personal hospitality largely made up for it, the London we met in 1922 was far icier to the touch than the sociological and town-planning groups I had found in London in 1920.

Curiously I never got to know the English writers of my generation even casually, as I was to know their equivalents quite intimately in America; nor did I seek out any of the older generation of Shaw, Wells, or Chesterton.

As an erstwhile editor of 'The Sociological Review,' I was invited to a conference at Oxford with Sophia—I staying in New College, dining on roast beef and vintage wines, while she was put up at St. Hilda's Hall, where she was fed the usual Women's College pabulum. At the conference I had occasion once more to marvel over both Branford's sociological insights and his utter ineptness in dealing with his intellectual opponents, or those whom he chose to single out as 'enemies.' Yet my most vivid memory of that conference is not

315

of the speeches but of the loud scratch of Sybella Branford's goose-quill pen as she made notes at the secretary's table: that and the handsome, bearded face of John Linton Myres, the classic archeologist, and, not least, young Julian Huxley, then likewise bearded, looking like a handsome Renaissance Jesus. But it was only years later that Julian and his wife, Juliette, became our friends.

From Oxford, Sophy and I, following Branford's advice, went on a walking tour of the Cotswolds, through Witney, where the famous woolen blankets were made, and in those days were still stretched on lines in the fields around the factory to be shrunken and bleached in the open air. Before we started, everyone had warned us against the rains of October, and we had overloaded our knapsacks with extra clothing. But actually we tramped through a blaze of sunlight, staying first at Burford and then at Bybury—William Morris's favorite village—where we almost caused a domestic crisis by innocently asking for wrapping paper and string, so that we might send back to London some of our excess gear. The pleasant woman with whom we lodged the night, for the inn was full, at length found some for us in a neighbor's cottage! We walked on through Circencester, with its Roman relics, and finally landed up, one twilight, in the murky industrial town of Stroud, in a sordid Temperance Hotel, as depressing as our Doughty Street lodging house. But next day we got the soft-coal taste out of our mouths by walking on to Chipping Camden before returning to London.

The Branfords had moved from Hampshire to Hastings, again living in an ill-designed red brick Victorian cottage on the hilly moorland above the cliffs; and the weekend we spent with them remained for both of us a model of tactful hospitality, with complete freedom from compulsory sociability. Breakfast over, Sybella had said to us, "The village is to the right, the sea to the left. We lunch at one-thirty and shall see you then." Later, tea and dinner would bring us all together again for talk. We were as relaxed at the end of that weekend as we were at the beginning—though at no point could anyone ever accuse Branford of being a relaxed man. And while Branford was still hopeful about getting me to help Geddes organize his ideas in some readable, publishable order, there was no longer any question of my coming back on 'the Sociological Review.'

Meanwhile, the twelve hundred dollars we had set aside for our trip was dribbling away faster than we had counted on, but nothing daunted, we cabled Sophia's brother Philip for a loan and stayed on for the full time, neither of us feeling there was any reason for an earlier return. All in all, this break had served us both well.

Our long sojourn away from New York and all its associations had firmed and widened the common ground on which our marriage stood, if only because it opened up a world that began in some measure to correspond to our hopes and ambitions, now increasingly Sophia's as well as mine. For four whole months we had lived together closely, week by week, day by day, almost hour by hour; and both our mutual affection and our knowledge of each other's character and life experience had deepened. Yet eventually we found Auguste Comte's dictum still true—that a whole lifetime in marriage is hardly enough to enable two lovers to know each other. Even at the end, we both can testify from the perspective of our later years that surprises, both delightful and disturbing, may still be in store!

CHAPTER TWENTY-THREE

The Disciple's Rebellion

I

As the reader knows, I did not actually meet Patrick Geddes in the flesh until the spring of 1923, but there were many premonitory tremors and quakes before we met, for our correspondence became more frequent. As early as 1919 he had suggested that I collaborate with him in writing a book about contemporary politics: one of a dozen volatile suggestions for projects that never came to fruition either in my mind or in his.

In 1920, early in my stay at Le Play House, Geddes had cabled Victor Branford of his imminent arrival; his coming, in a matter of days, filled everyone there, from Branford down, with eager trepidation and anticipatory anguish. But his work in Palestine, where he was already employed on various planning schemes by the Zionist organization—it was he who selected Mount Scopus as the site for the University and, with Mears, drew up the original plan for it—kept him in Jerusalem.

Then, at long last Geddes decided in 1923 to come to the United States, a place he had not visited for a quarter of a century. He had then left behind, at least in the mind of my old 'Dial' friend, Robert Morss Lovett, the memory of his marvelously vivid talks at the University of Chicago. In fact, everyone who knew Geddes in his prime—including Auguste Hamon, the French biographer of Bernard Shaw—was wont to couple him with Shaw for his brilliant conversation, satiric wit, and quick, sometimes savage repartee. Verbally he was master of the disconcertingly unexpected: so one can easily guess why the gentlemanly Sir Edward Lutyens, finding his imperially monumental plan for New Delhi severely criticized by this unconventional professorial nobody, turned on him with a furious contempt, as Lutyens's biographer would later disclose.

Now Geddes, full of years and experience, felt drawn back to America, partly in the spirit that had governed so much of his life, that of the wandering scholar seeking fresh intellectual contacts, partly to chat with old academic friends, partly stirred perhaps by the hope that his young American disciple would turn out to be the person who, as 'collaborator,' would manage to transform the accumulated thoughts of a lifetime into an orderly, readable form. Then, too, he doubtless looked forward to the refreshment of a new scene and a new '*école libre*,' though the purlieus of the New School for Social Research, then on London Terrace in West Twenty-third Street, with an old red-brick house serving as faculty hostel backing it on West Twenty-fourth Street, could hardly be called a sufficient stimulus, that hot and humid summer, even though an ailanthus-shaded garden stretched between the two street rows.

My friend Delilah Loch, still Branford's part-time secretary, anxiously warned Sophia and me about how we should take him.

> Geddes must be accepted [she wrote], as a good Catholic accepts grief, with an open heart and no reserves, *if* he is to benefit those whom his presence scourges. He will brook no reserves. . . . I have lost much of Geddes from my flights, fears, and reserves. Stop dealing with him when you (or if you) must, but when you may, go with him fully. Don't forget he is an old man and lonely, and the very-most-vicious-cave-barbarian when sad, angered, or thwarted.

Delilah, in the last characterization, was doubtless remembering the terrible moment when she had interrupted a conversation between Geddes and Branford in order to find a much-needed ashtray. Geddes had seared her with contempt for this housewifely respect for ashes and this philistine indifference to the mood of thought, which must not be broken by concern for material arrangements. Delilah's advice was excellent; but it did not make for easier intercourse, nor did it prevent reserves, frustrations, and repeated flights. But in the matter of the ashtray incident I can't resist adding that Geddes had the backing of Emerson, who noted in his 'Journals' (1861): "The vice in manners is disproportion. 'Tis right that the hearth be swept and the lamps lighted, but never interrupt conversation, or so much as pass between the faces of the inmates, to adjust these things."

In the months before Geddes was to arrive, I had tried at his suggestion to arrange a full-fledged lecture tour for him, not realizing how impossible this was in late spring season or summer. But offers from the distant Midwest in May, at fifty dollars a lecture, with expenses, did not attract Geddes, so it all simmered down to a course of specially announced lectures at the New School, and a few dashes to other places: to Washington for a social workers' conference, to Worcester to see his old friend, Stanley Hall, to Cambridge to lecture for the landscape architecture students and compare notes with George Sarton on the history of science, and—for he never lost touch with biological research—to Woods Hole for a week with his scientific colleagues.

My first glimpse of Geddes was at the White Star Pier near Twenty-third Street, on the other side of the customs barrier: a little, narrow-shouldered man, frail but wiry, with a flowing, gesticulating beard and a head of flaring reddish-gray hair, parted in the middle: hot and impatient that warm morning, vexed that I had not gotten a ticket to take me past the barrier, talking in a rapid stream whose key sounds were muffled by the gray thicket of mustache and beard. To my still adolescent horror I noticed, as he turned his head, that he wore no necktie. I feared it might be his regular costume; but discovered later that in the haste of a belated packing that morning he had dumped all his neckties into his bag before he realized that he had not put one on. Still, Geddes's head, with its great crown of hair and the equally bulging crown of the brain case, was reassuring. Even at first glance he seemed thought incarnate.

He spoke with a fine Edinburgh diction, perhaps the clearest and purest English that is spoken anywhere in educated circles: and except when he deliberately imitated braid Scots, there was not, disappointingly to me at first, even a burr in his speech. Yet for a man who relied so heavily on the spoken word, Geddes was guilty all his life of a singular oversight: he had never mastered the art of making himself audible, either on the platform or in closer quarters. He never realized that his beard muffled every sound, and that he couldn't be followed, even if one were sitting close by, without the greatest difficulty. On walks, when he talked in profile, whole paragraphs and chapters were lost on the air. Everyone complained of this obstacle, and there were certainly difficulties enough in following his agile thoughts without this extra handicap: yet no one apparently had dared to bring it to Geddes's attention—or at least could persuade him to change his ways.

I would not say that there was anything willful in this: the sound of one's voice is so much a part of one that few people have the faintest notion of their own speech till a tape recorder, to their consternation, plays it back; and Geddes came before the day of tape recorders. Perhaps the explanation is that he shared his beloved Carlyle's contempt for mere verbalism; but if so, no one except Carlyle ever put that contempt in so many words—or made so little effort to see that those words, when uttered, should be effective. Not heeding my warning, the editors of the 'Survey Graphic' hired a steno-typist to take down Geddes's New School lectures: but the weird product of that effort, though it finally got into print, exacerbated both Geddes and Paul Kellogg. It certainly didn't justify the expense.

Somehow, our companionship got off on the wrong foot; and we never managed to fall in step afterward, though we tried more than once to begin all over again. Geddes commanded all my time that summer, for he had sent me a *pour boire* in advance so that I might devote myself to him during the next few months, instead of deviling at reviews and articles for 'The Freeman' or 'The New Republic.' But neither of us knew how to make use of our opportunity. Partly, no doubt, this was due to my own awkwardness and ineptitude; but also it came from his never taking the time to get acquainted, in the way that Victor Branford had tactfully done in 1920 on my first visit to him in Hampshire. Instead Geddes started out by making a direct demand on me I was so unprepared emotionally to fill that I put up my guard and never thereafter fully lowered it.

On the day after his arrival, in the basement lounge of the New School, which gave out on the garden, he took me squarely by the shoulders and gazed at me intently. "You are the image of my poor dead lad," he said to me with tears welling in his eyes, "and almost the same age he was when he was killed in France. You must be another son to me, Lewis, and we will get on with our work together." There was both grief and desperation in this appeal: both too violent, too urgent, for me to handle. The abruptness of it, the sudden overflow, almost unmanned me, and my response to it was altogether inadequate, not so much from shallowness of feeling as from honesty. For I knew enough of his son, Alasdair, through Branford's memoir and other people's memories of him, to know that there was no essential likeness between us, in temperament or in background, in our modes of life or in our potentialities. If Alasdair's schooling, thanks to Geddes's theory that he could provide a better education at home than anyone could get at school, had been more irregular than mine, he was also inured to a far more varied and adventurous kind of life, for he had shipped for a cruise on a fishing boat, had tramped with a fiddle through Europe, making friends with simple people through his music, and had served as a balloon observer in the War, before a chance shell, dropping behind the lines when he was off duty, killed him.

Though Alasdair had indeed served as P.G.'s assistant in arranging his Town Planning Exhibitions, he definitely had a mind and a will of his own: so that the father's hopes of making him a docile junior partner who would carry through his hundred unfulfilled projects and tasks were unfounded. Those who knew both father and son realized that in this respect the imperious old man was willfully dreaming. He had not actually taken Alasdair's measure any more than, at this moment of paternal adoption, he was taking mine. The pathos of that fearful assumption and adoption was not lost on me at the time; nor have I ever recalled that moment without a shrinking within over my own stilted response.

The effect of this encounter was unfortunately to cover over and freeze up some of the natural warmth I felt toward him. In his need to falsify our relations and warp them in accordance with his own subjective demands, he also gave me a clue to a certain blind willfulness that in some degree, and often at the most inopportune moments, had undermined not a little of his own work. But the lesson I learned then carried into my own life: for when I was faced with a similar grief I was careful not to seek from my students, even by an indirect appeal, the response I would no longer get from my own son.

2

From the beginning our collaboration proved abortive: in fact, it never reached the initial stages of its conception. Yet my sense of Patrick Geddes's 'greatness' survived the whole summer I spent in his company, and if my criticisms of this or that aspect of his thought seem captious, or my admiration stinted, I beg the reader to modify that impression by this broader admission. Much of what I must say about Geddes applies equally, I find, to not a few other men of genius I have known: to Frank Lloyd Wright, for one, and to Adelbert Ames; for in one way or another one must pay for their extraordinary gifts: the very self-absorption that sustains their work, along with a godlike self-confidence, breaks down normal social attachments.

Genius, just because of its originality, tends to be self-isolating; and the less its departures are understood and accepted, the more self-protectively inviolable becomes the resulting solitude, and the more difficult it is to overcome the solecisms that result from this isolation. My mature experience with Adelbert Ames, in the forties, parallels my youthful relations with Geddes.

Back in the thirties, at Dartmouth, when Ames's pioneering researches in optics were taking shape, he had demonstrated to me some of his ingenious experiments that showed—conclusively, I believe—that pure sensations do not register automatically, by a reaction similar to the chemical changes in a photosensitive film; that every sensation is a perception that draws on the past experience and the present purposes of the organism. Whatever the physical conditions, they register only through interpretation, and through the total response of the whole organism. Human value and purpose have played as great a part in forming the 'objective world' as number, sensation, and abstract pattern. All these 'objective' phenomena are refined products of human history, not aboriginal components. On that basis we were in full agreement.

After the Second World War, when I lived in Hannover for a few years, I saw much of Ames, and he then wanted desperately the help of someone who would put his observations and theories into viable literary form: so more than once he tentatively suggested that I might join him in this task. But by this time, Ames had worked his own interpretation into a kind of solipsism: since he could produce illusions at will under experimental conditions, the 'external' world had come to seem an illusion, wholly dependent upon the observer. Reality, no less than beauty, seemed to lie in the eyes of the beholder. The very exquisite shapes of his experiments kept him from realizing that the apparent uniqueness of each person's perceptions resulted from the abstraction of the experiment itself, for by isolating the eye—and usually a single eye at that—he prevented the whole organism from coming into operation as it normally would.

When I tentatively broached some of my doubts to Ames, he shrank back into his private shell: the collaboration he begged for did not in fact allow for any criticism and rectification. Though I asked for the privilege more than once, he never invited me to go through his series of experiments a second time. Despite our underlying agreement, he was not prepared, I realized, to examine my criticism. The criticism that might have helped him should have come at a far earlier stage. Now it was necessary for him to go it alone, or at least accept aid only from those who would take his findings unreservedly. So it had been earlier with Geddes.

I used to come to Geddes at the New School before ten o'clock in the morning, and would leave at four or five to call for Sophia at 'The Dial' for a later dinner, myself usually in a stage of fatigue approaching exhaustion; for this Ancient, who lived, like the ultimate creatures in Shaw's 'Back to Methuselah'—a play published that year—in a vortex of thought, had enough energy to tire out "fifty fast-writing youths" like myself, even if the strain of listening so long to smothered, only half-caught sentences was not enough by itself to drain one's vitality. But unfortunately this daily intercourse did not bring us closer; and I was never alert enough at the end of the day to put down even a fragment of all that he had told me and taught me, though I had had the ambition, before we met, of using this period to gather materials for his biography. He did, of course, tell me much about his past, as he might tell some chance acquaintance in a railroad train or a restaurant; but he was averse to making any systematic effort to review his life: "Time for that later," he would say, and by later he meant after he was dead.

To show how closely Dewey's educational influence had paralleled his own doctrines, I took him one day to my friend Caroline Pratt's City and Country School in West Twelfth Street. I had expected him to be enthusiastic about a plan of education that shied away from abstractions and verbalisms and even delayed reading till need and interest turned the pupil toward it: a plan, moreover, that sent groups of children out to various parts of the city to explore its daily life and recapture it in paintings, blocks, and stories. Was this not Geddes's Regional Survey realized in education?

To my surprise, Geddes fastened, instead, upon what he considered a radical weakness—the absence of any firsthand contact with nature, in plants, animals, museums, and gardens, and made such swift scarifying criticisms that after this I hardly dared to introduce him to any of my other friends. Fortunately, his contact with my fellow members of the Regional Planning Association of America, on his long weekend at the Hudson Guild Farm, had proved memorable. We all retained a picture of him, sitting cross-legged, like an Indian guru, under a great oak, which almost turned, under the spell of his stories, into a banyan tree, telling us about his town planning in India—and how as 'Maharajah for a day' he had banished the plague from Indore.

Somehow, it is symptomatic of the strain and tension that existed between us that, after promising to spend a whole Sunday afternoon with my wife and me in our little apartment on Brooklyn

Heights, visiting our home for the first time, he entirely forgot the engagement and never even phoned. Characteristically, he was always forgetting engagements, or making two or three for the same hour: but he and I both realized that this particular oversight, on a day when he had nothing else on his calendar, was a Freudian slip. I was annoyed, too, that the one day we visited the American Museum of Natural History together, it was for the sake of two young sons of a chance acquaintance he had met at a dinner party, not for my sake. Had I given up a summer of my own time, just to take the leavings of his days? As you see, there were two demanding, self-absorbed egos to reckon with.

3

Frustrated, indeed exasperated, I felt the time had come for a show-down. So finally, early in July, I stayed away and wrote him, not without trepidation, the following letter: ". . . In one sense, I have the feeling that we have yet to *meet*. We both have been aware of the obstacles to meeting: but it is rather hard to climb over them, partly because of the gap between our generations and our varieties of secular experience, and partly because my respect for you is so great that it reduces my mental reactions in your presence to those I used to feel in the presence of my teacher when I was twelve years old—that is, complete paralysis!

"Putting this last matter aside, there is a real barrier to understanding between us in the fact that you grew to manhood in a period of hope, when people looked forward with confidence to Tennyson's 'great world spinning forever down the ringing grooves of time'; whereas I spent my whole adolescence in the shadow of war and disappointment, growing up with a generation which, in large part, had no future. Your pessimism about the existing state of civilization as portrayed in IX [one of Geddes's diagrams] does not prevent you from still working eagerly at the problem of the transition to 9 because your own career still has a momentum acquired under an earlier period of hope and activity; and so perhaps you don't realize the paralyzing effect of that pessimism, which is inherent in the situation, upon those of us whose personal careers have not yet acquired any momentum.

"Rationally speaking, there is as much chance of doing good work today as there ever was; rationally speaking, a work that is worth doing is worth doing for itself without regard to the possible mischances of war, famine, or whatnot; rationally speaking, all the interests that we had acquired before the war are just as important and as valuable as they ever were. True enough: but something of the impulse has gone; whatever one's conscious mind accepts is not strong enough to stir the unconscious; our efforts are no longer, as the saying is, whole-souled.

"If I found this bitter sense of futility in myself alone I should be tempted to attribute it to an unsatisfactory personal experience; quite the contrary, however, my own career has on the whole been a happy and eventful one; and the forces which undermine its satisfaction are at work in almost every intelligent and sensitive person I know between the ages of twenty-five and forty. Those who are younger than I am differ from my generation in the sense that they are 'realists' who have no hope for the morrow whatever and no faith or interest in the polity at large; whilst those who are over forty are still living, as it were, on the capital acquired during the days of hope, and if their store is rapidly running out they manage to scrape on from day to day. Our sense of a 'calling,' our sense of any one task to which we could profoundly dedicate ourselves, is gone; and until we can recover this sense a certain intensity of devotion to our professions is the only thing that prevents our lives from being altogether inconsecutive and dispersed. I have fought against this drift of things from the very moment I detected it in myself; but it is like trying to lighten one's bosom of the pressure of the enveloping air; and I see no way of healing the crippled psyche except by trusting to some slow and obscure process of cure. It is no use saying, 'Be different!' For we are like the sick man that Saadi mentions whose only desire was that he might be well enough to desire.

"You came over to America, without, I suppose, any sufficient awareness of this change which, apart from any mere difference of age, separates a large part of the younger generation from the older:

you came over, too, with a somewhat over-idealized portrait of me in your mind, as a vigorous young apprentice who might work at the same bench with you for a while, and keep on at the task when you had gone back from America. You are naturally disappointed to find me bound up with literary vocations, and to find that by natural bent and by training I am of the tribe of Euripides and Aristophanes rather than of Pythagoras and Aristotle; a trait which is, possibly, a little obscured by the fact that mere necessity and convenience oblige me to get my living, from day to day, with the Sophists of journalism. Faced with an actual me, you have naturally tried to make me over into the idealized portrait, whose aims and interests and actions were more congruent with your own; and, instinctively, I find myself resisting these frontal attacks, although my defenses have again and again fallen down before unpremeditated movements on my flank!

"In the light of this difficult adjustment between the Ideal and the Actual, it would not be at all surprising if the original portrait had turned into a Caricature—that of a clever young hack writer, rather sullen in temperament and unamenable to conversation, who had no other interest in life than that of turning out a certain number of sheafs of copy per diem. The inability of this creature to follow your talk for more than a couple of hours at a sitting you could, in the light of caricature, attribute to a lack of interest or—worse still!—to a general lack of synthetic intelligence, whereas it is only the obvious reaction of a thorough visual to an auditive method of presentation. And so on.

"Plainly neither the ideal nor the caricature corresponds to the real creature; and one of the things that has hindered our work together is, perhaps, that you began with one and shifted to the other, without our ever having (except in passing moments quickly forgotten) the chance to meet. If instead of thinking of me as a quack journalist you'd conceive of me rather as a young scholar who publishes his notes and lectures instead of speaking to a class: and if you'd see that I have chosen to get a living in this manner because it is for me the one means by which I can work at my own pace and keep at least a third of my time free for thinking and studying of a different sort, there might still be a little exaggeration, but towards the truth. Eutopitects build in vain unless they prepare the mind as well as the ground for the New Jerusalem; and nothing you have said has shaken in me the belief that the best part of my work must be in the first field rather than in the second, although it may be true that I shall do the first task more sanely and adroitly if I have had a little direct experience of the second; and I have so far admitted this as to go ahead with the plans of the Mohegan Colony. . . ."

In his reply Geddes rose to the occasion, as he so often did at critical moments, with overwhelming insight and magnanimity: not angry, but sorry over his own apparent failure to 'take me in'; realizing "only too sadly" the gap between our generations: his, heady even now with the hopes of endless progress through science, technics, and education: mine, war-shocked, disillusioned, discouraged, unconsciously anticipating the even more formidable barbarisms that were to follow. At the end he emphasized his interest in my development "as no mere exponent of mine." How that latter admission reawakened my love and admiration!

When we again came together, we had one illuminating, almost ecstatic day, which I recorded in my notes. But then, alas! he fell back once more into the old soliloquy, and repeated once more the old irrelevant demands, wanting me to take over this or that half-finished theme as a "legacy" from his "mingled heaps," ideas he himself, he knew in his heart, would never put together in any viable form no matter how long he might live. As the moment for his departure came nearer, our relations got even worse: I kept asking for the living kernel of his wisdom, and he insisted that I should swallow a heap of husks. Though I tried hard for a while to treat the latter as food, I could not deceive myself. He himself had taught me the difference.

Only now, looking back, do I realize all we might have done together. Had we spent some part of our days rambling in Central Park, dropping into the menagerie, revisiting the Museum of Natural History, or exploring the historic images and symbols in the Metropolitan Museum of Art, these shared experiences might easily have evoked by association the richness of Geddes's own mind, once he allowed it to roam freely outside his graphic enclosures. But from having hoped for too much from me as his 'collaborator,' he still had, even after meeting me, the same curiously constricted view of my interests and capabilities, which he had exposed in a letter I discovered when sorting Branford's files in 1957.

"I hope," he wrote Branford then, "Mumford does not feel I want to make a planner of him or biologist: no such idea: what I suggested was that with his vivid writing he might easily get the United States public to understand the use of Civic Exhibitions." When I came upon this letter, I was dismayed, indignant—and saddened. Civic exhibitions indeed! It was emphatically in biology and city development that he had something unique and personally valuable to pass on to me. What I have learned about cities did not come from his Cities Exhibition, for I never saw any part of it. Nor did it spring from conning his graphs or memorizing his categories. How blind Geddes was not to realize that from the beginning it was in biology that he had made his most lasting contribution to my education—and even more profoundly to my life.

For all this, that summer had some good moments, brief but memorable. Though my direct contact with Geddes was confined to such a short period, nothing that he had written or correlated in graphs had an influence on my thinking nearly as profound as he in his own person had on my life. Among books, Plato's 'Republic,' Emerson's 'Journals,' Whitman's 'Democratic Vistas,' Melville's 'Moby Dick,' Ruskin's 'Munera Pulveris,' Zimmern's 'The Greek Commonwealth,' Whitehead's 'Science and the Modern World,' to mention only a handful, left a deeper impression on me than any single work of Geddes's. But the impact of his person shook my life to the core.

The most impressive thing about Geddes, even at sixty-nine, was the sense he still conveyed, as Branford did, too, of what it is to be fully alive; so it was not a surprise to me, though it was a scandal to some of his friends, to find him at seventy-three, taking as his second wife a woman considerably younger. He was seeking something more, I have reason to believe, than mere companionship and care. And it was by this magnificent aliveness that Geddes towered above those around him.

Gladys Mayer was right. Blake would have understood Geddes, but Bentham would not have; for even Geddes's old-fashioned rationalism—and he had not a little of that—was too impassioned to satisfy its classic later exponents. "I and mine do not convince by arguments: we convince by our presence." If Geddes had only accepted that dictum of Walt Whitman's more fully, he might have conserved for better uses some of the time he actually frittered away in his endless graphic demonstrations and arguments. His presence was what counted; and if there had been long periods of silence, interspersed with longer periods of listening, it might have counted more!

It was true that the very intensity of his vitality, its exorbitance, made impossible demands upon those about him. Even the New School itself, under the shrewdest of directors, Alvin Johnson, found it impossible to contain this explosive personality. Johnson, I should explain, had rather grudgingly offered Geddes the temporary use of a guest room, till he should find more permanent quarters; but since his bedroom would remain vacant, Geddes saw no reason why he should leave it: he was quite content with the house and the rear garden and Professor Harry Dana's companionship, and had no mind to change them for a less congenial settlement house or a hotel.

So Geddes had not merely stayed on all summer, but had taken possession of the academic quarters of the school, room by room, opening up the bales of charts and diagrams he had sent over in advance, and spreading out his papers. For Geddes loved to work on large tables—he said this was the aristocracy's secret of mastery!—and here he had as great a space to work on as in the Outlook Tower. In short, Johnson found that he had a scientific Bartleby on his hands, as loquacious as Bartleby was silent, but just as difficult to dislodge. Yet with all this paraphernalia of preparation, nothing came of Geddes's graphic demonstration: it was mere gymnastic. The unformed theses, the unwritten books, mostly remained unformed and unwritten.

It would have been flattering to think that Geddes had brought his boxes of graphs and charts over for my special benefit: but the truth is that they were a standard part of his travel equipment, like the cabinet of medicines an invalid dares not leave behind, even if he never touches one. But since I was present, Geddes took advantage of the opportunity; and it was in one of the New School classrooms, hung with charts, piled with memoranda, that my sense of frustration came to a climax, just a few days before Geddes sailed. I still smart over the feeling of rebellious humiliation in my breast—I was then almost twenty-eight—when he demanded, while he was busy elsewhere, that I spend the morning setting down on the blackboard, one after another, all the graphs and charts of his that I had mastered, including not a few that I rejected entirely.

That exercise made me feel as if I were back in elementary school again! But I had lost my old docility, and though I went through this exercise grimly, and did it thoroughly enough to earn his approval on his return, I never felt further from him than at that hour. This was the complete antithesis of the bold, challenging, insurgent, vitalizing mind that I had been drawn to: as autocratic, as tyrannously Teutonic, as that of Carlyle. Secretly I still looked forward, as reward for this final submission, to at least one day of his undivided attention. But it never came.

The final evening P.G. was in New York—he was to sail at midnight—he had made an engagement to have dinner with Lillian Wald and the sisters Lewisohn, as I remember; and he left to me the dreary task of packing his bags and papers—those heaps of clothes, those middens of notes and charts, those shelves of new books! An English artist, Stephen Haweis, who had long been influenced by Geddes, dropped in for a last chat, and he, too, was disappointed at finding the master absent. Years later Haweis recalled to me the remark I had made then, in the midst of my packing: that it was like putting the contents of Vesuvius back into the crater after an eruption.

By the time eleven o'clock came, I was tired, and too sick at heart to retain the reproachful fury I had felt earlier in the evening. When Geddes came back, I found a taxi and put his bags into it, but I refused to accompany him the few blocks to the pier. For a moment, he began to protest and urge me, but he must have sensed my bitter disappointment, for he let me go. We shook hands hastily on the sidewalk and the taxi rolled off. Though we met briefly in 1925 and corresponded at irregular intervals up to the month of his death in 1932, this parting was really our final one.

CHAPTER TWENTY-FOUR

Regional
and Dramatic Sallies

I

By 1919 my private surveys of cities and landscapes, beginning with
my native habitat, Manhattan Island, and extending to Boston, Philadelphia, and Pittsburgh, ceased to be lonely. Gradually I found myself drawn closer to a circle of professionally trained people who
shared my interest in the entire human environment, and sought
not merely to conserve its visible beauties but to do justice to our
fuller cultural potentialities in the planning and building of cities.

Even before 1918 I had somehow stumbled upon the 'Journal
of the American Institute of Architects,' for already its editor, Charles
Harris Whitaker, had opened its once impeccable pages—until then
filled with graceful descriptions of the historic monuments of Europe, unsullied by any contemporary innovations in building—to a
series of articles on the new war housing for munitions workers in
Britain. Though my bold but inevitably amateurish designs for the
'JAIA' Housing Competition in 1917 had naturally failed to interest
the judges, this did not keep me from submitting to Whitaker early
in 1919 an essay entitled 'The Heritage of the Cities Movement'—an
historic survey partly cribbed from Branford and Geddes.

Whitaker's prompt publication of this paper led to my dropping
in on him at the fine old Octagon House in Washington—now en-
shrouded by a presumptuous complex of office buildings—on my
first visit to that city in 1918. This was the beginning of a friendship
that opened many avenues to my early career and presently made

me as much at home among architects and urban planners as among writers and editors. When in 1920 Whitaker moved the 'JAIA' to New York, I found myself in easy contact with other kindred spirits he had attracted, though they were older than I by at least a decade or two.

As yet I had few visible gifts in either writing or the graphic arts, but from the time I was eighteen on, I never went for a walk alone in either city or country without a haversack, a pad for taking notes, a sketch block, and sometimes a camera. Long before I responded to buildings as practical or symbolic constructions, I was jotting down my visual impressions of rooftop watertanks, sheetiron cornices, spindly tenement fire escapes—or chance human figures. My early watercolors now tell me that two great structures made a profound esthetic impression on me. One was the original rough-hewn 'Romanesque' form of St. John's Cathedral, whose low dome then dominated the crest of Morningside Park: the other was the contrapuntal dynamics of steel and stone that characterized the original Brooklyn Bridge, before its lines were marred by Steinman's motor-road beneath.

From the outset my unacademic habits of mind broke through departmental isolationism: so I valued architecture and engineering, not just for their practical benefits and achievements, but as fresh esthetic expressions of modern culture. My brief essay 'Machinery and the Modern Style,' published in 1921, antedated the English translation of Le Corbusier's more authoritative exposition of the esthetic potentialities of stripped machine forms, which appeared in 1927. Later, in the Bampton Lectures at Columbia University in 1951 (published as 'Art and Technics'), I developed these complementary ideas more fully.

Reviewing my oldest memorabilia, it now seems to me that intuitively, certainly unwittingly, I was preparing myself for a new, still unidentifiable and unnameable career: one which at first could be described only in negative terms, since it involved at one point or another, a more active interplay of human capabilities than was envisaged by any closed system of formal or specialized education. Actually, it has taken me a whole lifetime to single out, to assemble, to evaluate, to reorganize, and to integrate the varied components of my own education. That, in fact, is what this whole autobiography is about: *the ways and methods and goals and meanings and rewards of a lifetime education.*

Yet, as I look back on my development, certain seminal ideas had already been implanted before I could anticipate their future significance. Witness a Random Note dated 1919: "My present interest in life is the exploration and documentation of cities. I am as much interested in the mechanism of man's cultural ascent as Darwin was in the mechanism of his biological descent." Once anchored in my mind, this idea took many different forms.

As early as 1916 I had already begun to absorb the key texts that were to inspire the leaders of the Regional Planning Movement in America and Britain: Geddes's 'Cities in Evolution' and—even more formative in some ways than Geddes's papers—Ebenezer Howard's 'Garden Cities of Tomorrow' and Kropotkin's 'Fields, Factories, and Workshops.' This new social vision was translated in an essay I wrote in 1917 entitled 'Garden Civilizations: Preparing for a New Epoch.' Therein I observed that the "amorphous, shapeless, bloated, unbounded Mass City that we know so well today seems destined to go the way of those saurian monsters which once encumbered the earth. . . . The statistician who figures that the population of New York City fifty years from now will be twenty million has counted the census reports but he knows nothing of that movement toward decentralization which is not only carrying manufactures from the old centers of population, but will also, perhaps, through Garden City projects, carry populations with them."

One of my most significant departures was also one of my earliest: an extensive note, 'The Function of the Philosophic Mind,' which dates back to 1916. Though the tone of this note was light and quizzical, it dared to raise the ultimate problem of philosophy, the Meaning of Meaning, which at length either leads one to the Meaning of Life—or annihilates everything, including nihilist attacks, from Hume's to Sartre's, upon both meaning and life itself. It was only when I reprinted that note in 1975 in 'Findings and Keepings' that I at last realized how basic it has been not only to my early thinking but to my entire development.

Far less impressive in itself, but immediately more significant, is a long-forgotten memorandum I recently found on a half-sheet of manila paper in a 1921 folder of letters, unidentifiable as mine but for a single passage which contains the words "High Street, White-hall, and the British Empire," for that shows it was written by me after my sojourn in Le Play House in 1920. The opening note deals with the historic background of cities: *I. The Pageant of Cities in History. II: Where the Great City Stands. III. The Role of the Seven Romes and their Overthrow. IV. What the American City Might Be.*

The second note has to do with social and individual development: *I. The Seven Dramas of Life. II. The Olympic Motives in Life. [Influence of P.G.!]*

The third note has to do with certain tendencies in American society: *I. Shall New York Rule America? II. Recolonizing America (with ideas rather than people). III. Regional Versus Imperial Development. IV. Prophets Without Honour: Thoreau, Whitman, Poe, Clemens.*

In transcribing these notes now I have not sought to cover up their naïve ambitiousness. What is now more relevant is that they prospected a large part of the territory I was presently to cover in the four fresh interpretations of American culture that began with 'Sticks and Stones' in 1924 and culminated in 'The Brown Decades' in 1931. Whatever else these early jottings may show, it was more than mere literary facility that fitted me to become a working member of the new organization that Whitaker, Benton MacKaye, and Clarence Stein were about to bring to life.

2

Now back to the beginnings of our Regional Planning Association. Soon after Sophia and I returned from Europe in the fall of 1922, Whitaker introduced me to Clarence Stein, and we two became friends so readily, so inevitably that neither of us could recall the occasion when we first met face to face. Even before Whitaker had introduced us, though, Stein had become aware of my active exploration of the whole urban environment. Possibly what underlay our quick response to each other was the fact that we both had had an irregular academic education and had been frustrated alike by ill health and by inner conflicts in choosing our vocations.

Stein's maturation had been much tardier than mine, for unlike me, he had been too frail as a child for regular schooling, and his first vocational commitment was to Interior Decoration, which he chose to study in Paris. Stein's family had originally lived in Rochester, where his father had made a comfortable fortune manufacturing burial caskets. But Stein was not interested in that form of minimal housing: so finally his sensitive esthetic gifts turned to architectural design.

As with me, Stein's handicaps and delays turned out in the end to be advantages. By 1915 he had designed the new mining village of Tyrone, New Mexico; and with his work on the handsome structures of the San Diego Exposition that same year, he had become the chief designer in the office of Bertram G. Goodhue, then the only American architect who could be mentioned in the same breath as Louis Sullivan or John Wellborn Root, those giants of the eighties.

In later life there was a certain delicacy in Stein's trim figure and fresh complexion which made strangers underrate his abilities and his driving force. With his combination of sensitivity and unflagging energy, Stein was not unlike my Scots friend, Farquharson. And he was like Alick, too, in that he had a rare gift for recognizing and utilizing special abilities in others, along with a facility for directing them into channels of social service.

As if to compensate for the delicacy of his appearance, Stein had a taste for smoking heavy black cigars, coupled with the masculine trick, once dear to city editors and politicians, of talking without removing the cigar from his mouth. This common touch perhaps lessened the social gap between Stein and Al Smith when the latter became Governor of New York. Smith not only fathered Stein's proposal to create a Housing and Regional Planning Commission for the state of New York, but in 1924 made Stein its Chairman. That masterly stroke was the first American recognition of the need for a coherent policy in housing and environmental planning.

Shortly before this, in 1921, Stein had been made Chairman of the new Committee on Community Planning of the American Institute of Architects: then an unprecedented architectural innovation in both its scope and purpose. Stein took advantage of his post by promptly publishing in the committee's department of the 'JAIA'

337

Benton MacKaye's proposal to link together a fifteen-hundred-mile walking trail between Maine and Georgia: the now famous Appalachian Trail.

No single member of the group that in time became the formally organized Regional Planning Association could have embarked alone upon these ambitious and far-reaching efforts to overcome the limitations of contemporary urban thinking. Without Whitaker's receptive response to MacKaye's proposal, it is indeed doubtful if the manuscript would ever have been published, or if published, would have enlisted so many sympathetic collaborators so soon. Moreover, without Stein's new department in the 'JAIA,' our ideas would have lacked professional authority and backing.

Actually it was the providential conjuncture at the right moment of Whitaker, MacKaye, Stein, and—I must add—myself that produced a kind of fusion reaction that released energy and light. Where two or three are gathered together something happens that no individual ego, however inspired, knowledgeable, constructive, or imperious, can bring into existence.

3

Our first formal meeting coalescing as a recognizable group took place in the office of Robert D. Kohn, a close associate of Stein's, who had already left his unmistakably masculine stamp on a few distinguished pre-1920 buildings, notably the offices of 'The New York Evening Post' in Vesey Street and the new Meeting House of the Ethical Culture Society.

Besides Whitaker, Kohn, MacKaye, Stein, and myself, our founding group included Stuart Chase, by profession an accountant: John Bright of Philadelphia, Frederick Lee Ackerman of New York, and Henry Klaber of Chicago, all socially motivated architects: Frederick Bigger of Pittsburgh, an urban planner; A. L. Bing, a semiretired capitalist who had made a fortune in real estate and was now ready to take the lead in experiments to improve housing for the lower-income groups; and Henry Wright, who was perhaps the best qualified member by virtue of his wide professional training as a landscape architect and community planner, and his varied regional experience in Kansas City, St. Louis, Philadelphia, and Ireland. In our early days we also included Nils Hammarstrand, whose scholarly studies of historic cities in the 'JAIA' were then outstanding.

Though at this first meeting we adopted a neat, formal constitution, it served only as a point of departure—a method of selecting and inducting new members. Our Manhattan meetings with accessible members at lunches or dinners were so frequent that we habitually worked toward an inner consensus rather than a formal show of hands. Before long we added Mrs. Edith Elmer Wood, a hardheaded critic of low-grade standardized housing for underpaid workers: while thanks to MacKaye's personal relations with 'The Survey' staff, Robert Bruere and Dr. J. K. Hart, a loyal exponent of John Dewey's philosophy of democratic education, soon rounded out our group.

Though from time to time we invited potential members to our major conferences, I doubt if we ever could count more than twenty active members. Our last important accession came in 1931, when young Catherine Bauer joined us, soon becoming our Executive Director and Research Assistant to Stein. This was before her critical talents in promoting modern architecture and housing had won her the title that our German colleague, Walter Curt Behrendt, bestowed on her, with a friendly twinkle: "Catherine the Great."

Although Whitaker's diverse intellectual interests had already engaged some of us, it was Stein who used his Community Planning Department in the 'JAIA' to marshal us together and put us to work; and he did this with the skill of a resourceful general deploying a limited number of troops to take over a large territory. So as early as 1923 I found myself received as an equal—actually also as Executive Secretary—of the new organization we formally called the Regional Planning Association. Our cumbrous title was an effort to separate our aims and proposals clearly from those of the Russell Sage Foundation's quite different conceptions in its many-volumed study, 'A Regional Plan of New York.'

I have named and identified our membership for a definite purpose: to show how few we were, how diverse our cultural interests and our professional qualifications, how experimental our approach, and how modest our personal claims. Whatever the range of our abilities, there were no prima donnas in this original group. In spirit we answered to Aristotle's definition of a good society: "a community of equals, aiming at the best life possible." And at no later point were we tempted to enroll a large national membership, with a permanent paid secretary, a limitless, nonselective mailing list, and heavy endowments from rich individuals or great corporations. Far from it! Our efforts were helped rather than hindered by the fact that we never had more active members than could meet comfortably in Clarence Stein's New York apartment.

4

Before going further with the activities of our Regional Planning colleagues, let me say a word about my new friend Benton MacKaye. Certainly it was no accident that the man who fathered the Appalachian Trail was a lean, wiry Yankee, the youngest son of the famous actor, dramatist, and theater designer, Steele MacKaye. Benton had spent his early years in New York, but when he was eight, his family moved to Shirley Center, in the New England of Benton's ancestors, much as Robert Frost had been taken back East from his early urban habitat, San Francisco.

As so often happens with the twice-born, Benton became more of a Yankee than the purely native breed. With his eaglelike profile, his black hair, his gift for picturesque epithets and oaths, his campfire stories, he seemed the archetypal Yankee—almost the stage Yankee. Though he once confessed to me that he had never read Thoreau until he came upon him in the pages of my 'Golden Day,' he figures in my mind as Thoreau's close continuator: tart as a wild apple, sweet as a hickory nut—though to more Philistine minds he often must have seemed, in Benton's own lingo, "as wild as a wolf, as crazy as a loon."

Like Thoreau earlier, MacKaye had studied at Harvard at the beginning of this century, under Nathaniel Shaler and William Morris Davis; and one of a dozen things that brought us together was the fact that I, too, was familiar with Shaler's dynamic formula, *"structure, process, and stage,"* and had equated it roughly with Geddes's "organism, function, and environment." After teaching at Harvard a few years, MacKaye had joined the Forestry Service during Theodore Roosevelt's second term, thereby becoming one of "Gifford Pinchot's Young Men."

Forestry in those days also attracted other dedicated young men, like Aldo Leopold. The colleagues of Benton I met later all had that fine edge and outline we call character. Most of MacKaye's official time, until the end of the First World War, was spent 'in the field'— or rather in the woods. When he left the Forestry Service, after the early death of his wife, Benton retired into his mind; and though he had qualified for only a small pension, he did not waste his time in making a living, but subsisted, like Elijah, on such fodder as the ravens brought him.

Benton had first discussed his new proposal for the Appalachian Trail at Whitaker's country home in Mount Olive, New Jersey, which was not far from the Hudson Guild Farm, where the social workers from its Settlement House in the West Side Chelsea district had established a vacation habitat for their working-class members. As if their ultimate coalition was preordained, Clarence Stein was taken on as architect for the Guild's new cow barn! No happier mixture of social opportunities and roles could have been found than on the Hudson Guild Farm itself: the very place where the Appalachian Trail, our wider Regional Planning proposals and our new experiments in housing were incubated and broke through their separate shells.

It was here that the members of our Regional Planning Association met one weekend in early April of 1923—a memorable weekend. For our meeting coincided with the monthly Saturday-night Square Dance the local farmers held there, continuing a tradition they had never abandoned. The local carpenter was the caller. We 'outsiders' were permitted to join in; but, alas! we stumbled and fumbled our way through the rounds of the first dance, helplessly laughing at our own awkwardness. But the old fiddler was properly outraged by our behavior. In the middle of the second dance he stopped playing, held up his hand, and called us all to order. "You city folk seem to think this dancin' is fun. Well, it ain't. If you can't get down to business, clear off the floor!"

That just rebuke sobered us up; even better, it improved our manners by making us readier to take our country neighbors and their lingering folkways more seriously. From then on country dancing became part of our weekend conference programs—we even met for it on occasion in the city.

By the most helpful of accidents, the first meeting of the Regional Planning Association at the Hudson Guild Farm that April had coincided with the arrival of Patrick Geddes in the United States. As his unofficial, part-time secretary, I had the honor of introducing him to our group at the opening conference.

Though few of our associates had had any direct contact with Geddes himself or with his varied planning initiatives, they recognized him as the authentic Father of regional planning: so his presence cast a symbolic halo over that first conference. Geddes's insurgent vitality at sixty-nine—before his debilitating illness the following year in India—made even our most vigorous members seem anemic. Despite the desolation produced by his son's death in 1916, followed soon by his wife's, Geddes was still the man who in a few months had dictated his challenging two-volume report 'The Planning of Indore'; and who in the same decade had written his sympathetic biography of Sir Jagadis Chandra Bose, the Indian physicist.

Geddes stayed on at the farm for two days after the conference disbanded, and it was then that a special link between Benton and Geddes was sealed. They took a six-mile walk together to the railroad station to catch P.G.'s train to the city: a walk repeatedly interrupted by Geddes's darting off to the roadside to collect botanical specimens, or further running a risk of missing his train by halting to explain at length, in his special Geddesian dialect, that MacKaye's subject was *geotechnics* and his vocation that of a geotect, not a regional planner! So—and this was characteristic of Geddes, too—they had to run the last hundred feet for him to catch the train!

Perhaps I should add here that I never agreed with Geddes's amendment; and so, when I served as editor and sub-rosa collaborator with Benton for his book 'The New Exploration,' I persuaded him to use 'regional planning' as a more dynamic term that would be more intelligible and useful to both publisher and reader. Benton nevertheless stuck fondly to 'geotechnics' and felt justified when, years later, he discovered the word itself in a new dictionary.

5

While the first meeting of the RPA at the Hudson Guild Farm set the stage for MacKaye's ambitious wilderness project, Clarence Stein and Henry Wright, backed by the financial resources and humane purposes of Alexander Bing, embarked on a series of studies for a small-scale experiment in community planning. To come abreast of British housing and planning they made direct contact with Ebenezer Howard, whose conception of the Garden City was such a radical departure from conventional practice that even Unwin and Parker, the planners of Letchworth, the first Garden City in England, had only partly done justice to Howard's ideas. Today, half a century later, there are still reputed experts in urbanism who have never read far enough in Howard's 'Garden Cities of Tomorrow' to appreciate his most original planning conceptions in the chapter 'Social Cities.'

Without losing time in searching for an ideal site or attempting by legal means to modify New York's obsolete and wasteful gridiron plan of 1808, Stein and Wright went into action at once to see what improvements could be made immediately in the layout and equipment of a small urban community within the New York metropolitan area. Partly because the postwar housing shortage still prevailed, Bing formed the limited-dividend City Housing Corporation, and promptly bought enough acres of cheap waste land in Long Island City, lying between the Long Island Railroad yards and a bleak Catholic cemetery, for immediate experiment.

This was pragmatic idealism with a vengeance! But after a fumbling start with the equipment of the first block of houses and apartments, the social purpose of this new enterprise brought forth human responses which in turn stimulated and guided the designers. By 1930 Sunnyside Gardens, as the community was called, had aleady fostered a diversified social life that even the best one-class suburbs by their very nature lacked.

During this period I developed a closer relation with the whole field of planning and building by serving on the AIA Committee on Community Planning—without salary—as Editorial Secretary. This was a postgraduate opportunity that no existing school could then have offered me. Not only did I attend all the meetings of the committee and become acquainted with a well-sorted group of architects whose day-to-day experience provided an internal view of the whole political and technological process, but I was able to round out their personal memoranda and written recommendations with some of my own hoarded notes about buildings, neighborhoods, and experimental social proposals.

6

What could better reveal the informal, unfettered approach of our RPAA associates than the ultimate effect of his Appalachian Trail proposal on MacKaye himself. Without waiting for any formal confirmation by our members, Benton took a bold step to define our new conceptions of communal and regional planning by discussing with Robert Bruere, then Education Editor of 'The Survey,' a social-workers' review, the possibility of dedicating a whole number of its graphic monthly edition to regional planning. In its boldness and comprehensiveness this was as audacious a proposal as that of the Appalachian Trail itself. Our ideas had scarcely pecked their way through the shell before they began laying eggs!

Though doubtless Benton had mentioned this project to Stein, as far as my records show, it was undertaken entirely on Benton's initiative. Cannily enough, 'The Survey' scheduled this regional planning number for May 1925, to coincide with the meeting in New York of the International Townplanning and Garden Cities Association: the *first* since 1914 to include delegates from the defeated Central Powers. Once the proposal had crystallized, Benton left it to

344

me to distribute the articles among the best qualified members of our group and whip them into shape for publication. My earlier experience had fitted me for this task, for the individual articles needed some editorial cement to hold them together and keep them focused on our common objectives. This was almost a test of their viability.

What a busy period followed! In the midst of it, my mother became critically ill, and for a week I had to spell her nurse by establishing a temporary worktable in her dining room in order to keep pace with my scheduled editorial tasks. They were more various than the reader might imagine, for they included my drawing in pen-and-ink a series of symbolic tailpieces to embellish the text, as well as an impromptu diagram of regional relationships.

To illustrate both the basic problems and our fresh approach to still unexplored opportunities, I recounted the successive states of movement and settlement, of cultivation or mal-exploitation in our country, beginning with our more or less balanced early agricultural settlements, then following the stages of population expansion and technological exploitation and communal dispersal. These past stages, the agricultural, the industrial, and the financial-metropolitan, brought us into the 1920s, and I now suggested that a *fourth migration* had become not only possible but necessary, indeed imperative. *Possible* because of a growing sense of man's actual, age-long role in changing the face of the earth: *necessary* because the wanton waste and misuse of our natural, our racial, and our cultural resources threatened our many potential and conceivable gains. Whatever the inevitable limitations of this thesis, its most serious fault was that it was half a century in advance of current thinking, and in not a few essentials is still ahead.

But proposals in the regional planning number of 'The Survey' made so little impression on our American contemporaries that it never appeared in book form, even after paperbacks had become common, until half a century later Carl Sussman gathered its main articles together in a book entitled 'Planning the Fourth Migration.' This was the title of my critical exposition on our assumptions and proposals.

Halfway through our work on this number, however, Paul Kellogg, the Editor-in-Chief, became a little panicky, for he conceived the function of 'The Survey' to be that of reporting or interpreting visible events or active social movements; whereas our dubious innovation was largely that of presenting nascent ideas and potentialities before they had taken concrete form—still less had been realized: in brief, the ideas of regionalism, not sectionalism, nationalism, or imperialism, of biological, technological, and cultural diversity, not uniformity, automatism, regimentation, and power. None of the significant improvements we sought was yet in existence, though they had been partly foreshadowed in various older cultures. We did not expect that any of our interwoven proposals would be achieved within a single lifetime by following any pat collective formula or doctrine. Kellogg's doubts gave way before our enthusiasm and the 'Survey Graphic' came out with its Regional Planning number. Though at times MacKaye's exposition of his own philosophy might seem a little wooden or oversimplified, it was eventually he, not Whitaker or Stein or myself, who first neatly identified our common purpose in his book, 'The New Exploration,' which came out in 1928.

Though I was qualified to play a special role in widening the outlook of the Regional Planning Association, once our views were sufficiently defined to be carried out in practical experiments with community plans and buildings, with my lack of professional status I could only be an understanding outsider. Yet because I was financially pinched in 1924, I took on Stein's assignment to compile a factual report on European advances in housing legislation. But since this task proved more fitted to the talents of a college sophomore, I thenceforward rejected all similar opportunities. In 1926 I even turned down without misgiving Stein's invitation to redraft more effectively the now classic final report of the New York State Housing and Regional Planning Commission. Whatever I still had to contribute to regional and community planning, my scope, my outlook, and my self-education were not those of a specialist restricted to a single field.

7

These engrossing activities of our Regional Planning program had
diverted some of the concern from that area of my life which centered on Sophia and the peripheral problems of marriage.

During the critical years 1924 and 1925, I was still weighing my
open alternatives as a man of letters and a scholar. At bottom the
choice was between narrowing the field of my interests and thereby,
if possible, getting a sufficient income to support a family; and following my own bent to explore one or another as yet meagerly cultivated area of life that called to me—even if this meant imposing a
severe discipline upon Sophia as well as myself in every part of our
daily round—especially in counting both my pennies and my time.

This was not an easy choice. Heaven knows that until 1927 I still
tried hard enough to get a paying half-time post as editor of this or
that magazine, or to be taken on by a national lecture bureau to be
yanked hither and yon over the Ladies Club circuit, like an actor on
the road doing one-night stands. No, thank you! One taste of that
had been enough. I preferred starvation to such a harum-scarum
existence. Mine was now Whitman's Call of the Open Road and even
more, the Open Mind, ready to explore life in every meaningful
direction.

While I was weighing my various alternatives as a writer, I had
the good fortune to draw from Delilah Loch, my Le Play House
mentor, a letter so understanding that it served to rouse all the inner
resources of my mind.

> I have a very deep sympathy and some understanding
> [she wrote] for your difficulty in getting at the real
> desire or desires of your creative capacity, and still more of
> delivering yourself to the creation born of that desire. The
> sheer need to earn one's living, the presence of little daily
> demands, do most terribly fill up one's hours and leave small
> capacity for worthwhile work when they are dealt with. I
> am not sure whether *fear* is not sometimes an element in
> allowing small things to intervene. The Dionysian demon-
> deity does most terribly rend, tear, and exhaust those whom
> he enters, and knowing this, one may fear a little to submit

to his possession, not consciously, but just putting up barriers to the soul for small things to do. May grace (and cash) be given you to surmount these things and get to your real work.

Bless Delilah! That perfectly timed letter re-enforced such insights as even my early plays and philosophic reflections had already disclosed.

Actually I was turning thirty before I became fully aware of the complexities that life itself was now exposing me to, however I might try to keep myself in check. Po-Chü-i's admonition loomed before me: "Between thirty and forty one is distracted by the Five Lusts." But as early as 1924 this challenge had been awakened by a covey of young women who were now part of our enlarging circle of common friends. In their company I was aware that what began as easy, conversational friendships might sometime burgeon with unexpected provocations and invitations. My impulse to go back to the playwriting I had abandoned was possibly an evasion of 'danger' on my part—an unconscious effort to bypass fresh emotional challenges while projecting in a play some of their subjective inner pressures.

That impulse was probably strengthened by my meeting Aline MacMahon, a young actress of about my own age, at a dinner party in Clarence Stein's family home, where as a bachelor he was still living. Well before this I had become aware of Aline's talents through her dashing performances in the Neighborhood Playhouse 'Grand Street Follies,' where her takeoffs on a series of Broadway stars were sometimes better than the original exemplars. That permanent company was good enough to draw Uptown People to the Playhouse's remote and rundown neighborhood; and all too quickly the Shuberts would recognize Aline's abilities with a handsome Broadway contract, without having enough sense later to pick out a play that would do justice to her ripening talents.

Though that dinner may have been our very first personal contact, I must sheepishly admit that I have no visual images whatever of the evening, or any way of accounting for the impression I made on Aline. What *did* happen that evening? Was I so excited over this chance for comparing notes with a budding actress that I let my

348

tongue run away with me? Did I dare to talk about my early play-writing? Actually more than eight years had passed since the Washington Square Players had been favorably enough impressed by my frothy one-act comedy about Leonardo da Vinci to call me in for an encouraging talk about more suitable future work for them. Did I even mention to Aline my pre-Civil War play, 'The Brownstone Front,' which I had first outlined as a sort of American variation of Arnold Bennett's 'Milestones'? I can't imagine how the slow-moving first act I had written in 1917 could have excited Aline! But even less was I prepared for the result of that evening on her; for the letter she sent me next day simply said: *"Write a play for me!"* Those words were a beautiful thunderbolt.

Until then I had never met such an outwardly attractive and inwardly reserved creature—except Sophia—and one Sophia is enough for any man! Nor could I guess that our brief exchanges, usually by letter, over more than half a century, would retain the same candor, the same detachment, and the same sensitive homage to each other's specific abilities: no more—but no less either—with the passage of time. (If I were a licensed playwright, I think a delicate Henry Jamesian comedy could be made of that!)

In the same private note I jotted down after getting Aline's heady invitation, I was honest enough to admit "I welcome this suggestion, but it comes with an ironic effect, for I have spent the day wondering how far my career as a dramatist was a mere adolescent shimmer, and how far it reflects the inner reality of me. Six or eight years ago this invitation, almost a demand, would not have produced a five-minute quandary: I should have sat down and finished the play—or begun half a dozen plays! Today my imagination lags; and in this lassitude doubts enter. I long for time to squander in free experiment, or in *waiting for some deep emotional impetus.* A play without an impassioned idea—that would be a denial of all my ideal purposes."

And yet—how this timely invitation beckoned me! Before I knew it, the needed emotional impetus had come from within. I suddenly rose to Aline's challenge. Unfortunately I was driven, as a condition for writing anything at all, to wedge the writing of the play into two autumn months. This prompted me to use the too leisurely first act, conceived in the spirit of a romantic idyll, in almost unaltered form.

Aline's response to the finished play when she read it a year later bowled me over. Had she ripped the play apart, thrown half of that wordy first act into the wastebasket, and remodeled the characters or dismissed the climactic final scene as improbable, I would still have been grateful. Her letter showed how closely she had read the script, though, and her actual response was more favorable than the unrevised play deserved. She wrote, "The play is more beautiful than my dreams. And I want to play it more than I can say. I am really in a state of rapture over it. Especially since reading the last act aloud. Alice's speeches are such heavenly theater—the sort that made Mrs. Pat Campbells and Ellen Terrys!" To her credit, these feelings did not override Aline's sense of the theater, for she regretted that the two climactic scenes were shaped in words, not in action. By presenting a purely verbal resolution of the Eternal Triangle I had muffed a flesh-and-blood opportunity.

A whole generation later, long after Aline had married Clarence Stein and so become part of our circle, when her half-time devotion to Hollywood had given her an independent place both as a film star and as a versatile dramatic actress of the stage, she still remembered my bitter idyll, 'Wild Asters and Goldenrod,' well enough to ask my consent to her showing the play to two or three managers who respected her judgment. The response to that still unrevised play was so favorable that one of the possible producers wanted to meet "the young author" at once to discuss revisions. But my mind was so far away from the theater by the 1950s that I precipitately retreated. The young man who had written that play had too long ago vanished. There was no one left with whom a discussion might take place.

Strangely enough I had never shown Aline the long play, originally called 'The Bridge' but now entitled 'The Builders of the Bridge,' I had so effortlessly written on Martha's Vineyard in 1927; for all too readily I had taken for granted that a work that had been tossed off so swiftly needed drastic revision. (How many admirable first drafts, I now wonder, have I in the course of my whole life mottled or spoiled by needless revisions?)

When Aline at last read the printed play, in my 'Findings and Keepings,' her original interest in my potential talent as a playwright revived even more intensely than before. One scene after another captured her imagination, not least the dizzy love scene on the spidery approach to the half-finished tower high above the river. Without hesitation she asked my permission to offer the play to Joe Papp; and he kept us both in suspense for a whole year until he confessed that, though tempted, he could not take it on; it would require at least a year of his time and he was already committed to half a dozen other plays.

CHAPTER TWENTY-FIVE

The Generation of
the Twenties

I

Now I must go back to my early career as a writer, for I, too, belonged to the new generation. Young writers, indeed educated young
people generally—at least the saving remnant!—look back to the
1920s as a time of vivid promise and audacious performance in
American literature. Many of one's contemporaries then—Eliot,
Faulkner, Hemingway, Edmund Wilson—by now have attained,
temporarily, the stature of gods, or at least of Nobel laureates; and
by comparison some of the new figures of a later day seem mis-
shapen, ill-nourished, almost poisoned—as if fed on moldy bread.

Though part of this magnification and beatification is the in-
verted effect of distance, the impression is not altogether false; and
in describing my own part in this decade I shall try to portray those
common interests and attitudes that, for all our diversities of character and background, made us willy-nilly the special 'generation of
the twenties,' quite as definite an entity as 'the generation of the
seventies' in Russian culture.

When I look around my native city for some concrete symbol of
the literary life of the twenties, I find myself centering on a single
street, Thirteenth Street between Sixth and Seventh Avenues. That
street belonged in part to an older era of three-story brick houses
whose passing Henry James deplored when he revisited New York
at the beginning of the century. There was a white porticoed church
in the middle of the north side, dating, as its fluted wooden doric

columns showed, from the early Greek revival, a style which was lingering on into the 1840s; and though the tone of the street had been lowered by a later intrusion of tenement houses, and none of the dwellings adhered to the more delicate ornament of an earlier day on King or Varick Streets, Thirteenth Street still had character.

If one had stood long enough on the sidewalk, one might, some time in that decade, have seen the editors of the monthly 'Dial,' climbing the front steps at 152, next door to an undertaking parlor; or on a Wednesday noon one might have seen a straggling line of editors of the newly established 'Freeman' going to lunch at the nearby Civic Club. In a few steps one might bridge all but the ideological distance between Michael Gold on the 'New Masses' and Henry Hurwitz, the editor of the 'Menorah Journal,' then a vigorous, well-endowed review for which I occasionally wrote. True, the saloon on the southwest corner of Sixth Avenue soon closed, but a quite reasonable Italian speakeasy survived all through that decade. In my personal circle, I must, however, note, speakeasies were reserved for occasional treats, for both our thoughts and our erotic impulses effervesced easily enough without the need for a liquid booster.

'The Freeman' was started within a few months of the new monthly 'Dial'; and Walter Fuller, an old Manchester man, was its first managing editor. We liked each other at once when we discovered our common interest in Patrick Geddes, and Fuller not merely introduced me to Van Wyck Brooks, that shy, bright man, but gave me, just before my first visit to England, what was then invaluable advice about coming to terms with the English.

Fuller had originally been sparked—yes, 'sparked' is the exact word!—by Geddes in the days when the latter held forth at Thomas More's garden in London in Chelsea, after helping to rescue Crosby Hall, More's old City mansion, from the ruthless commercial demolitioners. Fuller was always brimming with ideas, pulling them forth like newborn rabbits from his hat, or darting after them in the air with birdlike eagerness. Though he wrote nothing, he helped to establish in 'The Freeman' the air of urbane catholicity that saved it from becoming what it at first threatened to be, an organ that recognized only one enemy, the political state, and held fast to only one remedy for all human ailments, the Single Tax—both of these the odd intellectual prepossessions of that strange mixture of cultivated sophistication and primal naïveté, Albert Jay Nock.

There was a slight air of mystery about 'The Freeman' from the first, and that air never left it. There were nominally two principals at the beginning, Francis Neilson, an English parliamentarian who had married into the Chicago meat-packing industry, and Albert Jay Nock; but though the first supplied the working capital, it soon became plain whose editorial yes and no counted. Enigma teasingly surrounded this central figure, Nock. Rumor had it that he had once been a professional baseball player; and to make matters queerer, he was also supposed to have been an Episcopal clergyman. There were people who swore they had met him in one or the other role; and by now there is, I believe, evidence to show that they were not fibbing. But these possibilities were surely no stranger than still another rumor, more open to verification: that in 1914 he had been sent abroad by William Jennings Bryan, then Secretary of State, as his personal representative to report back on the political situation: in fact, he had been for Bryan a sort of early Colonel House.

If one considers that sophisticated Tory, Nock, he with his quiet elegance in dress, with his quick courtesies and his wry silences—his tightened lips did all the speaking—in the presence of vulgarity of any sort in manners, in clothes, above all in ideas: what could have brought him so close to Bryan? Since Nock never concealed his abiding contempt for all writers of the sociological school, like H. G. Wells or Sinclair Lewis, and for all political thought that did not rest on the ideas of either Henry George or Franz Oppenheimer—a now almost forgotten German social theorist—this association with the bucolic Bryan seems improbable.

Yet part of Nock's sophistication, as so often happened with Americans of that day (it was queerly true of my friend Thomas Beer, too), was in fact a cover-up for a kind of homespun simplicity. Only the simpleminded could still think, for example, that the Single Tax was a sufficient answer to the age-old problems of wealth, poverty, exploitation, power, injustice; and only, again, a very simpleminded soul could believe that the educational needs of contemporary society could be clarified—and satisfied!—by letting the mass of the population sink back again into illiteracy, whilst restoring to the elite the rigorous study of Latin and Greek.

Surely that was Bryanism of the most hayseed kind, with only a slight disguise and without Bryan's goodness of heart; for beneath all these propositions rested, in Nock, a quite insolent sense of his own superiority over the mass of contemporary human animals, especially those of the liberal persuasion.

Though at first Nock cast a stony eye on me, openly disliking my sociological interests, and looking with even more acrid distaste on my occasional sociological neologisms, he tolerated me in time; so that the greater part of my sporadic work came out in 'The Freeman,' in unsigned editorials and 'Journeyman' paragraphs, as well as in signed reviews and articles: on a few occasions I even took Brooks's place in writing a substitute column ('Ex Libris') for his 'Reviewer's Notebook.' One of them was a then unfashionable appreciation of Santayana's five-volume 'Life of Reason.'

Toward the end of my association with 'The Freeman,' when I offered the early chapters of 'Sticks and Stones,' Nock became positively enthusiastic, and suggested that I drop around to the office and "talk about writing in general." When I accepted his invitation, he asked me whether I remembered his repeated suggestions that someone should write a genuine history of civilization in the United States, and what would I think about undertaking the task myself.

In a stroke Nock wiped out every earlier snub or disparagement in extravagant words I would blush to repeat here, though my original notes lie before me. Nock finished by saying, "I should like to see you do such a book, and if you have a mind to, we can perhaps . . . "—he was thinking of his friend, Sir Edgar Speyer, as a possible angel . . . "find some way of subsidizing you." Much later, he repeated this proffer of aid for a larger work in the same vein as my essay, 'The Buried Renaissance,' published in 'The New Freeman.'

The fact that I never followed up either offer may secretly have nettled him, but my reluctance was not due solely to the magnitude of the task he set before me, a task for which I knew I was not yet ripe: it was also doubtless due to my distrust of such outside financial

355

props, with their tendency to weaken one's self-reliance. I had not read my Emerson in vain; and perhaps I had in addition a certain pride that I had so far made my way without the benefit of even a single introduction—for somehow the various friendly intercessions that *had* been made had never produced any favorable results. But the spirit that prompted the offer sustained me for a longer period than the money would have done; and because of the terms in which it was couched, it may have contributed, with later incitements I shall tell about, to quickening the audacity needed to tackle 'The Renewal of Life' series.

Behind this handsome gesture of Nock's—in later years we drifted apart and he attacked with scathing contempt my antifascist, anti-isolationist position—was the impersonal kindliness that suffused this period. Temperamentally, he felt no closer to me than Voltaire felt toward Rousseau; but this did not keep him from recognizing such abilities as he admired and seeking to further them. Throughout the voluminous correspondence files I have kept, I find this generosity of spirit abundantly reflected in letter after letter, sometimes from my elders, like John Macy, who paused in the midst of a parallel book he was writing to counsel me astutely about 'The Golden Day'; sometimes from my nearer friends, like Van Wyck Brooks, Paul Rosenfeld, or Thomas Beer, the admirer of Stephen Crane and Joseph Conrad.

Insecurity, competitive rivalry, inordinate greed for quick money and flashy publicity had not yet crippled the more generous impulses of our contemporaries. There was a personal trustfulness and helpfulness that sprang perhaps out of the common hope and the common pride we all shared. This partly counteracted our cynicism, our withdrawal, our disillusion. Even when I took a critical attitude toward the ideological postulates of some of those who had helped me, for example, Charles Beard, I could do so with sufficient personal fondness to maintain, until the more serious breach of the Second World War, our warm relations.

Years before Nock's last expression of interest, he gave me one of the best pieces of advice I've ever received, when I confessed that I was trying to make a choice between various posts that had opened for me. "Don't ask yourself which of these jobs seems better to you now," he said. "Before you make any decision, first ask yourself: 'What do I really wish to do? What do I want to make of my life?' If you answer that honestly, you may find, Mr. Mumford, that you don't want to accept any of these jobs. The ideal decision comes first: the practical one will come by itself when that is made." Along with the admonition from Talcott Williams about money, this was the most shrewdly clarifying counsel a young man like me could have received; and I continue to hand it on, confirmed by my own experience, to young people who consult me about their prospects.

2

But I owe still another debt to 'The Freeman': for during those years it brought me closer to Van Wyck Brooks, in a friendship so solid that it survived our sundry intellectual and political differences, some of which flared into quarrels whose flames were smothered only by the love that underlay our mutual respect. That upright, compact figure, of the same Dutch-English ancestry as Melville and Whitman, was a seemingly healthier, solider version of the Brooks I had imagined from my reading of his essays in 'The Seven Arts.' (Yet even then, his alert, birdlike shyness fought with his genuine liking for people and for sociable relaxation.) 'The Seven Arts' had in 1917 assembled many of the leading writers of the next decade and had given a foretaste of the new spirit we stood for: at once unashamedly declarative of our national identity yet equally cosmopolitan. Brooks and Randolph Bourne were the two critics who then made the deepest appeal to me; and though Bourne had died in 1918, Brooks remained loyal both to his memory and to the social ideals they shared.

Now that some of the most daring departures of that period have become commonplaces of history and criticism and daily literary practice, it is hard to convey the excitement that Brooks's early work aroused, or how ice-breaking, as in a spring freshet, his criticisms of our older American idols, even Emerson, then seemed. We could no longer take the American past on hearsay, or feel confident

357

of the good judgment of our elders, who too often favored the wishy-washy genteel. Before we could accept that gift horse, we had to examine the creature's mouth; here Brooks was our leader, and his tense urbane prose sounded like a bugle, advancing at a gallop.

Even before we met, I felt close to Brooks, but his shyness in person provoked an equal shyness in me—though during some of the grimmest passages of his life I was more fully informed about his inner difficulties than I ever have been with any other man. Because of his neurotic breakdowns in the twenties, it was a one-sided relation with his wife, Eleanor, as our intermediary. Our intimacy thereafter was always, so to say, on a family level, which included our wives and children, neither of us giving or taking confidences that we accorded to people who meant far less to us.

This is not to say Brooks did not in the early twenties influence my work. When I was hesitating about whether to return to America from London in 1920, it was not only the image of my future wife, or the need for earning a sufficient income, but Brooks's voice, in 'A Reviewer's Notebook,' that helped to draw me back.

Fortunately the wall that too often rose between us in our face-to-face meetings sometimes became a mere picket fence in our correspondence. A few of our early letters provide pertinent footnotes to the period: particularly those we wrote each other from 1924 to 1926, when we began revaluing and reclaiming an older America—he at first in his 'Emerson' and I in 'The Golden Day.' Quite independently we found ourselves establishing Emerson as the central figure of that intellectually adventurous generation. And it was Brooks's bringing me to the attention of Alfred Zimmern that led to my giving in Geneva the series of lectures that provided an underpinning for my writing 'The Golden Day.'

The fact that Brooks was even then succumbing to a depressing, work-blocking neurosis, marked but not caused by his inability to write a conclusive last chapter for his 'Emerson,' was one of the serious literary disasters of the period: for it left the critical leadership, if one excepts a few writers like Waldo Frank and Edmund Wilson, mainly to socially irresponsive if not reactionary minds, seduced by the poetic talents of T. S. Eliot.

By the time Brooks returned to the scene in 1931, it had become almost a condition of his recovery that he restrict himself to constructive and affirmative themes. In a letter written in October 1931 he held up to me the example of Gibbon, as an incitement to write a far more comprehensive "great, grand, and immortal History of American Culture!" Though he aimed those encouraging words at me, the writer who responded to them was Brooks himself; for only a week later he confessed that this correspondence had reawakened in his own mind an idea he had cherished for years: to embark

Van Wyck Brooks

on a history of American literature in two or three volumes, which he could spend the rest of his life writing.

Curiously, one of the most pregnant analyses of Brooks's achievements, his shortcomings, and his potentialities was made at a quite early date in the essay his friend Paul Rosenfeld published in 1924 in 'Port of New York.' The first part of this critique does ample justice to the sheaf of essays, beginning with 'America's Coming of Age,' that had established Brooks as a leader of the new generation; but already, in touching on 'The Ordeal of Mark Twain,' Rosenfeld detected that Brooks had arbitrarily superimposed an extraneous thesis upon the evidence, and had quarreled with Clemens for not overcoming the negative pressures of his environment—which, in fact, was Brooks's own personal problem. Percipiently, Rosenfeld had recognized in Brooks an indifference to rising contemporary writers: even worrisome signs of spiritual withdrawal. Here Rosenfeld exhibited the kind of imaginative critical discernment that Brooks himself had shrunk from providing. Yet it may be that some of the things that Rosenfeld justly said touched off the desolating sense of failure that haunted Brooks during the harrowing years that immediately followed the writing of his 'Pilgrimage of Henry James.'

With Brooks, as with so many people who have successfully emerged from the hell of a neurosis and the purgation of a psychoanalysis, a valuable component of his youthful self was extirpated during this ordeal. Brooks kept his inner stability by an inexorable routine of reading—a book a day, on top of his writing!—a practice that allowed no time for despairing negations, guilty self-reproaches, or demonic incursions. This routine was so necessary, and it succeeded so well in restoring his composure once he was past the critical danger point that it partly insulated his mind from the evils that were enveloping the whole world. Brooks covered his withdrawal by running for Congress as a Socialist and giving himself nominally to every 'good cause': even, as it turned out, to such a patently bad cause as the League of American Writers.

This self-protecting optimism was perhaps the price of Brooks's health: but it tended to muffle his response to contemporary realities, and even caused him to identify his ingenuous hopefulness with the true American spirit.

I have often praised Brooks's 'Makers and Finders' series for presenting many aspects of American life and thought that no one had ever explored before. His method of drawing on works of the imagination for data hitherto disregarded by the historian was in itself a highly original contribution. Unlike so many of Brooks's academic critics, I still do not underestimate that achievement. This said, I must admit that one may go through the entire series without finding any passage, even when Brooks was dealing with Melville or the Civil War crisis, which reflects, by so much as a passing allusion, the parallel trepidations and tragedies of our own time.

The truth is that Brooks, philosophically speaking, was an

innocent, or what is almost the same thing, a man of the eighteenth-century 'Enlightenment,' entirely at one with its Pelagian assumptions about the innate goodness and rationality of man and the inevitability of human progress. Impatient with those who interpreted the events of our own time in the less sanguine terms of Herman Melville, Brooks was as confident as any of the Illuminati that the power of light, though it might occasionally flicker, was destined to overwhelm the 'Power of Blackness.'

Now, since these hopeful assumptions have been the foundation of a large part of the American experience, they only increased Brooks's capacity to retell American history in the very images and sounds that most American writers—especially the lesser ones—had used up to our own time to describe or express or, all too often, gloze over their own experience. Actually, Brooks's limitations brought him close to this material, and his unique termite facility for extracting nourishment from the cellulose of minor books made up for the inability of his new method to do justice to those great works of art whose very essence is that they transcend "their race, their moment, and their milieu," even while they are making the fullest use of these animating conditions.

Doubtless some of these adhesions and aversions were there from the beginning; for Brooks once shamefacedly confessed to me his youthful admiration for such secondary English writers as A. C. Benson, then popular among the genteel. So his friendships with people of more mordant habit of mind, first with Randolph Bourne, then with me, were instinctive efforts to compensate for something lacking in his early domestic background, though certainly not in his own shattering later experience. As a young man he had severely criticized the pragmatism of William James, put off like so many of us by James's vulgar marketplace metaphors; but his own development, his own breakdown, and his own compensatory optimism curiously paralleled that of this philosopher, as in another way it paralleled that of a more resolutely healthy spirit, Longfellow, who had from an early moment looked into the face of death and evil but had never—except when he translated Dante—been able to make it an integral part of his vision.

Though I have perhaps partly accounted for what a newer generation finds lacking in Brooks's later work, this does not do justice to the fact that he once seemed, as no one else did, to be the central figure—the "little colonel," as Rosenfeld once fondly called him—of contemporary American literature. He was the embodiment of a promise that had hitherto not been visible in any single latter-day writer: the promise sounded in Longfellow's Bowdoin Commencement Address, in Emerson's 'The American Scholar,' in Whitman's preface to 'Leaves of Grass': the promise of an authentic American literature, freed from its Colonial apron strings, not indifferent to Europe or any other culture, but no longer politely subservient and self-deprecating. Brooks occupied that place by sheer force of personality: he was dedicated to literature, as a craft, as an art, as a social responsibility—as men in other ages had been dedicated to religion or to royalty. The writer's task absorbed his whole being, and all other occupations and interests were for him relatively trivial.

Someday a patient student will find a subject for a better Ph.D. thesis than the usual run by tracing Brooks's personal influence on the writers of his generation. When he adds them up, the list of people whom Brooks stimulated, incited, challenged, and aided will probably astonish in its length even survivors like myself: for his interest in other writers, even unlikely ones, was inexhaustible, and his passion for sociable intercourse caused him to give his time all too generously to those who sought him out.

Without any apparent effort, Brooks was a selfless man; and without resorting to the more courtly gestures of politeness, such as our mutual friend Spingarn was capable of, he was likewise the perfect gentleman: reticent about his own affairs, but patiently interested in those of other people; observing all the traditional courtesies for gentlemen from Confucius to Louis XIV, never complaining, never mentioning illness or death; never harsh, never visibly angry, never extravagant in speech, never overbearing, but still immensely at ease with more Rabelaisian characters like Hendrik van Loon or Jo Davidson or Carl Sandburg, with their vulgar humor or hearty obscenities.

In the later years of our friendship, long after the period I am describing, I had more than one occasion to benefit from Brooks's magnanimity; for in 1940 I privately attacked his position, then neutralist, or rather anti-British, on the war; and still later, in 1947, I made an issue of the American Academy's presentation of a gold medal to Charles Beard, the historian, only to realize belatedly that it was Brooks who, again in his utter innocence, had put forward Beard as a candidate.

With people like John Gould Fletcher and Frank Lloyd Wright friendship did not survive similar attacks unimpaired, even when we resumed relations; but with Brooks, his charity, his patience, his quintessential sweetness poured unguents on the wounds I had inflicted. In short, I am tempted to say he was one of those rare men who, by the special quality of their own nature, hold no grudges and make no enemies. But that would not be quite true; for his best qualities made enemies of those who, like James Farrell, lacked them; and, almost comically, in his persistent feuding with T. S. Eliot, Brooks not merely forfeited his own urbanity but lost his critical sense. Brooks so detested Eliot's snobbism, his affectation of an essentially Gallic royalism, his Anglophile identification with the British Establishment, that he failed to recognize Eliot's merits as a poet and critic.

At the moment I write these lines my friend Van Wyck lies at the brink of death: unable to recover from the shock of a whole series of futile surgical operations that have been performed on him for grave cause the last five months. The ruddy, healthy man I have known for more than forty years has wasted away: a frightened child, too weak, nay too appalled for speech, peeps out from under his lifted eyebrows. When our eyes meet, they do not dare to converse, lest they utter a truth neither of us wants to face. Always shy, always distant, he has retreated into depths I cannot fathom.

My sadness is heightened by my consciousness of his having, just before his first operation, begun work on a biography of me. Though he knew I was writing the present memoir, he brushed this aside, for he still wanted to have his own say in some more extensive way than he had already given utterance to. My gratitude for this last gift of his was, I confess, mixed with apprehensions and doubts, which even his generous essay in 'The Writer in America' had not banished. But once started, he was dauntless. Almost the last time I saw him, he asked me to jot down some further details about my life, to fill out the chronological synopsis he had requested just a month or so before, when he was already too weak to spend even an hour a day in his study.

Though I began by recalling our original meeting, I have leapt over forty years to our final parting. And while I started by acknowledging my personal debt, I find that what I have written is something less than a friend's unashamed eulogy: it is almost—though but in barest outline—a critical appraisal. Yet what could I still say about him in mere words of praise that would equal what I have said here in establishing Brooks's character and his personal influence? For it is by the light of Brooks's own ideals, his resolute craftsmanship, his unshakable honesty and integrity that I have characterized him. And that gives the measure of his contribution to my generation.

CHAPTER TWENTY-SIX

Our Great Expectations

I

Among the contributors to 'The Freeman' in its first two years, despite the fact that he proclaimed himself a liberal, an allegiance Nock could not abide, was Harold Stearns, a strange young man with enchanting blue eyes and the sort of smile Scott Fitzgerald attributed to Gatsby, which would sweetly emolliate his pasty face and make one forget he hadn't shaved. He was soon to become the symbol of American escapism in Paris, and he hung on there for over a decade, never earning quite enough to cover his drinking and betting, by imposing a sort of maintenance tax on his American friends and acquaintances passing through—though somehow, I must quickly add, he respected my poverty or my innocence sufficiently never to borrow a sou from me. But he introduced Sophia and me to Calvados, that scorching Norman apple brandy, in the very cellar Villon is supposed to have frequented, and what is more, conducted us to a rear garden—I wish I could remember where!—from which one got the best view of Notre Dame across the Seine.

Stearns had been at Harvard a year or so after Walter Lippmann, and left legends of his brilliance and his Shelley-like audacity—including that of the night when, on a dare, he dashed into Harvard Yard naked, to prove something or other about modern *mores*, or merely to abash the puritanical past. He had been an editor of 'The Dial' just before my brief day; and I must have met him first through Clarence Britten.

Stearns has the modest distinction of being the originator of a new literary fashion in the United States—the making of symposiums; for if I am not mistaken, his 'Civilization in the United States' was the first of a long list of such volumes. If there had been others published in America before, we should not have first discussed our plans in terms of the famous English religious symposium, 'Essays and Reviews,' which came out in the 1860s.

In January 1921, after talks with Britten and me, Stearns summoned a group of us to his dingily hospitable basement at the south end of Jones Street to discuss a project he had vaguely in mind for making a united critical onslaught on all the shabby mediocrities and false moralities of our American contemporaries. He was so impassioned in his negotiations that he somehow infected all of us with his own discontents, though they might never have taken such intransigent form in him but for the inconveniences of Prohibition.

There were nine of us at that original meeting; and at one point we even contemplated editing a new polemic encyclopedia in the fashion of Diderot, an outrageously immodest enterprise, for none of us had the concentrated intellectual passion or equipment that Denis Diderot applied to that monumental work. We recognized our disabilities quickly enough.

We had sufficient in common, nevertheless, in negative sentiments if not in positive ideas, to meet again; and in fact we met on Sunday evenings throughout the whole winter, every fortnight; sometimes we dined together beforehand, and always, at the meeting, Stearns would provide a jug of Marsala from an Italian bootlegger nearby. One night, I remember Stearns had had a good headstart on us, with an earlier jug, and by the time the evening had ended, he was flat on the floor asleep. Like so many respectable undertakers, we picked up his limp body and laid it on the daybed, covering him with an overcoat, and solemnly filed out of the room, hoping he wouldn't freeze before morning came.

That winter furnished the best sustained conversation I can recall over any period in America; for the group included such masters of the art as Clarence Britten, so witty, deft, and urbane; and even that voluble, long-bearded Irishman, Ernest Boyd, did not for more than a few minutes at a time overwhelm us by his derisive contentiousness. Hendrik van Loon was then on the brink of his first success, 'The Story of Mankind'; and to stem his flood of coarse Dutch-flavored anecdotes, there was Van Wyck Brooks, Paul Rosenfeld, Walter Pach, Geroid Robinson, and J. E. Spingarn: men devoted to art and thought, who could be relied on to bring the argument back to the point at issue. Not least Spingarn, slim, saturnine, aristocratic, aloof, whom I was soon to know more intimately as both friend and neighbor, whose mind cut with a rapier's delicacy to the core of any intellectual problem.

I was the youngest member of the group, once John Dos Passos had dropped out; and I sometimes came to these Sunday meetings, at the end of a day's walk with Sophia in the Westchester Hills, in a tweed suit, with my trousers encased in muddy canvas leggings—so that one of our less distinguished members, with a stab of journalistic malice, later characterized my appearance as that of the mining engineer hero in a western movie.

For me, this experience was a postgraduate course in literature and philosophy, full of intellectual stimulus; so I rarely missed a meeting. And the fact that the older men kept on coming, too, proved that this group filled a need as deep as that which brought into existence the famous Saturday Club that Emerson helped to found. Unlike the venerable Saturday Club in Boston, however, we had two women in our circle: Katharine Anthony and Elsie Clews Parsons.

Two books were composed in the course of that winter; and the better one vanished in Harold Stearns's basement in the act of expression. We played devil's advocate to the conventions of our civilization: a useful task. But our only real unity was in that which we rejected. Among the older men the will to create had seemingly trickled away. 'Civilization in the United States,' the volume that did appear, turned out to be largely an assessment of the handicaps and harassments, the vulgarities and stupidities of American life: almost a Menckenian counterblow to Croly's 'The Promise of American Life' and Waldo Frank's 'Our America.' As for myself, certainly the most hopeful member of the group, by youth, by temperament, by positive philosophy, I was too ignorant at that moment, even in the field

I had chosen for my essay, 'The City,' to do justice to the original contributions of Olmsted and Richardson, still less to those of Sullivan and Wright, for I then knew the latter two only by name, through Claude Bragdon's book, 'Architecture and Democracy.'

An able psychiatrist Stearns knew, Dr. Kempf, refused to join our group when he found that so few members were married, and so few of these had children: he doubted our maturity. That refusal then seemed more than a little patronizing; but by now I have come to understand what he meant by it. Some of us were to spend no small part of our lives bringing to light the achievements of our predecessors and spiritual ancestors. Yet we all, at bottom, loved our country, whatever our reserves might be. Even the Teutonophile Mencken, for all his contempt for the American "booboisie," was to give years to his one scholarly contribution, 'The American Language.' That was a witness to how tight the family bond was.

Randolph Bourne had led the way here, both in his early acrid comments and his later pride over America's genuine achievements; and part of what we did was justifiable as a bit of preliminary housecleaning and rubbish-removing, before our generation moved in. With youthful brashness I tried to revive the group a few years later; but the first soggy meeting in our cramped Brooklyn Heights flat dampened all further efforts.

I can remember sitting in on various other projects for symposiums at intervals during the decade that followed. Few of these efforts came to anything, for they usually lacked the very component that had made ours so noteworthy, the actual face-to-face meeting: a symposium in true Platonic style.

None of these collapsed projects could have had such an unexpected outcome, however, as one that Van Wyck Brooks, Walter Fuller, and I met to discuss one autumn evening in 1921. We proposed to issue a series of paper-covered books, one a month, on the model of the French *Cahiers de Quinzaine*.' Fuller, who could always be relied on for Latin quotations and Roman history, proposed to call these books Scipian Pamphlets, to contrast the bold departures and frontal attacks of the great Scipio with the evasive, retreating tactics of Fabius and Britain's latter-day Fabians. With the nonchalance of inexperience, we figured that with a modest circulation of two or three thousand, we could cover expenses and print all sorts of valuable work that would otherwise go a-begging. But none of us had the free time or the practical flair necessary to launch that enterprise.

Six months later I mentioned our abandoned scheme to a Mr. Samuel Craig, then the business manager of 'The Dial'; and within a few years, thanks to his diligent efforts, it came to life after various metamorphoses—originally the editorial board was to consist of Brooks, Conrad Aiken, Mary Colum, and myself—as the Literary Guild. Our modest plans had been done over into a pattern more acceptable to our profit-oriented economy, and the original board was disbanded before it met. I cannot say that I am proud of having had any part in this development, even at the seminal stage; for the only aspect of our original idea that remained was the paper covers in which Literary Guild books at first were bound. I record this incident for the light it throws on the insidious deflation of ideal possibilities that went on all through this decade, with increasing swiftness toward the end.

2

It was only in this general atmosphere of heady conversation, intellectual adventure, and emotional release that such a yearbook as 'The American Caravan' could have emerged without the kind of benevolent financial backing that 'New Directions,' its chief latter-day successor, had. The guiding spirit in this new enterprise was Paul Rosenfeld, then at the height of his literary and personal influence; for his hospitalities and generosities gave tactful encouragement to the widest circle of writers, musicians, and artists, from Sherwood Anderson to Kenneth Patchen, from Aaron Copland to Roger Sessions and Edgar Varèse; and he was capable of appreciating the original achievements of men as radically different from himself in temperament as Charles Ives, at a time when few music lovers took Ives's musical compositions seriously or had indeed ever heard of them.

369

In 1926 Rosenfeld and I had found ourselves discussing one of our mounting discontents: "What was wrong with 'The Dial.' " How petulant, how unreasonable, how wanting in decent gratitude that complaint seems now! But we had a point, for 'The Dial' too often turned down promising American writers in favor of Europeans of no greater merit or magnitude. Hence our desire for a more genially responsive attitude to our native talent. Remembering Walter Fuller's notion, remembering, too, my friend Avrahm Yarmolinsky's description of the influential Russian Yearbooks of bygone days, we both cottoned to the notion of ourselves publishing an American Yearbook, a project that Rosenfeld had already discussed at length with Kreymborg the previous summer at Stieglitz's summer home on Lake George.

That was the beginning of 'The American Caravan.' Yet it tells something about the sketchiness of our several American backgrounds then that we had hit upon the idea without suspecting that similar yearbooks had been in existence in our country back in its "Golden Day," even before the Russian ventures, and were catholic enough in taste to serve as repositories for some of Hawthorne's stories.

But how easy it was to find a backer in those days! And how helpful, indeed how indulgent, was Lee Furman, our publisher, though I fear we often viewed his very moderate concern for commercial solvency with suspicion, if not righteous hostility. Our intermediary in this venture was Sam Ornitz, the author of a memorable document on New York corruption, 'Haunch, Paunch, and Jowl.' Ornitz had grown up in the toughest part of the East Side, and he had the thick, smashed nose of an ex-prizefighter: yet somehow he had emerged with a respect for letters. For a while he was literary editor of the Macaulay Company, an offshoot of a cheap reprint house which now commissioned him to foment original literature. To our surprise, we found ourselves with a contract for the Yearbook, and even with an editorial den of our own in the Macaulay Company's offices on Fourth Avenue. In fact, the deal was consummated so swiftly that we were uneasy over our very success: could we perhaps have stood out for even better terms?

The fact that the first 'Caravan' was taken by the Literary Guild was one of those pieces of blind poetic justice that are so skillfully metered that the actors, unaware of their appointed roles, deliver their lines as if they were prose. Kreymborg, Rosenfeld, and I— Brooks went to England for analytic therapy and dropped out permanently before we even made our first selections—spent a good part of the next few years, not merely selecting manuscripts, but attempting by letters and personal meetings to give contemporary writers, whether young or old, the kind of critical understanding that is even more encouraging than praise.

We sought to shame the conventional magazines with their cut-and-dried requirements as to subject and length; we looked with special zeal for 'difficult' works, too long for magazines, too short for book publication: particularly the short novel (novella), the form in which Henry James had done some of his best work. With Marianne Moore's 'Dial' loftily indifferent, with 'Broom' gone, and 'The Little Review' more uncertain of appearance than ever, untried writers remote from popular taste had no place to publish until 'The American Caravan' appeared—except in Paris. But though we were especially open to literary experiments, before such experiments ceased to be experimental, we sought with a majestic effort at open-mindedness to favor no one school or method or age group.

Our purpose was to establish a common ground where the new and the old, the traditional and the adventurous, the younger writers and the more sympathetic older ones could meet. But we were not cowed by established reputations, even those of the avant garde. Though Rosenfeld had published an appreciative criticism of Gertrude Stein's work, she for long nourished a grudge against our 'Caravan' for turning down the manuscript of 'Four Saints in Three Acts'—épatant on the stage, it turned out, with the Stettheimer sisters' decorations and Virgil Thomson's music, but dull to read. More sadly, Ezra Pound, for a similar refusal, hurled such screamingly dirty abuse at us by letter that, for the honor of the human race, we threw it into the fire.

Every year the unpublished Walt Whitmans and Stephen Cranes beckoned us on and yet eluded us, though writers who had already begun to find themselves, like Katherine Anne Porter, William Faulkner, and Hart Crane appeared in our pages; and out of sheer good will even Robert Frost, Conrad Aiken, or John Gould Fletcher would give us, on occasion, a new poem. Frost indeed once chided us for surrendering so much of our own time, virtually gratis, to this enterprise, when we should have been zealously guarding the hours for our own work. Possibly he was right.

3

In recollection the winters shift to Rosenfeld's apartment at 77 Irving Place, south of Gramercy Park, handy to a cooperative cafeteria and to Lüchow's restaurant. Behold us in Rosenfeld's old-fashioned living room, with its plum-colored carpet, its dark sagging bookcases, its grand piano on which perched the suave, demure Chinese goddess Kwannon, and its walls, covered with old Hartley paintings in his Ryder manner, a Marin watercolor, a small pear by O'Keeffe, a pinky-blue oil by the comically bumbling Oscar Bluemner, and a few posterlike canvases by E. E. Cummings.

The middle of the floor was the only empty space in the room, and that was important, because it was on the floor we used to lay the manuscripts for final selection. Here Kreymborg sits, with his back to the high windows, reading poetry aloud in a perfectly modulated voice that unfortunately does more than justice to the poorer poems—though when he confronts a poem he does not like, he is not above killing it by reciting it with an increasingly German accent. We listen: we are impressed or not impressed—but at least we read every promising poem aloud before we make up our minds.

Those happy Saturday afternoons! How I wish I could by so many words bring them back again: for what mattered was the immediate touch and feel of our comradeship, not merely between us as editors—we of course had our little tiffs and swallowed differences—but between ourselves and the whole circle we touched, at least a few times every winter, at one of Rosenfeld's evening parties, whose gaiety was the sheer capering of free minds, glad in one another's company, even when behaving childishly, as Cummings sometimes did. As Rosenfeld once remarked of the League of Composers' concerts: "You invariably see all your friends together in one room . . . and that is always ravishing." It was Rosenfeld who spread that ravishment to all of us.

Copland might play the music he had written for one of Ezra Pound's poems, his raucous voice accompanying the music: "Love in idleness: love in idleness: nought else on earth is worth the having." And at one of those early parties I met that handsome bullyboy, Ernest Hemingway, tall, rosy-cheeked, still beardless, and got a clue to the psychal injury that had permanently lamed him when I found that in the first few minutes of our conversation he began describing to me the black opalescence of dead bodies that had been putrefying on a battlefield.

What quick insights one got in that salon atmosphere of Rosenfeld's! No Frenchwoman of the Eighteenth Century knew how to mix her guests more deftly. Yet no woman ever doubted Rosenfeld's persuasive masculinity; for just as some fat men are gracefully light on their feet in the dance, so Rosenfeld, plump though he undoubtedly was, by all accounts was equally charming and attractive as a lover.

In the end, however, our editorial councils, with all their attendant sociabilities, which I enjoyed at the time and now look wistfully back on, irritated Rosenfeld more than a little; and to keep my panegyric in perspective, I shall now quote for contrast his account of our meetings, written in the very heyday of the 'Caravan' in 1928.

> Our meetings last year were veritable kaffeeklatsches among old women. First, kisses. Next, dinky little presents, exchanged as if they were Koh-i-noors. Then all the gossip and the news, announced with the gravity and punctiliousness of senatorial and diplomatic announcements. Then a little business, and finally the coffee.

Sufficiently true to be momentarily devastating. But again I must add hastily, to keep the record close to the actualities of the twenties, that the kisses were figurative. Nothing more perhaps than Kreymborg and I swearing fondly at each other in German: *"Du alter dummer Kerl, du! Was hast du denn diese Woche gemacht?"* This Weber and

Fields dialogue, without the nose twisting and belly prodding, satisfied some silly fragment of us, old New Yorkers that we were.

4

Paul Rosenfeld, not Van Wyck Brooks, was my closest literary friend: so I feel obliged to round out my account of 'The American Caravan' with a few words about Rosenfeld himself. When he sits for my portrait, he is always dressed in a good brown suit, which not merely accentuates the auburn of his neatly laid hair and trim mustache, but the high color of his full, rosy cheeks. He had always been pleasantly stout—animatedly, never lethargically so: all in all he was a runcible man. In good weather Paul kept in form by Sunday walks in the country—a practice not yet made impossible by the lethal parade of motorcars.

Alfred Stieglitz's photograph of Rosenfeld, with troubled, almost haunted eyes, was, it turned out, prophetic: but though Stieglitz took hours to achieve that result, as Paul told me, it actually did the whole man no more justice than would a mere candid camera shot, for it entirely missed the wit and sparkle, and the inner joy of life his face conveyed until the sad closing years, when publishers and magazine editors—except those of the Catholic 'Commonweal'—rebuffed his work.

Since Rosenfeld's novel, 'Boy in the Sun,' follows closely the story of his own youth, I need not go into that; but he must have been a spoiled child as well as a sensitive one: quick to anger over trifles, given to unexpected sulks—and yet just as easily placated and restored to his tender, effusive self. Though, incredibly, he had been sent to a military school in Poughkeepsie, he was not trained to face hardship or poverty, or even to earn his own living: hence the Depression of the thirties, when his investments and his professional income dwindled, hit him hard. But in a decade of Bohemian irresponsibility, he performed his duties as a citizen with punctilio, even enduring without complaint all-too-frequent calls for jury duty. For all his sensitiveness, for all his thinness of skin, he was firm on essential matters of literary or moral principle. If he had occasional lapses in judgment, they were honest blind spots, such as his over-valuation of his mistress's short stories, which he appraised under the magnifying glass of love.

Rosenfeld was the heart and soul of our enterprise; and what a good critic, what a responsive, work-inciting editor he was! He reached out to a work of art with every organ of his body, not merely with his eye or his ear, yet always with a full play of mind, capable of exquisitely recording his feelings and at the same time offering reasons for his judgments. Over the years, my respect for Rosenfeld's critical acumen grew, and I learned to doubt, or at least to reconsider, my own judgment when I differed with him.

This applied equally to my own work. When I sent him 'The Condition of Man' in 1944, I eagerly awaited his criticism and hoped for some measure of praise; but months went by before I heard from him, for, he confessed, he found writing me difficult, since my book delighted and yet dissatisfied him. "I felt its point of view right," he said, "but ineffectual, since it made a moral issue of the matter of regeneration; and I felt that all movement comes from connection with a new object, or a new connection with an old, and found yourself taking to what I feel to be a moral exhortation. . . . All that you say is true. But a *constatation* [authentic statement] is not necessarily an act."

That criticism was more salutary than any praise; and though I took it to heart slowly, the more I considered it, the more dissatisfied I grew with the final chapter of that book. Unfortunately, this did not keep me from repeating the same error even more blatantly in 'The Conduct of Life.'

Partly perhaps because of age, Rosenfeld was closer to Kreymborg than I ever became, and saw much more of him: but while he valued the birdlike twitter of Kreymborg's early poetry and marionette plays, his doubts about Alfred's later development as a poet and his position as a man of letters increased as time went on. It was typical of Rosenfeld's courage as a critic that he not only exacted as high a performance of his friends as of anyone else, but dared to say so, and the more promising the work, the more severe his judgment. His letters to Sherwood Anderson, explaining his attitude toward Waldo Frank—letters now in the Newberry Library in Chicago—recall the greatness of spirit he brought to the task, though Anderson himself at first thought Rosenfeld's criticism, as Frank always did, an act of hurt pride or revenge. Let me quote a few lines, for Rosenfeld's surviving letters deserve to be more widely known: they have the kind of precious candor and self-respect one values in Chekhov's.

> Don't think for a moment that I wrote this because of the failure of D.M. [Frank's 'Dark Mother']. If I thought the failure of the D.M. merely a fluke, an ill chance, I would let the book pass unnoticed. But I perceive something at the base of the faulty esthetic of the work that is the very devil in Waldo, in me, in everyone. I hope to hit it wherever and whenever I catch sight of it. I hate it in myself, and I give everyone the right to point to it whenever they spy it. For Waldo is beginning to catch sight of it; he knows it is in him; he is even trying to fight it. But he will never fight it hard until he knows it is his very enemy. And he will not know until he sees someone like myself daring to sacrifice friendship, esteem, etc. in order to convey it to him.

The devil that Rosenfeld referred to was the imperious, overblown ego, which insistently claimed for itself the homage due to a thousand nameless forces, spiritual activities, and personalities that, in their totality and finality, transcend the individual ego and make the artist himself, not an end, but an instrument of higher purposes. Rosenfeld well knew to whom or what this homage belonged, and perhaps in his humility before every expression of the creative impulse, in his eager desire for even a peep at the creative act itself in the divine moment of conjunction and conception, he failed to utilize his own fullest energies or do justice to his own talents.

As Edmund Wilson pointed out, in the postmortem *Festschrift* that Jerome Mellquist piously gathered together, Rosenfeld wantonly dispersed his powers in a hundred appreciations of the work of others, instead of concentrating them in a few mature works of his own. Thus Robert Frost's criticism of our 'Caravan' editing applied particularly to him. His crowning book—finished but for the last few pages—remains, alas! unpublished: the novel called 'Concert in Rome.' My failure to find a publisher for it still tantalizes and rebukes me.

But something of Rosenfeld's eager spirit is present in all the best work of the twenties; and the people who were untouched by that spirit, like Hemingway, whose pathology Rosenfeld so brilliantly diagnosed in 'Men Seen,' might have overcome their private maladies and continued their growth into full maturity if they could have swallowed the astringent medicine that Rosenfeld offered them.

5

Much that went on in the twenties does not, I realize, correspond to the characterization I have given here: but only historically unsophisticated minds can make themselves believe that a decade or a century may be treated as a uniform block. At the height of the Victorian period Tennyson, the poet who now seems to us the quintessence of the Victorian spirit, was rejected by his close contemporaries as a dubious if not dangerous innovator. And who incarnated the Eighteenth Century—Voltaire or Rousseau? Thomas Paine or William Blake?

Yet there was a substratum of experience that more or less affected everybody, even when they were unaware of it or rejected it. The 1914 war had left my generation, even those who had taken no active part in it, in a state of shock: the unthinkable had happened, and from now on nothing would be quite unthinkable. As is natural in shock, we withdrew into a dugout of our own making; and as so often has happened in such a compensatory response to the horrors of war, that private retreat set the stage for a public orgy. The conventions and ideals that hitherto had been accepted as a normal and necessary covering for the raw *id* were flung aside as hypocrisies and frauds: no longer rejected merely as ideas, but rejected in practice. All the joys of life were reduced to liquor and sex: drink to the point of anesthesia, sex to the point of impotence or fretful exhaustion.

This was the age of the flapper: she whose stockings were rolled right below the knee, without benefit of garters, and whose sole undergarment was a 'step-in,' a shift so contrived that, at the slightest relaxation of her posture when seated, her Mount of Venus was exposed to even unprying eyes. Many a university lecturer in a science demonstration theater found his attention prickingly distracted by this spectacle. The more subtle feminine arts were now at a discount: the approach was direct to the point of crudeness, with a kind of boyish frankness that went with the flattened breasts and lean buttocks, without need for girdles but with extra tight brassieres to suppress even the suspicion of bosomy roundness.

On current theory, all the ills of life might be interpreted, if one chose to read Freud that way, as due to a damming up of the libido and to unconscious sexual repression. If so, the cure was easy: demolish the dam! Out with the censor! Or as Charcot prescribed in Freud's presence: "A penis inserted every night in the vagina." (But note: Charcot himself, even in addressing his colleagues, still sufficiently respected the censor to put this prescription in Latin!) 'Freud' and bootleg liquor played into each other's hands: what might not be condoned on moral grounds, if one still had a twinge of conscience, became almost a matter of duty if considered as hygiene. The immediate moment was what counted: to drink life to the dregs and to pretend that the dregs were particularly to one's liking. "Let's have another drink" became a monotonously stock refrain in Hemingway. That perhaps was the beginning of today's Instant Culture.

This almost therapeutic sexuality, with its insidious devaluation of the whole wide gamut of human relations rooted in love, affected even those who by habit and self-discipline sought to maintain, with whatever current modifications, more time-seasoned standards of conduct. It left a mark on literature in the early work of writers as conscientious as Joseph Wood Krutch—the author of that once ultimate bible, or at least the 'Science and Health,' of this period: 'The Modern Temper' (1929). Later, I hasten to note, Krutch himself changed profoundly in his outlook, but that book remains as authentic a period piece as T. S. Eliot's 'The Cocktail Party,' in which something like nostalgia mingles with revulsion. The constant pressures in daily life explain possibly, up to a point, the sudden unlocking of energies that took place; analogous to what happened to Victor Hugo, who reacted to intense dolor and grief with the compensatory expression of an insatiable sexuality. As with woman's new form of dress, the postwar *mores* brought a welcome measure of open-eyed frankness, hitherto conspicuously lacking in both our life and our literature. So even our disillusion fed in some degree on that newly released energy.

6

And yet, after one has made allowances for the more sordid or meretricious qualities of the twenties, much that was valuable remains. It was, one sees now, a period of surging energies mingled with desperate hopes, though these hopes were no longer tied to utopian social improvements. Even in the American publishing world there were many publishers who still had a sufficient sense of their duty to literature to publish books because they merited publication, not because the publisher was deluded by prospects of sales. On those terms Donald Brace nursed Virginia Woolf, on repeated visits to England, through three of her most original books, despite their feeble reception and circulation before she had her first American success.

This was a healthy atmosphere for the writer; and the publishers I knew personally then, Maxwell Perkins, Frank Hill, Curtice Hitchcock, John Farrar, Horace Liveright, B. W. Huebsch—to say nothing of Donald Brace, Alfred Harcourt, and J. E. Spingarn—were an honor to their guild. Such people are not bred in the corporate bureaucracies and Wall Street conglomerates that now dominate the scene.

Beneath the ripples of literary fashion, the dominant note of the twenties was the recognition of our national identity and personal idiosyncrasy in the arts. This is what bound together my generation, apart from the central experience of the First World War and its aftermath. That discovery of our own formative part in establishing a fresh tradition recalled to us the period of Hawthorne's and Emerson's youth; and it was obliquely expressed at an early moment in Brooks's 'America's Coming of Age,' and more emphatically in John Macy's 'The Spirit of American Literature.'

Now this faith in our national potentialities began to seep into music, the theater, architecture, and painting as well. This is what Waldo Frank sought to focus more clearly in 'Our America,' and then more maturely in 'The Re-discovery of America'; and my own 'Sticks and Stones' and 'The Golden Day' played a similar part, which is today more easily recognized than it was by my contemporaries.

Most clearly and confidently this spirit was expressed by Constance Mayfield Rourke, whose studies of our native expressions in the arts, notably in her 'American Humor,' would—had she not met death too early through a wanton accident—have led to the monumental work she had planned on all our folk arts, which would have complemented, reinforced, and subtly revised Brooks's 'Makers and Finders' series.

This was not the first time such an expression of inward assurance had welled up in our country; was it not the motive force of Cooper's novels? One finds it no less assertively expressed there than it was by Whitman, likewise in the intimate letters of the young Henry James, he who in a later period was as much identified with Europe and England as with his own country. In 1867, writing to his friend Thomas Sergeant Perry, did James not say:

One feels—I feel at least that he [Sainte-Beuve] is a man of the past, of a dead generation, and that we young Americans are (without cant) men of the future. I feel that my only chance for success as a critic is to let all the breezes of the west blow through me at their will. We are Americans born—*il faut en prendre son parti*. I look upon it as a great blessing; and I think that to be an American is an excellent preparation for culture. We have exquisite qualities as a race; and it seems to me that we are ahead of the European races in the fact that . . . we can deal freely with forms of civilization not our own, can pick and choose and assimilate and in short aesthetically, etc. claim our property wherever we find it. To have no national stamp has hitherto been a regret and a drawback, but I think it not unlikely that American writers may yet indicate that a vast intellectual fusion and synthesis of the various national tendencies of the world is the condition of more important achievements than any we have seen.

Henry James never entirely lost that vision, however blurred it might become by his ever closer identification with England; at all events, he had already expressed at that early moment the best spirit of my generation. Long before I myself had read James's words, I vibrated to the same expectation, since Emerson and Whitman had pointed the way. To call this 'chauvinism' is absurd; for it ignores the fact that this generation subjected our country to as severe a critical examination of its weaknesses and defects as any country had ever received: so relentless, so unsparing, so persistently negative that it was often grossly unjust, as I was in my ruthless denigration of the saving virtues of the Puritan and the Pioneer. The point is, however, that this drastic criticism was itself a product of our self-confidence, and the surest witness to our Great Expectations.

Even the writers who turned their backs on their native country during the twenties had returned from their exile, many of them, before the great financial crash of 1929 had depleted their incomes. Reversing Carlyle's old dictum, they could now say: "Here or no-where lies our Europe."

And if, in rejecting the esthetic and moral hand-me-downs of our more diffident elders, we sought to fashion new garments cut closer to our measure, or felt obliged to establish our identity afresh, it was in order to have a national self mature enough to enter, as an equal, into communication and cooperation with other regions and cultures and personalities. In short we felt part of the common world, which some of us still believed was actually materializing before our eyes. There is much more I am tempted to say about the ambience of art and literature during the twenties, but I would blur the image if I overcrowded it with a hundred remembered details. Until the decade came to an end, it was still possible to believe that our crea-tivity—however intermittent, however erratic, however febrile—would eventually overcome, or at least deeply modify, our country's equally visible materialistic self-absorption.

CHAPTER TWENTY-SEVEN

Fulfillment in Geneva

I

When Sophy and I returned from Europe in 1922 we started at a very low point indeed, for we had barely moved into a cramped two-room apartment on Brooklyn Heights, where Clinton Street joined Fulton, before I came down with trench mouth and a septic sore throat: a combination that in those days was often fatal. This dangerous ailment was then treated by an equally dangerous method; for when our Dr. Stratford, who came all the way from West Seventy-ninth Street to Brooklyn to examine me—how incredible that ready response would be today!—found his mild gargle did not work, after a *second* house visit he turned me over to a dentist who used a drastic military (World War) remedy: swabbing the gums with cyanide of mercury, a chemical so poisonous that even a few drops, if swallowed, produce instant death. (No one had yet guessed that pure peroxide of hydrogen kills streptococci quite as surely, in a less menacing way.)

We lived on Clinton Street for two years. But the forty dollars we could afford for rent, at a time when my earning powers still averaged little more than fifteen dollars a week the year round, provided only minimal facilities: the kitchenette lacked both a sink and an icebox; and the rumble of the elevated railroad in the rear ruffled our sleep. We invented an early 'room divider' by framing the wide opening between the two rooms with narrow bookcases, later enhanced by a background of color—a red-and-orange embroidery

382

Patrick Geddes brought us from India—and so we made the place cheerful to the eye. Sophia overcame our chief culinary handicap by souring each day's bottle of milk, after we'd taken the cream off for our coffee—in those days milk was not homogenized, but even pasteurized milk still soured decently!—and she would hang up the curds in the evening to drip, so that the next morning we had cottage cheese instead of butter for our toast.

We usually dined nearby at one of the last of the city's old-fashioned Eating Houses, Joe's, with an encyclopedic bill-of-fare and the best of sea food fresh from Sheepshead Bay. Not the least attraction was its genial, efficient waiters, many of them self-conscious 'characters' whom we got to know so well that ten years later, when I would lunch at Joe's with our son Geddes, they would ask about Sophy. Yes, even twenty years later, when we went there with our young daughter, Alison, one or two of the waiters would still identify us.

The winters in this flat were tolerable; but we couldn't say as much for the summers. Both summers of 1923 and 1924 were grievously hot; and the latter was made hellish by the wholesale repairs being done at night on the Fulton El right under our rear window—all the worse because our apartment was directly under the hot tin roof, and the smell of burnt fat from the lunchroom below made the heat and the noise all the more sickening.

Somehow we survived by staying out late every night on Montague Street Plaza, facing the harbor, for we loved the neighborhood itself. By going down to the foot of Montague Street, we could get a glimpse of the Manhattan skyline and a whiff of the salt air, if the west or south wind was blowing: even the hoot of the tugs and steamers sent promissory shivers of release.

But when in the autumn a group of rowdies rented the flat below ours and roistered far into the night, Sophy and I felt we had had all we could endure. Fortunately, Charlie and Gene Whitaker, who were planning to spend three months in Europe, offered to turn over to us their partly remodeled old farmhouse in Mount Olive, New Jersey, rent free: with no more onerous duties than stoking the furnace and caring for a dozen hens. So eager were we both for a long draught of country air that Sophia again took a three-month leave of absence from 'The Dial.' Overnight, we ceased to be mere hikers and country visitors: we had our first authentic experience of rural life.

Mount Olive turned out to be a sort of second cousin to the Vermont farm of my boyhood: diminished in scale, depleted in richness; and yet diagrammatic, too, for though the hills were lower and the valley narrower, the Twelve Opossums Farm (Whitaker's private pun on the Twelve Apostles) was partway up one slope. And like my Vermont model, Whitaker's house already had a library with files of 'Punch' as a substitute for the 'Illustrated London News.' Our nearest neighbors, from whom we daily fetched our milk in cans, were a little under half a mile away; while to replenish our groceries we used to tramp, I with my Tyrolean knapsack on my back, for a good six miles along the dirt road to Bartley, where there was a lone country grocer not far from the lone railroad station, both seemingly stranded.

The solitude and serenity of winter in the country was a new experience for us. We arrived when the snow was freshly fallen on the ground, and the footprints between the chicken house and the kitchen told us that a neighbor—he who would teach me the right grip and slip in chopping a tree with an ax—had been in to feed the chickens and stoke the coal furnace. We had much to learn about the simplest routines of country living; but we took to every part of the life with a feeling that we had at last come home.

At that time we were so pinched for money that when, one late afternoon I came back from a dental visit in New York to find the snow already a foot deep and still thickly falling, I decided to walk the five or six miles from the Hackettstown station, instead of paying fifty cents for a taxi. The snow fell more heavily, the sky got darker, the way wearier with every slogging step; and I finally reached the lonely farmhouse—Sophia had stayed over in New York—so spent that I could scarcely boil myself an egg. Since I was then already in a weakened state from the infected tooth, my erratic heart might have given out, but for the few ounces of brandy my mother had given me—heaven knows who had given it to *her*!—for medical emergencies. The whole next day, indeed, I passed in a torpor, though the snow had stopped falling during the night and the sun had come out. Yet that dogged tramp through the clinging snow and those lonely hours count among my deepest images of country living: the hardship itself gave it a tang.

This period was also the first time that Sophia had assumed the tasks of a housewife and made her initial experiments in baking. I still remember my shameless glee over her first effort to bake a pie, pinching and pounding the crust in her attempt to make it round, only to discover that when baked it was almost as hard as the pie plate itself. My mother's advice: "A light touch makes a light crust," alas! arrived too late.

Our common responses to rural sights and sounds and daily routines did almost as much to consolidate our marriage, to make it steadfast if not unshakable, as the subsequent birth of our first child: and indeed the one secretly made us ready for the other.

The Whitakers came home a few weeks earlier than they had expected, and we all lived together under the same roof for a fort-night. This gave us a postgraduate course under experts in country living that later visits—as guests, we always helped with the garden—carried further.

2

When Sophia went back to 'The Dial' after this interlude, we reso-lutely decided to scour the neighborhood for more viable quarters, this time on the port side of Brooklyn Heights. That September we found just what we wanted in an old brownstone with a slight Gothic touch, at 135 Hicks Street, now deservedly marked as an historic building. There we had a one-and-a-half-room basement apartment, with an open fireplace, and a share in a rear garden which gave on the sandstone Gothic church behind—that tawny Belleville sand-stone from New Jersey which has none of the chocolate dinginess of the Hartford variety! The small rear alcove, whose only ventilation came through an airshaft, we dedicated to typing and dressing. (We found later that that airshaft served our upstairs neighbors on the

nearer floors, too, for they were amused by overhearing our sometimes bawdy repartee while undressing for bed.)

Our new neighborhood was as genial an example of both urbanity and community as Boston's Mt. Vernon Street area. Our Fourth
Street flat in Greenwich Village, with its next-door stable, and our
Clinton Street flat, amid a mishmash of beanery, laundry, tailor shop,
all without backyards or gardens, had conformed to Jane Jacobs's
half-baked prescription for 'urban liveliness.' But Hicks Street, then
so humane and serene with its nearby assortment of restaurants,
markets, and shops, at hand but not under one's nose, met our need
for esthetic comeliness and social variety. Small wonder many of our
younger New York friends had begun to move over to the Heights.
Our Hicks Street quarters were visually so attractive that we forgot
at first that our single living-dining-sleeping room was fit only for
'bachelor life,' and its space could not be stretched or twisted to accommodate a baby even if the little creature was immobilized in a cradle. Though it did not solve our coming housing problem, our winter
in Hicks Street at least gave us the promise of a better life, along
with the confidence needed to face cheerfully the inevitable ordeals
of parenthood.

Suddenly everything began to go right. By 1925 my first two
books, 'The Story of Utopias' and 'Sticks and Stones,' had, despite
their modest sales, established me as a writer who without any fan-
fare had nevertheless 'arrived.' Not merely the weeklies but the more
adventurous monthlies, like 'Harper's' and the new 'The American
Mercury' were well-disposed to my offerings. The previous winter,
in addition, I had edited the regional planning number of the 'Survey Graphic.' Things went right with Sophy, too! In the fall she had
begun to serve mornings as an apprentice teacher and helper in the
nursery group at the Walden School, carrying on her 'Dial' work in
the afternoon. I gave a course on literature once a week at the same
school and guiltily earned as much in a day as she did in a week. To
cap it all, early in the winter of 1924, she conceived. That *was* a
rewarding winter for both of us!

The gala spring of 1925, before our baby was born, came to an
unexpected climax: Alfred Zimmern was prompted by Van Wyck

Brooks to invite me to the International Summer School he was instituting at Geneva. My welcome assignment was to give a short course of lectures on American literature. Instead of providing a bare minimum fee, Zimmern offered more for a single month than Sophia and I together were wont to spend in five months. At such an opportune moment, the money itself added an unexpected luster to the invitation. This double accolade, which was even more a double challenge, served to swing me back to my permanent orbit as a man of letters, preparing me for an even larger and broader career by inciting me to come to terms with my own American heritage. In hastily preparing these lectures, I drew special sustenance from the original writers and scholars whom our more timid, anglicized mentors had either disparaged or ignored.

3

From the moment in 1924 when we decided to throw caution to the winds and to try to have a child, our sex life began to improve, too, for the business of becoming one flesh was not interrupted by the prelude and the aftermath of contraceptives. The delicious abandon of it brought both a physiological and a psychological reward. But for all our inner readiness, Sophia did not conceive at once. After a few impatient months we even consulted a gynecologist to make sure that there were no anatomical obstacles. He cheerfully advised patience, and added, after examining my semen under the microscope, that the spermatozoa were so lively he felt prompted to exhibit them to his classes at the medical school, as a rare but happy example of how an active spermatozoon should behave to ensure its swift climb and successful penetration into an ovum.

But suddenly, when Sophia skipped a period, we found ourselves panicked: this was it! So much so that Sophia took three pathetic doses of castor oil, that old wives' prescription for bringing on menstruation. But the castor oil, thank Heaven! was ineffective and the panic did not last. With the acceptance of my prospective parenthood, a new life began for me, too. Yet I dare not minimize what a large break that was, or what hazards it presented to my survival as a writer, or with what inner misgivings and withholdings I took it on: a reluctance that only time, experience, and love could eventually overcome.

In my case, this tardiness in assuming parental status doubtless was accentuated by my own lack of a visible father to admire or resent, to imitate or rebel against. In addition, my reluctance was abetted by my early admiration for Bernard Shaw's 'rational' attitude toward marriage: the product of his arrest at adolescence. Even before the days when we started openly discussing the possibility of having a child, Sophy had once idly asked me if I did not sometimes wish I could support her as well as giving a monthly stipend to my mother. And I had replied nonchalantly, in my best Shavian style, that I had no such wish whatever: was she not a strong, healthy girl, capable of supporting herself?

Before our baby was born, I had begun indeed to revamp this maleish career-centered attitude toward love and marriage. But I felt no active desire for children, as so many young men feel today, even to the point of taking part as vicarious midwife in the birth of their children, until our son Geddes was born. Yet even after that, too easily seduced by a false dichotomy of Plato's, I for long treated the Children of the Flesh and the Children of the Spirit as rivals: and more than once I put the claims of the latter first. *Peccavi!* I know better now!

Sophia and I were so little prepared for the moment of childbirth that, though we had calculated the date of our baby's arrival with fair accuracy, he caught us by surprise. When Sophy awoke one night toward midnight with her first birth pains, she thought that they were only indigestion from the chicken salad and tongue she had eaten copiously at a family party—it was the Fourth of July of 1925—at my mother's home the evening before. (Perhaps that food, indeed, played the part of the tripe that enabled Gargamelle to bring forth Gargantua.) Since her indigestion curiously came in waves, we at last awakened to its real nature; her doctor, oddly enough, had neglected to give her any information or instruction on this point. But we were both too indecisive and too considerate of our obstetrician's sleep to phone him before seven in the morning, when the pains were coming at very frequent intervals.

As it turned out, we reached the Brooklyn Hospital, adjacent to Fort Greene Park, with little time to spare; and the doctor did not arrive, for a reason never adequately explained, till after the baby was born. As an unfortunate result, an inexperienced intern, in a panicky moment, performed a forceps delivery so clumsily that our infant's head was flattened at the rear, and took endless months to fill out properly.

In the spirit of Bernard Shaw's Bluntschli, instead of pacing back and forth to await the birth, I calmly walked to my mother's home on nearby Cumberland Street and tucked in a solid breakfast. There was another half-hour to wait after I returned, enough time for me to write a properly apprehensive note on the feelings of a young man whose first child is being born. But it was not until a little later, when I beheld the crumpled, beet-faced, quite ugly little creature, that I became aware of the change that had taken place, not just in my status, but far more profoundly in my feeling about life. Fatherhood stirred me in a fashion I had never anticipated. Though it took more than this realization to make me truly and fully a family man, it was a beginning.

Those early weeks were full of anxiety: for our infant, reacting no doubt to the rough treatment he had received at birth, curled into an invisible womb again, and refused to open his eyes or eat for more than a few seconds at feeding time: indeed, it became my duty gently to flick the soles of his feet—and what big feet they were!—to awaken him again; and for a day or two his state was so precarious that he was put in an incubator. This early tension about his feeding became chronic later on when it turned out that he had an allergy to milk albumen, which it took several years to overcome, by patiently adding drop by drop of milk to his formula. But at the beginning Sophy was still close enough to the older generation to oppose the fashionable bottle-cum-formula, and to demand, reinforced by her mother's insistence, a continuance of breast feeding, even though at first she had to express the milk herself in order to make sure that Geddes—for that's the name we perhaps too piously bestowed on him—would imbibe it.

The luxury of ten days in the hospital after childbirth had not yet been destroyed by the pressures of space and the rise of costs—

to say nothing of the discovery that surgical cases heal more quickly if they do not remain immobilized in bed. Poor as we were, Sophy still had earned for herself the privilege of a private room. But what a panic was in both our breasts when we brought the little one back to Hicks Street: alone with him, entirely responsible—and neither of us had ever diapered a squirming baby! Even worse followed: Sophy came down with a severe attack of jaundice and was too weak to wash the diapers. Her plight would have been pitiable—there were no diaper services or public washing machines in those days—had not the wife of our janitor, out of the goodness of her heart, taken on this job for the next few weeks. (It shames me that I do not recall this woman's name.) Sophia's innate stoicism during that harrowing period before I was due to sail for Geneva rose to this trial, as it was repeatedly to do later.

Those were tense days for both of us, despite our deepened tenderness; and the prospect of my so soon leaving would have been unbearable had Sophia not made provision to move out to Flatbush with her baby to spend the summer with her parents in their porch-shaded house.

As for me, I started out for Switzerland without guessing how much I myself was irretrievably losing: two precious months of our son's infancy! Yet this voyage was the almost magic fulfillment of a wish I had uttered a year before, when Sophy and I had gone on a Sunday walk. "What I would like now," I had said then, "would be for you to have your baby, and for me to go off for a while to Europe, to think over my future work." Not knowing it then, I was proposing to repeat a flight from parenthood similar to what William James had more than once staged in his own life. That there was anything incompatible or untimely in these wishes did not occur to Sophy or to me: but that they would actually be fulfilled precisely as we had wished, did not occur to us either.

The moment for parting was not easy: the 'Aquitania' was to sail at midnight, and the driver of the taxi I finally snared around nine o'clock gave my going an extra sinister turn, for his approach to the bridge to Manhattan was by way of a dark waterfront street, empty except for a lone garage that looked like a gangster's hideout. When at length I asked him what he was up to, he confessed he was lost;

he didn't know where the Bridge was; so the nightmare of my being robbed and murdered vanished, and soon, following my directions, we came safely to our destination.

This traumatic half-hour before reaching the pier had a paradoxical effect: my lonely reaction to this scary threat had drawn a safety curtain over the scene I was leaving behind. Once I stepped aboard the 'Aquitania,' all my natural anxieties about Sophia and the baby dropped away. I began to enjoy the smooth ocean passage over the velvety July sea as I had never before been able to, for everything about the ship, even in second class, represented to me—and still does—perhaps the highest point reached in British steamer design. And to carry my paradoxical regeneration even further, the greater the physical distance between me and Sophia, the closer we came together.

4

Most of the correspondence between Sophy and me during my two months in Europe concerned our child, and that story I have already told in 'Green Memories'; but since I've spoken so freely about our misgivings and frustrations, I must now add something of the fresh consummation that the birth of the baby brought about. We fell in love all over again, this time with equally fervent passion on both sides; and the depth and delight of this new-found union, no less than the wonder of little Geddes, added to the brilliance of the Geneva sunshine when I would pause on the bridge over the Ile de Rousseau to watch the swans feed. That love irradiated every moment of our separation. Yes: we were indissolubly united both in the flesh and in spirit: the sacrament of marriage had taken effect! "Why should I go wander?" I asked in a little verse to Sophy:

> Adventure lies at home;
> My sweetheart is the planet
> Whose surface I would roam.

Sophy's letters expressed the same feelings, with equal certainty, equal serenity, equal rapture: "I feel full to bursting with love for you and though I know it sounds silly, still I could die happy now

391

and with no regret except that of leaving life—what I have had out of it would do me for eternity." Each of us at that moment, secure in the anchorage of our marriage, had his own kind of fulfillment: Sophy in her hour-to-hour absorption in our baby; and I in the intellectual and emotional stimulus of my new environment, in the companionship of the Zimmerns and their assistants, Rolf Sohlmann, who in time became a distinguished Swedish diplomat, and Jean de Menasce, who had one of the best-endowed and most subtle minds I have ever met. With Jean's seething mixture of national, racial, and cultural allegiances—Egyptian, French, English, and Jewish—who could guess that he would finally become a Dominican Father and a world authority on the ancient Persian religions, with a special chair at the Sorbonne?

The Pension Mirabeau, where I stayed, was just around the corner from the Conservatoire de Musique, where the Zimmerns' school held forth; and below, at the corner, was the very café in which Lenin had plotted the Russian Revolution. Near at hand on one side was the wide Plain Palais, where an appetizing open market was held twice a week; and on the other side was the Promenade des Bastions, beneath the wall of the Old Town. For all its Protestant limitations, Geneva was then a comely city, with one aspect facing John Calvin and the other pointing to Jean-Jacques Rousseau, its two most famous citizens. The flower markets, the daily swims in the translucent green waters of Lake Geneva, then still fit for bathing at a *plage* nearby, the endless discussions before lunch over beer or vermouth in the cafés, all blended together in a perfect month: one of those marvelous months that add extra years to a lifetime.

Some of the friends of that period drifted away, not to turn up again until they became refugees from Hitler. But my friendship with Father Jean de Menasce quietly ripened even during the periods when we did not meet or even exchange letters. In the fifties, after a lapse of years, my visits to Paris were vivified by repeated talks with Jean, then living in a convent at Neuilly; and our underlying unanimity of feeling and thought about the world crisis, about the catastrophic nuclear policies of the United States and Soviet Russia, about the general moral collapse bridged the superficial differences in our ideologies and institutional allegiances. With Father de Menasce I felt as I was later to feel about Pope John XXIII: given two Pope Johns I could become a Catholic; three might even turn me into a Christian.

Each time we met and parted, I felt a deep sense of gratitude over intercourse with such a soul. In the 1950s, his life had been devastated by a series of heart attacks that left him increasingly paralyzed: yet despite this, on the last visit Sophia and I paid him, he took us haltingly on a tour of the grounds, to show us a new build-

Jean de Menasce

ing. After our saying good-bye to Jean on the steps of his domicile, I turned around and asked him to give us his blessing; and all three of us knew in our hearts this was a final farewell.

Not the least of my memories of that Geneva summer was my meeting with a sixteen-year-old girl, an auditor, not an accepted student: a slip of a girl, with ivory white skin and black hair, fragile but palpitating with life, so that one could even see her heart beating wildly beneath her dress. Too wayward for formal instruction either in literature or in music—though her mother was a pianist—she had nevertheless composed music and written poems; and when I inquired after her poetry, she gravely led me to a bench in the Promenade des Bastions and read to me out of a loose-leaf book a shy sample; poems delicate, fragile, haunting, like her own person.

These poems were artless, as artless as Emily Dickinson's early poems, and astonishingly original: so extraordinarily good that the following winter my fellow editors unanimously welcomed them for 'The American Caravan.' Happily, she was not in the least an imitator of her elusive forerunner: I doubt if she had even read Emily's poems. She just *was* another Emily Dickinson, of Queens, not Amherst, of Russian Jewish, not New England lineage, yet too much like a creature of fantasy to give any promise, it seemed then, of a long stay on earth—all the more because her naïve, untutored spirit was so wildly daring that she almost, the next winter, ran off with that psychotic French novelist, Céline.

Josephine Strongin was her name; and Jo and I came to know each other well during the next twenty years: I at first in a deliberately avuncular, protective role, full of a love that never became insistent; she in an increasingly intimate fashion, willfully demanding a more passionate response than I could give her, wanting the homage due her femininity even after she had married a young businessman and produced a child. All the while I sought only to preserve the breathless enchantment she had cast over our first session together. Unfortunately, it was as impossible for her to sustain this diaphanous tie indefinitely as it was to recreate in her later verses the untaught and untrammeled spirit that had created the original images and rhythms of her earliest poems.

5

My lectures were a trial for me and doubtless for the audience, for I had little experience in lecturing. But that granted, they went well: at least the first one did, if only because of the shock I gave my European student audience when I said that all the qualities they regarded as peculiarly American had had their origin in Europe, from the crassness of capitalism to the barbaric disorder of romanticism. That lecture became the first chapter of 'The Golden Day.'

394

But a few minutes before I was to give my second lecture I realized that I had left my notes at my *pension;* and at one panicky moment in the midst of this impromptu lecture I had a rare but not uncommon experience: the next sentence would not come. I somehow broke through this block, and when I told Zimmern later about my plight, he pushed aside my apologies with the advice *always* to leave my notes behind.

Zimmern himself had been one of the heroes of my adolescence: he gave me a passport, good for a lifetime, to Greece and the Hellenic spirit; and though I never sat under him as a student, I have plenty of other evidence to show that he was an ideal teacher, stimulating, keen in appreciation, yet rigorous in criticism, holding up to his students high standards of intellectual and moral self-discipline. He had broken with the academic complacency of the universities by scandalously running off with Lucie, the French Calvinist wife of a fellow university professor in Wales, in a fashion that oddly paralleled D. H. Lawrence's marriage with Frieda. "We could have been lovers without attracting attention," he once explained to me. "The scandal was that we were so much in love that we wanted to be married." As for Lucie, she had, even in her late forties, the charm and spluttering passion of a certain kind of Frenchwoman, steeped in music and politics, with swift prejudices against persons and equally swift attachments, and a sense of the comic that was always at ease with my own lighthearted sallies.

Both Lucie and Alfred hated to have him identified only as the author of 'The Greek Commonwealth,' although ironically that was perhaps to remain his masterpiece; and it preserved his early connection with Oxford, to which he returned after the First World War to teach politics. For they both knew, just as Geddes and Branford knew—though Toynbee did not—that Oxford, like every other university, was suffering from complacency and self-worship, iridescent with decay; and so they sought in their summer school in Geneva to introduce students from every part of the planet to the realities of their common world, and to infuse their intellectual discipline with the passion and feeling that the bureaucratic spirit of our time ejects from our academic studies no less than from the routines of daily life.

To win Zimmern's interest and approval became a criterion of success for my own books. If sometimes I felt that he and Lucie took the daily tumult of events too seriously, and were perhaps too sanguine about the realities of Anglo-American leadership, already badly slipping in the thirties, I nevertheless respected Zimmern as I respected his old master, Gilbert Murray, whom I never, alas! met, except in the printed page.

More than one benefit effortlessly came about through this invitation to Geneva, almost as sometimes wonderfully happens with lovers while locked together in an embrace. For the first time I came face to face with teachers and scholars, poets and students from Oxford, Paris, Salamanca, whom I had hitherto known only in the shadows of their written works. Within a few months these actual contacts, even when superficial—like the curl of disdain over my diffident German on the face of a young Hannoverian aristocrat!—taught me more than a year of restless traveling and sightseeing would have done. There are passages in 'The Little Testament' whose liberated prose tells the effect on me better than the tarnished memories that have survived.

My days at Geneva were so beautifully rounded that I seized the excuse of a dying tooth to turn down the Zimmerns' suggestion that I accompany them to Prague, as a sort of personal secretary, to attend a Central European student conference; and I now regret having missed my first and last opportunity to visit that lustrous medieval-baroque city. But this best of months came at last to an end, punctuated by a reading I gave one evening of American poetry, from Whitman to Frost and Sandburg: a performance that almost broke down when I read 'Out of the Cradle Endlessly Rocking,' for my voice choked up out of homesickness and longing for my mate.

6

Meanwhile, in letter after letter, Sophia had already been introducing me to the new world of parenthood—the world of fixed schedules, feedings, diaperings, babblings, listenings, bathings, and anxious hoverings, with all the normal parental relaxations of fondling and petting taken all too gingerly. Current psychological doctrine then strictly opposed those very attachments that are the basis of love, security, and healthy growth! Quailing before the admonitory images of Watson and Freud, Sophy had almost been apologetic, in writing to me, about stealing a kiss from the back of her baby's neck, but had been haunted by the lines of Blake I used to recite: "Every time I steel myself to let the infant shriek and not to mind it, I hear a soft throbbing voice reading:

> 'Can a mother sit and hear
> An infant groan, an infant fear?
> No, no! never can it be!
> Never, never can it be!' "

The single-minded concern of lovers with each other and with the new way one ego impinged on another had now to give way to an-

Señor Madariaga

other reality, not a close dyad but a more open triad, a family. And just as a writer at work on a book has one ear cocked at all times to catch the inner voice that may be whispering a new phrase or flashing forth a new idea, so will a mother, in the midst of the most intimate conversation, intellectual or carnal, have an ear cocked for a baby's breathing or crying, or suddenly remember, in the midst of a confidence, some forgotten household duty upon which the baby's welfare, an hour hence, supposedly will depend. From the moment of my return when I embraced Sophy, I sensed that I had only exchanged a procession of phantom lovers for a solid flesh-and-blood rival, more constant in his presence, more insistent in his demands. From the outset, fortunately, I had an equal share in this ménage à trois: for as soon as I held our baby in my arms, I, too, succumbed.

During the Geneva separation Sophia and I had become so closely bound together in spirit that the letters we exchanged bear witness to the forgivable defect of most love letters: the very intensity of our passion made our declarations too repetitive to produce any effect on a neutral reader save boredom. Wordsworth's condition for poetic expression, that it should be infused by an emotion *"recollected in tranquillity,"* puts most intense love letters outside the public realm. At the height of our new intimacy I realized this and said so in a letter to Sophia after we had been parted six weeks: "I've just come away from a lecture by a Spanish man of letters named Salvador de Madariaga; and the wretch spent most of the time reading us Spanish tortas. That's not the sort of thing for a young man to listen to when his dear of dears is far away. Listen yourself:

> *Love me little by little*
> *Be not in haste*
> *For I would have you love me long.*

and then this:

> *Love is uphill*
> *And down dale together.*
> *I shall go uphill*
> *Though it be hard work.*

Life is so down-daley now inside of me, dearest—if only I can preserve a little of this till I embrace you and we begin to live together with our bratling!" That climactic letter was almost incoherent with passion. And in the final sentence I ended almost as the torta had begun:

> *Love me slowly, Love me deeply*
> *Love me long.*

Naturally, it has taken the remainder of our life together to transform this invocation into a time-tested reality.

CHAPTER TWENTY-EIGHT

Emancipation
in Edinburgh

I

The last time I came together with Patrick Geddes was at the end of
the summer of 1925, on my way back from Geneva. This was my
first opportunity to visit Edinburgh and explore alone the city with
which he had so long been identified. This time Geddes and I lived
under the same roof at the Outlook Tower, and I slept on an improvised cot amid bookcases and boxes of notes in the library in the
very stone tower, capped by a castellated turret in baronial style,
whose contents at once typified in conception all Geddes stood for:
the regional outlook, the urban focus, the unification of all the dispersed and dissociated aspects of our present jumbled technocratic
culture.

The dark, craggy outlines of the old city, with its towering stone
tenements and its pinnacled churches; the dank, murky atmosphere
in the old closes; the patent animal odors and the wild gleams of
beauty, mingling like the foul words that might stream forth from
the fresh, lovely faces of the nubile slum girls; the surly puritanic
note of John Knox juxtaposed, to so say, with the defiant erotic vitality of Mary Hamilton, the king's mistress in the ballad—all this
left an impression even more ineffaceable than my meager breakfast
talks with Geddes in the cozy little kitchen with its open-fired coal
stove. But he had left his mark all over the Old Town: there were
traces of him in the most unexpected places. So much so that an
urchin eager for a penny grabbed me by the hand to point out a

bust of Socrates Geddes had placed over an entrance and asserted: "Luv, that's the Professor." In a city of professors, as I discovered when he took me to a Rotary Club luncheon where he spoke to an audience that stayed respectfully beyond their strictly set hour, he was still notably *the* Professor.

I had plenty of time for exploration during this five-day visit, for at that moment Geddes was concentrated on his difficult relations with the Zionist organization, writing constant letters and memoranda: so, after breakfast, he would turn me over to his son Alasdair's old mountain-climbing companion, Mabel Barker, whom I knew of old from the week Sophy and I had spent in the Tyrol. Surefooted as a goat, she shamed me by skipping down the steep far slope of Arthur's Seat whilst I was trying a gingerly descent on all fours. That was a vivid week; but it was only at meals, or over a dram of neat whiskey before turning in for the night, that I got anything out of Geddes, except for a single ramble we took to Calton Hill on the final afternoon—as if he wished to make amends for bidding me visit him without providing sufficient free time for closing the gap between us.

At that period the Outlook Tower was an all-but-deserted place, kept going through the financial support of a small, loyal group of admirers and the exertions of Mrs. Galloway, the housekeeper, a ruddy-faced woman with a grimly reassuring sense of humor. "A woman of the people," Geddes told me, "but a lady": a combination still possible in Scotland, but never in England. I was at home in this Scots atmosphere, for the democracy worked both ways; after a supper party at the Tower, where I met Hugh McDiarmid, the new Scots poet—an anti-Burns man—the one woman with a title, Lady Whitson, took her place in washing the dishes as easily as an American university wife might, and far more easily than most American women of either her wealth or position.

Geddes conducted me through these half-dismantled chambers, from which he had been absent for more than a decade. The contents and arrangement of this laboratory-museum-library had filled me with excitement when I had first read about them, for one started at the top with an actual view of Edinburgh and the heavens above, and then as one descended story by story, one passed from city to region, from region to country, from country to commonwealth, from commonwealth to the world, with every sort of cartographic device and bibliographic aid so that, theoretically, one got a rich and full picture, at least in outline, of the physical and social world. But now, as if to jeer at Geddes's actual presence, everything had crumbled and fallen apart: here and there in the rubbish, one might find a time-browned historic chart mournfully meaningful, reminding one of heady discussions and high intellectual hopes before the First World War.

Geddes showed me the dusty piles of unsorted manuscripts, mostly records of his lectures, too rapid and unexpected in content to be taken down accurately by even the swiftest of court stenographers, lectures that never more than hinted at the living essence; and everywhere were bins of teasing notes, mostly on folded paper, that pointed to ideas, often brilliant, that had never been transformed into more communicable discourse once the original voice had vanished. *"Ay de mi!"* Geddes would say with a deep sigh of desperation.

> How am I to get these graphs and notes in order? A lifetime's accumulation, never really sorted out. I need your help, Mumford. My health is better now, but my doctors say that a winter in Edinburgh or London might kill me before my time. So it's time to be tidying up these idea middens, and that not too tardily. Bring your wife and bairn over next winter, when I am settled again in Montpellier. I need you, and while you're working with me, you can get your Doctorat Etranger at the University—an excellent place—and become a professor yourself. Writing is a poor trade. We professors have it easier and live longer. All you need is to present a creditable thesis in French.

At moments when he appealed for help there was a soft, womanly pathos about Geddes that contrasted with the almost ferocious virility of his usual self: he would shrug his shoulders, fling out his arms with a gesture of hopelessness and sometimes a film would cover his sorrow-laden eyes, bringing him close to tears—tears of frustration? of self-pity? of desperation? Loving him despite the distance between us, grateful to him for all he had given me, I could not help being moved by his plight; and as the years went on, these calls and these appeals became more urgent, for his hope of mastering the job himself ebbed with his increasing age.

Well before this, fortunately, I had steeled myself to resist Geddes's blandishments. I realized that 'helping Geddes' would be a career in itself: a career that would need the patience of a saint, the single-mindedness of Browning's Grammarian, the physical stamina of an athlete; and even then would be so full of frustrations and humiliations that it might come abruptly to an end before anything was accomplished. Merely to plow through these dead notes would have been the task of a lifetime; and to make sense of them one would have needed constantly to refer to Geddes himself, without any genuine prospect that his memory could now requicken the glowing moments when six separate ideas fused into a dazzling unity.

Yes: he who wanted to help Geddes would have to relive Geddes's life, but that would only recreate the very predicament that now caused these demands for succor. Forty years before, Geddes needed and might have used someone as devoted as Boswell—and far more self-effacing—to wing his flying words. Too late, far too late, he found Phillip Boardman, whose record of Geddes's conversations sometimes seems as authentic as Geddes's own letters or memoranda in the biographies by Amelia Defries or Phillip Mairet.

If I had needed confirmation of my doubts about my ability to satisfy P.G.'s demands, a brief incident, when we surveyed Edinburgh from the top of the Tower, would have set me straight. Geddes delighted not only in the view from the terrace but in the view inside provided by the old camera obscura; for it cast on a table in the darkened room the image of the city so that it came out in brilliant colors, without the blinding overhead light that leaches colors in direct sunlight: a pure impressionist result. I had long practiced the trick of half-shutting my eyes to a landscape to get the same effect; so I was reluctant to accept Geddes's dictum that what I now saw on the table had a special beauty I could not possibly have realized without this optical device. Then we went outdoors. Instead of letting me take in the landscape in my own way, he insisted on my seeing it through his eyes, standing behind me and holding me by the shoulders, almost savagely demanding that I pick out of the panorama exactly what he was seeing, and respond to it in the same way.

That settled it. Much as I admired Geddes, much as I had profited by his devastating sallies, I would not see Edinburgh or anything else through his eyes.

On the last morning Mabel Barker and Geddes walked me down to the Waverley Station, and his final words increased the sense of distance between us. Apart from repeating his old plea that I achieve a doctorate and take an academic post, he put forth an idea that was even further from any conceivable reality: that I might someday become a United States ambassador, carrying further the work that James Russell Lowell had done at the Court of St. James's in Geddes's youth. All the way down the hill Geddes's familiar suggestions kept buzzing in my ears, and at every step the distance between us widened again, making me impatient for the moment of getting aboard the train. When I finally got to my seat, I took out my notebook and recorded, in detail, what I have been summarizing here: that all possibility of any closer relation with Geddes was over; and I even guessed correctly that I would never see him again.

Though that judgment left me somewhat desolate, it brought a sense of release. I was about to turn thirty, and my tutelage was over: indeed, years before this I had begun to stand on my own feet, and I needed only this last contact with Geddes to realize how independent I necessarily had become; so that though I would continue to draw upon his ideas and his example in many ways, on my own terms, for my own purposes, any closer relation would have turned, inevitably, into a hostile one, as with a child whose parent is not wise enough to cast him loose. I was not willing to arrange the dried flowers of Geddes's thought into lifelike bouquets: but I could use what he had accumulated to form the compost out of which new ideas would grow in my own garden.

The proof of my feelings, even before I put the case to myself in so many words, was my failure to be captured even for a moment by Geddes's burgeoning plans for creating a series of residential colleges at Montpellier in the south of France. From the first, that project seemed to me a folly, for even when part of his second wife's modest fortune was poured into the scheme, there was no prospect of a permanent foundation, and without Geddes himself a residential college was no college at all, but at best another dormitory.

Geddes was captivated not only by the historic position of Montpellier itself, but by the open heath he had bought that gave him ample scope for building and not least for arranging his graphs and charts in the form of gardens. The fact that this parched land had no water supply of its own and, for the first half-dozen years, was too far from the city to be attached to a municipal water supply did not deter him from inviting Sophia and me to stay with him, though our child was still in the diaper stage. When he came by a windfall of some seven thousand dollars, in compensation for the loss of his Cities Exhibition, he invested it in a château, to boot, as a weekend retreat from a college that was itself a rural retreat from Montpellier. In short, the whole enterprise was a white elephant, and it produced in Geddes's fertile mind a whole herd of little white elephants.

In that final phase Geddes was not so much a scientist or a philosopher as an imperious but too long frustrated Master Builder. This was his last opportunity to convert his dreams, his plans, and his graphs into solid stone structures and ideologically conceived gardens that would testify concretely to his ideas when he was no longer there to explain them. In a sense he was building his tomb, or rather, a city of the dead, for his ideas. But actually the Montpellier project, I realized, was an evasion: an excuse for not completing the task too long postponed, that of translating his graphs into some coherent verbal form that would both explain and justify the endless hours and days he had spent—beginning at four and five in the morning—seeking wild truths in the too well-fenced zoo of his ideology.

This activity, this urgency, this adding more colleges to the burden of running a single one, covered up Geddes's constant despair: for in his heart he must have realized that the task he had left for the end of his life would never be accomplished. He would fasten on one person after another, demanding their 'help,' their 'cooperation,' their 'criticism,' but all he really asked for was their ear and their docile assent, so that once again he could go through the old exercises, now stereotyped beyond addition or correction: so self-sufficient in his mind that they discouraged rather than aided any wider application.

In view of Geddes's increasing senescence, the available means, and the prospective results, the whole Montpellier scheme was a wanton fantasy. But by the time it seized him, he was more exhausted and depleted than I then realized, for a severe fever he had suffered in India in 1924 had permanently undermined his vitality and probably shortened his life. Now, looking back on that period, I am inclined to think more charitably of those last years, for after all they did not prevent him from finishing with J. Arthur Thomson their long-contemplated opus, 'Life: Outlines of Biology.' This massive work, the summation of a lifetime of personal experience and an immense command of scientific resources, does better justice to Geddes's mind as a biologist than the specific but often subjective explications that accompany his more questionable graphs.

In trying to account for Geddes's strenuously extroverted activities during the last decade of his life, I have not hesitated to call a spade a spade; but it will give a better measure of Geddes's true dimensions if I now bring forth evidence to show that, in his best moments, he could be even more unsparing of himself in self-criticism. I draw upon a letter written to Branford as late as October 1929, with a first sentence that characteristically begins: "Council of war!—How to get over walls which keep us out of reach of other minds—effective reach of them anyway!" Then, after various considerations in his usual manner for marshaling old friends or holding a conference, he says:

Is not everyone we can think of as completely absorbed in his own thought and work as to be practically *inaccessible* inside his own walls? Are we not all prisoners? . . .
Is this then the social situation we are trying to under-

stand all this while—that "the individual, in each breast, is tyrannous to sunder them!" Even though there remain good feeling, as reminiscence, are we not—more or less all—like men distressed to the verge of bankruptcy, who know not where to turn? Yet even these often find someone to turn to after all, and thus weather the storm—but—in this world of social thought and endeavour—are not each and all more or less in the same solitary search—like so many explorers diverging in an Arctic wilderness—and mostly to be lost before reaching shelter, or survival till the return of chilly spring?

Despite the respectable looking minorities—who form a So. So. [Sociological Society], a Le Play House, an O.T. [Outlook Tower] or a college here—and who have some small tenaciously surviving results to show—what *real* advances have we in any direction of thought clarified to common agreement, or of action, or any real co-operation or resulting social effect? Have we anything more than little groups on a seat—on the Embankment at night—weary people so far gregarious, yet each unable for common understanding, much less cooperative activity—unable to buy, or even desire, each other's little wares, which they'll go on hawking again tomorrow—without social result!—and never an offer of real employment.

Unable to change his ways—for who was now more a prisoner than himself?—Geddes could nevertheless clearly see where they had led him, and were still leading him. That willingness to face the worst, without self-deception, was deeply in the grain of his scientific tradition and honorably counterbalanced his many more willful moments.

3

As I look through Geddes's letters during the period that followed our meeting in 1925, I am saddened by two things: the repetitiousness of their ideas and suggestions and, even worse, their irrelevance, their failure ever to reach the plane of easy personal intercourse, though often full of friendly concern about Sophia, his godson, Geddes, or my own health. But his own early expectation never quite vanished. As late as April 1931 he wrote me: "I have no colleague, executor and heir to whom I can look with any substantial hope but you." And one of his very last letters, just a few months before he died, made a final plea for 'collaboration,' *as between equals*!

Unfortunately, the collaboration was to consist in my finding in America funds for carrying out his scheme for building an American residential college, along with his Scots and Indian colleges! This appeal came at a moment when America was almost touching the bottom of the Great Depression, and I wrote what I fear was a brutal reply: for I reminded him of his own doctrine that men come before physical structures, and I reproached him for squandering his vital energy on these proliferating building projects. This answer must have shaken him; and his reply in turn shook me, though its stern beginning abruptly changed: "Dear Mumford—no! Lewis my son!"

In 1932 Geddes at last accepted the knighthood that, as a proud republican of the Victorian age upholding the independence of science from royal favor, he had declined twenty years before; and he stayed on in London for the ceremony, despite his doctor's warnings of its probably fatal consequences. That April I planned to begin in Germany a four months' study tour of European housing and technology, and I had made arrangements to spend a week or ten days with Geddes at Montpellier, to come face to face with the work that had occupied him for the past seven years. In my heart, I shrank from this final encounter, knowing how it would in the end only more glaringly disappoint this frustrated old man. Yet I was inwardly unprepared for the announcement of Sir Patrick Geddes's death, which appeared in the New York papers just a week before I sailed for Europe.

The Master of my youth was dead! That finally ended the dream of faithful discipleship and helpful collaboration which had never come down to earth in either of our lives. But, as the reader knows, the tragedy of our parting bore for me an earlier date.

4

Yet when my youthful dream faded, some of the reality that had originally stimulated it remained. Released from the pressure of hopes and pleas I could not fulfill, I was able henceforward to draw freely on those parts of Geddes's life and work that still nourished me and incited me to go further along lines he had often fleetingly indicated but never followed up. I could, in a series of essays and introductions, call the attention of my contemporaries to those parts of his thought they seemed most in need of. While I could never write the biography he had nominated me to write, those critical appreciations have perhaps aided, almost as much as any full-length study could, in placing Geddes in the niche he now occupies—though I fear that there is still a popular academic tendency to reduce his rank to that of a mere father of modern town planning. That depreciation of his many-faceted mind I have never shared.

As for my own obligations to Geddes, they are both closer and remoter than most people who have compared our ideas have discovered: closer in personal indebtedness, remoter in intellectual adhesion. Some of Geddes's ideas I have carried further and transformed: some of his favored prepossessions, like his singular devotion to Comte, I never shared, even as a young man: and some, like his Graphic Synthesis, his Chart of Life, which he regarded as his central contribution, I have rejected as an arbitrary and sterile counterfeit of his living philosophy.

But I have no desire to discount my debt even when, like Aristotle before me, I must contradict or correct my master. When in the 1950s Carl Sauer asked me to be co-chairman of the Wenner-Gren Conference on Man's Role in Changing the Face of the Earth, I knew far better than anyone else how much I owed to Geddes for that invitation. For it was from Geddes that I first heard the name of our great American geographer, George Perkins Marsh, whose original work on the earth as modified by human action, 'Man and Nature' (1864), Geddes had come upon in the seventies; and it was in all probability the little memoir I had written on Marsh in 'The Brown Decades' that helped draw the attention of Carl Sauer and other American geographers back to the pioneer they had neglected.

Some touch of Geddes's aboriginal energy and vitality, then, remains present, I would hope, even in my work today; though, as with a radioactive particle good for a generation, only a half-life is left. At the time I first encountered his thought, I was—as already noted—at the beginning of a period of mild invalidism, not too dissimilar from one Geddes had gone through at a somewhat later point. Without his example I could easily have drifted into a purely bookish life, short in tether, prudently bridled. That might have been the smooth road to conventional academic achievement. But my life took a different course; and it is in part to Geddes that I owe this difference. To me, the lesson of his example, both encouraging and admonitory, was worth—peace to all his more faithful disciples!—a cartload of his graphs and diagrams.

Gladly, however, I leave the last word on Geddes to a mature contemporary—indeed, a colleague of his—D'Arcy Wentworth Thompson, the many-sided author of a biological classic, 'Growth and Form.' When the biography of Thompson by his daughter appeared, someone raised the question of why there was no mention of Geddes in that work, though they had so many general points of resemblance: both original minds, but only half-appreciated, almost unheeded by their peers. In the correspondence that followed in 'The Times Literary Supplement,' Ruth Thompson cited one of her father's colleagues, who recalled a discussion that had taken place after Geddes's death, when a few members of the faculty who had known him were assessing his life and influence. Geddes and D'Arcy Thompson had never been close, partly perhaps because Geddes had been only a summer occupant of his Dundee chair, yet Thompson led the group in his vivid appreciation of Geddes's gifts.

"But D'Arcy," protested one of the participants, "you speak as if Geddes had been the best man of all of us!"

"*Well*," said D'Arcy Thompson quietly, "*wasn't he?*"

CHAPTER TWENTY-NINE

Sunnyside Pioneering

I

Back in 1924 we had decided that rents in Greenwich Village or Brooklyn Heights, the only parts of inner New York that attracted us, would be too steep for our purse; so we settled on the sole place that seemed possible for us—the new housing development that Clarence Stein and Henry Wright were now planting at the barren, weedy edge of Long Island City, walled by railroad tracks. I had inspected the first unit a year before, and we decided to invest in a cooperative apartment there. Because of the architects' concern to keep costs low, the rooms were small, the fixtures cheap and at first downright old-fashioned in design: but even in this early block of row houses and three-story apartments, there was an inviting emptiness, with gardens, play space, and young trees lining each side of the street. That helped make up for what was lacking in the interiors.

For the next eleven years we lived in this enclave in the midst of an industrial desert and watched the houses march from one block to another, becoming more commodious and more comely as experience taught the architects the futility of petty economies, since in any event they could not bring their housing costs down to the level that the lowest-paid workers could afford, as they had at first hoped. When we moved to Sunnyside, only one block and a row had been built: this was a tiny patch of urban order in the chaos of railroad yards and goat pastures, on the edge of Long Island City's air-polluting factory district. But it was already unlike any of the blocks that speculative builders were beginning to put up: witness Matthews Model Flats, which provided neither central heating or hot water! Even the first unit at Sunnyside had a playground with a somewhat premature tennis court in the center of it. From the beginning, furthermore, the project mingled one-, two-, and three-family houses, along with cooperative apartments.

The wasteland around Sunnyside was formidable; for it had been held for speculation for more than a generation, and though there was still a degenerate farm nearby when we moved there—a few cows would be driven past our windows twice a day, and we used to take our baby to a nearby chicken yard, to watch the rooster crow— our surroundings were so depressing that, for the sight of green, we sometimes would be driven Sundays to walk through nearby Calvary Cemetery. But as this new housing grew under our friends' direction, it created its own environment; and if you knew your way about, you might follow a footpath through a network of rear gardens and green lawns for almost half a mile, with all sorts of charming vistas. Only trimmed privet hedges then separated the private plots; and the density was low enough to permit younger children to gambol on the inner green—pure Breughel!—while the older ones had a more specialized playing field not far away.

Among the many dire pronouncements that wiseacres made when Sunnyside was founded was the dictum that New Yorkers had no interest in gardens, and that no one, for the sake of keeping the rear greens open, would walk a quarter of a mile to the garages that were at first provided at the edge of the tract. (These prophets still remain stone-blind to the meaning of the suburban exodus.) As so often happened, the wiseacres were wrong: their predictions, based on past experience, did not apply to fresh possibilities. New Yorkers who had never bothered to raise even a potted geranium in their apartments worked at their little pocket handkerchiefs of gardens as if this had been a lifelong passion. Within a few years the atmosphere of Sunnyside was neither desolate or yet suburban; and by now the place is an oasis of green.

What made this neighborhood unit uniquely good, apart from

the comeliness of its design, was the fact that, like Greenwich Village and far more than Brooklyn Heights, it was a mixed community, in which one might mingle without undue intimacy with one's neighbors. Manhattan was sufficiently close at hand for us to enjoy the advantages and opportunities that it could supply, beginning, of course, with our means of earning a living; and we were less than twenty minutes from Times Square, by subway, and only half an hour by bus, in those precongestion days, from the great Public Library on Fifth Avenue. In addition, we could get much companionship and social intercourse in an area within the walking distance of a three-year-old child: from tennis to social dinners, or just casual droppings-in without even the necessity of a phone call.

But we had still another advantage: the variety of houses provided for people with a variety of occupations and incomes, ranging from a grocer's clerk with an income of fifteen hundred dollars a year to physicians and lawyers who earned more than ten thousand—then a quite decent professional sum. This gave the place exceptional educational opportunities, for people who live in one-class neighborhoods all too easily lose their sense of social realities. If I became vividly aware in the early thirties of the immediate menace of fascism in the United States, and the attraction it often had for Irish and Italian Catholics, from even reputedly liberal members of the ecclesiastical hierarchy on down, it was because we were once awakened in the middle of the night by a drunken Irish woman across the way, seemingly a decent enough woman when sober, but with an ugly tongue when under the influence of liquor. She ended a party she had been giving by coming out on the terrace, cursing the Jews at the top of her voice, and threatening that Hitler would finish them off. Had I lived only near people of my own kind, that early alert, so much more penetrating than any newspaper account, might never have reached my ears.

2

The years we spent in Sunnyside were not merely sustaining to our family relations. They confirmed by experience many of the things my friends and I in the Regional Planning Association had begun to speculate upon and actively promote as necessary for renovating our great overgrown metropolises, with their overpowering impersonality and loneliness. (*Anomie,* the French sociologists called it.)

Sunnyside would not have been conceived in the way it actually was had these ideas not already come into existence. Their translation into practice, so far from disillusioning us, worked rather in the opposite direction, at a time when all the forces in our society were moving toward anonymity, impersonality, conformity, regimentation. At the end of this was the crime-inviting emptiness of high-rise housing projects—witness the dire fate of the Pruitt-Igoe 'model housing' in St. Louis!—or the dreary down-to-earth blankness of the Levittowns. In contrast, Sunnyside enhanced its human character.

In town planning circles during the fifties there were numerous denunciations of 'the neighborhood' as no longer a natural unit of the city: usually made on formal theoretic grounds, by people who had never lived in an active neighborhood, and who attributed to it a fantastic isolation and self-centeredness and parochialism that is only true of the low-income industrial groups of a big city like Paris, who are confined by poverty to their *quartier.* But there is no argument that can be made against a neighborhood that does not apply equally to a metropolis or a nation. Whenever the social idea miscarries, impassable barriers and forbidding frontiers arise.

Even in the most barren urban wasteland vestiges of neighborhood mixture and self-sufficiency remain in the relation of customers and shopkeepers, sometimes maintained beyond a generation. And I know from our varied experiences of Greenwich Village, Brooklyn Heights, and Sunnyside—three genuine neighborhoods—how essential this unit is to the improvement of urban life. For in all healthy growth, organized forms—cells and organs—are the basis for maintaining a dynamic equilibrium and controlling the growth of the larger organism. The 'urbanologists' who still dismiss the neighborhood are the same breed that was sure that onetime apartment-house dwellers would never develop a taste for gardening.

But if Sunnyside was to teach me in the most direct way possible, despite its sometimes irritating limitations and handicaps, how good a well-planned quarter of the city might be, it also taught me another lesson that bites deep into the story of all man's efforts to

413

solidify his most vital impulses by translating them into brick and stone. Buildings are vehicles of the spirit only so long as the spirit that produced them remains alive and at intervals renews itself. After the spirit departs, there is something derisive and ironical in the structure left behind.

Sunnyside still stands: but in the general bankruptcy of the thirties, marked by the bitter and disruptive rent strike, the spirit that built it and brought so many people together, all so expectantly, so hopefully, almost vanished. But not quite! Our daughter noted much later that the Sunnyside students in the High School of Music and Art formed an identifiable, cohesive group: outstanding in ability, poised and balanced. In those modest gardens not just flowers but healthy human beings could and did grow—and perhaps will keep on growing.

Often on my trips between Boston and Washington, the train has taken me—but all too swiftly—past Sunnyside Gardens in its Long Island detour; and I would fasten my eyes to the windowpane, eagerly, to see how well the houses have stood up, and how the slim trees now have grown so heavy in foliage that they almost choke off the light from the front rooms. Yes, much of the original charm remains, thanks to the pride of those who first took over Sunnyside, thanks even more to the original imagination of the planners and their financial sponsor, Alexander Bing. But the story of what was planned and what has survived was told by Henry Wright in his 'Rehousing Urban America' (1934) and by Clarence Stein in his later 'New Towns for America.' The present sketch is only a personal footnote to that story.

As a family, Sophia and I were always more than a little cramped for space at Sunnyside; and one room in the cooperative apartment we lived in for the first couple of years had to serve as my bedroom and my study. I had not improved things by proposing that two rooms be turned into one, so that I might have a workplace where I might occasionally stretch my legs. Our long room in Hicks Street had spoiled me; and I ignored the fact that in claiming so much space for myself I caused Sophia to sleep in the living room, which one entered directly from the hall, and when I had company in the evening, she, while still a nursing mother, needing sleep, had to place a screen before her bed.

But, as we found out, there were many compensations for both of us. While some of our new neighbors proved interesting friends, many of our old friends were drawn to Sunnyside and became neighbors, as did two of Sophy's sisters and their husbands; and it was a delight to have all these people within walking distance. On a much later occasion in Berkeley, we had the same good fortune with our new colleagues in the University, and our old friends, the Wursters and the Meiklejohns, enjoying a kind of spontaneity and easy familiarity, freed from the tyranny of the engagement pad and the calendar, that gave refreshment to an old fondness. At Sunnyside, whilst our baby was young, we were even able to go visiting evenings without hiring a baby-sitter; for we had only to wheel his carriage to a friend's house and leave it on the porch.

After a couple of years, however, the lack of space and internal privacy irked us: so we moved to the westernmost portion of Sunnyside: to a five-room house that was part of a series of terraces, running through from one street to the next, designed in this case by Frederick Ackerman—one of our Regional Planning group. When we had watched these rows going up, we had asked each other: "Who would ever live in such rabbit hutches?" The surprising answer was: *We would!*

By the time the houses were built, the first row, which had a wide green in the rear as well as a narrow terrace with poplars between the facing rows, was really charming. So, though we were still looking forward to a bigger family, we thoughtlessly settled for this inadequate house, mainly, I fear, on esthetic grounds, since more ample six-room houses, at an advance of only ten dollars a month, were available. In the end our mistake served us well: if we had had enough space in 1935, when our daughter, Alison, was born, we might never have decided to establish a year-round base in the country.

In our early years at Sunnyside, we actually lived under double constraint. Our most obvious limitation, besides the initial one of cramped space, was my slim income: during the first year there our expenses were thirty-two hundred dollars—prices were still war-inflated as compared to the decade before or the decade after—while our total income was only twenty-nine hundred dollars. According to Mr. Micawber's classic principle, this implied misery. The disparity was so obvious that my mother offered to forgo part of her monthly check, meager though that was.

Gradually our income became sufficient: within two years after 1927, indeed, it almost doubled. But even then we were forced to watch our pennies, and rarely could look ahead confidently more than a month. The word 'security' had no place in our vocabulary, and it wasn't till we were both past sixty that we gave serious thought to what might happen to us in our old age—or, before that, if either of us should fall seriously ill. True: in the earliest years, we had more than our fill of spaghetti and beans, but like Henri Quatre's prosperous peasant, we had a chicken in our pot every Sunday—unfortunately not always a very fresh chicken, for at least once, I still recall, it stank of formaldehyde, so that even the first dubious bite proved uneatable.

During this pinched period, I would walk along Fifth Avenue, after a visit to Liveright, my publisher, or a luncheon with the editors of 'Harper's,' juggling mentally the checks that should be coming in during the next couple of months from new articles, as against expenses that were far more certain. The "archaic Greek smile" by which one of my friends characterized my expression at that time may have been due, not to any inner sense of security, but to the discovery that both ends would actually meet! Sophia's modest demands for clothes and household accouterments made our condition easier: but she could no longer go around, as she had done in the brashness and the beauty of her youth, with so slim a wardrobe of homemade dresses: a minimum for everyday wear, and only one for parties.

Still, in describing our lean economy at this time, I find I have been exaggerating the penalties and have not sufficiently taken into account all the alleviating circumstances, apart from the natural overflow of our great city's life. Yes: we knew the constraints of poverty, but they were lightened by a growing group of more prosperous friends whose hospitality added a color to our lives we could not have otherwise enjoyed. What 'The Dial' did first for Sophy in opening delectable glimpses of a gayer world, Clarence Britten, Robert Lovett, Morris Crawford, J. E. Spingarn, Clarence Stein, and Lee Simonson did for us later: taking me to lunch at their clubs, inviting us to literary soirées, or providing us with free seats for the theater. Before long I was at home in a whole gamut of clubs, from the Harvard to the National Arts and the Manhattan clubs, without having to belong to any or pay dues! Obviously this was not the sort of poverty that dogged writers like George Gissing.

In addition, I must note the larger hospitalities offered during the thirties by the Spingarns in splendid parties at the Cotton Club in Harlem and their New Year's Eve balls. Likewise the princely indiscretions of Tom Beer, who in 1932, before his mid-thirities breakdown, provided a first-class passage for me to Europe instead of the second class I had put in for, under the pretext that his agent had a special skill in arranging such matters.

To return to the daily life of Sunnyside: something our age has still to pay effective attention to is the wear and tear of a two-generation family during the child-bearing years, when the wife and mother is on twenty-four-hour duty, and often, during the periods of teething and illness, cannot count on an unbroken night's sleep. When servants were cheap and plentiful, even poor families—I am thinking of Emerson's widowed mother—did not lack some daily help and relief: how else could Mrs. Emerson, with her big family, have reserved for herself a whole hour after breakfast, behind a closed door, inviolate from intrusion?

Until Sophia began working, first at the local nursery school in the early 1930s, then at other experimental schools in New York, she sometimes found her daily life a little lacking in personal stimulus; and the more active and independent our child became, the less need there seemed to be for her constant attendance—though the family of three or four children she then still hoped for would have fully justified her choosing motherhood and wifehood as her main vocation. Unfortunately, the ten-year delay before the birth of our second child—a delay caused by a miscarriage in 1926 and then another in 1928, plus the exigencies of my writing life—produced an increasing sense of frustration. It was not so much the harassment of domestic work that bothered her, since I took on a fair share of the daily household tasks, including cooking. But there were the inevitable moments when Sophia wistfully looked back to her editorial days on 'The Dial,' as much for the easy personal intercourse with the contributors who hovered about as for the work itself.

This problem is evaded, not met, by the old-fashioned feminist solution which would give a full-time outside job to the mother and let her hire a substitute mother for the daytime, to take her place. Nor is it solved, in any satisfactory fashion, by the day-care center, which liberates the mother by confining the child and isolating it from its parents. In the first case the substitute mother might have as much ground for complaint as the liberated one, except that she is paid in cash. Here I would offer Fourier's "Butterfly Principle"—frequent changes of work throughout the day rather than full time at any one occupation. If all our communities were planned for three generations, and the houses grouped with a view to mutual aid, there could be a fuller sharing of domestic tasks; and it should be possible for a mother to have time off for her own purposes or for her professional pursuits, knowing that other mothers or experienced older people would be on duty to share the care of her children, informally, as she in turn would do for them. When our daughter, Alison, lived in an intimate community in Brooklyn, she was the member of such a group and described its advantages in a lively article in 'Woman's Day'—a magazine widely circulated in supermarkets.

3

When Sunnyside began to grow, no one had anticipated that in a few years its layout would help to generate a more active social life once people of different vocations, interests, and appetites were drawn so conveniently together. The finishing touch to the essential idea of community came, not from the architects but from the nascent groups of neighbors who wanted community rooms for many different purposes: for social parties, for political discussions, for literary evenings, for dancing and activities in which two or three score of people might take part. Result: The well-lighted leftover space in the cellars of the apartment houses became the magnetic core of Sunnyside's community life, before the larger Community House was built. At a minimum expense for kitchen equipment and room enclosure the residents supplied something precious the architects had originally forgotten—that Man, as Aristotle observed, is a political animal!

If it had not been for all the social opportunities that Sunnyside in time offered, its many early disadvantages—the dreariness of the surrounding area, the poisonous effluvia from factory chimneys, the lack of decent nearby school facilities—would have driven many of us away, well before the great exodus of the mid-thirties occurred. But not even in Cambridge or in Stanford or Hanover, three admirable university towns, have we ever found better intellectual companionship, or more vivid, enlivening discussions. Even the local politics of running the nursery school, or attending to the upkeep of the common inner green, added an extra essential political dimension to our lives.

As I write this account the liveliest memories of these local meetings come back to me. Whether they fostered poetic recitations or political debates, they proved something even more important: namely, that with a little leeway for experiment, the democratic process would still function provided the local unit allowed a mixture of political, religious, and social beliefs—and of occupations, too. This makes for a more satisfactory all-round life, based on personal participation, than any one-class community, however wealthy, can offer.

As for evening parties and dinners, one particularly remains in mind, perhaps because crystallized in a poem of Babette Deutsch's. One night at the Yarmolinskys', when Avrahm, out of an acid skepticism that sprang from his dedication to the Life of Reason, said at one point: "Spirit? What is spirit? Who can define it? It's only a word." None of the counterattacks from the other writers present budged him from his position; but as it happened, our young friend Josephine Strongin was one of that group, and when she left early, Avrahm and I both gallantly accompanied her to her Richmond Hill home in a taxi. All evening that frail, palpitating butterfly of a poet fluttered around our heavy thoughts; mischievous, dancing, luminously inarticulate. Finally Avrahm and I, alone in the cab returning to our party, began to compare notes about the lovely pixie we had left at her door. "Why," said Avrahm, with awe in his voice, *"she is pure spirit!"*

I put that moment alongside a more communal scene, to stand for a hundred other impromptu meetings and relaxed encounters that atoned for all that was harried or humdrum in our preoccupied lives. This was a night in winter when the snow, which had been falling all afternoon, mantling the gabled roofs, outlining the branches of the plane trees, haloing the street lamps, turning bushes into huge white mushrooms, ceased falling around ten o'clock. Then, as if by a whispered command, we neighbors all sallied forth on the streets, hushed in their whiteness, with not even the track of an auto visible: plowing our way through the inner courts, tossing snowballs at each other, licking samples of the fresh snow, pausing silently to take in the muted rosy beauty of the night sky over Manhattan, by turns breathless with delight and shouting with laughter as we encountered some familiar face, ruddy with the same intoxication. We embraced one another then, and we embraced the world in the pure joy of being: knowing life at that moment held nothing better.

Such a spontaneous explosion of high spirits in a spotless snow-drenched world came to Sophia and me once again—around the Common in Cambridge a quarter of a century later. This was like a miraculous second induction into a polar paradise, before evil had invaded the world, a world whose virginal whiteness knew no Moby Dick.

The occasions of this sort that Sunnyside made possible were sometimes repeated, after the Second World War, when, under pressure of need, various prefabricated villages were built for veterans returning with their families to college. But we have still to think the whole problem through, in terms of both more varied human needs and suitable architectural structures; and good as Sunnyside was, neither it nor its later offshoot, Radburn, went as far in providing variety, both social and esthetic, as the best of the later British New Towns would do.

CHAPTER THIRTY

'Sticks and Stones'

I

I began this digging into my past life and work in the autumn of 1956 and wrote a first draft of this book. In another spurt of writing in the winter of 1962–3 I elaborated and filled out part of this account. But not until a dozen years later did I discover that I had composed some sixteen or eighteen chapters with hardly more than a passing reference to one of the most constant and significant phases of my experience—my response to architecture in its most fundamental and inclusive aspect—what W. R. Lethaby had summed up as "Form in Civilization."

When I discovered this omission, I almost laughed aloud. How had it been possible for me to deal with the very years in which my study of the culture of cities was making a deep impress on my outlook and plans, inciting many appropriate activities, without a word about what was constantly awakening my responses and reflections? The joke became even more blatant when, in sorting the various literary oddments and reflections I put together in 'Findings and Keepings' (1975), I read, as if for the first time, the almost forgotten series of notes on buildings I had begun as early as 1915, as an incidental part of my survey on foot of my whole metropolitan environment. Was this a chance oversight—or was I hiding something from myself?

What makes this oversight more puzzling is that, when I wrote about my explorations of the metropolitan region and my becoming a founding member of the Regional Planning Association, the very group that was rethinking the problems of urban living, I owed an immediate debt for both, as the reader knows, to the same man, Charles Harris Whitaker. Whitaker did more to open the windows to the fresh currents that were stirring in architecture than perhaps any other leader in America except Gustav Stickley, the editor of 'The Craftsman.' When Whitaker took over the 'Journal of the American Institute of Architects' in 1913, similar minds in Germany, Switzerland, Holland, and England were working to the same end.

My earliest notes about architecture were at first merely random esthetic observations and pencil sketches of cornices, balconies, fire escapes, or the incongruous water tanks on the roofs of pretentious apartment houses. But quite early these notes were followed by more functional descriptions of innovative modern buildings, such as the Riverside Model Tenements near Brooklyn Heights (1896), which had no dark or airless rooms and provided a generous inner quadrangle that served both as park and drying green. But I was likewise impressed by a large building on the East River specially designed for tenants with tubercular histories; for its balconies and French windows not merely welcomed fresh air but drank in the morning sun. Though such happy experiments were rare, I quickened to them at once.

But to be honest I must admit with a blush that the first time I visited Ogunquit in 1915 I was charmed to 'discover' an unusually straightforward shingled house, newly built, which seemed to me a fresh specimen of modern design. So innocent was I then of architectural history that I did not realize that with its second-story overhang, its diamond-paned windows, and its unpainted clapboards, it was a close approximation of a seventeenth-century model.

When much later Henry-Russell Hitchcock, a well-trained young Harvard scholar, asked me for a more detailed bibliography than the one I had provided in 'Sticks and Stones,' he was baffled by my admission that it was on my urban and rural rambles, not in libraries, that I had mostly encountered the buildings I had written about. Direct observation and experience were the neglected complement I added to such systematic (academic) knowledge as was available in books.

My earliest article on modern architecture, or to put it more correctly, on the sources of modern form, appeared in a *nonprofessional* magazine—namely, 'The New Republic,' in 1921. It was entitled 'Machinery and the Modern Style,' for at that time it was not yet fashionable to speak of 'the' Machine. Since, except as incidental background, my early articles in Whitaker's JAIA bear witness as much to the editor's charity as to any studious qualifications of mine, I now ask myself, wonderingly, what on earth impelled Alvin Johnson in 1923, as the Director of the New School for Social Research, to invite me to outline a series of lectures on contemporary architecture, to be given by various leaders in the field. And what preposterous audacity caused me to outline a series on the *history* of American architecture, for which the only plausible collaborator, it turned out, would be myself? But that was what happened! Johnson agreed to my giving the course alone: and I spent six months or so in an effort to absorb enough from books and magazines to unify and bring into focus my still all-too-unballasted observations.

Viewed in any light, this was a dubious adventure, both in Johnson's first conception and even more in my overconfident response: for the historical and critical analysis of post-Colonial American architecture was only beginning. No general historic interpretation of this field, comparable even to Barrett Wendell's history of American literature, as yet existed. As for the course itself, this was, unless I am mistaken, the first to be offered anywhere on the whole panorama of American architectural development. A mere sketch? Yes, decidedly! But often an artist's quick pencil outlines will have a vitality that the laboriously finished painting may lack.

Fortunately, I was spared the humiliation that might have followed had I actually given the course I had put together by the fall of 1924. My first lecture proved humiliation enough: only half a dozen auditors appeared. Naturally the new class was dropped. I have given my share of unsuccessful lectures in my time, and once at the Columbia Forum, when I espoused the program of our country's immediate resistance to the totalitarian onslaughts of Nazi Germany, the members of the audience began, by the middle of the lecture, to walk out on me. Never did my heart sink so low, however, as when I said "Good night" to that handful of listeners in the New School and realized that neither I nor my subject had appealed even to this small self-selected group. But like General Foch's at the Battle of the Marne, my reaction to the threat of defeat in those days was to counterattack at once. As soon as I had swallowed my disappointment, I set about to salvage the failure by spending the winter writing out my proposed lectures for immediate magazine publication!

At first, while outlining the lectures, I had put together a few premature and laborious chapters for a book I hopefully conceived as a contribution to the series of paperbacks that the editors of 'The New Republic' had recently launched—before any but the two Boni brothers had taken the potentialities of paperback publication seriously. In offering a sample of this manuscript to Herbert Croly, the editor of 'The New Republic,' I too confidently hoped that the subject itself would have a special appeal to him, since he had been an editor of 'The Architectural Record' until 1914. But Croly's experienced eye probably detected the weakness of my synopsis and even more seriously of my architectural background. At all events, he turned the proposed work down.

The following autumn Alvin Johnson generously renewed his offer; and here I must record a debt of gratitude to the woman who underwrote this invitation: Esther Johnson, then chief of the circulation department at the great Central Library on Bryant Park. We had had little more than a pleasant nodding acquaintance at the check-out desk: but it was enough to awaken her interest in my career and enlist her sympathies. Without telling me of her intentions, she rounded up enough members of her staff to ensure my having the minimal audience required for my second New School sally.

Though lecturing has remained a side road in my career, the fact that I had presented such a course gave me my first slippery foothold in the academic world and helped pave the way for the invitations that have followed at intervals throughout my life. What good fortune for me that such an animated and dedicated career woman as Esther Johnson was behind me! Another such was Laura

Bragg, the director of the Berkshire Museum at Pittsfield—who likewise gave me timely help and encouragement when I most needed
them. Both these women responded to my talents and mothered my
reputation. They exemplified a specially valuable breed of New
Woman, for their professional dedication had not inhibited their deep
maternal impulses in the service of the mind.

3

The value of my second plunge into a New School course was to
restore my self-confidence as a potential lecturer. Better still, my crisp
early articles in 'The Freeman' and in Whitaker's 'JAIA' served as
chapters for a new kind of book, 'Sticks and Stones.' The success of
that book not merely opened up my many-sided professional career
better than a limited Ph.D. thesis would have done but established
my place as a wide-ranging critic. This came all the easier, I must
modestly note, because outside of a limited academic area—and the
contributions of a few members of the older generation like Claude
Bragdon and Irving Pond—there were then no serious competitors,
since the most competent of our architectural historians and critics,
Montgomery Schuyler, had died.

The first acknowledgment of my status as an interpreter of contemporary architecture came almost at once through an invitation
from Hamilton Owens, then editor of the Baltimore 'Sun,' to spend
a week gathering impressions for a series of four architectural articles for his paper. The first of these was an appreciation of Baltimore's early domestic tradition, particularly its human scale and its
lively orange and scarlet brick façades. The greater part of its old
buildings, I pointed out, had plainly been designed for human beings,
and as a result the older streets were "a mad carnival of color."

In my next article, 'Deserts versus Gardens,' I dwelt on the contest that perpetually goes on between the desert (paved streets, backyards, alleys, transportation arteries) and the garden; and pointed
out that when the garden has the upper hand, even the meanest
house on a tree-lined street possesses a modicum of charm. To recover the garden, people too readily gave up the advantages of the

city by moving to the suburb. But there was, I suggested, "a middle ground between the overspacious platting which only the very well-to-do could afford in settings like Roland Park and Guilford, and the abject and monotonous streets which the commercial builder is now rapidly planting over the vacant squares of Baltimore."

In my final article, entitled 'How to Ruin Baltimore,' I suggested that the surest way to do this was to imitate the congestion of skyscraper office buildings in a central district, as in New York and Chicago, where the designs will be so inexorably determined by financial values that they might as well be turned over to the office boy—or as one would say nowadays, to the computer. "To ruin Baltimore . . . to destroy its suburbs and turn its streets and avenues into catacombs," I summed up my advice in two words: "Build skyscrapers."

I have never had reason to go back on that timely judgment, and I am pleased now to find how rapidly my ideas on building and planning had matured in the very act of writing 'Sticks and Stones.'

My next invitation came from the Woman's Club of Grand Rapids, seconded by other invitations from Chicago: so I spent a month in the Middle West shuttling each week between the two cities, talking critically out of my still unripe knowledge about architecture as applied to these cities. From my Grand Rapids meetings I profited in more ways than one, first by my opportunity to supplement my earlier tour of a furniture factory in High Wycombe in the Chilterns by a close look at Grand Rapids products at a time when 'Grand Rapids' was almost a synonym for 'American furniture manufacture.' There I found that the most advanced specialized machines were used to turn out already obsolete forms—fake museum specimens like spiral table legs—which a further change in fashionable taste next year would make obsolete. The handicraft of the original Dutch artisans in Michigan had largely been displaced by machines, though furniture making was still almost a family industry. The wives of the owners not merely visited the factories frequently but influenced—hardly less than the designers—the seasonal choices of French or Italian or Spanish or Jacobean models.

This early encounter with a Woman's Club suggested to me then that the hidden private purpose of such afternoon lectures was to provide more interesting overnight guests for the bored wives and daughters of the more well-to-do manufacturers, bankers, and lawyers. Actually I found myself feeling more at home in the factories than in my hosts' dining rooms.

Doubtless the memory of my last dinner in Grand Rapids reenforced my growing resolution to eschew lecture tours. On this final occasion the dinner was held at the Country Club, in order to accommodate more guests for the farewell party. The night was bitter cold, and the snowed-in clubhouse was even colder; our party sat alone in the desolate long dining room, as if a blizzard had stranded us. The fact that the men were in dinner jackets made the human atmosphere even chillier and more constraining. Once we were seated, silence settled over the party; and I was too worn out and withdrawn to do anything to break the ice: no one dared to test that ice by even a banal observation, to see if it would hold our weight. When the silence finally became unbearable, our hostess suddenly turned to me and said brightly: "Don't you think, Mr. Mumford, that we all neglect epistemology far too much nowadays?" I still don't know what the right answer to that question could be: but later, when I had time to reflect, I guessed that the unfamiliar word had escaped from the mouth of the previous lecturer the week before. To be honest, as well as charitable, however, I must admit that this incident has served me many times at other parties to do precisely what it was unable to do in Grand Rapids—to break the ice!

But in contrast, my first Chicago experience was highly stimulating and profitable. In Chicago, Clarence Stein's architectural friends, Ernest Grunsfeld and Henry Klaber, had just set up an office together; and Chicago itself on immediate contact opened up my whole architectural horizon. For the first time I beheld the confident contemporary forms of the great school of Chicago architects who had begun to flourish there in the eighties, awakened and challenged by the powerful examples Henry Hobson Richardson had given them in the Marshall Field warehouse and the Glessner mansion: an influence so many-sided that the first house young Frank Lloyd Wright built for himself derives directly from Richardson's shingled houses. Until then, the names of these robust Chicago ar-

chitects, with the exception of Sullivan and Wright, were almost unknown to me; and their buildings had scarcely cast a shadow on my
consciousness. But now at last I beheld the great achievements of
the eighties and early nineties; Adler and Sullivan's Auditorium Hotel and Theater, the Monadnock Building (Holabird and Root), the
later Schlesinger and Meyer Building (Louis Sullivan), to say nothing
of many other buildings now destroyed, which were equally full of
the same masculine vigor.

None of these significant works was dealt with in 'Sticks and
Stones.' Soon afterward, however, Thomas Tallmadge, the Chicago
historian of this period, treated fresh works of the Chicago School
as if they had diminished in importance when put alongside the
fashionable simulations of the neoclassic leaders like Daniel Burnham, Charles Follen McKim, and Stanford White. I had failed to
exploit—indeed I had not even riffled through—this rich material
in my first survey. If I had any earlier image at all of the Chicago
School, it derived mainly from Claude Bragdon's appreciation of
Sullivan or, at a still further remove, from the bitterness of Sullivan's
one-sided account in his 'Autobiography of an Idea.' There, in the
act of recounting the frustration and neglect of his own work, Sullivan dismissed much of the excellent work done between 1890 and
1910 by a slightly later generation, as if the Chicago World's Fair
had immediately blighted everything. Beneath the surface, his Autobiography reveals less about the state of architecture than about
his wounded ego and his misspent sexual life.

Not strangely, one of the first persons to do justice to the innovations of the Chicago architects was a European, Eric Mendelsohn, and at our first meeting in 1927 he expressed his enthusiasm
to me. By good luck, my chief guide to these buildings was the same
architect who had shown them to Mendelsohn, Barry Byrne, who
had started his apprenticeship in architecture as an office boy for
Frank Lloyd Wright. As a Catholic architect, Byrne was seeking for
an adequate symbolic alternative to the Gothic and Baroque clichés
of the architects the Catholic hierarchy usually favored. Byrne sought
an expression equally fit for a cathedral, a church, and a parochial
school, and not unfit either for secular architecture. But with char-

acteristic modesty, it was not until Byrne and I had become friends that he was ready to show me his own work.

Meanwhile, through Ernest Grunsfeld I had studied some of Wright's classic 'prairie houses' in Riverside, and had admired his fertility of invention, though my favorite house, the Cheney house, has fewer of his spectacular earth-flattened prairie forms, with their heavy overhangs and low ceilings, and more of a classic serenity and formality than his willful genius usually favored. It took much further study for me to come to grips with Wright's work in all its protean manifestations; so it was not Wright's innovations but the sturdy vernacular of the Chicago School, with its command of external space and interior form, that first awakened me and dominated my original reactions.

The crude vigor of Chicago, rising from the ashes of its Great Fire in 1873, had taken many disorderly and wasteful forms: in the tangle of deliberately disconnected railroad systems; in the sprawling mass of stockyards whose stench penetrated the best residential quarters; in the pollution of its waterways and the sacrifice of its lakefront to rail traffic. But that rampant vitality had given its architects and engineers the courage to make structural innovations, like the floating foundations for skyscrapers in areas where no solid rock was near the surface; and it led to the invention of steel-frame construction, with its curtain wall which freed useful interior space from the progressively heavier masonry needed for the support of mounting stories.

Whatever the misuses of the steel-framed skyscraper as an agent of congestion and an automatic inciter to higher land values, for a short while it had liberated the more creative spirits in American architecture. The Chicago that I saw in the twenties was no mere "Hog Butcher for the world": in the university it would give scope to John Dewey in education, to Thorstein Veblen in sociological economics, to George Mead in philosophy—and to Sandburg, Dreiser, and Sherwood Anderson in literature: not least to the galaxy of architects whose work was an unconscious synthesis of the emerging age, in its hopeful embryonic manifestations.

After I came back East, I turned my experience to account by writing a series of articles for 'Architecture,' then a vigorous review edited for the house of Scribner by Henry H. Saylor. These essays were reprinted by McGraw-Hill in 1975, thanks to Martin Filler's initiative, along with later articles in 'The Architectural Record,' under the title 'Architecture as a Home for Man' in celebration of my eightieth birthday.

At a time when Fiske Kimball, a devotee of classic and Renaissance formalism, was still dismissing the esthetic and constructional innovations of the Chicago School as barbarous, my essays were the first open-eyed estimate of those Chicago pioneers whose work was worthy to be placed alongside the equally bold planning and building of Olmsted and Richardson in Boston. With Montgomery Schuyler's unwavering appreciation of the buildings of Sullivan and Wright, and Wright's estimate of his own work in 'In the Cause of Architecture,' I had the honor of closing a long period of critical neglect when I carried my appraisal further in 'The Brown Decades' in 1931. Since then a huge literature has grown up around the work of the Chicago School, thanks to the later studies of Carl Condit and others. No wonder the present generation finds it hard to realize how many of the great classics of modern architecture were still standing in Chicago and Buffalo during the twenties without being considered worthy of appreciative notice, still less treated with critical discernment. (Today many of those buildings have been destroyed and supplanted by towering urbanoid anthills.)

4

And now, to round out the account of these humble beginnings in urban and architectural studies, I must say something about my encounters with Frank Lloyd Wright, that architect of genius who loomed so high above the American horizon between 1890 and 1950. In the twenties, when I became personally acquainted with him— indeed, before I had had more than a fleeting glance at his buildings—his planet was in all but total eclipse. He was one of the handful of people I have known who, through the direct impact of their personalities, I would place on the same level as Patrick Geddes. Yet that very force, I must ruefully admit, remained at the end—as with Geddes—an obstacle to the deeper and closer attachment that both men at one time or another openly sought.

Our first contact came about through my book 'Sticks and Stones,' for Wright had written me, unexpectedly, an appreciative letter about it. At the time I wrote that book I was so little acquainted with Wright's buildings that I dared mention them only in passing. Even when in 1925 I had contributed a pathetically meager and tentative article on Wright's significance for Henric Wijdeveld's presentation of his work in Wijdeveld's Dutch architectural review, 'Wendingen,' I still lacked even a literary acquaintance with Wright's work. But Wright himself opened the door to me; and he followed up his letter, in 1927, by inviting me to lunch with him alone in his favorite New York hotel, the Plaza.

One could not be in the presence of Wright for even half an hour without feeling the inner confidence bred by his genius. Certainly it was no flattering appreciation of his work by me that had led him to seek me out. Nor had I approached him in turn with the handicap of being a worshipful disciple: we met under the sign of friendship, which erases distinctions and inequalities. There was, I found, a curious softness about Wright's face that somehow brought the word 'corn-fed' immediately to one's mind: a sort of family resemblance to Sherwood Anderson that increased my pleasure later when, at the Guggenheim Museum's big show of Wright's work, I discovered that while Anderson was still in a publicity agency in Chicago he had written the copy for an advertisement of a prefabricated house Wright had designed.

Wright and I were never more friendly and at ease than we were at that first exploratory luncheon; he was disarmingly candid: almost painfully so, as sometimes happens more easily with a stranger than with an old friend or future associate. He confessed at the beginning that he was financially broke; indeed he had come to New York to find someone who would purchase his collection of Japanese prints, so as to stave off his ever-threatening creditors. But before long he was also unrolling the story of his second marriage, with the older woman who had rescued him from his desolation, indeed, restored him to life after that grim holocaust at Taliesin in which Mrs. Cheney, who had left her husband to live with Wright, was murdered with an ax wielded by a demented butler as she and her two children fled from the house he had set on fire.

Wright survived the gruesome murder of his beloved mistress as he survived the shattering publicity that resulted from his later persecution by his second wife, who became an avenging angel when he left her for Olgivanna, his younger final mate. None of the tragedies of his life, none of the harassing episodes that had followed, had corroded his spirit or sapped his energies: his face was unseamed, his air assured, indeed jaunty. Was he, then, lacking in sensitiveness or sensibility? Yes and no! More probably, I am driven to believe, his ego was so heavily armored that even the bursting shell of such disastrous events did not penetrate his vital organs. He lived from first to last like a God: one who acts but is not acted upon.

Perhaps this explains why, for all the friendliness that developed between us, we never became intimate: strangely neither of us ever saw the other in his own home, nor did we ever spend so much as a whole evening together in conversation. So I never had direct contact with the central creations of his family and working life: Taliesin East and Taliesin West. This was not for lack of good will on Wright's part—or on mine. In the early thirties he actually invited me to take up residence in Taliesin to help him run the school he had started there. This came after he had prudently withdrawn his earlier invitation to his admiring Dutch friend, Wijdeveld. With good reason, Wright suspected that 'Dutchy's' ego and even his original talents in architecture, stage design, and typography were too insistently visible to blend with his own.

Our relations were not merely friendly; in the early thirties, before I had begun to weigh Wright's work and his underlying philosophy more circumspectly, they were affectionate—as Wright's letters to me testify. But Wright could not understand my unwillingness to abandon my vocation as a writer to have the honor of serving his genius; and he was puzzled, almost nettled, over my unreadiness to break into my own work at any given moment to be his guest.

For all that, during the next dozen years, I did my best to put

433

forward Wright's name and extol his achievement, at a time when he was still being passed over for commissions only he could have audaciously filled—including the two world's fairs, Chicago in 1933 and New York in 1939. The failure then to turn even a single exhibition building over to Wright, who was in every sense a great exhibitionist, was revelation of the limitations of fashionable taste in the thirties—both that of the exponents of the so-called International Style and that of Wright's more favored rivals, whose work now bears the derisory name of Art Deco.

Though I never made an exhaustive firsthand study of Frank Lloyd Wright's entire work, I kept my eyes open for his buildings wherever I traveled, whether in Buffalo, Minneapolis, Los Angeles, or Palo Alto. And by good luck I had the opportunity to examine closely two of his most original structures—the Midway Gardens in Chicago and the Larkin Building in Buffalo—before both were torn down. The exuberance, the imaginative energy visible in these designs—even after the structures had been deserted—overweighed the chronic technical lapses and human oversights that had become as much a mark of Wright's character as is a mole on the cheek of a beautiful woman.

With Wright's extravagant gestures, his princely airs, his confident dismissal of other historic architectural epochs, along with his open contempt for most of his peers—likewise his disgracefully unparental jealousy of younger followers as possible rivals—went an innate desire to dominate and subdue those around him. So after our early meetings, my relationship to him became one of wary mutual respect: the rebellious disciple who had refused to see the panorama of Edinburgh from Geddes's Outlook Tower through his master's eyes was equally rebellious, though smilingly so, when Wright reproached me at lunch for not following his example. He was pained, for example, one hot day, when I insisted on having my favorite Irish whiskey on ice rather than in plain water—or at another time, for my not walking with my toes pointed outward—an old military style which Wright still favored against the more natural 'Indian walk' of my generation!

Yet Wright and I were both steeped in that part of the Ameri-

434

can tradition which had found literary expression in the culminating phase I had called the Golden Day: the period that found its voice in Emerson, Whitman, Thoreau, and Melville, and that then, in the generation after the Civil War, found concrete expression in buildings, parks, and the suburban communities of Frederick Law Olmsted. For both Wright and me the source and exemplar of that indigenous culture was Emerson; and though our roots were in our native soil, we, no less than Emerson, drew spiritual nourishment from remote cultures and lands: Emerson himself from Persia and Brahmin India, Wright from the newly discovered architecture of the Aztecs and Mayans, I from China and pre-Platonic Greece.

But if this common ancestry drew us together, between our conscious personal and political philosophies there were wide gaps. Like old Geddes, Wright demanded a complete, uncritical acceptance of his outlook and his way of life. To question his pre-eminence in any sphere was to become a defector. At an early stage I sensed that if our friendly relations became too close, I would surrender my right as a critic to pass an unfavorable judgment on any of his sacred beliefs or achievements. In certain vital places these differences in temperament and outlook went deep. So in time my relation to him was not a little like that of Chekhov to Tolstoy. In order to retain our admiration for the master, both Chekhov and I were forced out of self-respect to maintain a certain spatial and psychological distance.

In the late thirties our different political views widened the gap between Wright and me; and over the issues raised by the Second World War, we, alas! inevitably parted company. Such fissures in friendship were not unusual then; for I lost more than one friend or associate, at least temporarily, through my militant opposition to Hitlerism and Stalinism, as well as to all other demoralizing later forms of dictatorship, including that of the Pentagon, the Atomic Energy Commission, the F.B.I., and the U.S. Central Intelligence Agency. And though I was able to remain friends with Robert Frost, who was as bitter an isolationist as Wright, this was possibly because we both discreetly smothered our differences in silence.

To Wright's public denunciation of the handful of Americans

like myself who at that time advocated active military resistance to Fascism and Nazism, I replied with a passionate counter-indictment. In that crisis our friendship had come to an end; so much so that I did not open till years later the New Year's messages he continued to send me. But I smiled grimly when I received a greeting from him—sent at a time when there was a stringent paper shortage—in an envelope eighteen inches long, containing a folded greeting on heavy paper twice the length of the envelope! During the early forties that insolent symbol seemed final.

Happily, we came together again soon after Wright's great exhibition of his life work in Florence in 1950, the first of such choral triumphs punctuated by gold medals. He sent me a catalog inscribed, "In spite of all, your old F.Ll.W." When I saw this, I turned to Sophia and said: "I've just written a book in which I've said that without a great upsurgence of love, we shall not be able to save the world from even greater orgies of extermination and destruction. If I haven't enough love left in me to answer Wright in the same fashion as this greeting, I'd better throw that book out the window." So I wrote him, repeating my words to Sophia; and he answered in his characteristically generous fashion by sending me an inscribed print of a winter scene by Hokusai. And neither of us referred to that breach thereafter.

How consoling it would be to report that from this time on we drew closer, and that, as a by-product of our restored friendship, it would be I and not a young colleague, Henry-Russell Hitchcock, who would attempt the first definitive criticism of Wright's architecture, for by then Wright's imagination, released and exalted by the opportunities offered him after the Second World War, was enriching the vocabulary of modern forms. If at this time architecture had been my dominant concern, I might, perhaps, have been tempted to make such a study. But what had already happened to the world around us since 1935 made it clear by 1945 that though Nazism had been undermined in the end by the delusions of its psychotic leaders, Hitler had nevertheless won the war. Well before the end, Nazism's methods had infiltrated the minds and plans of his enemies and had begun to dominate the science, the technology, and the politics of the so-called Nuclear Age. I did not think that architecture, as the favored masters of modern form still conceived it, would serve as an instrument in our salvation. But without such a change in the American political and moral climate, a closer relation with Wright would be impossible. By 1950 we were each too firmly rooted in our individual allotments and commitments.

My difficulty in doing complete justice to Wright's achievements in architecture was based on the fact that, the better I knew his work, the more I found in its whole span to admire—no one else could rival him in sheer fertility of imagination and constructive innovation—and the more I found to question in his unwillingness to admit, as copartners in shaping the design, his individual clients, the contributions of his disciples or rivals, or the communal traditions that support and enhance every work designed to meet the varied needs of life. Too often with Wright showmanship took precedence over workmanship, and dramatic originality often flouted tested experience. If, on my estimate of Wright's early buildings, the Cheney house shows Wright at his human best, was this perhaps, I have asked myself, due to the fact that in this building the client he passionately loved had had an active influence over her lover's design?

My reservations about Wright's most characteristic insignia came to a head in my response to the retrospective exhibition held on the site of the still unbuilt Guggenheim Museum, in a temporary building Wright himself designed. In viewing his whole life's work, I now had the good fortune to have Wright himself as my commentator and guide. But in seeing his life, so to say, spread before me, with his voice as a persistent undertone, I realized as never before how the insolence of his genius sometimes repelled me: notably in his transforming the tempting site of Pittsburgh's Triangle, a hillside plot formed by the dramatic juncture of the Allegheny and Monongahela Rivers, into a typically Wrightian "fun" area. That exhibitionistic idea was hardly more worthy of so grand a site than the unplayful mass of mediocre buildings later erected there.

Despite all such doubts and reservations, what remained, what indeed dominated this exhibition was, for me, still magnificent: so rich, so resourceful, that it seemed the work not of a single individual over a limited period of time but almost of a whole culture, over a century-long span. Not merely that, but Wright had met and conquered his rivals at their own game. In Fallingwater, designed for Edgar Kaufmann, he had created a dynamic multi-dimensional composition that made Le Corbusier's buildings seem flat cardboard compositions; while in the Johnson Wax Laboratory at Racine, Wisconsin, he had experimented with untried glass forms that made Mies van der Rohe's blank glass façades look blanker than ever. So I spelled out my critical evaluation of Wright's *oeuvre* in two 'New Yorker' Sky Lines: the first favorable, the second tempering my praise with questions, though seeking to do justice, in spite of Wright's belligerent Americanism, to his truly universal bequest from other cultures and other ages.

Wright read my first article in a plane; and he became so angry about it that he then and there wrote me a letter that trembled with rage as if from some mechanical vibration. His references to me were all in the third person—"He says that"—as if it were a Letter to an Editor. To settle matters, he dismissed me—whom he had once put on a par with his favorite writer, Emerson—as a "mere scribbler," an "ignoramus"; and he was sure, he said, that his clients would rise up in their wrath to denounce me. This looked like the second end of our friendship.

When I answered him promptly, I told him that I respected his greatness too much to belittle it by sweetening my critical appreciation with undiluted praise; and that I had written about him in the same unsparing manner in which I had written in 'Green Memories' about my young son's life, out of admiration and love. When I reached the end of the letter, I was about to sign it in my usual fashion, but a sudden impish impulse prompted me to sign it instead in the style of Frank Lloyd Wright himself: "With all respect and admiration, as from one Master to another, Ever yours . . ."

Wright tacitly accepted that explanation and that declaration of equality. At all events, he made no comment on my second article, despite its unsparing severity. Possibly in the meantime too many of his admirers had praised my first article as a fine tribute to his life and work—which it actually was.

438

At the end, alas! I missed my final chance for a warm reconciliation with Wright when he invited me to take Robert Moses's place at a dinner in Chicago where Wright himself was to be the chief speaker. As usual, I was reluctant to break into my work; but I had already drafted an acceptance when a closer reading of the invitation made me realize that this dinner was part of an effort to launch Wright's design for a 'Skyscraper a Mile High.' In that project all of Wright's egocentric weaknesses were crystallized in an ultimate fantasy, conceived as if by a lineal descendant of Kublai Khan. What a monument of futility—even more absurd, humanly speaking, if that were possible, than the later World Trade Center in New York. Naturally, I could not lend myself to a proposal that violated every canon of Wright's own conception of an organic architecture, as well as my own. If this was what old age had done to Wright, I had no desire to exalt his mummified remains.

5

Not a long while after this I was scheduled to give a public lecture at the University of Pennsylvania, where I was then Ford Research Professor; but up to the last week I had hesitated to choose the theme of the lecture. Almost at the last hour, the theme announced itself. The news of Wright's death came to me that morning. On approaching the old building of the School of Design I saw that the flagpole above the entrance showed the American flag at half-mast; around the mast itself the students had suspended black streamers of mourning. The students' swift response touched me: and I realized that there was only one possible subject for the lecture that night— Frank Lloyd Wright's life and work.

Though I have given many extemporary lectures, good and bad, I can remember only two in which all the deeper resources of my experience as well as self-knowledge were brought to bear. One of them was to a small class in biography at Dartmouth, under Professor Arthur Wilson: my subject was Vincent van Gogh. And the other, even fuller, profounder, and infinitely more audacious, was this lecture on Frank Lloyd Wright. In it I did something like justice to both his actual and his potential greatness; and at the same time I related his work to the vicissitudes of his personal life; and not least to the insidious temptations to which his success alike as a creative architect, as an outstanding public figure, as a seminal personality, had laid him open.

Speaking to the young audience, especially about their future careers in architecture, I pointed out that Wright's expansive ego, his own uncritical self-love, his naïve self-righteousness had made him too lenient toward his own weaknesses and errors, and too ready to transfer self-reproach to a hampering family, to jealous rivals, to unscrupulous imitators, to inefficient or recalcitrant workmen, to unimaginative clients. While he preached 'democracy,' his practice was that of a Renaissance despot; for he built *himself* into every building, and even in the intimacies of the marital bedroom of the Hanna house, Wright's presence was inescapable. What is more, he regarded the minimal modifications necessary to meet practical exigencies he had not foreseen as an insult to his genius.

Though I never favored Walter Gropius's ambitious concept of 'total architecture' in this increasingly totalitarian world, I must admit that my Wright lecture came near to being, in quite another sense, 'total criticism,' since I did not spare myself any more than I spared Wright. As with my Van Gogh talk, there is no record of what I actually said: not so much as a penciled scribble. And even if the words had been recorded on tape, the lecture itself, with its passion, its exuberance, its harassing search for truth, likewise in my self-exposure and self-criticism, which underlay the very words I addressed to Wright, would all be missing. This was not a psychoanalytic diagnosis: it was a dramatic act, set within the vast theater of Wright's own genius. If that was not to be my last word on Frank Lloyd Wright, it deserved to be. And the highest honor my own life could possibly receive would be to serve as the subject for such a drastic, ego-transcending performance by a mind capable of meeting my work on equal terms—"As from one Master to another!"

CHAPTER THIRTY-ONE

'The Renewal of Life' Series

I

October 1930 opened a new period in my life. By some caprice of fate the next decade, which shattered the American economy and favored the negative forces in Western civilization, proved a favorable turning point in my career. It not merely concentrated and magnified all my potentials for further development, but put them to work. Almost as if I were following a musical score, the overture to this new phase of my life was two essays. One of them was part of the symposium sponsored by 'The Forum' on 'What I Believe,' later published as 'Living Philosophies.' Had I framed this credo before writing my biography of Herman Melville, it would have edged away from dealing with the more basic religious and cosmic questions, for until I had wrestled with Melville I had never formulated my reasoned beliefs or even been sufficiently conscious of my oversights and evasions.

The other essay, 'Our Present Dilemmas: 1930,' remained unpublished for almost forty years, until I included it in 'My Works and Days.' For reasons I cannot remember or even guess at, I never revised the original copy for publication. But if a better contemporary diagnosis of the existing forces and counterforces in civilization was published elsewhere at that time, I have still to find it. At the outset I said: "The likelihood of witnessing an even more ghastly war than the last one is a constant possibility." The situation "is certainly much worse than it was in a world so comparatively unorganized for war as was that of 1914: that innocent world, without passports or visas or poison gas, without compulsory military service in either the United States or England. . . . That was indeed an innocent world. . . . Let us not make the mistake of thinking that we are still living in it."

Already the smell of danger was in the air, the tramp of 'marching men' was becoming ominous in Japan, in Germany, in Italy, not least in Soviet (Stalinist) Russia, though it had first taken form as an American symbol of the liberation of labor in Sherwood Anderson's so-named novel! By this time the world-embracing hopes that had proliferated in the Nineteenth Century had begun to shrivel.

The most foresighted picture of the eventual fate of twentieth-century civilization had been presented as science fiction in H. G. Wells's 'The Time Machine' in 1895. But it was so frightening in its prophetic accuracy that a decade later Wells himself repudiated it. Indeed, he actually advised his later readers in so many words *to act as if it were not so*! Yet in 'The World Set Free,' a year before the First World War broke out in 1914, Wells had depicted for the first time the destruction of a whole city by a single atom bomb. (Quaintly enough he pictured the handy little bomb as being dropped from the open cockpit by the aviator himself.)

Early in this same decade my scattered articles on architecture in 'The New Republic' had drawn the attention of the editor of 'The New Yorker,' Harold Ross, and he suggested that I take on their quite unique department, the Sky Line, whose outgoing critic had unfortunately involved the magazine in a losing libel suit. Perhaps my knowledge of literary law, thanks to two brothers-in-law—Philip Wittenberg and Sidney Fleisher—who had specialized in this field, reassured Ross, and he tried me out in a critique of the new plans for Rockefeller Center, then called Radio City.

My delicately acrid comments did not disqualify me: so Ross took me on for monthly reviews. At first these articles were elemental and brief: only the designs of new bars and lunchrooms competed for attention with a few belated skyscrapers like the McGraw-Hill Building or the Cornell Medical Center. But they tested my critical competence: if I could make a discriminating esthetic judgment about the design of a modern lunchroom, I could perhaps handle Michelangelo or Le Corbusier!

My increasingly friendly relations with Ross and his coeditor, Katharine White, opened up other areas and even included my earliest incursions into autobiography: 'A New York Childhood' and 'A New York Adolescence.' But before that, from 1932 to 1937, it led to my also taking on a weekly department, the Art Galleries. This wide-ranging commission sharpened my esthetic perceptions and broadened my sociological background. My first publishable essay as an art critic had come out in 'The Freeman' in 1920 while I was still in London: an interpretation of the Turners and Blakes at the Tate Gallery. The dazzle of light in the later Turners, not just the sun-drenched landscapes but even the interior at Petworth House, told me something about both nature and man that Western civilization was forgetting—or had overlooked: the reality of man's inner life. This was the reality that Sigmund Freud had sought to penetrate in 1900 in his 'Interpretation of Dreams.'

This personal absorption of the messages of modern art was more significant than most of my rapid reviews could convey. But in time I realized that the contemporary departures of painting and sculpture, from Picasso and Brancusi to Gabo and Henry Moore, were making the new generation aware of profound transformations both within the psyche and in visible Western society. This explained more about the emerging future than most of the current documents and statistical summaries, to say nothing of newspaper reports, upon which supposedly hardheaded specialists in every field were forming their views of the future. But note: the first scholar to predict accurately the radical disintegration of modern civilization was that profound student of art, Jacob Burckhardt. (See his work, belatedly published in English, entitled 'Force and Freedom.')

Let me shorten the account of my own subjective education with two samples, one trivial, the other—as it turned out—significant. In 1935 I briefly commented in 'The New Yorker' on the work of an unknown painter, Alice Tenney: a newcomer, at least in New York. Of one of her canvases I wrote: "The V-shaped composition of the scene in the grocery store, with the green-faced grocery clerk and customers, might better have been reserved for a lynching." The artist wrote me: "Strangely enough, the picture which you mentioned of a 'lynching' was *painted* also in the same breath as the lynching, so to speak. I suppose it recalled a certain emotion which wouldn't come out in the lynching picture, but first found an escape in a stronger picture of a less strong subject matter." The artist's unconscious, when denied, had persisted in telling the shocking story that the hand had refused to paint!

The earliest eruption of latter-day subjective art had taken place at the great Armory Show in 1913, which first presented Marcel Duchamp's 'Nude Descending a Staircase.' Its more scandalizing departures were marked publicly by jeers, labored witticisms, explosive indignation, and even manifestations of visible nausea. I was then too young and callow even to visit that exhibition, let alone respond to it, but thanks partly to Alfred Stieglitz's later pioneering shows at '291' and 'An American Place,' I learned fast. By 1915 I was deep in Freud, inducted by Bernard Hart's once classic 'Psychology of Insanity.'

When, in 1936, I had an admirable opportunity to summarize what I had been experiencing and learning in a review of the Surrealist Show at the Modern Museum, I traced part of the movement back to Goya's dismaying confrontation of the horrors of war and human cruelty in the 'Caprice' etchings. After surveying the entire range of 'modern art' from the lavatory scrawls of Dada—the new art to end all art—I wrote: "It would be absurd to dismiss Surrealism as crazy. Maybe it is our civilization that is crazy. Has it not used all the powers of the rational intellect, all the hard discipline of the practical will, to universalize the empire of meaningless war and to turn whole states into fascist madhouses? There is more here than meets the eye. Demons, for the modern man, are no less real than electrons; we see only the shadows of both flitting across the screen of visible reality. Surrealism makes us conscious of this fact, it arranges the necessary apparatus. Before we can become sane again, we must remove the greatest of hallucinations—the belief that our society is sane now.

"Here Surrealism, with its encouraging infantile gestures, its de-

444

liberately humiliating antics, helps break down our insulating and self-defeating pride. Even in perverse or sinister or silly forms, the Surrealists are restoring the autonomy of the imagination."

My weekly reviews of contemporary art had made me realize that, as with all organic processes, there was an integrating and yet at the same time an insistent disruptive factor visibly at work throughout modern life. The artist who alerted me most to the coming ordeals of Western civilization was, inevitably, Pablo Picasso, whose lightning transformations and cultural journeys and imaginative flights encompassed both the restless creativity and the increasing perversity of our disoriented civilization.

In the final illustrations for 'The Condition of Man' (1944), I concentrated the conclusions I had reached through my studies of modern art before they were dismayingly confirmed in the slow time bomb that began to sizzle once more in 1939. In the plate entitled 'Drama of Disintegration,' I chose four paintings by Picasso to tell the story. His work, I noted, "is a series of shocks, and with each shock part of the structure of our civilization is revealed—and disintegrates. At the outset haggard Columbines and famished Harlequins connect him with the surviving play world of Baroque society. Then comes the primitivism of Negroid Idols as human masks: an effort to re-assert our waning vitality by a return to primitive sources: almost synchronous with the rise of Jazz. After that come his exhibitions of dizzying technical virtuosity, comparable to those of a great circus performer on the high trapeze: cubism, neoclassicism, contortionism, and finally such a geometrized nonentity as Picasso's Figure in a Red Chair, a kind of esthetic guessing game. A new shock every season!

"Suddenly, a profound emotion overcomes Picasso: the actual horrors of the Fascist uprising in Spain torture him. Hence the powerful symbolization of woman's utmost misery in his many studies for the Guernica mural. At the climax of that experience, Picasso achieved his ultimate masterpiece: the Guernica mural itself. Here, as in the more exhibitionist other phases of Picasso's art, he brought forth a truer image of the world we are actually living in than the so-called documentary realists."

445

For symbols in the last plate of 'The Condition of Man,' entitled 'Renewal or Catastrophe,' I chose three paintings by Vincent van Gogh. One, the circular daily exercise of prisoners, epitomizing the fate of a generation that accepts its man-built prison walls and knows no way out, either by climbing over or breaking through. The second, two walkers in a moonlit landscape, dominated by a towering poplar: man's opening destiny, toward love, comradeship, freedom. Van Gogh had written: "The best way to know God is to love many things. Love a friend, a wife, something, whatever you like. *But one must love with a serious sympathy, with strength, with intelligence.*" The third painting, of dark clouds and ominous crows flying over a cornfield, presents the tragic alternatives the human race now faces— Van Gogh's last act. Insanity and suicide.

2

The Wall Street crash, in October 1929, had put an abrupt end to the sales of my 'Herman Melville,' which had come out in May that year. Five thousand copies had been sold, but the remaining five thousand were eventually remaindered. Now for the first time, Sophia and I had a brief taste of affluence; but instead of taking time to relax, I began at once the task of turning my Dartmouth lectures on American art into a series of articles for Scribner's. These, in 1931, became my third book, 'The Brown Decades: A Study of the Arts in America: 1865–1895.' Even if a larger audience had already existed, the Depression would partly account for the fact that this book sold only sixteen hundred copies, while the unsold four hundred copies yawned—I did not say yearned!—for readers.

Since no other new theme as yet held me, I decided to assemble a series of variegated essays written in the twenties which, with only slight revisions, would provide a thinly painted but readable background for the larger work of synthesis that I still shrank from. The essays, whatever their merits, were as scattered as their possible audience, and the manuscript I submitted was little more than a neat summation of my past thinking. What brought it up to date was only its title: 'A Preface to Action.' When I submitted this outline to my publisher, I was not prepared for Alfred Harcourt's response. But the letter he wrote gave me the key that opened the door to the next twenty years of my working life. Harcourt wrote me:

> I have read most of the pieces in 'A Preface to Action' and others have done the same. We are all in agreement that from various points of view, it would probably be a mistake to make a book of these pieces now. It is all right—in fact it's fine—for you to experiment with these political, economic, and social themes in articles and in magazines, but they hardly strike me as ripened, rounded, and thought through sufficiently for you to want to stand on them as book material in these times, for which these essays seem to me not quite ripe. Several considerations beside the material itself lead me to this advice. 'The Brown Decades' was, in a sense, a group of essays. I think it might be better for your career as an author to have the work a more substantial and integrated affair than 'A Preface to Action' would be.
>
> If the book on 'Form' should be slow in coming and if more essays do collect under your wing, it would be all right to return to the charge next autumn. Perhaps there would be a group of essays on both literary and artistic subjects that would form a book, leaving the political and economic essays for a later and more homogeneous volume when the ideas had ripened and been modified, both by your further thoughts and by events.
>
> I don't want to be at all dogmatic about this view— merely frank and helpful, with your whole career, rather than this one book in mind. If you really think you have a volume that means you at this stage of your development and which you'd like to have printed, do say so, and we'll be glad to take your word for it.

Without hesitation I responded to Harcourt's salutary advice, completely disarmed by the last paragraph, which so generously— and so astutely—left the final decision to me. Harcourt made me realize that I had been funking the challenge to draw all my expanding interests and reserve energies into what might eventually prove to be a lifetime task.

Though my study of Melville's development had, as I got fur-

447

ther into his difficulties and dilemmas, opened up my own unconscious repressions, I had kept myself 'under wraps,' as jockeys used to say of a horse they held back until reaching the home stretch. I had reason to hold back. As I had written to Josephine Strongin as early as January 1928, "I feel like a diver on the edge of a high diving platform, ready for the exhilaration but a little afraid of it." And a little later I wrote to her: "Every once in a while some larger idea rises before me, and I walk around it and quietly look at it and say to myself: Yes, I'll return to you in a little while, and then we shall see! Patience! I am not ready for you yet."

Even earlier, in 1925, in fact, I had exposed this inner reluctance when I wrote to my friend Delilah Loch: "If we are to have a vision to live by again it will have to be different from all the past efforts of religion and philosophy, and yet it will have to learn from them and contain them. . . . a synthesis of, not of knowledges, for that is impossible except in abstract forms, but of attitudes and experiences which will lead out into the life through which even the darkest parts will become assimilable and humanly self-sustaining. To tell the truth, I am a little frightened when I contemplate the size of my task. If it is to be done at all, it will have to call forth every particle of energy and experience I possess; and I shall have to venture forth on uncharted waters, in the face of an adverse gale—that is to say, in directly the opposite quarter from that of my own generation, whose more sensitive members all say that we must swallow chaos and may never know order again."

The larger idea I had avoided tackling received its impetus from an opening that incited me to further work in a field I had so far explored only in scattered notes and articles: the impact of technology on modern life. This new concentration resulted from an invitation by Professor Robert MacIver early in the thirties to give a course at Columbia University in the evening, in the division then called Extension Teaching, now University Studies, entitled the Machine Age in America. No academic courses similar to mine as yet existed in the United States, though I had written more than one brief essay on the influence of modern science and technology on the arts, beginning with a piece in 'The New Republic' called 'Machinery and the Modern Style.'

But my choice of technics as the opening theme of the series I was soon to begin work on was not due solely to MacIver's invitation. As the reader knows, my boyhood interest in the radical technological advances of our age—the Wrights' airplane and Marconi's wireless—had prompted me to choose a technical high school. But my interests from the beginning were cerebral and imaginative, rather than technologically inventive and practical. My response to technology was never more specialized than my responses to literature and painting had been. From my youth on, my technological studies were never separated formally from my interest in architecture and cities—or eventually, today, the entire cultural history of *Homo sapiens*.

This diversified approach took many forms, as my Random Notes from 1915 on testify. My concern with the whole technical and social complex gave a dimension to my thought that the usual specialized approach lacked; and this flowed over into my imaginative life. From reading Vasari's 'Lives of the Painters' years before Leonardo da Vinci's immense 'museum' of technological and scientific discoveries had been disinterred and deciphered and translated, I had singled out Leonardo as one of my heroes, first in a one-act play I wrote, entitled 'The Gorgon's Head,' named after one of his imaginative tricks in painting. And as my chapter on Leonardo in 'The Myth of the Machine' demonstrates, I remained equally appreciative of both his inventions and his singularly prophetic imagination—for I realized, better than most of my specialized colleagues are yet ready to admit, that many of Leonardo's worst dreams have turned out to be the very realities of our darkening age, whose presence few dare to face. It was Leonardo's superior, all-embracing mind that from the first fascinated me, not the cold, laborious perfectionism of the painter, whose Bacchus and John the Baptist are identical images.

What the course I gave at Columbia from 1932 to 1935 did was to urge me to widen my entire technological and social perspective. By then I knew enough to realize how much I had still to learn by a more systematic exploration of the whole field. Except for the work of Thorstein Veblen, the American literature of technics was singularly sparse. Even Stuart Chase's pioneering study 'Men and Machines' did not appear before 1929. But already I knew enough of the decisive earlier European contributions, from Karl Buecher's to Franz Feldhaus's, to sense how much I had still to absorb through visiting the technical museums of Vienna, Paris, London, and above all, Munich.

Once again I felt the need for a period of detachment and solitude, as well as for fresh stimuli from new scenes and other people. Years before the first part of Arnold Toynbee's many-volumed 'A Study of History' was published in 1934, I had anticipated in my own person that his significant study 'Withdrawal and Return' was the essential key to the most creative periods of every historic culture. With individual thinkers that withdrawal might come about in many different ways: through illness or physical disablement (Abelard or Loyola), compulsory imprisonment (Cervantes), voluntary retreat in the desert (Jesus) or the monastery (Thomas Aquinas) or solitary winter quarters (Descartes). But such latent periods of creativity—if not to remain sterile and inert—demand a return to the social complexities, the day-to-day involvements, and the personal challenges of a living society. For beyond the temporary withdrawal and return rises a further need for continued creativity: renewal.

As soon as I reached this point in my thinking, I realized my comprehensive study 'Technics and Human Development' was already beginning to call for a related group of books, presently to be entitled 'The Renewal of Life' series.

CHAPTER THIRTY-TWO

Ordeals of Reality

I

With the publication in 1926 of 'The Golden Day: A Study in American Experience and Culture,' my work had attracted the attention of readers and editors who had not been concerned with my earlier forays in Utopias or architectural history. George Santayana's unsolicited private letter in response to that book, characterizing it as "the best book about America, if not the best American book" he had ever read, was accompanied by his unsought but generous permission to be quoted publicly. Similar praise had at last made more than one editor aware of my potential capabilities as a literary critic and possibly a biographer. In 1927 John Farrar, then with Doubleday Doran, quickened me with the suggestion that I write a brief study of Herman Melville for a series he proposed to start. I had already turned down my friend Robert Lovett's invitation to do a critical study of William Blake for a proposed Men of Letters Series, for it was Melville who now attracted me.

Until then my interest in Melville had fastened mainly on his 'Moby Dick': indeed, as yet he had played no part in my thinking comparable to that played by Emerson, Whitman, or Thoreau. But in mulling over the theme, I soon realized that this could be no modest literary study: it would have to examine Melville's entire work, going more deeply into his whole life and covering broader ground than the only biography which as yet existed: Raymond Weaver's study of Melville, 'Mariner and Mystic,' not published until 1921.

Though Weaver had done indispensable work in ferreting out original letters and Melville's then unpublished notebooks, and by 1924 had assembled and edited Constable's complete edition of Melville's works, there was still much to be done, for Weaver had glided over the last thirty years of his life. Obviously this would be no spare-time task for me if I were to tunnel beneath the superficially romantic details of Melville's life. Harcourt's prompt offer of a contract for the biography (Doubleday Doran had ultimately turned down the idea) enabled me to settle down to work: a task both hastened and handicapped by my need for an early financial return, since Sophia and I were already looking forward to another baby.

But before I could give my mind completely to Melville, part of my time was engaged with Paul Rosenfeld and Alfred Kreymborg in launching 'The American Caravan,' and—as if that were not enough!—in working for four or five weeks on the first draft of a new play, whose epical pretensions were possibly stimulated by my first reading of Tolstoy's 'War and Peace.'

Early in the spring of 1927 Sophia and I decided to spend the summer on Martha's Vineyard. We found a shabby little shack on a lonely heath in sparsely settled Chilmark, a mile away from the dunes that faced the sea, and more than another empty mile from the little harbor opposite, at Menemsha, where the fishing boats came in. A good jumping-off place for both mainland New Bedford and seaward Nantucket: the geographic starting points of 'Moby Dick.'

The first few nights in our lonely quarters Sophia found it difficult to fall asleep because of the insistent thump of a nearby pump, which I was unaware of. I suggested she wake me the next time she heard it, and one night she did, saying, "Listen! Don't you hear it now?" I listened. "You idiot, that's the sound of the ocean beating against the cliffs." Thereafter we both slept placidly.

It was indeed primitive living, for the only household convenience was a pump at the kitchen sink, whose water could not be drunk, while the outhouse was sixty or seventy feet away, and the crystal spring from which I toted our drinking water was even farther off. But the very primitiveness of the setting, its strangeness and its loneliness, proved more stimulating than harassing. Though we visited the Vineyard and the Cape on many later occasions, we never again had such a drenching in the nakedness of natural scenes, natural forces, natural acts.

During these three months on the Vineyard, Sophia and I enjoyed just the right balance of society and solitude, of swimming and basking, of dreaming and acting, while the incidental hardships or disruptions of domesticity kept us close to basic realities. Our friends at the Chilmark end of the island were few and far between. The nearest, our Sunnyside neighbors, the Aschers, were a mile of

New Bedford

moorland away, hedged in by poison ivy, barberry bushes, sweet fern, and somewhat more edible blueberries; while a handful of other responsive friends—Helen Marot and Caroline Pratt, Sally and Boardman Robinson (the latter illustrated a handsome edition of 'Moby Dick'), and Rita and Tom Benton—were scattered about the landscape. But no one had a telephone, and except for Helen Marot, no one had a car either: everyone walked. When on one occasion we needed a doctor to attend to our two-year-old, who had scalded himself by spilling a cup of hot tea seized from the serving counter,

Sophia had to run and stumble a breathless mile to find a phone, while I applied first-aid treatment.

The established routine of our days, once the after-breakfast chores were done, was that we separated, Sophia to be busy most of the morning with washing diapers and small clothes, tending the house, looking after little Geddes, until she could walk or carry or wheel him down to join me at the beach. Meanwhile I would have retired to an even smaller shack, hard by the outhouse, where I would spend the next two or three hours composing the play I had dimly conceived two years earlier. Then I would go off to the beach and await Sophia and Geddes.

This was the right place for both that play and my coming work on Melville. For the sea was our constant companion. Its presence, night and day, whispering or roaring, soothing or threatening, advancing or retreating, was the best possible prelude to my writing my play. I have the first anticipatory note I put on paper: even that fragment was more than faintly autobiographic.

"2 June 1925. Future work. Plan play, woven around the building of the Brooklyn Bridge. Show the conflict between the man, intent upon *getting his work done,* and the woman, intent upon extracting happiness and companionship out of the day's mixture. Her case as well as his. His insatiable restlessness. Hers, too, is one of the lives sacrificed in the building of the Bridge. All this against the sordid background of the seventies."

So, early in August, instead of settling down to a closer study of Melville's work, I found myself scribbling a few penciled notes outlining the characters and actions of this play, now called 'The Builders of the Bridge.' Yet as soon as I wrote the first scene, I had no need for those notes. Morning after morning my unconscious took charge of the whole process, digging into every part of my past life for the raw material which it automatically transposed into realistic scenes and encounters, some going back into my childhood—though one of the most striking episodes, a dizzy love scene high on the pier of the still-unspanned bridge, anticipated a future encounter.

So spontaneous was the conception of this drama, so brief its gestation, so swift and painless its birth, that when I had written the final scene less than a month later, I did not dare believe that the play was even half-finished. These serene mornings in my shack, with the characters and scenes and lines flowing from my fingers, seemed too good to be true: I had never before written such a polished first draft. Soberly I put the play aside for future revisions by my less intoxicated, more responsible self. So it remained in my files, mute and inert, until Elmer Newman dug it out for his 1970 bibliography of my work.

Not until then did I appreciate how effectively I had transcended both the limits of the neat, old-fashioned drama up to Eugene O'Neill and the dumb motion picture before the sound track was added. Still less did I realize that, in turning back to my study of Melville, I was renouncing a potential career as a dramatist, for I never mentioned the existence of the play even to my experienced theatrical mentor, Aline MacMahon, until I was ready to include it, with an account of its genesis, in 'Findings and Keepings.'

Whatever the merits of 'The Builders of the Bridge' as drama may still be, no one will ever have a valid insight into my character and history who does not recognize in Jefferson Baumgarten and Robert-Owen Binns the two complementary sides of my own nature, as well as the story of my marriage with Sophia, beginning with that note made in 1925. By September, however, when we prepared to go home, I was already pregnant with Herman Melville: so I let Sophia and little Geddes go back to Sunnyside alone, while I spent a few days exploring New Bedford, which was still, in many quarters (like the Whaleman's Chapel, the scene of Father Mapple's sermon), the town young Melville knew. I could not guess then that Melville's tragic exploration of his depths would in time unbare parts of my own life which I had never been ready to face.

2

Once Sophia and I were back from our summer on Martha's Vineyard, I followed a stimulating but grueling routine: for I not only read, sometimes for the first time, the later minor books of Melville, which I had until then no more than skipped through, but I had to read and reread, almost line by line, 'Moby Dick' itself—until I could think and feel in the same mood as Melville, while holding some part of me aloof enough to discriminate between the golden nuggets of his mind and baser minerals in the same stratum. Not the least significant of these books, and one which threw a new light upon his nature, was his ambitious, two-volume novel in verse, 'Clarel,' a work so buried in silence that the great Forty-second Street Library had cleared its rare copy off the shelves, and through the timely intervention of my friend Avrahm Yarmolinsky—curator of the Slavonic Department there—turned it over (gratis) to me. Though the book came out in 1876, *I was the first person to cut its pages!*

Apart from taking advantage of Raymond Weaver's pioneer exhumations of Melville's papers, I benefited by his chivalrous readiness to place still unprinted data at my disposal in 1928. Thanks further to the hospitality of Melville's granddaughter, Eleanor Melville Metcalf, I spent a few days at her summer home in Edgartown, where I read Melville's original journals; a task lightened by my experience with equally illegible letters from my friend David Liebovitz, which helped me to decipher Melville's otherwise baffling script. I even had a pleasant, genteel interview with Melville's surviving daughter, Mrs. Frances Thomas, who, I found, had unmistakably inherited her father's small, whalelike eyes. Only one condition limited that interview: on no account might I even mention her father's name! That silence reopened the dark chapter of Melville's long alienation from his family.

Meanwhile I was working on the first draft of my study of Melville, the actual writing of which alone would have been quite enough to fill those two years. Yet in addition I wrote a long, three-part article on regionalism for the 'Sociological Review,' published a succession of magazine articles, actively served as coeditor of 'The American Caravan,' and carefully edited, with occasional interpolations of my own, Benton MacKaye's path-breaking work, 'The New Exploration,' after spending a few days with him in his Shirley Center home for the first time.

Since I then had no foundation grant to amplify my income or permit me to slacken my pace, by the time I had finished the final draft of my 'Herman Melville,' in the late summer of 1928, my energies were badly depleted, and they were to be drained still further by my having to prepare the six Guernsey Center Moore Lectures I was committed to give, solely from notes, at Dartmouth that November. Never before had I worked under such heavy pressure for so long, or dared to draw so heavily on my resources. The stage was set for at least a liberating illness as the only means of getting a rest!

Troubles, as Shakespeare knew, "come not singly but in battalions," and with a kind of Melvillian fatality both Sophia and I from November on went through the most desolate year of our whole lifetime until our son's death in 1944. Almost anything can happen at such a juncture—and almost everything painfully did.

Sophia had a second miscarriage in November of 1928, which though earlier averted, had in the end taken place. Meanwhile I, before I started to give my Dartmouth lectures, developed a carbuncle on my left hand. By innocently caressing the back of Sophia's neck I had likewise infected her with an even more painful carbuncle. I had engaged to lecture for a fortnight in January 1929, in Denver, but before I left, my always sensitive throat again became infected and swollen, and after I stopped off in Chicago for further medical treatment, the harsh weather suddenly prompted me, in blind desperation, to cancel the long-made Denver engagement and take the earliest train back to New York.

This turned out to be the happiest decision I could have made. When I got back to Sunnyside, I found that not only was Sophia prostrated by the flu and being looked after by her mother, but our little boy was down with a prolonged fever and what turned out eventually to be a dangerous double mastoid. I hesitate even now to sketch the next five months: this whole tale too darkly reminds me of the pyramid of fatalities at the end of Hardy's 'Jude the Obscure,' which suddenly turns the tragedy into a farce. I have recounted this ordeal in 'Green Memories' and will not dwell on it further.

On the surface, Harcourt's publication of 'Herman Melville' that spring could not have been better timed. By May, our child, though still in the hospital, was beginning to recover—thanks to a tardily ordered blood transfusion. In addition, the immediate success of my book was underwritten by Carl Van Doren's choice of it for the Literary Guild's new paperback editions. The gala cocktail party that marked this publication for a few hours effaced from our consciousness the ordeal Sophia and little Geddes and even I had been through. For Sophia and me the celebration itself had an even headier effect than the unrestricted flow of bootleg liquor and gay embraces; but that persisted only long enough to end with a wistful touch of loving intimacy in the taxi before we got back to the Manhattan Hospital.

Unfortunately, the effects of those harrowing nine months were not so soon shaken off. By the time we could bring our child home again a month later, we were ourselves so deeply exhausted that, willy-nilly, we felt inwardly estranged, with nothing in common except our distance from each other; and I found myself beginning to seek elsewhere some show of the warmth that we could no longer evoke in each other.

Despite my inner disruption, I went to Geneva in mid-July to lecture again for a week at Zimmern's school. This time I stayed with the Zimmerns at the old Baron Necker house in the rue Jean Calvin—exactly as I had *imagined* five years before in 'The Little Testament of Bernard Martin'! But this trip proved a fiasco, too. In sudden desperation I fled back to Sunnyside, thereby rudely cutting short Sophia's relaxing few weeks with little Geddes on the Vineyard, where she had found a sympathetic married woman of her own age with whom she could exchange confidences freely. That abrupt return did not help either of us.

3

The spring when 'Herman Melville' appeared found me rereading Dante and rethinking his 'Divine Comedy,' with the aid of Karl Vossler's masterly interpretation of Dante's life and work, of medieval culture, and even more of human destiny in both time and eternity.

In October the following year I was to become thirty-five years old: not quite midway, as it turned out, in the journey of my life. At this point, like Dante, "I found myself in a dark wood where the straight way was lost, verily in a wild and stubborn wood" where phantom monsters and teasing nymphs lurked. But again in Dante's words, "to treat of the good things I found there, I will relate the other things that I discovered."

During the approaching decade, though I was to have more than one glimpse of both Inferno and Paradiso, I was destined to endure a longer period suspended in Purgatorio, for which confinement and ultimate release I was to be ultimately rewarded, not by Dante's vision of supernal beatitude, but by a wide-awake return to the common earth, where heaven and hell and all that lies between are, in varied and uncertain measure, everyone's lot from cradle to grave. Up to this point one part of my nature had been untried and unformed. Even as a writer, until I wrote my study of Herman Melville, I had never pushed myself to my limits. And by the same token I had never let any nascent intimacy with the few attractive young women who crossed my path draw me away from Sophia or take possession of me except in fleeting daydreams.

One day in 1929 Cap Pearce, at that time one of the junior editors at Harcourt Brace, introduced me to the young woman who was then doing their unconventional book jackets and advertising layouts: Catherine Bauer. At our first lunch together that October, we tentatively matched ideas about art, advertising, and architecture; and then, or soon after, I discovered that she had read my 'Golden Day' a few years earlier, while exploring France on a bicycle and flirting in Paris with a young Frenchman. My revaluation of American culture in that book had piqued her curiosity and, it turned out, eventually stirred her to come home. Her fresh sensibility attracted me more than the curve of her breasts under her tight jersey.

Still our friendship did not ripen quickly, for that winter we both had various distractions that kept us from even lunching together often—I my infected teeth, and Catherine a love affair that was beginning to wilt. At that period Catherine was a classic example of the contemporary *jeune fille americaine*: a new species first identified in embryo by Henry James in, among other tales, his story of Daisy Miller. Catherine's basic credo, I found, was an ancient Stoic motto, "Nothing can hurt me," only slightly amended by a popular song that ran: "I'll try anything once, and if I like it, I'll try it again." Yes: *ready for anything then* indeed—except love and marriage! If outwardly Catherine seemed more uninhibited sexually than I, it was perhaps because, as I found later, her casual yieldings so far had told her not to expect too much from them.

Both physically and psychologically Sophia and Catherine were poles apart: for Sophia's almost classic Greco-Oriental beauty was the antithesis of Catherine's definitely Germanic cast. Catherine was a type I had never before been attracted to, the type one finds in the paintings of Lucas Cranach the Elder: with the same high forehead, the same upturned nose, the soft body curves, the blond hair of the medieval German woman—though spiritually there wasn't a touch of the medieval woman in Catherine. Certainly to serve men dutifully and bear children was not her central purpose in life, however gamely she would in time do both.

Not strangely, the contrasts between Catherine and me were even greater, for she felt close to the Renaissance painter, Bronzino, whom she had studied at Vassar, while my favorite painter of the same period was Paolo Veronese, he who had magnificently presented both sacred and profane images, both Faithful and Unfaithful Love. By temperament and experience Catherine and I were opposites, almost enemies. But our eventual intimacy enabled both of us to profit from our polarity; and this, I can see now, broke through some of my own prudent limitations and helped release my throttled energies further for the major tasks I was at last ready to undertake.

The fact that Catherine and I at first had been in quarantine as lovers, incited another kind of intimacy in our frequent letters and in walks about the city, viewing and appraising the buildings I would later describe in 'The Brown Decades.' From the start, our very differences incited the free play of our minds: we plunged and leaped in a sea of ideas like two dolphins—with dolphin smiles, too, over our own quips and sallies—before our bodies were ready for any other kind of play.

At that low tide in our marriage, facing a bleak, sandy waste, what Sophia and I required was a marital holiday from each other, long enough for the tide to turn and deepen the waters enough to enable us to swim together again. We both needed time apart to recuperate internally. To effect such a simultaneous transformation, almost a miracle was needed; and something like one began to take place in the spring of 1930.

Actually the notion of a marital vacation had been broached to us a few years earlier by an earnest middle-aged European physician who had sought us out in Sunnyside to discuss his ideas; for he wanted independent confirmation of his belief that he had conceived a veritable panacea for preserving and prolonging a satisfactory marriage. By a vacation he meant, not embarking on a passing love affair, but a period of complete detachment, of solitude and irresponsibility, afloat in space and time. Though Sophia and I had politely discussed the doctor's ideas with him, we did not consciously swallow his prescription. But who knows, it may have worked! And by the same token, though we did not plan it that way, Catherine and I also needed time to pass our tentative love affair in review, before it became more peremptory or pushed us any further. So that June each one of us started on an experimental separation.

Sophia, nettled if not outraged by my undisguised interest in Catherine, had earlier decided that she needed a clean break, a period by herself, in order to come to terms with this new situation and with her own innermost needs, not least her still latent desires and unfulfilled hopes. Happily, that spring of 1930, both Sophia and Catherine had found themselves economically unfettered, and spontaneously each was seized by the same impulse: to take a vacation alone in Europe! What was left over from the Melville royalties after our grim winter now made Sophia's plan easy to effect: while Catherine had received an award from her Vassar Alma Mater, which would enable her to spend the whole summer in Germany, to come abreast of current innovations in architecture and housing.

Sophia was lured to Germany and Austria by the prospect that the intelligent young German woman who ran our Sunnyside Nursery School would join her a few weeks hence on a walking tour in the Black Forest. She would in the meantime go to Berlin to visit my friends Walter Curt and Lydia Behrendt there. Unfortunately the Behrendts were off on a vacation, and Sophia found her two years

461

of high school German were more inadequate for her needs than she had expected. Even more disappointingly, she discovered, when Hedwig joined her belatedly, that her companion's main purpose in travel was to waylay any promising male who came in her path: an active walking trip was not on her agenda.

Until Vienna, where she had letters of introduction to a gay, intelligent group of people, with some of whom she started lasting friendships, Sophia found much of her vacation—except for the ocean trips—somewhat of a letdown. To make her plight worse, my letters were too full of Catherine to be reassuring. If Sophy had not yet found her essential self, she wasn't sure then that I was not losing mine. Yet she emerged from the trip with more self-confidence than she had had when she embarked on it.

As for Catherine and me, our letters, until the end of the summer, brought us closer to each other's actual lives as real persons than any quicker intimacies could have done. Yet in a corner of her mind lurked the hope that once Sophy had come back to Amenia, Catherine might have a fling with me in the Europe she had been describing with such gusto. Naturally enough, considering Catherine's past and my present, it didn't work out that way. Quite casually, in August, Catherine wrote me that she had gone to bed with a German architect who had visited some housing with her. Though this made no difference to her, it did to me. Sophia, in contrast, on her last night in Bremen before sailing home, had firmly said "No" to a tall attractive man she had been dining and dancing with, who conveniently occupied the room next to hers in the hotel.

Soon after Sophia's return in July I had confided my predicament to Paul Rosenfeld, who was close to both Sophia and me: for I was in the midst of the classic medieval scholastic dilemma—that of the ass equidistant between two haystacks! The factor that made an active triadic relationship possible was singled out by Paul in a letter he wrote from Lake George in August 1930.

> The situation is doubtless being resolved not only in you but also without you: Sophia and Catherine will have to settle it, since you have so little sense of division; or accept a relation that has always had the sanction of nature and

sometimes of Society. Meanwhile let me say that where your writing hangs its hat is what is Home Sweet Home for you: that is nature's Amen. For the rest of us anything that makes you feel like working is our good; and anything that diminishes your energy is our foe. . . . I am sorry for the pain; I know it is unavoidable; but I do not think that the presence of pain indicates the presence of tragedy in any shipwrecking form.

By the time Catherine came back in October, our differing conceptions of sexual loyalty had opened a breach in our still tentative relations and deflated any lurking amorous prospects. Catherine was defiant but disconcerted over my aloofness. Though during the next month we visited old haunts together, both of us remained remote, detached, politely ironic.

With Sophia, on the other hand, just the opposite kind of change had taken place. Even before Catherine's return, the underlying realities of our marriage had reasserted themselves in both of us. The brisk autumn weather and our increasing enjoyment of our country-loving child, now in full health, ready to serve as our 'mushroom hound' when we all went foraging for mushrooms in the neighboring pastures, both restored our marital security and spiced our pleasures together. By now it was Catherine who was on probation, not Sophia. The fact is that Sophia and I were now closer than ever. So our once seemingly stranded marriage began to roll back on an even keel, with Catherine, it turned out, often serving as ballast!

Once Catherine had accepted the permanence of my relations with Sophia, she, too, was released. Suddenly in mid-November, without rhyme or reason, still less plan, with Catherine taking the initiative, the icy distance between us melted, and she discovered for the first time, after her superficial earlier ventures, that she was no longer coolly permissive, but actively responsive. So Paul Rosenfeld's prediction that the strains and stresses that had developed within me would be resolved by the women themselves—and without words, though not without occasional later breaking points—proved sound. For, in the course of the spring, when I was in bed with a severe cold, Sophia sweetly invited Catherine over one afternoon to brighten my dull convalescence, and before summer came, Sophia, without any word from me, turned our Sunnyside house over to Catherine to use while we were in Amenia.

In 1932, with my personal life in temporary equilibrium, I took up a much earlier suggestion of Victor Branford's that I enlarge the limited American background of 'The Golden Day' by going abroad and embarking on a more exhaustive study of creative European sources. For this purpose I applied for and received a Guggenheim Fellowship of $1,600 to cover four months by myself in Europe.

Quite by coincidence, Catherine, who had just reread 'The Golden Day,' independently made a similar proposal at the same time. She broached this with an apology for an idea she felt "she had no business in having at all and that would," she added, "quite ruin her life if I chose to act on it. . . . I used to think," she wrote,

> that it was almost criminal, after years of hard application and a period of probably harder work in England you should have rushed right back and got married, and never gone back again except for more work. But maybe that was all right. You are too profoundly imaginative and live a person to need such external stimuli to get started. That is just the point, in fact. You have such a God-given genius for fresh correlation . . . that you almost owe it to yourself to tie up the loose threads of Western Civilization. Perhaps all this is completely selfish after all! To me, and in your effect on me, your prime quality—and the thing that distinguishes you from everyone else—is a genius for establishing direct firsthand authentic contact with physical and mental reality. I could almost face not seeing you for a year just to have it.

After a reflection or two on the possibility of all this being a bad suggestion, Catherine ended up, characteristically, with: "And dear God! how infuriated, how bitter, how miserable I should be if you really acted upon it."

But almost at the same moment she played with an alternative proposal which, with fortuitous modifications, actually came about. "One grand gesture breeds others. . . . To be more feminine, more practical, it might be that Sophy and I could meet you at different points [in Europe] for a while. I hereby positively state that nothing would give me greater pleasure and profit than to take care of Geddes for a couple of months." Almost from the outset *that* scenario broke down.

4

Until March 1932, my own plans for four months of meditation and research in Europe had not included Catherine. But when the editors of 'Fortune' suddenly offered me $2,000 to write a series of articles on modern European housing, I was tempted by the possibility of getting Catherine to do the necessary research—since her trip to Europe two years before had sharpened her interest and ability in the field of architecture and the problems of housing—so that I might dash off the articles on my return from Europe. This was the classic flaw of trying to have one's cake and eat it. Catherine's research for me and my own plans for a first-hand study of European technology did not mesh; they mocked the reality of our personal intimacy.

Yes: Catherine did come to Europe, though earlier than we had agreed upon, thus slightly upsetting my schedule. But she had first stopped off on her way to meet me to have dinner in Paris with an old friend, and she arrived in Munich next evening with a violently upset stomach. So our first day together began with my seeking, before breakfast, a druggist who could guess what castor oil was in German. (Rizinusöl, if you ever need to know.)

But as between Catherine and me, it soon became evident that though we had various keen, interlocking interests, we had basically divergent temperaments, and different methods of work—and irreconcilable expectations of our thinkable futures, either professional or marital. Without any need for formal acknowledgment, the proceedings for our separation were already under way. To sum up: None of the members of our domestic triad got exactly what he or she had wanted or hoped for from this trip.

Without our anticipating or realizing it then, the neat, pragmatic division of labor between Catherine and me in Europe had proved the beginning of the end. Once I returned from my four months abroad I had to use much precious time turning her all-too abundant statistics and personal observations into the series of articles I had promised 'Fortune.' Meanwhile the fissures in my relations with Catherine were still widening.

The first week in March 1933, just before I planned to start writing 'Technics and Civilization,' Catherine and I had a shattering quarrel. But despite this I doggedly began on the opening section of its first chapter. Shortly after this we slipped back, falteringly, into our old groove. Yet inevitably other men were entering her life, both socially and with her work.

Ironically, Catherine's 'Modern Housing' and my 'Technics and Civilization' came out almost simultaneously in the fall of 1934. But neither of us could have guessed that the brief letters we exchanged then would be so remote, so noncommittal, so dispassionate as they actually were. Our polite silences told even more than words. In due time we recovered a still lively intellectual friendship—mainly through our common gift for letter writing—though the widening political and ideological gaps between us soon became as apparent there as our emotional remoteness. In a letter she wrote me in 1933, she said:

> There is of course a deep conflict between us. On the one hand your intensity, your idealism, your inherent feeling for perfection or nothing, your fine esthetic sense of the form and single strength of love—made up of a sum of things but still an identity in itself, not to be chipped off, not to be experienced unconsciously in ups and downs, in offs and ons, without being ruined!—these are the very things I admire most, respect most, love most, and, *yes, need most* in you. A capacity for such feeling in myself is the biggest, the most priceless thing, you have given me. You gave me perhaps the first intimation I ever had of what *incorruptibility* means. On the other hand (alas, for I am still myself!) I simply cannot help feeling that the girl does not exist, could not exist, who would not make you feel she had failed you, every now and then. Perhaps it is true. Perhaps it is just the price you pay for having fallen in love with an opposite.

And yet, all in all, what a wonderful shakedown that 1932 trip finally proved! And how rewarding my own recurring intervals of socially embellished solitude, from the moment I landed in Bremen and was introduced by Oscar Stonorov—the talented architect and sculptor I had met on the 'Europa'—to his circle of friends and one-time loves! And what a perfect initiation into Germany that had been, beginning with my visit to Lübeck, under the wing of Stonorov's old friends, the Vermehrens. In Lübeck I stayed alone (and later brought Sophia back to savor the same experience) at the Hotel der Stadt Hamburg, the very hotel Tonio Kröger had stayed at in Thomas Mann's story. And how fine a preparation for my later visit to Mann himself that was!

In a few weeks I went back to Munich alone to pick up the threads of my special technological interests, spending my days there exploring the inexhaustible riches of the Museum of the Natural Sciences and Technics. As a professor giving a course on Technics at Columbia, I needed no other introduction to the Director, Dr. Oskar von Miller. In discussing my further plans for study, it turned out that he and I had complementary views: he felt that German students of technology were far too '*theoretisch*'; and he admired the American engineer's readiness to take off his coat on the job and cope with the practical problems. But I realized as soon as he turned me loose in the museum's library that a large number of significant historical studies had been made, chiefly by German and French scholars, which no Americans in the field had as yet even heard of. Dr. von Miller met both my needs.

And now the Germany that I had fallen in love with earlier when I visited Lübeck alone, and later with Sophia, was about to be taken over by Hitler. For all that, the outlines of my book 'Technics and Civilization' were already firm enough, so that on the steamer that took Sophia and me back to America at the end of our stay abroad, I was able to sketch a new layout for the illustrations I had gathered.

Meanwhile I had met that marvelously wide-ranging, morally courageous scholar: Spingarn's old friend, Karl Vossler. Since I already had absorbed and written about his masterly study of Dante, we spent our time in more intimate, personal exchanges that rounded out the detached views we had of each other through our books. After a few hours together, he dipped into his library in order to

467

give me a book he thought I might find relevant to my present work, and asked me whether I had visited Thomas Mann. I said I hesitated to intrude on Mann, but I had in fact read 'The Magic Mountain' repeatedly since it had come out in English. "You should have a talk with him," Vossler said, picking up the phone. "If I tell him you have read 'The Magic Mountain' three times," Vossler assured me, "he'll invite you over. No author could resist such a reader!" And so it happened. When I rose to take my leave of Mann at the end of the stipulated half-hour, Mann begged me to remain, for he had been reading Ernest Hemingway, with admiration for his laconic style, so different from his own; and it also developed that he, too, appreciated Kipling's prose.

Those hours I spent with Vossler and Mann fulfilled—even more than Oskar von Miller's guidance—the inner purposes of my trip, apart from any practical effects they might have on the book which was now beginning to take form in my mind. When next day I started for Paris, I was still so buoyed up by every hour of this Munich experience that while waiting for the train I danced, rather than paced, back and forth on the platform.

CHAPTER THIRTY-THREE

The Great
Hiatus

I

"There are times when one spends perhaps a whole day, vaguely conscious that one has been through all its details before. Was it in a dream? Was it in the imagination? Or was it in actuality? I have had this feeling during the last year, and upon analyzing it, I find it has to do with a series of personal decisions and public events that came more or less to a head ten years ago. The aftermath of the War (First World) and the deflation of our recent prosperity were not altogether dissimilar events."

These words come from the browned manila pages of an unfinished essay I wrote in 1930. What astonishes me is the discovery that as early as the first year of the Great Depression, the bitter consequences of that economic stoppage were already visible. Yet it took years of beating, years of frustration and anguish, before most Americans would accept the fact that this disaster would not cure itself, that the proud, unsinkable 'Titanic' of the New Capitalism, as it was confidently called before the crash, had hit an iceberg and capsized. Henry Longan Stuart, my 'Commonweal' friend, liked to quote his old housekeeper, who used to say: "It all began with the 'Titanic'!" She was a more astute interpreter of these world-shaking events than academically more acceptable observers.

At the time the Depression started, I was President of the Sunnyside Progressive Nursery School, a cooperative founded by a group of parents with the beneficent aid of the City Housing Corporation.

Our teachers had been promised a raise when they began at a very modest salary, and they were indignant when I pointed out that no annual raise would now be possible: we should be lucky simply to keep going. "When times get better . . ." I promised: but times did not get better.

Freud long ago uncovered the psychological mechanism whereby people repress the memory of painful experiences; and this repression has worked so well that even children who were born immediately before the great Stock Market crash do not seem to have received from their parents any more than the barest hint of the anxieties and deprivations that so many families went through for more than a decade.

If one is to understand all that has happened since the Depression, one must recall in some detail what took place then. The widespread economic debacle leveled the living standard of the whole population. On its positive side this brought about a quiet but profound revolution in American life, completing the change instituted in Woodrow Wilson's administration, when the passage of the Income Tax Amendment to the Constitution made it possible to enact public legislation for redressing the grosser inequalities of income by providing essential public services hitherto left to the self-serving philanthropies of the rich or the caprices of the money market.

When in 1933 every economic prop collapsed, 'security' supplanted 'freedom' as the imperative if not the desired goal of the American economy. Even capitalists—as it turned out, the capitalists first of all!—sought to insure their gains by calling loudly for active financial assistance from the President they detested. Roosevelt's response to this demand—the National Recovery Act (NRA)—was worthy of Bunyan's Mr. Facing-Both-Ways: for under the guise of saving democracy it would have buttressed its reactionary totalitarian opposite. Fortunately, the prompt veto by the Supreme Court temporarily postponed this miscarriage of 'democracy.'

The fact that Sophia and I lived through this period naturally made us participants in all that went on. Yet I had some of the detachment of a foreign observer, for we were one of the rarer middle-class families whose always modest income was not affected by the

470

Depression: indeed, in buying power, it went up rather than down. So we never directly experienced the gnawing anxieties with which many of our friends—not least of course our neighbors in Sunnyside—actually lived. The worst that happened was that the magazine I began to write for regularly in 1932, 'The New Yorker,' facing dwindling pages of advertising if not fewer readers, was compelled to impose a 10 percent cut across the board for all its staff. If I was able to devote most of my working time to the first two volumes of 'The Renewal of Life' series, this was because my regular weekly contributions to the magazine served the same economic purpose that a permanent teaching post would have done—but with a far smaller sacrifice of time and effort.

As a student of Thorstein Veblen, I was not unprepared for the Depression itself: for the Business Cycle was the special study of one of his ablest pupils, Wesley Clare Mitchell; and an early friend of ours, Dorothy Swaine Thomas, had even written her doctoral thesis in the twenties on its social effects. But I had never shared the illusion of "permanent prosperity" with which the more sanguine minds had deluded themselves in the closing days of the twenties. The New Capitalism seemed to me as meretricious as what many people then boasted of as a New Renaissance in the Arts, supposedly springing from the same source. Does this seem suspiciously like hindsight masquerading as foresight? Then let me quote words written early in 1929 (six months before the Wall Street crash) to back it up. In reviewing Waldo Frank's 'The Re-discovery of America' in the 'Herald Tribune' book section, on March 31, 1929, I had written:

"Every Sunday . . . our metropolitan newspapers assure us that our American civilization is a great one. In art or in literature, or in the industrial organization of society, we are in the midst of a Renaissance! These announcements are very gratifying: but one has only to look closely at our new skyscrapers to see that at least three out of five are a disgrace to the profession of architecture; one has only to follow the season's output of books to discover that among the twenty geniuses who are hailed and hallooed about in February, it is doubtful if a single name will be recalled with a shrug of respect in December; and after one has read the lyrical ballads that are com-

471

posed about the benefits of mass production and the reign of universal prosperity, it is a little discouraging to walk half a mile from the heart of any large city and come upon a sordid environment whose physical destitution contrasts oddly with the happy ejaculations of the economists.

"From the fact that these paeans to modern civilization are repeated every week, one gathers that no one is really convinced; and one has reason to suspect that all our grand assertions and confidences are bottomed on a doubt. Indeed the most heartening sign of a Renaissance in America is that there is a considerable body of intelligent people who realize that a new order and mode of being do not yet exist, or, if they do exist, are still embryonic and hidden. These people gaze upon contemporary life without any comforting illusions; and what is more important they are not content to be overwhelmed by it and to drift blindly and trustingly in its currents. . . ."

There was plenty of visible evidence to confirm this skepticism, if only people did not turn their eyes away from it. In 1929 anyone who read the newspapers could not overlook the fact that two major economic groups—the farmers of the corn and wheat belts and the coal miners—were in serious straits, for their annual income was insufficient to sustain even their abjectly low standard of living. Many of our Sunnyside neighbors labored, however, under a quite different handicap. Not merely had there been a rise in the standard of living during the twenties, thanks to the spread of cheap motorcars, motion pictures, wireless sets, and vacuum cleaners, but they were tempted to the further expense of keeping abreast of the latest fashions in clothes and furniture by the incitement of installment buying; what the English mockingly call the Never-Never Plan. Not saving, but heedless spending, now became the specious key to consumer credit. Eventually, people like Sophia and me who lived strictly within their current incomes, in defiance of the system, were treated as bad risks, in fact, almost financial outlaws or nonpersons!

As the human plight became more hopeless, with banks insolvent, factories idle, farms and homes sold off to satisfy the mortgage holders, the incurable nature of the paralysis, on the terms then acceptable to the business community, became more evident. People's savings were soon used up, and with their savings gone, their self-confidence went, too. All over the country people were starving.

No one knew how to set the wheels going; those who knew least about it as a class were the bankers, the businessmen, the industrialists, whose rapacity and inordinate ambitions had largely brought on the catastrophe. Obviously it was those committed to the system itself who needed to be shocked into self-consciousness and self-appraisal before it could become humanly serviceable. In the succession of bankruptcies culminating in the Bank Holiday, which marked the exit of President Hoover in 1933 and the inauguration of Franklin Delano Roosevelt as President, the full extent of the damage suddenly became visible. How well I remember Madison Avenue on that strange business morning—as deserted of vehicles and office workers as if it were Sunday.

What was further demoralizing was the revelation of the unbusinesslike carelessness as well as the outright corruption that had accompanied this economic debauch. One of the accountants who had investigated the affairs of the bankrupt financier Ivar Kruger, the so-called Match King, was an associate of mine in the mid-thirties on the New York City Board of Higher Education, and he told the story of the many-million-dollar loan Kruger had obtained from a leading American bank on the security of forged Italian government bonds. "If only a clerk had gone over those bonds he would have discovered they were a clumsy fake," he said. "But I found the bank officials had put them away in their vaults without even examining them."

That there were probably still many conscientious businessmen and industrialists in the country goes without saying. Even in a diseased body, most of the organs may still be in working order till death draws close. But the money-making minority who were largely in control of our national market and who set the tone were not in fact to be trusted. The words 'prudent,' 'thrifty,' 'down-to-earth' could no longer be associated with bankers, any more than 'farsighted' could be associated with great industrial organizers.

Was there not something almost too neatly symbolic in the fact that the Ford Company—which had increased profits and even raised wages by concentrating on their Model T, the Poor Man's Automobile—changed over to a more impressive car in esthetic competition with its rival, General Motors, so soon before the financial crash occurred? Was it perhaps that year's wholesale layoffs, necessary for retooling the new model that caused an irreparable break at a critical link in the delicate economic chain? At all events, Ford took off the market the very kind of minimal car which even an amateur mechanic could patch up: just the car America sorely needed during the Depression! (Who could guess after this historic misreading of their economic prospects that the 'Big Three' of American motordom would in the 1960s make this same fatal error a second time?)

In keeping with this emphasis on showy sales appeal—later translated into sex appeal—the largely meretricious profession of Industrial Design (packaging) got its start. That new profession's plausible esthetic intentions were quickly betrayed, as Veblen might sardonically have pointed out, by the salesman's conviction that the package is more important than its contents.

3

During the thirties the air was full of timid home remedies and pretentious corporate panaceas. How I wish I had kept for the record even a tenth of the proposals for 'economic recovery' that came to me through the mails! They came from the widest variety of people: not merely congenital crackpots, but also once-sober leaders of business or law, now diligent in their idleness with sundry plans for legally controlling capitalist procedures and equalizing consumption. The means varied from annual issues of money that would lose value the longer one kept it to the distribution of 'credit' without respect to performance and productivity! The Technocrats, following How-

474

ard Scott, believed that a 'dictatorship of engineers' could restore and improve the economy better than those who in England, following Major Douglas, relied on a new kind of 'honest' currency. Still others, ignoring the lesson of the pre-Fascist Italian solution, favored the even simpler method of letting cooperatives of workers take over and run the idle factories!

At that time, Buckminster Fuller even believed he could solve the housing problem of the unemployed in New York by having them take over the Empire State Building. That newly built monument was bleakly empty, indeed quite unfinished above the sixtieth floor—or was it the fortieth? Characteristically, he failed to reckon with the cost of renovating—or maintaining—even the elevators needed to make the building habitable! Then there were the almost equally naïve minds who believed that what America needed was a new product, as marketable as the automobile had been twenty years before: so they proposed to get the economy going by manufacturing trailer houses, on the tacit assumption that if you could move your house, you could live on unoccupied land anywhere, and pay, at worst, no more than nominal rentals or taxes.

This proposal was a last pathetic effort—short of colonizing the moon!—to find a machine-age equivalent of the pioneer practice of moving on to fresh territory when the soil became exhausted or the neighbors crowded too near. The trailers and the trailer camps were eventually built: but the romantic dream of evading rents or mortgages and taxes—ignoring likewise the public need for drinking water and sanitary sewage disposal—by squatting and then moving on soon disappeared.

4

Little commonplace incidents sometimes give a better measure of catastrophe than a wide panorama of violence and desolation. Recall the lonely scene in Eisenstein's motion picture 'Potemkin': that of the solitary baby carriage, released from the hands of the dead mother who had been wheeling it, rolling helplessly down the long, corpse-strewn, otherwise empty steps leading to the Odessa waterfront.

Other such incidents have left an impression upon me, and I have occasionally used them in discussions with my students to convey something about our immediate past that no more extensive description, however factual and statistically supported, can do. One concerns a man of about my own age who stopped me one afternoon in 1933 along Central Park South. He was dressed in a sports jacket and plus fours, the fashionable suburban attire a few years earlier; and everything about him spoke of suburban comforts and suburban habits: the country club, the golf course, the family picnic. Very hesitantly he asked me if I could spare a dime—then enough to buy a hamburger on a bun. As it happened, I found only a half-dollar, and after a moment's hesitation gave it to him. He took the coin, but when he recognized it, he made a motion to return it to me. "Oh, no!" he protested, sizing me up as another middle-class man like himself: *"You can't afford that!"*

An even more shaming encounter still lingers in my mind. I was walking along Madison Avenue on a winter evening on my way to take a friend to dinner. Being a little early, I had no need to hurry. From behind me a respectable middle-class man, in black 'Sunday' clothes, came abreast and asked me if I could spare him something: he had had nothing to eat for a whole day. I rose superficially to the occasion by handing him enough to buy a simple meal. Though he quietly thanked me, he kept on walking beside me. What he wanted was what every human soul wants when in distress: another soul to listen to him. He had come all the way from Kansas, leaving his family behind, looking for work. Everywhere he had been turned down. He could not believe what had happened to him: the emptiness, the weariness, the starvation, the inability even to write to his family—all seemed unreal to him.

Like Job this man sought some rational answer to his misery. What had he done or left undone to deserve it? My meager words of sympathy were all too remote: the only response that could have warmed him would have been my willingness to stay with him for half an hour, sitting down with him at a nearby Child's, to relieve, if only with my presence, his desolation. But I failed him completely. After walking a few blocks listening to him, I looked at my watch, falsely pleaded lateness, and left him alone. I had forgotten my duty to my neighbor.

Spontaneously or willfully, most people have put such memories out of mind, even when they are old enough to have lived through this period. But in overlooking the psychological results of the Depression with its unsettlement of our American faith in the potential resources and putative wealth of our country, this silence does not do justice to the resilience many of our most humble countrymen showed then: to their adaptability, and their wryly comic defenses and comebacks. Some of these qualities showed up even in those pathetic colonies of destitute people that spread overnight on the bottle-strewn borders of our big cities: shacks put together out of discarded boxes and rusting pipes and odd lumber picked up anywhere, filched perhaps from half-finished buildings. The very name the inhabitants applied to their encampments—Hooverville— was a proof of their irrepressible humor.

Not the least of the acts that showed how grimly President Hoover was out of touch with his own countrymen—Hoover, the masterly succorer of the starving Russians in 1920!—was his command to the military to use physical means to turn back the limping Bonus Army—in England called more correctly Hunger Marchers—who had trudged to Washington to beg for relief from destitution and famine. Besides food and shelter, these bewildered, desperate people needed—like the man who had stopped me on Madison Avenue—a sympathetic ear. Instead Hoover showed them a frightened fist—as it happened, General Douglas MacArthur's fist.

Only ten years later, by a grim act of cosmic justice, this brutal humiliation of our Bonus Army was matched in the Philippines by the Bataan Death March, which followed MacArthur's 'unthinkable' defeat by the Japanese.

5

In March 1933, when Roosevelt took office, he still seemed politically a lightweight. Neither his cagey record as Governor of New York, nor his acceptance of the Democratic Party's national platform, nor his choice of political advisers, gave any hint of his later political adroitness, his adventurous readiness for experiment.

At what turned out to be the last general conference of the Regional Planning Association of America, we had sought to emphasize our diversified regional orientation by holding this meeting during the summer term at the University of Virginia. One of our purposes was to bring our group in closer contact with the new Southern Regionalists, whose academic home was Howard Odum's sociological laboratory at Charlottesville: in effect a notable American counterpart of Geddes's Outlook Tower in Edinburgh. Clarence Stein had gone up to Albany to persuade Governor Roosevelt to address a public session of our conference, but FDR needed no persuasion. It was on that occasion that Roosevelt was for the first time hailed publicly as "our next President" by Senator Byrd of Virginia.

Roosevelt delivered a surprisingly scholarly paper on the functions, the opportunities, and the problems of state government. In discussing it immediately afterward with my RPAA colleagues, I committed one of the sublimest gaffes of my whole career. That talk, I observed, was a model of its kind. Beautifully organized, rich in concrete observations and proposals, Roosevelt's address would have done credit to a top university professor. But it was obvious, I concluded, that *Roosevelt was no Politician!*

I had failed to take any account of Roosevelt's two special political assets. The obvious one was his facility—the facility of an actor— for dramatizing a political occasion and playing an appropriate role. Viewed coldly, FDR's ideas would often turn out to be commonplace or inadequate; it was the timing, the delivery, the right gesture, that did the trick. Roosevelt's outstanding social gift was his unique ability to give power and authority a more human guise, as in the intimacy of his Fireside Chats—"My Friends! . . ." He would even undermine the effectiveness of his political opponents by the almost childish chanting of their names: "Martin, Barton, and Fish!"

Fortunately, Roosevelt had a deeper psychological resource: the inner will that had not merely overcome the effects of his attack of infantile paralysis in early middle age but would enable him to face other dismaying situations with unflagging self-confidence and a reassuring voice. On one occasion he lost his grip on the rostrum, and fell flat on his face. When he was helped to his feet, he resumed his interrupted sentence. On coming to office, it was not the dubious economic measures the President proposed—the devaluated (sixty-cent) dollar—that counteracted the increasing popular distrust of both parties. No: it was the tone of Roosevelt's voice in his first Inaugural Address, his assurance that his countrymen had "nothing to fear but fear itself," that first tided over the crisis in public confidence. Through his own personal history FDR symbolized—and all the better if this operated only in the collective unconscious—the quickening assurance that *Paralysis can be overcome!*

This was Roosevelt's timely gift to his fellow men. Not only did it partly offset his own sundry misjudgments and specious compromises with both men and measures, but it allowed him sufficient freedom for furthering a chain of fruitful experiments after 1935—like the Civilian Conservation Corps, the Federal Public Works Projects, the Shelter Belts, the State Planning Boards, the Federal Housing Act, and the even more unprecedented Federal Arts Project. All these proposals gave discouraged unemployed people of widely different social classes and vocations the hope of economic survival without losing their self-respect. Fortunately, Roosevelt's earlier prescriptions for overcoming our economic inertia, like the National Recovery Act, by being nullified by the Supreme Court, had opened the way for these valuable constructive measures.

Strangely, the most enduring of Roosevelt's early constructive efforts was the very first on his agenda, his creation of the Tennessee Valley Authority. This was a foresighted effort to utilize the potential national resources of a great river basin, capable of generating electric power sufficient to pass beyond state lines and make use of underutilized human and natural potentialities. Though it took years to carry out this project and to work out experimentally the details for distributing both power and social advantages, it for long remained the most creative American image of democratic social reconstruction.

CHAPTER THIRTY-FOUR

The Domain of Troutbeck

I

Three years before I became a charter member of the group that wrote 'Civilization in the United States,' I had encountered J. E. Spingarn's Crocean views on literary criticism in the old fortnightly 'Dial,' which I had read in the Widener Library in Cambridge while qualifying in the regular Navy as a radio operator. Spingarn's espousal of Benedetto Croce's formalistic esthetic doctrines then had little appeal for me; I preferred William James's pragmatism. But it was his open contempt for the esthetic illiteracy of American scholars that led me as late as 1930 to spend half a year surveying the then-meager American literature of esthetics.

From the outset, it was our respect for each other's latent qualities that first drew Spingarn and me together. And it was our differences rather than likenesses that proved rewarding. Next to a close friend, there is no one so close as an understanding and sympathetic enemy! Though I altogether lacked his ambition for active military and political leadership, my earliest 'Random Notes' testify that I at least matched him in my self-confidence in my own potential creativity. From our first group meeting in Stearns's Varick Street cellar Spingarn and I had 'clicked.' So it was no surprise when early in November 1921 he asked three of us—Van Wyck Brooks, Ernest Boyd, and myself—to spend a weekend at his Dutchess County home to discuss our esthetic views: that focal point in his philosophy! Needless to say, we accepted.

To break the ice on our first Saturday morning together, Spingarn showed us Troutbeck's nearby acres, whose first owner was Myron Benton, the farmer-poet whose love for Wordsworth had prompted him to choose that name. After we had viewed the lay of the land and the nearby houses, the earliest dating back to 1761, Joel took us in his car as far north as the historic Red Lion Inn in Stockbridge, where we lunched and chatted idly, even comparing notes about old and new codes of table manners. By the time we returned to Troutbeck and had unpacked, we were all sufficiently at ease with one another to be ready to talk freely on everything under the sun, beginning—and ending!—with esthetics.

On that November weekend in 1921 neither the bleak countryside nor the new manor house stirred me. Though I had barely begun to write about architecture, my taste was sufficiently formed to reject the half-timbering and the overheavy slate roof. Even worse, their fashionable English architect had taken an informal Tudor cottage as his model and had blown it up in every dimension. When at the end of our first exploratory stroll Spingarn privately asked me how I liked the exterior, I hesitated before giving a polite, halfhearted approval. Visibly disappointed, he changed the subject and never referred to it again. That was characteristic of him! Despite his many gifts, Spingarn had an impatience and a smoldering pride that sometimes kept him from making the fullest use of his own gifts or opportunities.

Yet what a heady experience those two days at Troutbeck proved to be! How subtly they exposed our different cultural origins and life expectations, turning our abstract ideas into flesh-and-blood realities. Since I was already steeped in Plato's Socratic dialogues, our Troutbeck talks produced in me more than a whiff of that same excitement.

Though I made no notes of our discussions, either on the spot or later, in 1924 I somehow recaptured, with only minor embroideries, both the spirit and the content of those conversations. What is equally astonishing is the fact that, though the dialogue in any formal guise was then editorially taboo, Henry Mencken accepted my account of that weekend discussion for 'The American Mercury,' the new review he and George Jean Nathan had just launched. But the dialogue was then so out of fashion that the subeditor changed my title from 'Esthetics: A Dialogue' to 'A Palaver.' Spingarn sufficiently approved my title to use it as one of the earliest of the 'Troutbeck Leaflets' he had begun to publish. He even sent a copy of it to Benedetto Croce, who in response characterized our discussions as *"fine e elegante."*

Neither Sophy nor I could guess, when I returned from that visit to our dingy flat in Greenwich Village, that this brief dip into Spingarn's Troutbeck was destined to lay the groundwork for our entire family life for more than half a century. But when Spingarn, early in 1926, suggested that we spend the coming summer in The Maples—a roomy cottage then left free because Geroid Robinson was leaving it for a year's study of rural Russia before the Bolshevik Revolution—we jumped at the chance.

From then on, despite Spingarn's lingering invalidism, the budding friendship between us began to flourish. The range of his mind was as wide and generous as the contents of the philosophic and religious books that lined the walls of his library. During the next dozen years that mental largesse was matched by the quiet Country House hospitality of Troutbeck itself: tactful, never ostentatious, always ample, with gay evenings, charades, luncheons, picnic excursions, and even hayrides in season. For me, Spingarn, like the Adriano Olivetti I later encountered, corresponded to Aristotle's description of the *Magnificent Man:* one who uses his riches to some purpose.

2

Before going further into this history of our relations with the Spingarns and with Troutbeck itself, I must publicly apologize, at least to Joel's ghost, for using so pretentious a title for this whole chapter. Spingarn never referred to Troutbeck as an estate, or even as his property. For Spingarn it was simply "our place" or "the land," and he would have shuddered at the use of "Domain," though he valued the name of Troutbeck. What my quixotic title reveals is the impression made upon me by my childhood reading of Edgar Allan Poe: particularly by his moralistic but riotous fantasy, 'The Domain of Arnheim.' Only at this late date have I come fully to realize how much of my life had been subtly affected by experiencing the 'ideal' conditions Poe had laid down in that early essay. For here Poe admitted "four elementary principles." The first condition was Health: free exercise in the open air; the second was Love of Woman. Third, and very difficult to realize, as Poe knew, was Contempt of Ambition. Finally, hardest of all, was the Increase of Attainable Happiness in Proportion to the Spirituality of the Object. All these conditions were open to fulfillment in the Domain of Arnheim.

Health attainable by means other than activity in the open Poe believed scarcely worth the name. He pointed to the tillers of the earth, whom as a class he considered happier than others. Strangely that same need had been independently expressed in Herman Melville's even earlier description in 'Pierre' of the strenuous daily routine at Saddle Meadows. Spontaneously I followed this injunction in our first summer at Troutbeck. Once I had spent three hours at my desk in the morning, I would trot the mile to Troutbeck Lake for a brief swim before returning to lunch with Sophy. That jaunt expressed sheer animal delight, not any dogged pursuit of health.

The spirit that then captured me had already brought forth in 1924 my first three-act play about marriage, which revealed my pent-up emotional life. Thus, Poe's second condition for fulfillment, Love of Woman, filtered thereafter through every part of our lives.

To round out this sketch of his fabulous Domain of Arnheim, which was to transform both the grand landscape and the life that would flourish there, Poe quite abruptly came down to earth in a suitably modest complementary essay, which he entitled 'Landor's Cottage.' He described a building on a meager patch of land and an antithetic mode of life based on stringent economy, not unlimited riches. In our imagined Domain of Troutbeck our Leedsville farmhouse came to serve after 1929 as Landor's Cottage.

Troutbeck, the 'Big House,' which dominated the upland village of Leedsville—then the classic Chinese 'hamlet of ten houses'—nestled in the hollow below where Troutbeck Brook and the Webutuck River joined. As friends of the family, we had the freedom of the Spingarns' wide domain. What a domain it was! For its eight-hundred-odd acres—roughly the size of Central Park—embraced every aspect of the landscape, from the wooded top of Oblong Mountain, where rattlesnakes nested on rocky ledges, to Troutbeck Lake, fashioned from an old iron-ore bed, from a swamp at whose edges the beautiful leaves of the elecampane flourished, to the newly made road, which brought us past a remote ore bed to the further bridge over the Webutuck, and so back to Troutbeck proper—a circuit of about three and a half miles. In less than an hour's tramp we could sample the most varied experiences of nature. How we came to value that!

We had spent three summers—with one in-between season on Martha's Vineyard—in one or another old house in the village of Leedsville when in the spring of 1929 the new Literary Guild took my 'Herman Melville' for its popular edition. Unbelievably, six thousand dollars was now at our disposal! Instead of looking further afield for something that might perhaps be more to our liking, we decided to acquire one of a pair of rundown farmhouses that faced each other across the village road, each behind its traditional pair of 'bridal maples.' These farmhouses had been built around 1837, when builders had stopped copying older Georgian models but still provided no indoor sanitary facilities: a pump in the kitchen sink and an outhouse fifty feet away had to suffice. One house was, esthetically speaking, a plebeian version of the other; but when Henry Wright came up to advise us, he found it the better constructed. Moreover, its view of the hills above and down to the river in back was infinitely superior. So we readily agreed to the princely sum of twenty-five hundred dollars for the house and its acre of land.

Apart from a few older surviving houses, and a few old-timers themselves, Leedsville had little to boast of, being the home mainly of farm laborers and a couple of trappers who, in fact, had been tenants of the house we bought. The only dwelling that had any claim to charm was the very Maples in which we had spent our first Leedsville summer. Set well back from the road, behind a low stone wall, and within sight and sound of the Webutuck River, it had been our daughter Alison's dream house when she was a child. Fortunately, she was eventually able to acquire it and so has been our neighbor ever since.

After the setting of our two spacious summers in the Century Cottage, which had once been an inn on the old road between Amenia and Sharon, in whose attic we had found old account books still reckoned in shillings and pence, Sophia and I had said to each other, looking at the Leedsville Road, "Who would want to live here?" The answer was, as it had been in Sunnyside, "We would!"

4

We took possession of our property in the autumn of 1929, though it would be more correct to say that our land gradually took possession of us. The house itself was in a state of utter disrepair: the trappers had hung their pelts on big nails that broke what plaster still remained on walls and ceilings. There was a small weedy patch outside the kitchen on the south side that indicated there might once have been a vegetable garden there, and there was a clump of peony bushes and a few old-fashioned roses; but the remaining land was bare of almost everything but burdock and plantain.

But we gradually fell in love with our shabby house as a young man might fall in love with a homely girl whose voice and smile were irresistible. As with faces—Abe Lincoln bears witness—character is more ingratiating and enduring than mere good looks. No rise in our income has ever tempted us to look elsewhere for another house, still less to build a more commodious or fashionable one. In no sense was this the house of our dreams. But over our lifetime it has slowly turned into something better, the house of our realities. In all its year-by-year changes, under the batterings of age and the bludgeonings of chance, this dear house has enfolded and remodeled our family character—exposing our limitations as well as our virtues.

Early on, before I had studied historic architectural modes, I had once done a sketch of my private 'dream house.' It took the form of a tower with one great room to each floor and a sweeping outlook from the roof. Incredible to relate we eventually stayed a night in just such a house, when we visited Van Wyck Brooks and his second wife, Gladys, on Martha's Vineyard, in the silo her previous husband, Henry Billings, had redesigned to give them needed space: one room to a floor with a wide sweep of landscape visible from each. Their version of my 'dream house' delighted me, but it never tempted us away from our more prosaic beloved dwelling.

5

By 1936 Sophia, Geddes, and I were so enamored of country living that we decided to remove all our Sunnyside household goods to Leedsville, and so we had for the next six years, broken only by two winters, the full experience of the seasons and the ever-altering landscape. This gave us time to make the necessary transformations of the house and its immediate surroundings and, even more perhaps, of ourselves. But for the ominous threats of Mussolini, Hitler, and Stalin, this might have prolonged the halcyon period of our married life. Without such an underlayer of rural experience I could hardly indeed have written 'Faith for Living.' That book made it possible, I later learned, for many reluctant people in America and especially in England to face with resolution the malign forces they had once sought to belittle or conceal or even sympathetically condone.

For a decade or more the Spingarns' hospitality drew—not only to Troutbeck itself but to our village as well—a wide range of people, for there were a number of small cottages and farmhouses available then. What an interesting parade of personalities that was: artists, poets, novelists, journalists, anthropologists, psychologists, educators, and people serving in public life. Then, in the summer of 1940, when war was threatening, Antonio Borgese and his young wife, Elisabeth, Thomas Mann's youngest daughter—she of 'Disorder and Early Sorrow'—took a house in nearby Smithfield. It was Borgese who assembled in neighboring Sharon a militant group to discuss and outline a book eventually published as 'The City of Man,' in a vain attempt to open our countrymen's eyes to the inimical dangers that threatened the world.

All of us so greatly cherished our solitude for writing, or painting, or just thinking that one might often be lonely for fear of intruding on another. Happily there was Troutbeck Lake a mile away to bring us all together in the afternoon when we were ready to relax. The 'lake'—it was really only a pond—was the focal point for sociability. Grown-ups and children, including the village children, mingled at the dock or on the float, and we swam and paddled and sunbathed and talked endlessly. Early on we saw perhaps less of the Spingarns, either parents or children, for Spingarn was suffering a recurrence of the disabling illness that had thwarted his military career overseas, and Amy was much away, visiting, traveling widely abroad, or studying painting with Hans Hoffmann; while their four children, Stephen, Hope, Honor, and Edward, had their own lives to live. But in a few years that changed, and all the Spingarns—though Joel but rarely—came more frequently to the lake. We were truly a community, close to one another, and the lake was our social magnet.

6

If Troutbeck proved a genial setting for our works and days no less for Sophia than for me, it was even more so for our children; they were for all practical purposes born into it, and every aspect of the landscape was theirs. Although Geddes had spent his first eleven winters in Sunnyside, this rural background was the only place that had reality for him and satisfied him. It was a vast field not only for muscular activity and adventure but for wildflower picking and mushroom hunting when he was a little child, for fishing after he was five, for hunting with the older boys from the age of seven or eight, and for going out with his rifle, alone or with his friend John Duffy, after he was ten. It was Geddes's passion for hunting, as I told of in 'Green Memories,' that brought me closer to the wilder parts of the landscape and gave me a sharp taste of what I had barely smelled as a boy in Vermont.

In those hunting expeditions all that had moved me when I had read 'The Leatherstocking Tales' in my youth became, not a superficial impression, but an integral part of my life. Though except for the sake of Geddes's company I had no disposition toward hunting, I gained an insight into the primitive impulses that had produced the Romantic Movement in the arts—impulses that are but dimly understood by those who merely analyze the written words of a Rousseau, an Audubon, or a Cooper and have no sense of the experience that prompted their words.

As for our daughter, Alison, not only had she a passion for butterflies but she exercised a singular influence over them, for they would light on her hand without fear, and she could almost call them to her at will. Her only enemies in that world were spiders: but to offset that, she, like her brother, was quite at home with snakes, and handled those cold pets with a freedom which sometimes frightened visitors. We would then have said that she embraced the landscape most by domesticating it, for she and the Duffy and Farley girls and her cousin Erica, who spent her summers with us, established a homestead on an island in the river; they built a full-fledged cabin out of discarded boards and shingles on the hill behind the Troutbeck barn, and later a miniature village with a garden and a diminutive river running through it, hard by our side door. The last was a place so full of happy fancies that one could wish it to remain forever in existence without losing the very frailty and delicacy that made it so charming.

Both our children found the country environment responsive in a way that no city street can possibly be, no matter how fertile a child's imagination. But Alison had, in addition, the good fortune to get her early elementary education in a surviving one-room schoolhouse, under a capable, indeed inspired, young teacher, Catherine Kane, who took advantage of every resource the scene provided, getting the children to scoop up clay for modeling from the neighboring brook, and teaching 'company manners' by having the children play host at school parties for their parents.

7

Spingarn, the master of Troutbeck, died in July 1939, after a year's illness.

In more than one way this marked the passing of the old order, not merely in Troutbeck itself but in the whole landscape. That, of course, was part of the more widespread and devastating transformations that have since been taking place not only within our own country but throughout the world.

Amy attempted to keep Troutbeck up, but that proved all too difficult. The house itself was so large, and domestic help, both within and without, was becoming almost impossible to find. After a few years she withdrew to the Century Cottage. Time passed, Amy was growing old: she died in 1980 at the age of ninety-seven. For the last decades of her life she was visibly failing. But though her body weakened and she became exceedingly frail, part of her mind re-mained alert to the very end, and she continued to prove fascinating to young people, for she still had a wonderful facility both for draw-ing them out and for entertaining them with tales of her own early life—which of course was 'history' to them.

During Amy's final years we tried, Sophia and I, to call on her at least once a week, but conversation grew more and more difficult, owing to her increasing remoteness, so I offered to read to her from the manuscript of this book, knowing she was deeply interested in my past and wanted to hear about the early years, which dealt with the days she herself had lived through. Alison's easy chats with her had roused a great curiosity about my unhallowed parentage. One day I took over the completed chapter about my mother's life, and Amy listened attentively. When presently I came to a passage that referred to Summit, New Jersey, the town my biological progenitor, Lewis Mack, had grown up in, she brightened; her attention was obviously caught. "Mack . . . Summit . . . Why, I had cousins of that name who lived in Summit. My father's sister married a man named Mack and I used to be taken to Summit to visit them when I was a girl. *I must have met your father then!*" To our absolute amaze-ment, when Amy drew further on her faded memory, she was able to place him. "There were two brothers, one of them was named Lewis—there's always been a Lewis in our family—he was nicer than the other one. I liked him." It seemed incredible. We had been friends and neighbors—close neighbors—for over fifty years, and now for the first time we realized we were kin.

My long relationship with the Spingarns had been based solely on friendship, and since I had never had any unsatisfied curiosity about my fathering, nothing in my own sense of myself was inwardly altered. By now, too, all the younger members of the Spingarn family were scattered: Honor and her husband in the Virgin Islands; Hope, who had lost her East Indian husband, remained in England; Edward and his wife and Stephen were all in Washington; there could be no cozy family celebration. But Hope and Honor seemed pleased at the disclosure, as was our daughter, Alison. At most, Hope would sign her letters to me "Your affectionate cousin." But what would Joel have felt if he had known?

There is no need for me to speculate about what Joel's response might have been to our 'cousinship.' He was no more attached to his wholly Jewish ancestry than I was to my partial one through that briefest of liaisons which had begotten me. It was not the anomalous ties of blood but far more intimate affiliations that had brought us together. At the end of his last illness in 1939 he was, alas! too weak to allow me to visit him even for a tender wordless farewell. Not until 1972 was I finally able to describe and evaluate, in an article in 'The New York Review of Books,' the creative potentialities he himself had failed to explore or utilize in his lifetime. As my final tribute to our friendship I republished that essay in 1979 in 'My Works and Days: A Personal Chronicle.'

8

We still own some fourteen acres that stretch back to the Webutuck River. The transformation of the ramshackle house and our first weedy acre into a densely cultivated tract constitutes a vital part of the story of our marriage. It took us years indeed even to overcome our urban scruples against removing badly grown trees or thinning unwanted 'volunteers' as ruthlessly as we must pull out weeds, and it was longer before we could properly distinguish between the plants we wished to preserve and the perverse weeds that frequently grew alongside them. So often, in their first leafing, they seemed alike! Only later did I learn from Edgar Anderson's 'Plants, Man and Life' that the resemblance between weed and selected plant is not altogether haphazard, but often shows some genuine botanic relationship: rye first appeared as a 'weed' amid wheat or barley and prospered under much the same conditions, but spread northward as a cultivated plant by taking more readily to poor soil and colder climates.

Without any set intention on our part our acres eventually became, at the climax of our cultivation, a small cross-section of the potential rural environment, with a woodlot, a swath of cleared meadow, a vegetable garden, two asparagus beds, a raspberry patch, a row of currant bushes, strawberries, and assorted flowerbeds, encircled by a miniature woodland walk—a *Philosophenweg*, as our German friends called it—that leads to what was once an open view across the valley to the exposed flanks of Oblong Mountain, some twelve hundred feet high. Like our thriving library, our acres contained a little of everything, but nothing just because it was rare or expensive. In time Sophy and I discovered from experience that gardeners are natural communists: eager to share their bounties with their neighbors and friends. So eager, in fact, that for years a Dutch botanist, whom I knew only from his letters, sent us annually a package of his latest bulbs. Spingarn himself had early led the way by having his garden help plant a fine assortment of flowering bushes and small trees, charging us only enough to let us delude ourselves that we were paying for what we received. Even now our garden shows vestiges of our friendships, not merely with our village neighbors, but with the Spingarns, the Brookses, and the Josephsons, to name only those who immediately come to mind. Not our least debt is to the adventurous traveler who in the 1850s brought back from Ohio one of the first buckeye trees hereabouts—the horse chestnut—which flowered magnificently on our road for a whole century. Each spring we would wait eagerly for its blossoming and pay a ceremonial visit of homage. We ourselves never went out walking without a trowel and a carrying bag for what we might find in wood or field.

Having this counterpoise to our metropolitan heritage, Sophy and I could make the best of both worlds and discover through experience how each was necessary and complementary to the other. But at no point, I must emphasize, did we ever lose contact with the city, for my work on 'The New Yorker'—save during the war—demanded my presence in Manhattan for at least two days a week. Even in our most secluded and withdrawn years, the tides of urban life could always be heard in the distance and sometimes the storm-whipped waves lapped at our feet, never so close indeed as in those tense years toward the close of the Second World War when every night we huddled around our radio to hear Ed Murrow's opening words: "This is London."

Index

Literary Guild, 313, 368–69, 371, 458
'Little Testament of Bernard Martin, The,' 205, 258, 259, 290, 314, 396, 458
Liverright, Horace, 190, 191–92, 303–5, 379
'Living Philosophies,' 441
Loch, Dorothy Cecilia (Delilah), 255, 257–58, 313, 314, 319, 347–48, 448
Loeb, Jacques, 220
Lovett, Robert Morss, 184, 217, 225, 318, 417
Lutyens, Edward, 319

Macaulay, Rose, 315
MacDonald, Ramsay, 277
'Machinery and the Modern Style,' 334, 424, 448
MacIver, Robert, 448–49
Mack, Lewis, 29–31, 489–90
MacKaye, Benton, 336, 338, 340–44, 346, 456
MacKaye, Percy, 120
MacKaye, Steele, 340
MacMahon, Aline, 348–51, 455
Macy, John, 356, 379
Madariaga, Salvador de, 397–98
Mann, Thomas, 194, 286, 467–68, 486
Mann, William, 271
Mantel, Herman, 100
Marot, Helen: at 'Dial,' 217, 218, 222–23, 243, 244; later years, 246–47, 250, 453
Marshak, Alexander, 92
Mayer, Gladys, 153, 330
Mayhew, Henry, 151
McDiarmid, Hugh, 400
McKim, Charles Follen, 429
Mears, Frank, 152
Mellquist, Jerome, 376
Melville, Herman, 40, 191, 209–10, 435, 451–58; 'Clarel,' 456; 'Moby Dick,' 210, 330; 'Pierre,' 47, 248, 483; 'White Jacket,' 210 (See also 'Herman Melville')
Manasce, Jean de, 392
Mencken, H. L., 216, 368, 481–82
Mendelsohn, Eric, 286, 429
Metcalf, Eleanor Melville, 456
Mies van der Rohe, Ludwig, 12, 438
Miller, Oskar von, 467
Minné, Eleanor, 225–26
Mitchell, Wesley Clare, 220, 471
Moore, Henry, 443
Moore, Marianne, 371
Moore, Thomas, 44, 83
More, Thomas, 303
Morris, Wright, 89
Morse, Beryl, 103–19
Moskowitz, Belle, 162
Mumford, Alison, 36, 55, 78, 139, 231, 418, 485, 488
Mumford, Elvina Conradina Baron, 25–48, 50, 52–53, 57–58, 68, 69, 72, 294
Mumford, Geddes: army life, 87, 90–91, 196, 209; birth, 42, 388–89; childhood, 55, 62, 389–92, 396–98, 457–58, 487–88; death, 196, 323; schooling, 78
Mumford, John, 25–26
Mumford, Sophia Wittenberg: as cook, 43; on 'Dial,' 222, 224–26, 232, 245, 285–86, 305; LM courtship of, 224–40, 283–94; marriage, 117–18, 184, 187–88, 293–302, 305, 317, 382–92, 397–98, 452–54, 457–65; parentage, 32; Sunnyside Progressive Nursery School and, 78; at Walden School, 386
Murray, Gilbert, 143, 396
Myres, John, Linton, 316
'Myth of the Machine, The,' 101, 449 (See also 'Pentagon of Power, The'; 'Technics and Human Development')
'My Works and Days,' 441, 490

About the Author

LEWIS MUMFORD was born in Flushing, Long Island, in 1895. His first book, *The Story of Utopias,* was published in 1922; his more notable works include *Technics and Civilization* (1934), *The Culture of Cities* (1938), *The Condition of Man* (1944), *The City in History* (1961), the two volumes of *The Myth of the Machine* 1967, and *My Works and Days* (1979). Mr. Mumford is a member of the American Philosophical Society, the National Institute of Arts and Letters, and a fellow of the American Academy of Arts and Sciences.